Corporate Finance and Portfolio Management

CFA® PROGRAM CURRICULUM • VOLUME 4

LEVEL I
2008

Cover photograph courtesy of Getty Images.

Printed in the United States of America

10 9 8 7 6 5 4 3 2 1

ISBN 0-536-34182-6

2006160826

AG/JS

Please visit our web site at *www.pearsoncustom.com*

PEARSON CUSTOM PUBLISHING
501 Boylston Street, Suite 900, Boston, MA 02116
A Pearson Education Company

CONTENTS

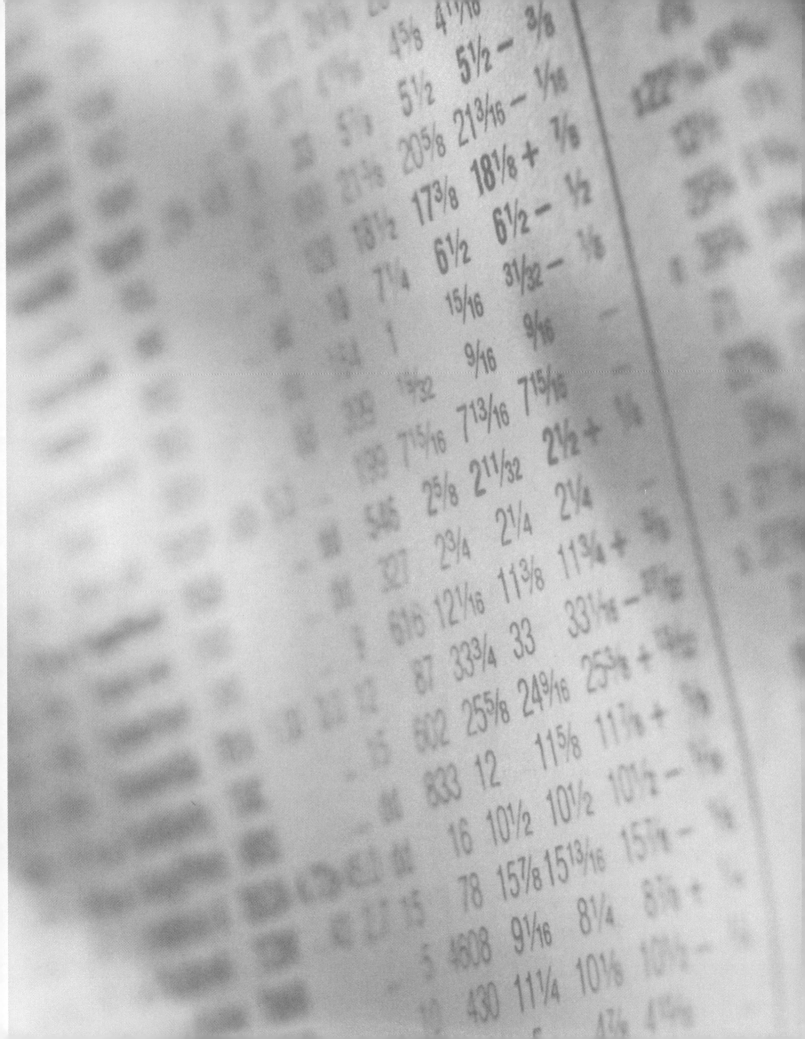

HOW TO USE THE CFA PROGRAM CURRICULUM

Congratulations on your decision to enter the Chartered Financial Analyst (CFA®) Program. This exciting and rewarding program of study reflects your desire to become a serious investment professional. You are embarking on a program noted for its high ethical standards and the breadth of knowledge, skills, and abilities it develops. Your commitment to the CFA Program should be educationally and professionally rewarding.

The credential you seek is respected around the world as a mark of accomplishment and dedication. Each level of the program represents a distinct achievement in professional development. Successful completion of the program is rewarded with membership in a prestigious global community of investment professionals. CFA charterholders are dedicated to life-long learning and maintaining currency with the ever-changing dynamics of a challenging profession.

The CFA examination measures your degree of mastery of the assigned CFA Program curriculum. Effective study and preparation based on that curriculum are keys to your success on the examination.

Curriculum Development

The CFA Program curriculum is grounded in the practice of the investment profession. CFA Institute regularly conducts a practice analysis survey of investment professionals around the world to determine the knowledge, skills, and abilities that are relevant to the profession. The survey results define the Candidate Body of Knowledge (CBOK™), an inventory of knowledge and responsibilities expected of the investment management professional at the level of a new CFA charterholder. The survey also determines how much emphasis each of the major topic areas receives on the CFA examinations.

A committee made up of practicing charterholders, in conjunction with CFA Institute staff, designs the CFA Program curriculum to deliver the CBOK to candidates. The examinations, also written by practicing charterholders, are designed to allow you to demonstrate your mastery of the CBOK as set forth in the CFA Program curriculum. As you structure your personal study program, you should emphasize mastery of the CBOK and the practical application of that knowledge. For more information on the practice analysis, CBOK, and development of the CFA Program curriculum, please visit www.cfainstitute.org/toolkit.

Organization

The Level I CFA Program curriculum is organized into 10 topic areas. Each topic area begins with a brief statement of the material and the depth of knowledge expected.

Each topic area is then divided into one or more study sessions. These study sessions—18 sessions in the Level I curriculum—should form the basic structure of your reading and preparation.

Each study session includes a statement of its structure and objective, and is further divided into specific reading assignments. The outline on the inside front cover of each volume illustrates the organization of these 18 study sessions.

The reading assignments are the basis for all examination questions, and are selected or developed specifically to teach the CBOK. These readings are drawn from textbook chapters, professional journal articles, research analyst reports, CFA Program-commissioned content, and cases. Many readings include problems and solutions as well as appendices to help you learn.

Reading-specific Learning Outcome Statements (LOS) are listed in the pages introducing each study session as well as at the beginning of each reading. These LOS indicate what you should be able to accomplish after studying the reading. We encourage you to review how to properly use LOS, and the descriptions of commonly used LOS "command words," at www.cfainstitute.org/toolkit. The command words signal the depth of learning you are expected to achieve from the reading. You should use the LOS to guide and focus your study, as each examination question is based on an assigned reading and one or more LOS. However, the readings provide context for the LOS and enable you to apply a principle or concept in a variety of scenarios. It is important to study the whole of a required reading.

Features of the Curriculum

- **Required vs. Optional Segments** - You should read all of the pages for an assigned reading. In some cases, however, we have reprinted an entire chapter or article and marked those parts of the reading that are not required as "optional." The CFA examination is based only on the required segments, and the optional segments are included only when they might help you to better understand the required segments (by seeing the required material in its full context). When an optional segment begins, you will see an icon and a solid vertical bar in the outside margin that will continue until the optional segment ends, accompanied by another icon. *Unless the material is specifically marked as optional, you should assume it is required.* Keep in mind that the optional material is provided strictly for your convenience and will not be tested. You should rely on the required segments and the reading-specific LOS in preparing for the examination.

- **Problems/Solutions** - *All questions and problems in the readings as well as their solutions (which are provided in an appendix at the end of each volume) are required material.* When appropriate, we have included problems after the readings to demonstrate practical application and reinforce your understanding of the concepts presented. The questions and problems are designed to help you learn these concepts. Many of the questions are in the same style and format as the actual CFA examination and will give you test-taking experience in that format. Examination questions that come from a past CFA examination are marked with the CFA logo in the margin.

2006 exam

- **Margins** - The wide margins in each volume provide space for your note-taking.
- **Two-color Format** - To enrich the visual appeal and clarity of the exhibits, tables, and text, the curriculum is printed in a two-color format.
- **Six-volume Structure** - For portability of the curriculum, the material is spread over six volumes.
- **Glossary and Index** - For your convenience, we have printed a comprehensive glossary and index in each volume. Throughout the curriculum, a **bolded blue** word in a reading denotes a term defined in the glossary.

Designing Your Personal Study Program

Create a Schedule - An orderly, systematic approach to examination preparation is critical. You should dedicate a consistent block of time every week to reading and studying. Complete all reading assignments and the associated problems and solutions in each study session. Review the LOS both before and after you study each reading to ensure that you have mastered the applicable content and can demonstrate the knowledge, skill, or ability described by the LOS and the assigned reading.

CFA Institute estimates that you will need to devote a minimum of 10–15 hours per week for 18 weeks to study the assigned readings. Allow a minimum of one week for each study session, and plan to complete them all at least 30–45 days prior to the examination. This schedule will allow you to spend the final four to six weeks before the examination reviewing the assigned material and taking multiple online sample examinations.

At CFA Institute, we believe that candidates need to commit to a *minimum* of 250 hours reading and reviewing the curriculum, and taking online sample examinations, to master the material. This recommendation, however, may substantially underestimate the hours needed for appropriate examination preparation depending on your individual circumstances, relevant experience, and academic background.

You will undoubtedly adjust your study time to conform to your own strengths and weaknesses, and your educational and professional background. You will probably spend more time on some study sessions than on others. You should allow ample time for both in-depth study of all topic areas and additional concentration on those topic areas for which you feel least prepared.

Preliminary Readings - The reading assignments in Economics assume candidates already have a basic mastery of the concepts typically presented in introductory university-level economics courses. Information on suggested readings to improve your knowledge of these topics precedes the relevant study sessions.

Candidate Preparation Toolkit - We have created the online toolkit to provide a single comprehensive location for resources and guidance for candidate preparation. In addition to in-depth information on study program planning, the CFA Program curriculum, and the online sample examinations, the toolkit also contains curriculum errata, printable study session outlines, sample examination questions, and more. Errata identified in the curriculum are corrected and listed periodically in the errata listing in the toolkit. We encourage you to use the toolkit as your central preparation resource during your tenure as a candidate. Visit the toolkit at www.cfainstitute.org/toolkit.

Online Sample Examinations - After completing your study of the assigned curriculum, use the CFA Institute online sample examinations to measure your knowledge of the topics and to improve your examination-taking skills. After each question, you will receive immediate feedback noting the correct response and indicating the assigned reading for further study. The sample examinations are designed by the same people who create the actual CFA examinations, and reflect the question formats, topics, and level of difficulty of the actual CFA examinations, in a timed environment. Aggregate data indicate that the CFA examination pass rate was higher among candidates who took one or more online sample examinations than among candidates who did not take the online sample examinations. For more information on the online sample examinations, please visit www.cfainstitute.org/toolkit.

Preparatory Providers - After you enroll in the CFA Program, you may receive numerous solicitations for preparatory courses and review materials. Although preparatory courses and notes may be helpful to some candidates, you should view these resources as *supplements* to the assigned CFA Program curriculum. The CFA examinations reference only the CFA Institute assigned curriculum—no preparatory course or review course materials are consulted or referenced.

Before you decide on a supplementary prep course, do some research. Determine the experience and expertise of the instructors, the accuracy and currency of their content, the delivery method for their materials, and the provider's claims of success. Most importantly, make sure the provider is in compliance with the CFA Institute Prep Provider Guidelines Program. Three years of prep course products can be a significant investment, so make sure you're getting a sufficient return. Just remember, there are no shortcuts to success on the CFA examinations. Prep products can enhance your learning experience, but the CFA curriculum is the key to success. For more information on the Prep Provider Guidelines Program, visit www.cfainstitute.org/cfaprog/resources/prepcourse.html.

SUMMARY

Every question on the CFA examination is based on specific pages in the required readings and on one or more LOS. Frequently, an examination question is also tied to a specific example highlighted within a reading or to a specific end-of-reading question/problem and its solution. To make effective use of the curriculum, please remember these key points:

1. All pages printed in the Custom Curriculum are required reading for the examination except for occasional sections marked as optional. You may read optional pages as background, but you will not be tested on them.
2. All questions/problems printed at the end of readings and their solutions in the appendix to each volume are required study material for the examination.
3. Make appropriate use of the CFA Candidate Toolkit, the online sample examinations, and preparatory courses and review materials.
4. Commit sufficient study time to cover the 18 study sessions, review the materials, and take sample examinations.

Feedback

At CFA Institute, we are committed to delivering a comprehensive and rigorous curriculum for the development of competent, ethically grounded investment professionals. We rely on candidate and member feedback as we work to incorporate content, design, and packaging improvements. You can be assured that we will continue to listen to your suggestions. Please send any comments or feedback to curriculum@cfainstitute.org. Ongoing improvements in the curriculum will help you prepare for success on the upcoming examinations, and for a lifetime of learning as a serious investment professional.

CORPORATE FINANCE

STUDY SESSION

Study Session 11 Corporate Finance

TOPIC LEVEL LEARNING OUTCOME

The candidate should be able to demonstrate a working knowledge of capital budgeting concepts and analysis. Candidates should understand how corporate finance concepts, such as cost of capital, cash flow and liquidity, as well as information obtained from financial statements are used in the valuation process, and be familiar with corporate governance issues and risks affecting companies.

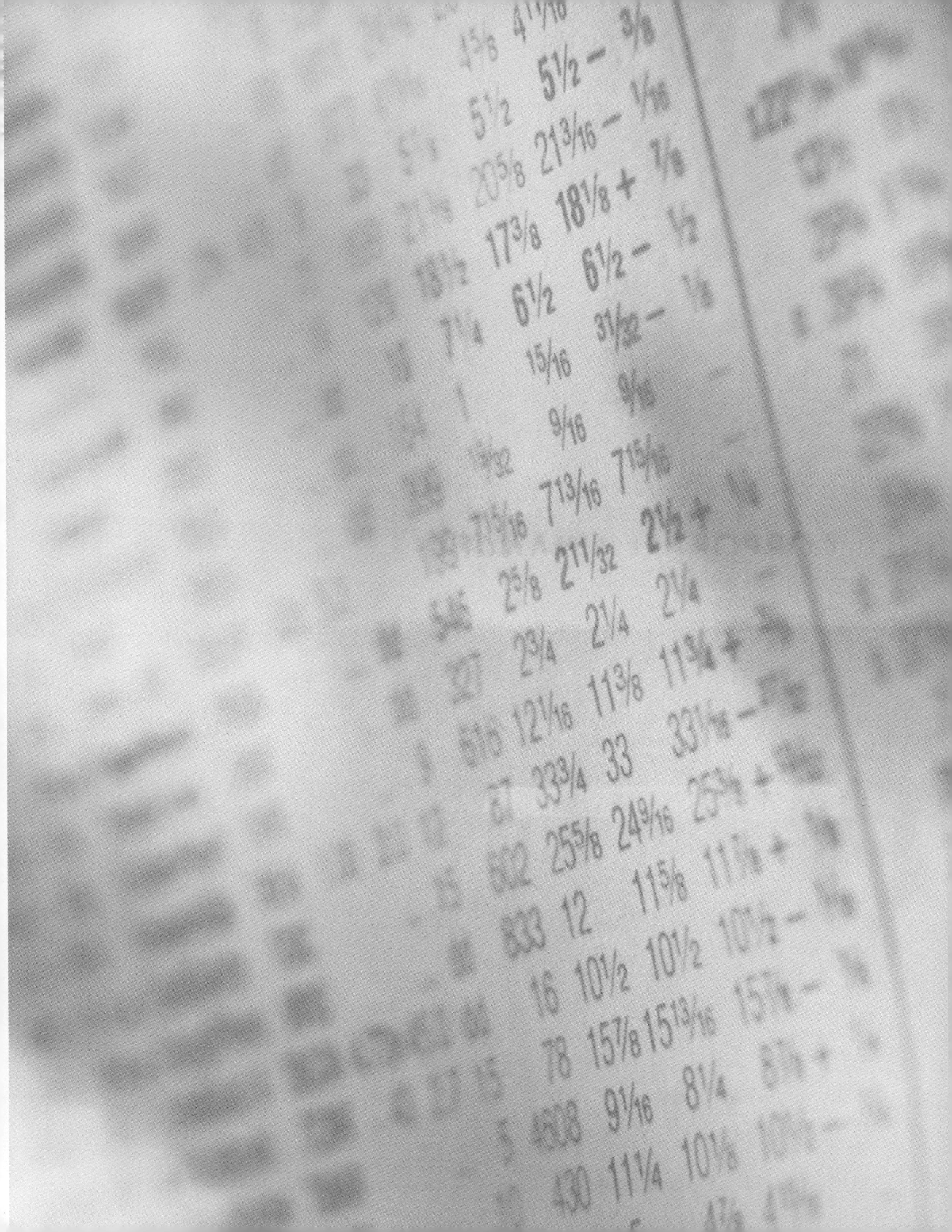

STUDY SESSION 11
CORPORATE FINANCE

This study session covers the principles that corporations use to make their investing and financing decisions. Capital budgeting is the process of making decisions about which long-term projects the corporation should accept for investment, and which it should reject. Both the expected return of a project and the financing cost should be taken into account. The cost of capital, or the rate of return required for a project, must be developed using economically sound methods.

Corporate managers are concerned with liquidity and solvency, and use financial statements to evaluate performance as well as to develop and communicate future plans. The final reading in this study session is on corporate governance practices, which can expose the firm to a heightened risk of ethical lapses. Although these practices may not be inherently unethical, they create the potential for conflicts of interest to develop between shareholders and managers, and the extent of that conflict affects the firm's valuation.

READING ASSIGNMENTS

Reading 44 Capital Budgeting
Reading 45 Cost of Capital
Reading 46 Working Capital Management
Reading 47 Financial Statement Analysis
Reading 48 The Corporate Governance of Listed Companies: A Manual for Investors

LEARNING OUTCOMES

Reading 44: Capital Budgeting

The candidate should be able to:

a. explain the capital budgeting process, including the typical steps of the process, and distinguish among the various categories of capital projects;

b. discuss the basic principles of capital budgeting, including the choice of the proper cash flows and determining the proper discount rate;

c. explain how the following project interactions affect the evaluation of a capital project: (1) independent versus mutually exclusive projects, (2) project sequencing, and (3) unlimited funds versus capital rationing;

d. calculate and interpret the results using each of the following methods to evaluate a single capital project: net present value (NPV), internal rate of return (IRR), payback period, discounted payback period, average accounting rate of return (AAR), and profitability index (PI);

e. explain the NPV profile, compare and contrast the NPV and IRR methods when evaluating independent and mutually exclusive projects, and describe the problems that can arise when using an IRR;

f. describe and account for the relative popularity of the various capital budgeting methods, and explain the relation between NPV and company value and stock price.

Reading 45: Cost of Capital

The candidate should be able to:

a. calculate and interpret the weighted average cost of capital (WACC) of a company;

b. describe how taxes affect the cost of capital from different capital sources;

c. describe alternative methods of calculating the weights used in the weighted average cost of capital, including the use of the company's target capital structure;

d. explain how the marginal cost of capital and the investment opportunity schedule are used to determine the optimal capital budget;

e. explain the marginal cost of capital's role in determining the net present value of a project;

f. calculate and interpret the cost of fixed rate debt capital using the yield-to-maturity approach and the debt-rating approach;

g. calculate and interpret the cost of noncallable, nonconvertible preferred stock;

h. calculate and interpret the cost of equity capital using the capital asset pricing model approach, the dividend discount model approach, and the bond-yield-plus risk-premium approach;

i. explain the country equity risk premium in the estimation of the cost of equity for a company located in a developing market;

j. describe the marginal cost of capital schedule, explain why it may be upward-sloping with respect to additional capital, and calculate and interpret its break-points;

k. explain and demonstrate the correct treatment of flotation costs.

Reading 46: Working Capital Management

The candidate should be able to:

a. calculate and interpret liquidity measures using selected financial ratios for a company and compare the company with peer companies;

b. evaluate overall working capital effectiveness of a company, using the operating and cash conversion cycles, and compare the company's effectiveness with other peer companies;

c. classify the components of a cash forecast and prepare a cash forecast, given estimates of revenues, expenses, and other items;

d. identify and evaluate the necessary tools to use in managing a company's net daily cash position;

e. compute and interpret comparable yields on various securities, compare portfolio returns against a standard benchmark, and evaluate a company's short-term investment policy guidelines;

f. evaluate the performance of a company's accounts receivable, inventory management, and accounts payable functions against historical figures and comparable peer company values;

g. evaluate the choices of short-term funding available to a company and recommend a financing method.

Reading 47: Financial Statement Analysis

The candidate should be able to:

a. calculate, interpret, and discuss the DuPont expression and extended DuPont expression for a company's return on equity and demonstrate its use in corporate analysis;

b. demonstrate the use of pro forma income and balance sheet statements.

Reading 48: The Corporate Governance of Listed Companies: A Manual for Investors

The candidate should be able to:

a. define and describe corporate governance;

b. discuss and critique characteristics and practices related to board and committee independence, experience, compensation, external consultants, and frequency of elections, and determine whether they are supportive of shareowner protection;

c. describe board independence and explain the importance of independent board members in corporate governance;

d. identify factors that indicate a board and its members possess the experience required to govern the company for the benefit of its shareowners;

e. explain the provisions that should be included in a strong corporate code of ethics and the implications of a weak code of ethics with regard to related-party transactions and personal use of company assets;

f. state the key areas of responsibility for which board committees are typically created, and explain the criteria for assessing whether each committee is able to adequately represent shareowner interests;

g. evaluate, from a shareowner's perspective, company policies related to voting rules, shareowner-sponsored proposals, common stock classes, and takeover defenses.

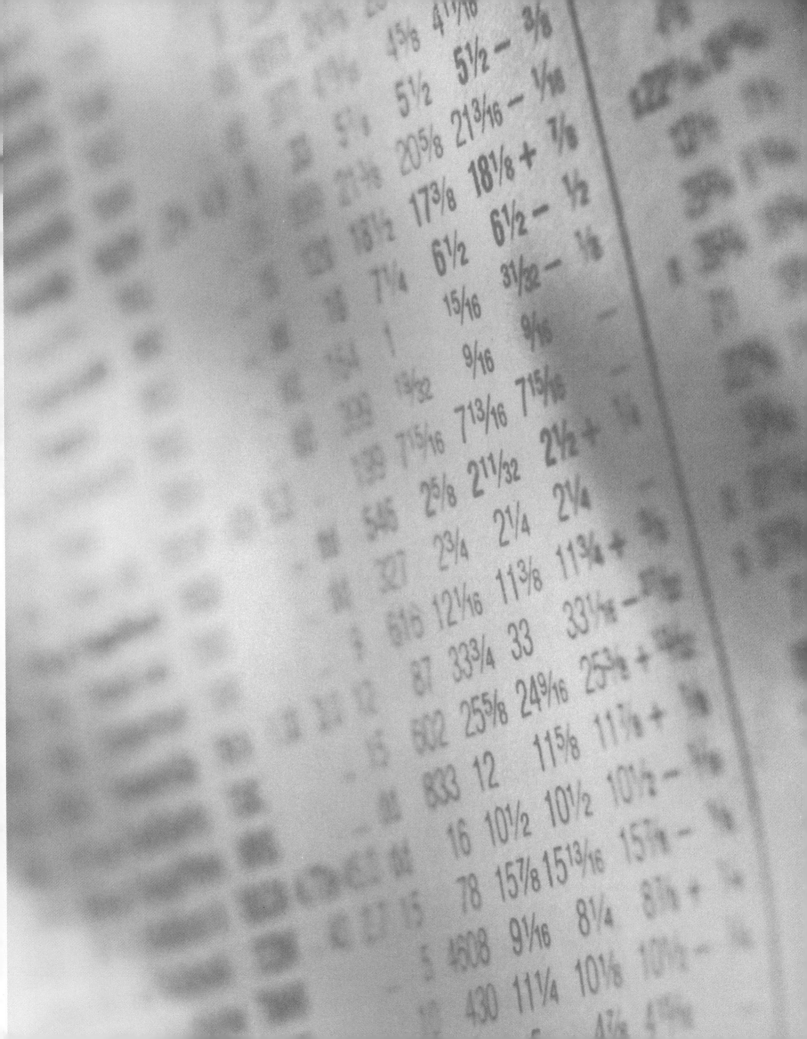

CAPITAL BUDGETING

by John D. Stowe and Jacques R. Gagné

READING 44

LEARNING OUTCOMES

The candidate should be able to:

a. explain the capital budgeting process, including the typical steps of the process, and distinguish among the various categories of capital projects;

b. discuss the basic principles of capital budgeting, including the choice of the proper cash flows and determining the proper discount rate;

c. explain how the following project interactions affect the evaluation of a capital project: (1) independent versus mutually exclusive projects, (2) project sequencing, and (3) unlimited funds versus capital rationing;

d. calculate and interpret the results using each of the following methods to evaluate a single capital project: net present value (NPV), internal rate of return (IRR), payback period, discounted payback period, average accounting rate of return (AAR), and profitability index (PI);

e. explain the NPV profile, compare and contrast the NPV and IRR methods when evaluating independent and mutually exclusive projects, and describe the problems that can arise when using an IRR;

f. describe and account for the relative popularity of the various capital budgeting methods, and explain the relation between NPV and company value and stock price.

INTRODUCTION 1

Capital budgeting is the process that companies use for decision making on capital projects—those projects with a life of a year or more. This is a fundamental area of knowledge for financial analysts for many reasons.

- First, capital budgeting is very important for corporations. Capital projects, which make up the long-term asset portion of the balance sheet, can be so large that sound capital budgeting decisions ultimately decide the future of many corporations. Capital decisions cannot be reversed at a low cost, so mistakes are very costly. Indeed, the real capital investments of a company describe a company better than its working capital or capital structures, which are intangible and tend to be similar for many corporations.

- Second, the principles of capital budgeting have been adapted for many other corporate decisions, such as investments in working capital, leasing, mergers and acquisitions, and bond refunding.
- Third, the valuation principles used in capital budgeting are similar to the valuation principles used in security analysis and portfolio management. Many of the methods used by security analysts and portfolio managers are based on capital budgeting methods. Conversely, there have been innovations in security analysis and portfolio management that have also been adapted to capital budgeting.
- Finally, although analysts have a vantage point outside the company, their interest in valuation coincides with the capital budgeting focus of maximizing shareholder value. Because capital budgeting information is not ordinarily available outside the company, the analyst may attempt to estimate the process, within reason, at least for companies that are not too complex. Further, analysts may be able to appraise the quality of the company's capital budgeting process—for example, on the basis of whether the company has an accounting focus or an economic focus.

This reading is organized as follows: Section 2 presents the steps in a typical capital budgeting process. After introducing the basic principles of capital budgeting in Section 3, in Section 4 we discuss the criteria by which a decision to invest in a project may be made. Section 5 presents a crucial element of the capital budgeting process: organizing the cash flow information that is the raw material of the analysis. Section 6 looks further at cash flow analysis. Section 7 demonstrates methods to extend the basic investment criteria to address economic alternatives and risk. Finally, Section 8 compares other income measures and valuation models that analysts use to the basic capital budgeting model.

2 THE CAPITAL BUDGETING PROCESS

The specific capital budgeting procedures that a manager uses depend on the manager's level in the organization, the size and complexity of the project being evaluated, and the size of the organization. The typical steps in the capital budgeting process are as follows:

- Step One: Generating Ideas—**Investment** ideas can come from anywhere, from the top or the bottom of the organization, from any department or functional area, or from outside the company. Generating good investment ideas to consider is the most important step in the process.

- Step Two: Analyzing Individual Proposals—This step involves gathering the information to forecast cash flows for each project and then evaluating the project's profitability.
- Step Three: Planning the Capital Budget—The company must organize the profitable proposals into a coordinated whole that fits within the company's overall strategies, and it also must consider the projects' timing. Some projects that look good when considered in isolation may be undesirable strategically. Because of financial and real resource issues, the scheduling and prioritizing of projects is important.
- Step Four: Monitoring and Post-auditing—In a post-audit, actual results are compared to planned or predicted results, and any differences must be explained. For example, how do the revenues, expenses, and cash flows realized from an investment compare to the predictions? Post-auditing capital projects is important for several reasons. First, it helps monitor the forecasts and analysis that underlie the capital budgeting process. Systematic errors, such as overly optimistic forecasts, become apparent. Second, it helps improve business operations. If sales or costs are out of line, it will focus attention on bringing performance closer to expectations if at all possible. Finally, monitoring and post-auditing recent capital investments will produce concrete ideas for future investments. Managers can decide to invest more heavily in profitable areas and scale down or cancel investments in areas that are disappointing.

Planning for capital investments can be very complex, often involving many persons inside and outside of the company. Information about marketing, science, engineering, regulation, taxation, finance, production, and behavioral issues must be systematically gathered and evaluated. The authority to make capital decisions depends on the size and complexity of the project. Lower-level managers may have discretion to make decisions that involve less than a given amount of money, or that do not exceed a given capital budget. Larger and more complex decisions are reserved for top management, and some are so significant that the company's board of directors ultimately has the decision-making authority.

Like everything else, capital budgeting is a cost–benefit exercise. At the margin, the benefits from the improved decision making should exceed the costs of the capital budgeting efforts.

Companies often put capital budgeting projects into some rough categories for analysis. One such classification would be as follows:

1. Replacement projects. These are among the easier capital budgeting decisions. If a piece of equipment breaks down or wears out, whether to replace it may not require careful analysis. If the expenditure is modest and if not investing has significant implications for production, operations, or sales, it would be a waste of resources to overanalyze the decision. Just make the replacement. Other replacement decisions involve replacing existing equipment with newer, more efficient equipment, or perhaps choosing one type of equipment over another. These replacement decisions are often amenable to very detailed analysis, and you might have a lot of confidence in the final decision.
2. Expansion projects. Instead of merely maintaining a company's existing business activities, expansion projects increase the size of the business. These expansion decisions may involve more uncertainties than replacement decisions, and these decisions will be more carefully considered.

3. New products and services. These investments expose the company to even more uncertainties than expansion projects. These decisions are more complex and will involve more people in the decision-making process.
4. Regulatory, safety, and environmental projects. These projects are frequently required by a governmental agency, an insurance company, or some other external party. They may generate no revenue and might not be undertaken by a company maximizing its own private interests. Often, the company will accept the required investment and continue to operate. Occasionally, however, the cost of the regulatory/safety/environmental project is sufficiently high that the company would do better to cease operating altogether or to shut down any part of the business that is related to the project.
5. Other. The projects above are all susceptible to capital budgeting analysis, and they can be accepted or rejected using the net present value (NPV) or some other criterion. Some projects escape such analysis. These are either **pet projects** of someone in the company (such as the CEO buying a new aircraft) or so risky that they are difficult to analyze by the usual methods (such as some research and development decisions).

3 BASIC PRINCIPLES OF CAPITAL BUDGETING

Capital budgeting has a rich history and sometimes employs some pretty sophisticated procedures. Fortunately, capital budgeting relies on just a few basic principles. Capital budgeting usually uses the following assumptions:

1. Decisions are based on cash flows. The decisions are not based on accounting concepts, such as net income. Furthermore, intangible costs and benefits are often ignored because, if they are real, they should result in cash flows at some other time.
2. Timing of cash flows is crucial. Analysts make an extraordinary effort to detail precisely when cash flows occur.
3. Cash flows are based on opportunity costs. What are the incremental cash flows that occur with an investment compared to what they would have been without the investment?
4. Cash flows are analyzed on an after-tax basis. Taxes must be fully reflected in all capital budgeting decisions.
5. Financing costs are ignored. This may seem unrealistic, but it is not. Most of the time, analysts want to know the after-tax operating cash flows that result from a capital investment. Then, these after-tax cash flows and the investment outlays are discounted at the "required rate of return" to find the net present value (NPV). Financing costs are reflected in the required rate of return. If we included financing costs in the cash flows and in the discount rate, we would be double-counting the financing costs. So even though a project may be financed with some combination of debt and equity, we ignore these costs, focusing on the operating cash flows and capturing the costs of debt (and other capital) in the discount rate.
6. Capital budgeting cash flows are not accounting net income. Accounting net income is reduced by noncash charges such as accounting depreciation. Furthermore, to reflect the cost of debt financing, interest expenses are also subtracted from accounting net income. (No subtraction is made for

the cost of equity financing in arriving at accounting net income.) Accounting net income also differs from economic income, which is the cash inflow plus the change in the market value of the company. Economic income does not subtract the **cost of debt** financing, and it is based on the changes in the market value of the company, not changes in its book value (accounting depreciation). We will further consider cash flows, accounting income, economic income, and other income measures at the end of this reading.

In assumption 5 above, we referred to the rate used in discounting the cash flows as the "required rate of return." The required rate of return is the discount rate that investors should require given the riskiness of the project. This discount rate is frequently called the "opportunity cost of funds" or the "cost of capital." If the company can invest elsewhere and earn a return of r, or if the company can repay its sources of capital and save a cost of r, then r is the company's opportunity cost of funds. If the company cannot earn more than its opportunity cost of funds on an investment, it should not undertake that investment. Unless an investment earns more than the cost of funds from its suppliers of capital, the investment should not be undertaken. The cost-of-capital concept is discussed more extensively elsewhere. Regardless of what it is called, an economically sound discount rate is essential for making capital budgeting decisions.

Although the principles of capital budgeting are simple, they are easily confused in practice, leading to unfortunate decisions. Some important capital budgeting concepts that managers find very useful are given below.

- A **sunk cost** is one that has already been incurred. You cannot change a sunk cost. Today's decisions, on the other hand, should be based on current and future cash flows and should not be affected by prior, or sunk, costs.
- An **opportunity cost** is what a resource is worth in its next-best use. For example, if a company uses some idle property, what should it record as the investment outlay: the purchase price several years ago, the current market value, or nothing? If you replace an old machine with a new one, what is the opportunity cost? If you invest \$10 million, what is the opportunity cost? The answers to these three questions are, respectively: the current market value, the cash flows the old machine would generate, and \$10 million (which you could invest elsewhere).
- An **incremental cash flow** is the cash flow that is realized because of a decision: the cash flow *with* a decision minus the cash flow *without* that decision. If opportunity costs are correctly assessed, the incremental cash flows provide a sound basis for capital budgeting.
- An **externality** is the effect of an investment on other things besides the investment itself. Frequently, an investment affects the cash flows of other parts of the company, and these externalities can be positive or negative. If possible, these should be part of the investment decision. Sometimes externalities occur outside of the company. An investment might benefit (or harm) other companies or society at large, and yet the company is not compensated for these benefits (or charged for the costs). **Cannibalization** is one externality. Cannibalization occurs when an investment takes customers and sales away from another part of the company.
- **Conventional versus nonconventional cash flows**—A **conventional cash flow** pattern is one with an initial outflow followed by a series of inflows. In a **nonconventional cash flow** pattern, the initial outflow is not followed by inflows only, but the cash flows can flip from positive to negative again (or even change signs several times). An investment that involved outlays

(negative cash flows) for the first couple of years that were then followed by positive cash flows would be considered to have a conventional pattern. If cash flows change signs once, the pattern is conventional. If cash flows change signs two or more times, the pattern is nonconventional.

Several types of project interactions make the incremental cash flow analysis challenging. The following are some of these interactions:

- **Independent versus mutually exclusive projects—Independent projects** are projects whose cash flows are independent of each other. Mutually exclusive projects compete directly with each other. For example, if Projects A and B are mutually exclusive, you can choose A or B, but you cannot choose both. Sometimes there are several mutually exclusive projects, and you can choose only one from the group.
- **Project sequencing**—Many projects are sequenced through time, so that investing in a project creates the option to invest in future projects. For example, you might invest in a project today and then in one year invest in a second project if the financial results of the first project or new economic conditions are favorable. If the results of the first project or new economic conditions are not favorable, you do not invest in the second project.
- **Unlimited funds versus capital rationing**—An **unlimited funds** environment assumes that the company can raise the funds it wants for all profitable projects simply by paying the required rate of return. **Capital rationing** exists when the company has a fixed amount of funds to invest. If the company has more profitable projects than it has funds for, it must allocate the funds to achieve the maximum shareholder value subject to the funding constraints.

4 INVESTMENT DECISION CRITERIA

Analysts use several important criteria to evaluate capital investments. The two most comprehensive measures of whether a project is profitable or unprofitable are the net present value (NPV) and internal rate of return (IRR). In addition to these, we present four other criteria that are frequently used: the payback period, discounted payback period, average accounting rate of return (AAR), and profitability index (PI). An analyst must fully understand the economic logic behind each of these investment decision criteria as well as its strengths and limitations in practice.

4.1 Net Present Value

For a project with one investment outlay, made initially, the net present value (NPV) is the present value of the future after-tax cash flows minus the investment outlay, or

$$\text{NPV} = \sum_{t=1}^{n} \frac{\text{CF}_t}{(1+r)^t} - \text{Outlay} \qquad \textbf{(44-1)}$$

where

CF_t = after-tax cash flow at time t
r = required rate of return for the investment
Outlay = investment cash flow at time zero

To illustrate the net present value criterion, we will take a look at a simple example. Assume that Gerhardt Corporation is considering an investment of €50 million in a capital project that will return after-tax cash flows of €16 million per year for the next four years plus another €20 million in year 5. The required rate of return is 10 percent.

For the Gerhardt example, the NPV would be

$$NPV = \frac{16}{1.10^1} + \frac{16}{1.10^2} + \frac{16}{1.10^3} + \frac{16}{1.10^4} + \frac{20}{1.10^5} - 50$$
$$NPV = 14.545 + 13.223 + 12.021 + 10.928 + 12.418 - 50$$
$$NPV = 63.136 - 50 = €13.136 \text{ million.}$$[1]

The investment has a total value, or present value of future cash flows, of €63.136 million. Since this investment can be acquired at a cost of €50 million, the investing company is giving up €50 million of its wealth in exchange for an investment worth €63.136 million. The investor's wealth increases by a net of €13.136 million.

Because the NPV is the amount by which the investor's wealth increases as a result of the investment, the decision rule for the NPV is as follows:

Invest if $NPV > 0$
Do not invest if $NPV < 0$

Positive NPV investments are wealth-increasing, whereas negative NPV investments are wealth-decreasing.

Many investments have cash flow patterns in which outflows may occur not only at time zero, but also at future dates. It is useful to consider the NPV to be the present value of all cash flows:

$$NPV = CF_0 + \frac{CF_1}{(1+r)^1} + \frac{CF_2}{(1+r)^2} + \cdots + \frac{CF_n}{(1+r)^n}, \text{ or}$$

$$NPV = \sum_{t=0}^{n} \frac{CF_t}{(1+r)^t} \quad \textbf{(44-2)}$$

In Equation 44-2, the investment outlay, CF_0, is simply a negative cash flow. Future cash flows can also be negative.

4.2 Internal Rate of Return

The internal rate of return (IRR) is one of the most frequently used concepts in capital budgeting and in security analysis. The IRR definition is one that all analysts know by heart. For a project with one investment outlay, made initially, the

[1] Occasionally, you will notice some rounding errors in our examples. In this case, the present values of the cash flows, as rounded, add up to €63.135. Without rounding, they add up to €63.13627, or €63.136. We will usually report the more accurate result, the one that you would get from your calculator or computer without rounding intermediate results.

IRR is the discount rate that makes the present value of the future after-tax cash flows equal that investment outlay. Written out in equation form, the IRR solves this equation:

$$\sum_{t=1}^{n} \frac{CF_t}{(1 + \text{IRR})^t} = \text{Outlay}$$

where IRR is the internal rate of return. The left-hand side of this equation is the present value of the project's future cash flows, which, discounted at the IRR, equals the investment outlay. This equation will also be seen rearranged as

$$\sum_{t=1}^{n} \frac{CF_t}{(1 + \text{IRR})^t} - \text{Outlay} = 0 \qquad \textbf{(44-3)}$$

In this form, Equation 44-3 looks like the NPV equation, Equation 44-1, except that the discount rate is the IRR instead of r (the required rate of return). Discounted at the IRR, the NPV is equal to zero.

In the Gerhardt Corporation example, we want to find a discount rate that makes the total present value of all cash flows, the NPV, equal zero. In equation form, the IRR is the discount rate that solves this equation:

$$-50 + \frac{16}{(1 + \text{IRR})^1} + \frac{16}{(1 + \text{IRR})^2} + \frac{16}{(1 + \text{IRR})^3} + \frac{16}{(1 + \text{IRR})^4} + \frac{20}{(1 + \text{IRR})^5} = 0$$

Algebraically, this equation would be very difficult to solve. We normally resort to trial and error, systematically choosing various discount rates until we find one, the IRR, that satisfies the equation. We previously discounted these cash flows at 10 percent and found the NPV to be €13.136 million. Since the NPV is positive, the IRR is probably greater than 10 percent. If we use 20 percent as the discount rate, the NPV is −€0.543 million, so 20 percent is a little high. One might try several other discount rates until the NPV is equal to zero; this approach is illustrated in Table 1.

TABLE 1 Trial and Error Process for Finding IRR

Discount Rate	NPV
10%	13.136
20%	−0.543
19%	0.598
19.5%	0.022
19.51%	0.011
19.52%	0.000

The IRR is 19.52 percent. Financial calculators and spreadsheet software have routines that calculate the IRR for us, so we do not have to go through this trial and error procedure ourselves. The IRR, computed more precisely, is 19.5197 percent.

The decision rule for the IRR is to invest if the IRR exceeds the required rate of return for a project:

Invest if IRR $> r$
Do not invest if IRR $< r$

In the Gerhardt example, since the IRR of 19.52 percent exceeds the project's required rate of return of 10 percent, Gerhardt should invest.

Many investments have cash flow patterns in which the outlays occur at time zero and at future dates. Thus, it is common to define the IRR as the discount rate that makes the present values of all cash flows sum to zero:

$$\sum_{t=0}^{n} \frac{CF_t}{(1 + IRR)^t} = 0 \qquad \textbf{(44-4)}$$

Equation 44-4 is a more general version of Equation 44-3.

4.3 Payback Period

The payback period is the number of years required to recover the original investment in a project. The payback is based on cash flows. For example, if you invest $10 million in a project, how long will it be until you recover the full original investment? Table 2 below illustrates the calculation of the payback period by following an investment's cash flows and cumulative cash flows.

TABLE 2 Payback Period Example

Year	0	1	2	3	4	5
Cash flow	−10,000	2,500	2,500	3,000	3,000	3,000
Cumulative cash flow	−10,000	−7,500	−5,000	−2,000	1,000	4,000

In the first year, the company recovers 2,500 of the original investment, with 7,500 still unrecovered. You can see that the company recoups its original investment between Year 3 and Year 4. After three years, 2,000 is still unrecovered. Since the Year 4 cash flow is 3,000, it would take two-thirds of the Year 4 cash flow to bring the cumulative cash flow to zero. So, the payback period is three years plus two-thirds of the Year 4 cash flow, or 3.67 years.

The drawbacks of the payback period are transparent. Since the cash flows are not discounted at the project's required rate of return, the payback period ignores the time value of money and the risk of the project. Additionally, the payback period ignores cash flows after the payback period is reached. In the table above, for example, the Year 5 cash flow is completely ignored in the payback computation!

Example 1 is designed to illustrate some of the implications of these drawbacks of the payback period.

EXAMPLE 1

Drawbacks of the Payback Period

The cash flows, payback periods, and NPVs for Projects A through F are given in Table 3. For all of the projects, the required rate of return is 10 percent.

TABLE 3 Examples of Drawbacks of the Payback Period

	Cash Flows					
Year	**Project A**	**Project B**	**Project C**	**Project D**	**Project E**	**Project F**
0	−1,000	−1,000	−1,000	−1,000	−1,000	−1,000
1	1,000	100	400	500	400	500
2		200	300	500	400	500
3		300	200	500	400	10,000
4		400	100		400	
5		500	500		400	
Payback period	1.0	4.0	4.0	2.0	2.5	2.0
NPV	−90.91	65.26	140.60	243.43	516.31	7,380.92

Comment on why the payback period provides misleading information about the following:

1. Project A
2. Project B versus Project C
3. Project D versus Project E
4. Project D versus Project F

Solutions:

1. Project A does indeed pay itself back in one year. However, this result is misleading because the investment is unprofitable, with a negative NPV.
2. Although Projects B and C have the same payback period and the same cash flow after the payback period, the payback period does not detect the fact that Project C's cash flows within the payback period occur earlier and result in a higher NPV.
3. Projects D and E illustrate a common situation. The project with the shorter payback period is the less profitable project. Project E has a longer payback and higher NPV.
4. Projects D and F illustrate an important flaw of the payback period—that the payback period ignores cash flows after the payback period is reached. In this case, Project F has a much larger cash flow in Year 3, but the payback period does not recognize its value.

The payback period has many drawbacks—it is a measure of payback and not a measure of profitability. By itself, the payback period would be a dangerous criterion for evaluating capital projects. Its simplicity, however, is an advantage. The payback period is very easy to calculate and to explain. The payback period may also be used as an indicator of project liquidity. A project with a two-year payback may be more liquid than another project with a longer payback.

Because it is not economically sound, the payback period has no decision rule like that of the NPV or IRR. If the payback period is being used (perhaps as a measure of liquidity), analysts should also use an NPV or IRR to ensure that their decisions also reflect the profitability of the projects being considered.

4.4 Discounted Payback Period

The discounted payback period is the number of years it takes for the cumulative discounted cash flows from a project to equal the original investment. The discounted payback period partially addresses the weaknesses of the payback period. Table 4 gives an example of calculating the payback period and discounted payback period. The example assumes a discount rate of 10 percent.

TABLE 4 Payback Period and Discounted Payback Period

Year	0	1	2	3	4	5
Cash flow (CF)	−5,000	1,500.00	1,500.00	1,500.00	1,500.00	1,500.00
Cumulative CF	−5,000	−3,500.00	−2,000.00	−500.00	1,000.00	2,500.00
Discounted CF	−5,000	1,363.64	1,239.67	1,126.97	1,024.52	931.38
Cumulative discounted CF	−5,000	−3,636.36	−2,396.69	−1,269.72	−245.20	686.18

The payback period is three years plus $500/1{,}500 = 1/3$ of the fourth year's cash flow, or 3.33 years. The discounted payback period is between four and five years. The discounted payback period is four years plus $245.20/931.38 = 0.26$ of the fifth year's discounted cash flow, or 4.26 years.

The discounted payback period relies on discounted cash flows, much as the NPV criterion does. If a project has a negative NPV, it will usually not have a discounted payback period since it never recovers the initial investment.

The discounted payback does account for the time value of money and risk within the discounted payback period, but it ignores cash flows after the discounted payback period is reached. This drawback has two consequences. First, the discounted payback period is not a good measure of profitability (like the NPV or IRR) because it ignores these cash flows. Second, another idiosyncrasy of the discounted payback period comes from the possibility of negative cash flows after the discounted payback period is reached. It is possible for a project to have a negative NPV but to have a positive cumulative discounted cash flow in the middle of its life and, thus, a reasonable discounted payback period. The NPV and IRR, which consider all of a project's cash flows, do not suffer from this problem.

4.5 Average Accounting Rate of Return

The average accounting rate of return (AAR) can be defined as

$$\text{AAR} = \frac{\text{Average net income}}{\text{Average book value}}$$

To understand this measure of return, we will use a numerical example.

Assume a company invests $200,000 in a project that is depreciated straight-line over a five-year life to a zero salvage value. Sales revenues and cash operating expenses for each year are as shown in Table 5. The table also shows the annual income taxes (at a 40 percent tax rate) and the net income.

TABLE 5 Net Income for Calculating an Average Accounting Rate of Return

	Year 1	Year 2	Year 3	Year 4	Year 5
Sales	$100,000	$150,000	$240,000	$130,000	$80,000
Cash expenses	50,000	70,000	120,000	60,000	50,000
Depreciation	40,000	40,000	40,000	40,000	40,000
Earnings before taxes	10,000	40,000	80,000	30,000	−10,000
Taxes (at 40 percent)	4,000	16,000	32,000	12,000	−4,000[a]
Net income	6,000	24,000	48,000	18,000	−6,000

[a] Negative taxes occur in Year 5 because the earnings before taxes of −$10,000 can be deducted against earnings on other projects, thus reducing the tax bill by $4,000.

For the five-year period, the average net income is $18,000. The initial book value is $200,000, declining by $40,000 per year until the final book value is $0. The average book value for this asset is ($200,000 − $0) / 2 = $100,000. The average accounting rate of return is

$$\text{AAR} = \frac{\text{Average net income}}{\text{Average book value}} = \frac{18{,}000}{100{,}000} = 18\%$$

The advantages of the AAR are that it is easy to understand and easy to calculate. The AAR has some important disadvantages, however. Unlike the other capital budgeting criteria discussed here, the AAR is based on accounting numbers and not based on cash flows. This is an important conceptual and practical limitation. The AAR also does not account for the time value of money, and there is no conceptually sound cutoff for the AAR that distinguishes between profitable and unprofitable investments. The AAR is frequently calculated in different ways, so the analyst should verify the formula behind any AAR numbers that are supplied by someone else. Analysts should know the AAR and its potential limitations in practice, but they should rely on more economically sound methods like the NPV and IRR.

4.6 Profitability Index

The profitability index (PI) is the present value of a project's future cash flows divided by the initial investment. It can be expressed as

$$PI = \frac{\text{PV of future cash flows}}{\text{Initial investment}} = 1 + \frac{\text{NPV}}{\text{Initial investment}} \qquad \textbf{(44-5)}$$

You can see that the PI is closely related to the NPV. The PI is the *ratio* of the PV of future cash flows to the initial investment, whereas an NPV is the *difference* between the PV of future cash flows and the initial investment. Whenever the NPV is positive, the PI will be greater than 1.0; conversely, whenever the NPV is negative, the PI will be less than 1.0. The investment decision rule for the PI is as follows:

Invest if	PI > 1.0
Do not invest if	PI < 1.0

Because the PV of future cash flows equals the initial investment plus the NPV, the PI can also be expressed as 1.0 plus the ratio of the NPV to the initial investment, as shown in Equation 44-5 above. Example 2 illustrates the PI calculation.

EXAMPLE 2

Example of a PI Calculation

The Gerhardt Corporation investment (discussed earlier) had an outlay of €50 million, a present value of future cash flows of €63.136 million, and an NPV of €13.136 million. The profitability index is

$$PI = \frac{\text{PV of future cash flows}}{\text{Initial investment}} = \frac{63.136}{50.000} = 1.26$$

The PI can also be calculated as

$$PI = 1 + \frac{\text{NPV}}{\text{Initial investment}} = 1 + \frac{13.136}{50.000} = 1.26$$

Because the PI > 1.0, this is a profitable investment.

The PI indicates the value you are receiving in exchange for one unit of currency invested. Although the PI is used less frequently than the NPV and IRR, it is sometimes used as a guide in capital rationing, which we will discuss later. The PI is usually called the profitability index in corporations, but it is commonly referred to as a "benefit–cost ratio" in governmental and not-for-profit organizations.

4.7 NPV Profile

The NPV profile shows a project's NPV graphed as a function of various discount rates. Typically, the NPV is graphed vertically (on the *y*-axis), and the discount rates are graphed horizontally (on the *x*-axis). The NPV profile for the Gerhardt capital budgeting project is shown in Example 3.

EXAMPLE 3

NPV Profile

For the Gerhardt example, we have already calculated several NPVs for different discount rates. At 10 percent the NPV is €13.136 million; at 20 percent the NPV is −€0.543 million; and at 19.52 percent (the IRR), the NPV is zero. What is the NPV if the discount rate is 0 percent? The NPV discounted at 0 percent is €34 million, which is simply the sum of all of the undiscounted cash flows. Table 6 and Figure 1 show the NPV profile for the Gerhardt example for discount rates between 0 percent and 30 percent.

TABLE 6 Gerhardt NPV Profile

Discount Rate	NPV € Millions
0%	34.000
5.00%	22.406
10.00%	13.136
15.00%	5.623
19.52%	0.000
20.00%	−0.543
25.00%	−5.661
30.00%	−9.954

FIGURE 1 Gerhardt NPV Profile

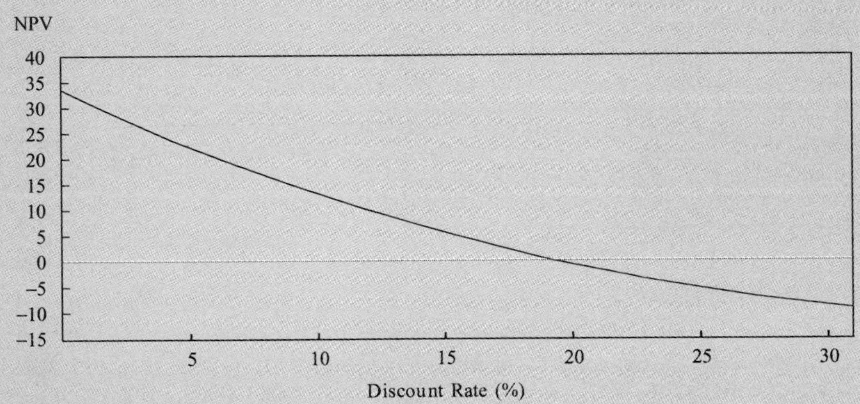

Three interesting points on this NPV profile are where the profile goes through the vertical axis (the NPV when the discount rate is zero), where the profile goes through the horizontal axis (where the discount rate is the IRR), and the NPV for the required rate of return (NPV is €13.136 million when the discount rate is the 10 percent required rate of return).

The NPV profile in Figure 1 is very well-behaved. The NPV declines at a decreasing rate as the discount rate increases. The profile is convex from the origin (convex from below). You will shortly see some examples in which the NPV profile is more complicated.

4.8 Ranking Conflicts between NPV and IRR

For a single conventional project, the NPV and IRR will agree on whether to invest or to not invest. For independent, conventional projects, no conflict exists between the decision rules for the NPV and IRR. However, in the case of two mutually exclusive projects, the two criteria will sometimes disagree. For example, Project A might have a larger NPV than Project B, but Project B has a higher IRR than Project A. In this case, should you invest in Project A or in Project B?

Differing cash flow patterns can cause two projects to rank differently with the NPV and IRR. For example, suppose Project A has shorter-term payoffs than Project B. This situation is presented in Example 4.

EXAMPLE 4

Ranking Conflict due to Differing Cash Flow Patterns

Projects A and B have similar outlays but different patterns of future cash flows. Project A realizes most of its cash payoffs earlier than Project B. The cash flows, as well as the NPV and IRR for the two projects, are shown in Table 7. For both projects, the required rate of return is 10 percent.

TABLE 7 Cash Flows, NPV, and IRR for Two Projects with Different Cash Flow Patterns

	Cash Flows						
Year	**0**	**1**	**2**	**3**	**4**	**NPV**	**IRR**
Project A	−200	80	80	80	80	53.59	21.86%
Project B	−200	0	0	0	400	73.21	18.92%

If the two projects were not mutually exclusive, you would invest in both because they are both profitable. However, you can choose either A (which has the higher IRR) or B (which has the higher NPV).

Table 8 and Figure 2 show the NPVs for Project A and Project B for various discount rates between 0 percent and 30 percent.

TABLE 8 NPV Profiles for Two Projects with Different Cash Flow Patterns

Discount Rate	NPV for Project A	NPV for Project B
0%	120.00	200.00
5.00%	83.68	129.08
10.00%	53.59	73.21
15.00%	28.40	28.70
15.09%	27.98	27.98
18.92%	11.41	0.00
20.00%	7.10	−7.10
21.86%	0.00	−18.62
25.00%	−11.07	−36.16
30.00%	−26.70	−59.95

FIGURE 2 NPV Profiles for Two Projects with Different Cash Flow Patterns

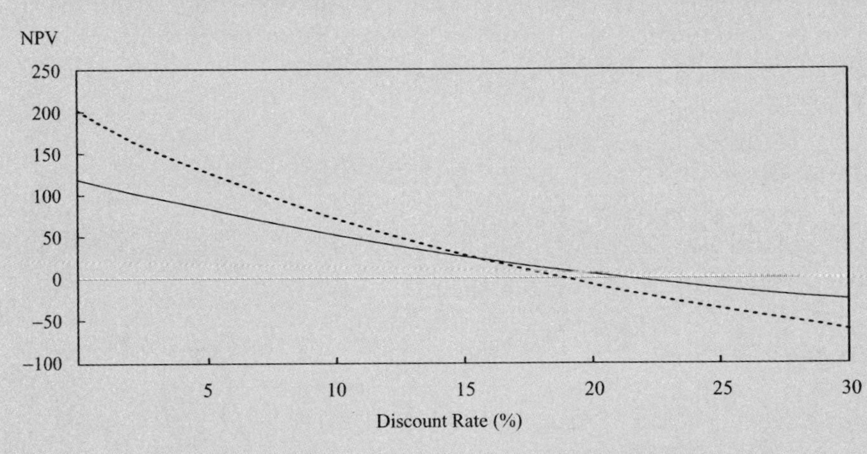

Note that Project B has the higher NPV for discount rates between 0 percent and 15.09 percent. Project A has the higher NPV for discount rates exceeding 15.09 percent. The crossover point of 15.09 percent in Figure 2 corresponds to the discount rate at which both projects have the same NPV (of 27.98). Project B has the higher NPV below the crossover point, and Project A has the higher NPV above it.

Whenever the NPV and IRR rank two mutually exclusive projects differently, as they do in the example above, you should choose the project based on the NPV. Project B, with the higher NPV, is the better project because of the reinvestment assumption. Mathematically, whenever you discount a cash flow at a particular discount rate, you are implicitly assuming that you can reinvest a cash flow at that same discount rate.[2] In the NPV calculation, you use a discount rate of 10 percent for both projects. In the IRR calculation, you use a discount rate equal to the IRR of 21.86 percent for Project A and 18.92 percent for Project B.

Can you reinvest the cash inflows from the projects at 10 percent, or 21.86 percent, or 18.92 percent? When you assume the required rate of return is 10 percent, you are assuming an opportunity cost of 10 percent—that you can either find other projects that pay a 10 percent return or pay back your sources of capital that cost you 10 percent. The fact that you earned 21.86 percent in Project A or 18.92 percent in Project B does not mean that you can reinvest future cash flows at those rates. (In fact, if you can reinvest future cash flows at 21.86 percent or 18.92 percent, these should have been used as your required rate of return instead of 10 percent.) Because the NPV criterion uses the most realistic discount rate—the opportunity cost of funds—the NPV criterion should be used for evaluating mutually exclusive projects.

Another circumstance that frequently causes mutually exclusive projects to be ranked differently by NPV and IRR criteria is project scale—the sizes of the projects. Would you rather have a small project with a higher rate of return or a large project with a lower rate of return? Sometimes, the larger, low rate of return project has the better NPV. This case is developed in Example 5.

EXAMPLE 5

Ranking Conflicts due to Differing Project Scale

Project A has a much smaller outlay than Project B, although they have similar future cash flow patterns. The cash flows, as well as the NPVs and IRRs for the two projects, are shown in Table 9. For both projects, the required rate of return is 10 percent.

TABLE 9 Cash Flows, NPV, and IRR for Two Projects of Differing Scale

	Cash Flows						
Year	**0**	**1**	**2**	**3**	**4**	**NPV**	**IRR**
Project A	−100	50	50	50	50	58.49	34.90%
Project B	−400	170	170	170	170	138.88	25.21%

If they were not mutually exclusive, you would invest in both projects because they are both profitable. However, you can choose either Project A (which has the higher IRR) or Project B (which has the higher NPV).

[2] For example, assume that you are receiving \$100 in one year discounted at 10 percent. The present value is \$100/\$1.10 = \$90.91. Instead of receiving the \$100 in one year, invest it for one additional year at 10 percent, and it grows to \$110. What is the present value of \$110 received in two years discounted at 10 percent? It is the same \$90.91. Because both future cash flows are worth the same, you are implicitly assuming that reinvesting the earlier cash flow at the discount rate of 10 percent has no effect on its value.

Table 10 and Figure 3 show the NPVs for Project A and Project B for various discount rates between 0 percent and 30 percent.

TABLE 10 NPV Profiles for Two Projects of Differing Scale

Discount Rate	NPV for Project A	NPV for Project B
0%	100.00	280.00
5.00%	77.30	202.81
10.00%	58.49	138.88
15.00%	42.75	85.35
20.00%	29.44	40.08
21.86%	25.00	25.00
25.00%	18.08	1.47
25.21%	17.65	0.00
30.00%	8.31	−31.74
34.90%	0.00	−60.00
35.00%	−0.15	−60.52

FIGURE 3 NPV Profiles for Two Projects of Differing Scale

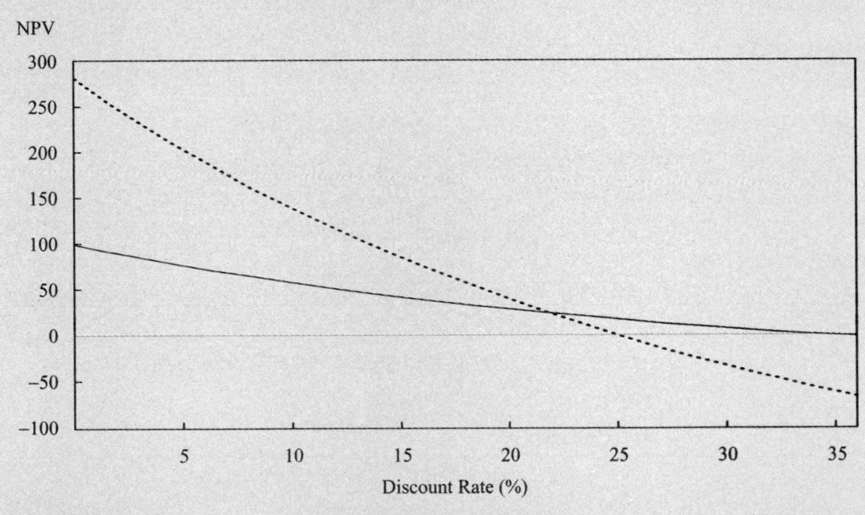

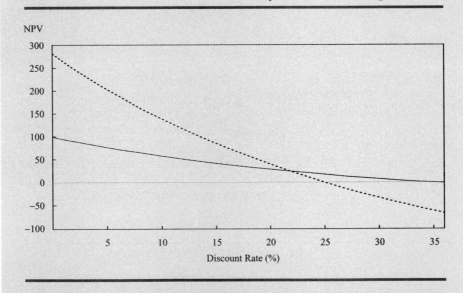

Note that Project B has the higher NPV for discount rates between 0 percent and 21.86 percent. Project A has the higher NPV for discount rates exceeding 21.86 percent. The crossover point of 21.86 percent in Figure 3 corresponds to the discount rate at which both projects have the same NPV (of 25.00). Below the crossover point, Project B has the higher NPV, and above it, Project A has the higher NPV. When cash flows are discounted at the 10 percent required rate of return, the choice is clear—Project B, the larger project, which has the superior NPV.

The good news is that the NPV and IRR criteria will usually indicate the same investment decision for a given project. They will usually both recommend acceptance or rejection of the project. When the choice is between two mutually exclusive projects and the NPV and IRR rank the two projects differently, the NPV criterion is strongly preferred. There are good reasons for this preference. The NPV shows the amount of gain, or wealth increase, as a currency amount. The reinvestment assumption of the NPV is the more economically realistic. The IRR does give you a rate of return, but the IRR could be for a small investment or for only a short period of time. As a practical matter, once a corporation has the data to calculate the NPV, it is fairly trivial to go ahead and calculate the IRR and other capital budgeting criteria. However, the most appropriate and theoretically sound criterion is the NPV.

4.9 The Multiple IRR Problem and the No IRR Problem

A problem that can arise with the IRR criterion is the "multiple IRR problem." We can illustrate this problem with the following nonconventional cash flow pattern:[3]

Time	0	1	2
Cash flow	−1,000	5,000	−6,000

The IRR for these cash flows satisfies this equation:

$$-1{,}000 + \frac{5{,}000}{(1+\text{IRR})^1} + \frac{-6{,}000}{(1+\text{IRR})^2} = 0$$

It turns out that there are two values of IRR that satisfy the equation: IRR = 1 = 100% and IRR = 2 = 200%. To further understand this problem, consider the NPV profile for this investment, which is shown in Table 11 and Figure 4.

As you can see in the NPV profile, the NPV is equal to zero at IRR = 100% and IRR = 200%. The NPV is negative for discount rates below 100 percent, positive between 100 percent and 200 percent, and then negative above 200 percent. The NPV reaches its highest value when the discount rate is 140 percent.

It is also possible to have an investment project with no IRR. The "no-IRR problem" occurs with this cash flow pattern:[4]

Time	0	1	2
Cash flow	100	−300	250

The IRR for these cash flows satisfies this equation:

$$100 + \frac{-300}{(1+\text{IRR})^1} + \frac{250}{(1+\text{IRR})^2} = 0$$

For these cash flows, no discount rate exists that results in a zero NPV. Does that mean this project is a bad investment? In this case, the project is actually a good investment. As Table 12 and Figure 5 show, the NPV is positive for all discount rates. The lowest NPV, of 10, occurs for a discount rate of 66.67 percent, and the NPV is always greater than zero. Consequently, no IRR exists.

[3] This example is adapted from Hirschleifer (1958).

[4] This example is also adapted from Hirschleifer.

TABLE 11 NPV Profile for a Multiple IRR Example

Discount Rate	NPV
0%	−2,000.00
25%	−840.00
50%	−333.33
75%	−102.04
100%	0.00
125%	37.04
140%	41.67
150%	40.00
175%	24.79
200%	0.00
225%	−29.59
250%	−61.22
300%	−125.00
350%	−185.19
400%	−240.00
500%	−333.33
1,000%	−595.04
2,000%	−775.51
3,000%	−844.95
4,000%	−881.62
10,000%	−951.08
1,000,000%	−999.50

FIGURE 4 NPV Profile for a Multiple IRR Example

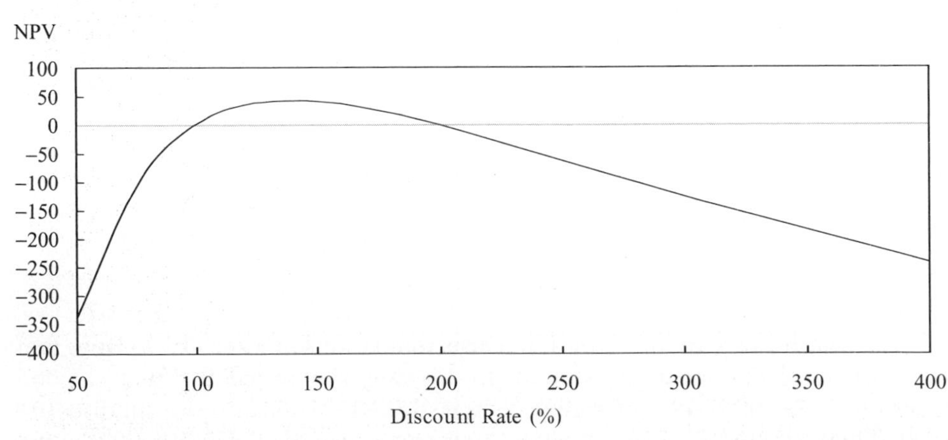

TABLE 12 NPV Profile for a Project with No IRR

Discount Rate	NPV
0%	50.00
25%	20.00
50%	11.11
66.67%	10.00
75%	10.20
100%	12.50
125%	16.05
150%	20.00
175%	23.97
200%	27.78
225%	31.36
250%	34.69
275%	37.78
300%	40.63
325%	43.25
350%	45.68
375%	47.92
400%	50.00

FIGURE 5 NPV Profile for a Project with No IRR

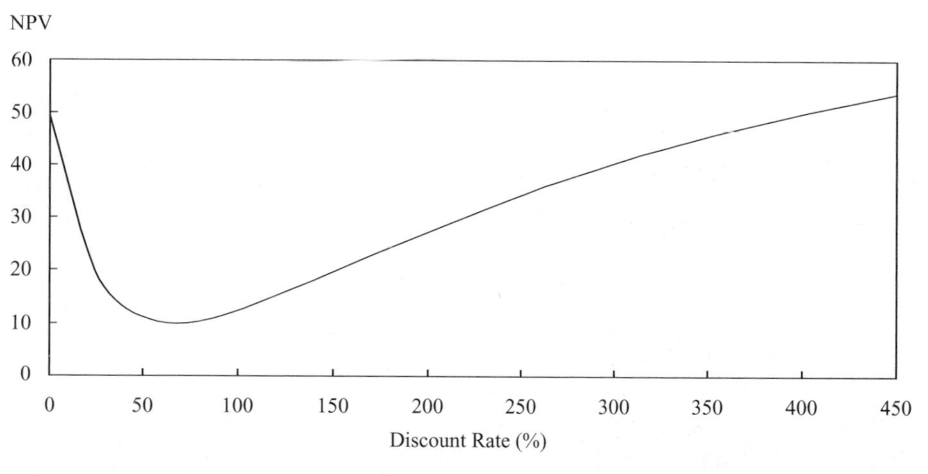

For conventional projects that have outlays followed by inflows—negative cash flows followed by positive cash flows—the multiple IRR problem cannot occur. However, for nonconventional projects, as in the example above, the multiple IRR problem can occur. The IRR equation is essentially an *n*th degree polynomial. An *n*th degree polynomial can have up to *n* solutions, although it will have no more real solutions than the number of cash flow sign changes. For example, a project with two sign changes could have zero, one, or two IRRs. Having two sign changes does not mean that you *will* have multiple IRRs; it just means that you *might*. Fortunately, most capital budgeting projects have only one IRR. Analysts should always be aware of the unusual cash flow patterns that can generate the multiple IRR problem.

4.10 Popularity and Usage of the Capital Budgeting Methods

Analysts need to know the basic logic of the various capital budgeting criteria as well as the practicalities involved in using them in real corporations. Before delving into the many issues involved in applying these models, we would like to present some feedback on their popularity.

The usefulness of any analytical tool always depends on the specific application. Corporations generally find these capital budgeting criteria useful. Two recent surveys by Graham and Harvey (2001) and Brounen, De Jong, and Koedijk (2004) report on the frequency of their use by U.S. and European corporations. Table 13 gives the mean responses of executives in five countries to the question "How frequently does your company use the following techniques when deciding which projects or acquisitions to pursue?"

TABLE 13 Mean Responses about Frequency of Use of Capital Budgeting Techniques

	U.S.	U.K.	Netherlands	Germany	France
Internal rate of return[a]	3.09	2.31	2.36	2.15	2.27
Net present value[a]	3.08	2.32	2.76	2.26	1.86
Payback period[a]	2.53	2.77	2.53	2.29	2.46
Hurdle rate	2.13	1.35	1.98	1.61	0.73
Sensitivity analysis	2.31	2.21	1.84	1.65	0.79
Earnings multiple approach	1.89	1.81	1.61	1.25	1.70
Discounted payback period[a]	1.56	1.49	1.25	1.59	0.87
Real options approach	1.47	1.65	1.49	2.24	2.20
Accounting rate of return[a]	1.34	1.79	1.40	1.63	1.11
Value at risk	0.95	0.85	0.51	1.45	1.68
Adjusted present value	0.85	0.78	0.78	0.71	1.11
Profitability index[a]	0.85	1.00	0.78	1.04	1.64

Note: Respondents used a scale ranging from 0 (never) to 4 (always).

[a] These techniques were described in this section of the reading. You will encounter the others elsewhere.

Although financial textbooks preach the superiority of the NPV and IRR techniques, it is clear that several other methods are heavily used.[5] In the four European countries, the payback period is used as often as, or even slightly more often than, the NPV and IRR. In these two studies, larger companies tended to prefer the NPV and IRR over the payback period. The fact that the U.S. companies were larger, on average, partially explains the greater U.S. preference for the NPV and IRR. Other factors influence the choice of capital budgeting techniques. Private corporations used the payback period more frequently than did public corporations. Companies managed by an MBA had a stronger preference for the discounted cash flow techniques. Of course, any survey research also has some limitations. In this case, the persons in these large corporations responding to the surveys may not have been aware of all of the applications of these techniques.

These capital budgeting techniques are essential tools for corporate managers. Capital budgeting is also relevant to external analysts. Because a corporation's investing decisions ultimately determine the value of its financial obligations, the corporation's investing processes are vital. The NPV criterion is the criterion most directly related to stock prices. If a corporation invests in positive NPV projects, these should add to the wealth of its shareholders. Example 6 illustrates this scenario.

EXAMPLE 6

NPVs and Stock Prices

Freitag Corporation is investing €600 million in distribution facilities. The present value of the future after-tax cash flows is estimated to be €850 million. Freitag has 200 million outstanding shares with a current market price of €32.00 per share. This investment is new information, and it is independent of other expectations about the company. What should be the effect of the project on the value of the company and the stock price?

Solution: The NPV of the project is €850 million − €600 million = €250 million. The total market value of the company prior to the investment is €32.00 × 200 million shares = €6,400 million. The value of the company should increase by €250 million to €6,650 million. The price per share should increase by the NPV per share, or €250 million / 200 million shares = €1.25 per share. The share price should increase from €32.00 to €33.25.

The effect of a capital budgeting project's positive or negative NPV on share price is more complicated than Example 6 above, in which the value of the stock increased by the project's NPV. The value of a company is the value of its existing investments plus the net present values of all of its future investments. If an analyst learns of an investment, the impact of that investment on the stock price will depend on whether the investment's profitability is more or less than expected. For example, an analyst could learn of a positive NPV project, but if the project's

[5] Analysts often refer to the NPV and IRR as "discounted cash flow techniques" because they accurately account for the timing of all cash flows when they are discounted.

profitability is less than expectations, this stock might drop in price on the news. Alternatively, news of a particular capital project might be considered as a signal about other capital projects underway or in the future. A project that by itself might add, say, €0.25 to the value of the stock might signal the existence of other profitable projects. News of this project might increase the stock price by far more than €0.25.

The integrity of a corporation's capital budgeting processes is important to analysts. Management's capital budgeting processes can demonstrate two things about the quality of management: the degree to which management embraces the goal of shareholder wealth maximization, and its effectiveness in pursuing that goal. Both of these factors are important to shareholders.

SUMMARY

Capital budgeting is the process that companies use for decision making on capital projects—those projects with a life of a year or more. This reading developed the principles behind the basic capital budgeting model, the cash flows that go into the model, and several extensions of the basic model.

- Capital budgeting undergirds the most critical investments for many corporations—their investments in long-term assets. The principles of capital budgeting have been applied to other corporate investing and financing decisions and to security analysis and portfolio management.
- The typical steps in the capital budgeting process are: (1) generating ideas, (2) analyzing individual proposals, (3) planning the capital budget, and (4) monitoring and post-auditing.
- Projects susceptible to capital budgeting process can be categorized as: (1) replacement, (2) expansion, (3) new products and services, and (4) regulatory, safety and environmental.
- Capital budgeting decisions are based on incremental after-tax cash flows discounted at the opportunity cost of funds. Financing costs are ignored because both the cost of debt and the cost of other capital are captured in the discount rate.
- The net present value (NPV) is the present value of all after-tax cash flows, or

  $$NPV = \sum_{t=0}^{n} \frac{CF_t}{(1 + r)^t}$$

  where the investment outlays are negative cash flows included in the CF_ts and where r is the required rate of return for the investment.
- The IRR is the discount rate that makes the present value of all future cash flows sum to zero. This equation can be solved for the IRR:

  $$\sum_{t=0}^{n} \frac{CF_t}{(1 + IRR)^t} = 0$$

- The payback period is the number of years required to recover the original investment in a project. The payback is based on cash flows.
- The discounted payback period is the number of years it takes for the cumulative discounted cash flows from a project to equal the original investment.
- The average accounting rate of return (AAR) can be defined as follows:

  $$AAR = \frac{\text{Average net income}}{\text{Average book value}}$$

- The profitability index (PI) is the present value of a project's future cash flows divided by the initial investment:

  $$PI = \frac{\text{PV of future cash flows}}{\text{Initial investment}} = 1 + \frac{\text{NPV}}{\text{Initial investment}}$$

- The capital budgeting decision rules are to invest if the NPV > 0, if the IRR > *r*, or if the PI > 1.0 There are no decision rules for the payback period, discounted payback period, and AAR because they are not always sound measures.
- The NPV profile is a graph that shows a project's NPV graphed as a function of various discount rates.
- For mutually exclusive projects that are ranked differently by the NPV and IRR, it is economically sound to choose the project with the higher NPV.
- The "multiple IRR problem" and the "no IRR problem" can arise for a project with nonconventional cash flows—cash flows that change signs more than once during the project's life.
- The fact that projects with positive NPVs theoretically increase the value of the company and the value of its stock could explain the popularity of NPV as an evaluation method.

PRACTICE PROBLEMS FOR READING 44

1. Given the following cash flows for a capital project, calculate the NPV and IRR. The required rate of return is 8 percent.

Year	0	1	2	3	4	5
Cash flow	50,000	15,000	15,000	20,000	10,000	5,000

	NPV	IRR
A.	$1,905	10.9%
B.	$1,905	26.0%
C.	$3,379	10.9%
D.	$3,379	26.0%

2. Given the following cash flows for a capital project, calculate its payback period and discounted payback period. The required rate of return is 8 percent.

Year	0	1	2	3	4	5
Cash flow	−50,000	15,000	15,000	20,000	10,000	5,000

The discounted payback period is

A. 0.16 years longer than the payback period.
B. 0.80 years longer than the payback period.
C. 1.01 years longer than the payback period.
D. 1.85 years longer than the payback period.

3. An investment of $100 generates after-tax cash flows of $40 in year 1, $80 in year 2, and $120 in year 3. The required rate of return is 20 percent. The net present value is *closest* to

A. $42.22.
B. $58.33.
C. $68.52.
D. $98.95.

4. An investment of $150,000 is expected to generate an after-tax cash flow of $100,000 in one year and another $120,000 in two years. The cost of capital is 10 percent. What is the internal rate of return?

A. 28.19 percent.
B. 28.39 percent.
C. 28.59 percent.
D. 28.79 percent.

5. Kim Corporation is considering an investment of 750 million won with expected after-tax cash inflows of 175 million won per year for seven years. The required rate of return is 10 percent. What is the project's

	NPV	IRR
A.	102 million won	14.0%
B.	102 million won	23.3%
C.	193 million won	14.0%
D.	193 million won	23.3%

6. Kim Corporation is considering an investment of 750 million won with expected after-tax cash inflows of 175 million won per year for seven years. The required rate of return is 10 percent. Expressed in years, what is the project's

	payback period?	discounted payback period?
A.	4.3	5.4
B.	4.3	5.9
C.	4.8	5.4
D.	4.8	5.9

7. An investment of $20,000 will create a perpetual after-tax cash flow of $2,000. The required rate of return is 8 percent. What is the investment's profitability index?
   A. 1.00.
   B. 1.08.
   C. 1.16.
   D. 1.25.

8. Hermann Corporation is considering an investment of €375 million with expected after-tax cash inflows of €115 million per year for seven years and an additional after-tax salvage value of €50 million in year 7. The required rate of return is 10 percent. What is the investment's PI?
   A. 1.19.
   B. 1.33.
   C. 1.56.
   D. 1.75.

9. Erin Chou is reviewing a profitable investment project that has a conventional cash flow pattern. If the cash flows for the project, initial outlay, and future after-tax cash flows all double, Chou would predict that the IRR would
   A. increase and the NPV would increase.
   B. increase and the NPV would stay the same.
   C. stay the same and the NPV would increase.
   D. stay the same and the NPV would stay the same.

10. Shirley Shea has evaluated an investment proposal and found that its payback period is one year, it has a negative NPV, and it has a positive IRR. Is this combination of results possible?

A. Yes.

B. No, because a project with a positive IRR has a positive NPV.

C. No, because a project with a negative NPV has a negative payback period.

D. No, because a project with such a rapid payback period has a positive NPV.

11. An investment has an outlay of 100 and after-tax cash flows of 40 annually for four years. A project enhancement increases the outlay by 15 and the annual after-tax cash flows by 5. As a result, the vertical intercept of the NPV profile of the enhanced project shifts

A. up and the horizontal intercept shifts left.

B. up and the horizontal intercept shifts right.

C. down and the horizontal intercept shifts left.

D. down and the horizontal intercept shifts right.

12. Projects 1 and 2 have similar outlays, although the patterns of future cash flows are different. The cash flows as well as the NPV and IRR for the two projects are shown below. For both projects, the required rate of return is 10 percent.

	Cash Flows						
Year	**0**	**1**	**2**	**3**	**4**	**NPV**	**IRR**
Project 1	−50	20	20	20	20	13.40	21.86%
Project 2	−50	0	0	0	100	18.30	18.92%

The two projects are mutually exclusive. What is the appropriate investment decision?

A. Invest in Project 1 because it has the higher IRR.

B. Invest in Project 2 because it has the higher NPV.

C. Invest half in each project.

D. Invest in both projects.

13. Consider the two projects below. The cash flows as well as the NPV and IRR for the two projects are given. For both projects, the required rate of return is 10 percent.

	Cash Flows						
Year	**0**	**1**	**2**	**3**	**4**	**NPV**	**IRR**
Project 1	−100	36	36	36	36	14.12	16.37%
Project 2	−100	0	0	0	175	19.53	15.02%

What discount rate would result in the same NPV for both projects?

A. A rate between 0.00 percent and 10.00 percent.

B. A rate between 10.00 percent and 15.02 percent.

C. A rate between 15.02 percent and 16.37 percent.

D. A rate above 16.37 percent.

14. Wilson Flannery is concerned that this project has multiple IRRs.

Year	0	1	2	3
Cash flows	−50	100	0	−50

How many discount rates produce a zero NPV for this project?

A. One, a discount rate of 0 percent.

B. Two, discount rates of 0 percent and 32 percent.

C. Two, discount rates of 0 percent and 62 percent.

D. Two, discount rates of 0 percent and 92 percent.

2005 exam

15. With regard to the net present value (NPV) profiles of two projects, the crossover rate is *best* described as the discount rate at which

A. two projects have the same NPV.

B. two projects have the same internal rate of return.

C. a project's NPV changes from positive to negative.

D. a project's NPV changes from negative to positive.

2005 exam

16. With regard to net present value (NPV) profiles, the point at which a profile crosses the vertical axis is *best* described as

A. the point at which two projects have the same NPV.

B. the sum of the undiscounted cash flows from a project.

C. the point at which two projects have the same internal rate of return.

D. a project's internal rate of return when the project's NPV is equal to zero.

2005 exam

17. With regard to net present value (NPV) profiles, the point at which a profile crosses the horizontal axis is *best* described as

A. the point at which two projects have the same NPV.

B. the sum of the undiscounted cash flows from a project.

C. the point at which two projects have the same internal rate of return.

D. a project's internal rate of return when the project's NPV is equal to zero.

2005 exam

18. With regard to capital budgeting, an appropriate estimate of the incremental cash flows from a project is *least likely* to include

A. externalities.

B. interest costs.

C. opportunity costs.

D. additional inventory.

COST OF CAPITAL

by Yves Courtois, Gene C. Lai, and Pamela P. Peterson

READING

45

LEARNING OUTCOMES

The candidate should be able to:

a. calculate and interpret the weighted average cost of capital (WACC) of a company;

b. describe how taxes affect the cost of capital from different capital sources;

c. describe alternative methods of calculating the weights used in the weighted average cost of capital, including the use of the company's target capital structure;

d. explain how the marginal cost of capital and the investment opportunity schedule are used to determine the optimal capital budget;

e. explain the marginal cost of capital's role in determining the net present value of a project;

f. calculate and interpret the cost of fixed rate debt capital using the yield-to-maturity approach and the debt-rating approach;

g. calculate and interpret the cost of noncallable, nonconvertible preferred stock;

h. calculate and interpret the cost of equity capital using the capital asset pricing model approach, the dividend discount model approach, and the bond-yield-plus risk-premium approach;

i. explain the country equity risk premium in the estimation of the cost of equity for a company located in a developing market;

j. describe the marginal cost of capital schedule, explain why it may be upward-sloping with respect to additional capital, and calculate and interpret its breakpoints;

k. explain and demonstrate the correct treatment of flotation costs.

1 INTRODUCTION

A company grows by making investments that are expected to increase revenues and profits. The company acquires the capital or funds necessary to make such investments by borrowing or using funds from owners. By applying this capital to investments with long-term benefits, the company is producing value today. But, how much value? The answer depends not only on the investments' expected future cash flows but also on the cost of the funds. Borrowing is not costless. Neither is using owners' funds.

The cost of this capital is an important ingredient in both investment decision making by the company's management and the valuation of the company by investors. If a company invests in projects that produce a return in excess of the cost of capital, the company has created value; in contrast, if the company invests in projects whose returns are less than the cost of capital, the company has actually destroyed value. Therefore, the estimation of the cost of capital is a central issue in corporate financial management. For the analyst seeking to evaluate a company's investment program and its competitive position, an accurate estimate of a company's cost of capital is important as well.

Cost of capital estimation is a challenging task. As we have already implied, the cost of capital is not observable but, rather, must be estimated. Arriving at a cost of capital estimate requires a host of assumptions and estimates. Another challenge is that the cost of capital that is appropriately applied to a specific investment depends on the characteristics of that investment: The riskier the investment's cash flows, the greater its cost of capital. In reality, a company must estimate project-specific costs of capital. What is often done, however, is to estimate the cost of capital for the company as a whole and then adjust this overall corporate cost of capital upward or downward to reflect the risk of the contemplated project relative to the company's average project.

This reading is organized as follows: In the next section, we introduce the cost of capital and its basic computation. Section 3 presents a selection of methods for estimating the costs of the various sources of capital. Section 4 discusses issues an analyst faces in using the cost of capital. A summary concludes the reading.

2 COST OF CAPITAL

The **cost of capital** is the rate of return that the suppliers of capital—bondholders and owners—require as compensation for their contribution of capital. Another way of looking at the cost of capital is that it is the opportunity cost of funds for the suppliers of capital: A potential supplier of capital will not voluntarily invest in a company unless its return meets or exceeds what the supplier could earn elsewhere in an investment of comparable risk.

A company typically has several alternatives for raising capital, including issuing equity, debt, and instruments that share characteristics of debt and equity. Each source selected becomes a component of the company's funding and has a cost (required rate of return) that may be called a **component cost of capital**. Because we are using the cost of capital in the evaluation of investment opportunities, we are dealing with a *marginal* cost—what it would cost to raise additional funds for the potential investment project. Therefore, the cost of capital that the investment analyst is concerned with is a marginal cost.

Let us focus on the cost of capital for the entire company (later we will address how to adjust that for specific projects). The cost of capital of a company is the required rate of return that investors demand for the average-risk investment of a company. The most common way to estimate this required rate of return is to calculate the marginal cost of each of the various sources of capital and then calculate a weighted average of these costs. This weighted average is referred to as the **weighted average cost of capital (WACC)**. The WACC is also referred to as the marginal cost of capital (MCC) because it is the cost that a company incurs for additional capital. The weights in this weighted average are the proportions of the various sources of capital that the company uses to support its investment program. Therefore, the WACC, in its most general terms, is

$$\text{WACC} = w_d r_d (1 - t) + w_p r_p + w_e r_e \quad \textbf{(45-1)}$$

where

w_d is the proportion of debt that the company uses when it raises new funds
r_d is the before-tax marginal cost of debt
t is the company's marginal tax rate
w_p is the proportion of preferred stock the company uses when it raises new funds
r_p is the marginal cost of preferred stock
w_e is the proportion of equity that the company uses when it raises new funds
r_e is the marginal cost of equity

EXAMPLE 1

Computing the Weighted Average Cost of Capital

Assume that ABC Corporation has the following capital structure: 30 percent debt, 10 percent preferred stock, and 60 percent equity. ABC Corporation wishes to maintain these proportions as it raises new funds. Its before-tax cost of debt is 8 percent, its cost of preferred stock is 10 percent, and its cost of equity is 15 percent. If the company's marginal tax rate is 40 percent, what is ABC's weighted average cost of capital?

Solution: The weighed average cost of capital is

$$\begin{aligned}\text{WACC} &= (0.3)(0.08)(1 - 0.40) + (0.1)(0.1) + (0.6)(0.15) \\ &= 11.44 \text{ percent.}\end{aligned}$$

There are important points concerning the calculation of the WACC as shown in Equation 45-1 that the analyst must be familiar with. The next two sections address two key issues: taxes and the selection of weights.

2.1 Taxes and the Cost of Capital

Notice that in Equation 45-1 we adjust the expected before-tax cost on new debt financing, r_d, by a factor of $(1 - t)$. In the United States and many other tax jurisdictions, the interest on debt financing is a deduction to arrive at taxable income. Taking the tax-deductibility of interest as the base case, we adjust the pre-tax cost of debt for this tax shield. Multiplying r_d by $(1 - t)$ results in an estimate of the after-tax cost of debt.

For example, suppose a company pays €1 million in interest on its €10 million of debt. The cost of this debt is not €1 million because this interest expense reduces taxable income by €1 million, resulting in a lower tax. If the company is subject to a tax rate of 40 percent, this €1 million of interest costs the company (€1 million)(1 − 0.4) = €0.6 million because the interest reduces the company's tax bill by €0.4 million. In this case, the before-tax cost of debt is 10 percent, whereas the after-tax cost of debt is (€0.6 million)/(€10 million) = 6 percent.

Estimating the cost of common equity capital is more challenging than estimating the cost of debt capital. Debt capital involves a stated legal obligation on the part of the company to pay interest and repay the principal on the borrowing. Equity entails no such obligation. Estimating the cost of conventional preferred equity is rather straightforward because the dividend is generally stated and fixed, but estimating the cost of common equity is challenging. There are several methods available for estimating the cost of common equity, and we discuss two in this reading. The first method uses the capital asset pricing model, and the second method uses the dividend discount model, which is based on discounted cash flows. No matter the method, there is no need to make any adjustment in the cost of equity for taxes because the payments to owners, whether in the form of dividends or the return on capital, are not tax-deductible for the company.

EXAMPLE 2

Incorporating the Effect of Taxes on the Costs of Capital

Jorge Ricard, a financial analyst, is estimating the costs of capital for the Zeale Corporation. In the process of this estimation, Ricard has estimated the before-tax costs of capital for Zeale's debt and equity as 4 percent and 6 percent, respectively. What are the after-tax costs of debt and equity if Zeale's marginal tax rate is

1. 30 percent?
2. 48 percent?

	Marginal Tax Rate	After-Tax Cost of Debt	After-Tax Cost of Equity
Solution to 1:	30 percent	0.04(1 − 0.30) = 2.80 percent	6 percent
Solution to 2:	48 percent	0.04(1 − 0.48) = 2.08 percent	6 percent

Note: There is no adjustment for taxes in the case of equity; the before-tax cost of equity is equal to the after-tax cost of equity.

2.2 Weights of the Weighted Average

How do we determine what weights to use? Ideally, we want to use the proportion of each source of capital that the company would use in the project or company. If we assume that a company has a target capital structure and raises capital consistent with this target, we should use this target capital structure. The **target capital structure** is the capital structure that a company is striving to obtain. If we know the company's target capital structure, then, of course, we should use this in our analysis. Someone outside the company, however, such as an analyst, typically does not know the target capital structure and must estimate it using one of several approaches:

1. Assume the company's current capital structure, at market value weights for the components, represents the company's target capital structure.
2. Examine trends in the company's capital structure or statements by management regarding capital structure policy to infer the target capital structure.
3. Use averages of comparable companies' capital structures as the target capital structure.

In the absence of knowledge of a company's target capital structure, we may take Method 1 as the baseline. Note that in applying Method 3, we use unweighted, arithmetic average, as is often done for simplicity. An alternative is to calculate a weighted average, which would give more weight to larger companies.

Suppose we are using the company's current capital structure as a proxy for the target capital structure. In this case, we use the market value of the different capital sources in the calculation of these proportions. For example, if a company has the following market values for its capital

Bonds outstanding	\$5 million
Preferred stock	1 million
Common stock	14 million
Total capital	\$20 million

the weights that we apply would be

$$w_d = 0.25$$
$$w_p = 0.05$$
$$w_e = 0.70$$

Example 3 illustrates the estimation of weights. Note that a simple way of transforming a debt-to-equity ratio D/E into a weight—that is, D/(D + E)—is to divide D/E by 1 + D/E.

EXAMPLE 3

Estimating the Proportions of Capital

Fin Anziell is a financial analyst with Analytiker Firma. Anziell is in the process of estimating the cost of capital of Gewicht GmbH. The following information is provided:

Gewicht GmbH	
Market value of debt	€50 million
Market value of equity	€60 million

Primary competitors and their capital structures (in millions):

Competitor	Market Value of Debt	Market Value of Equity
A	€ 25	€ 50
B	€ 101	€ 190
C	£ 40	£ 60

What are Gewicht's proportions of debt and equity that Anziell would use if estimating these proportions using the company's

1. current capital structure?
2. competitors' capital structure?
3. Suppose Gewicht announces that a debt-to-equity ratio of 0.7 reflects its target capital structure. What weights should Anziell use in the cost of capital calculations?

Solution to 1:
Current capital structure

$$w_d = \frac{€50 \text{ million}}{€50 \text{ million} + €60 \text{ million}} = 0.4545$$

$$w_e = \frac{€60 \text{ million}}{€50 \text{ million} + €60 \text{ million}} = 0.5454$$

Solution to 2:
Competitors' capital structure:[1]

$$w_d = \frac{\left(\dfrac{€25}{€25 + €50}\right) + \left(\dfrac{€101}{€101 + €190}\right) + \left(\dfrac{£40}{£40 + £60}\right)}{3} = 0.3601$$

$$w_e = \frac{\left(\dfrac{€50}{€25 + €50}\right) + \left(\dfrac{€190}{€101 + €190}\right) + \left(\dfrac{£60}{£40 + £60}\right)}{3} = 0.6399$$

Solution to 3: A debt-to-equity ratio of 0.7 represents a weight on debt of 0.7/1.7 = 0.4118 so that $w_d = 0.4118$ and $w_e = 1 - 0.4118 = 0.5882$. These would be the preferred weights to use in a cost of capital calculation.

2.3 Applying the Cost of Capital to Capital Budgeting and Security Valuation

With some insight now into the calculation of the cost of capital, let us continue to improve our understanding of the roles it plays in financial analysis. A chief use of the marginal cost of capital estimate is in capital-budgeting decision making. What role does the marginal cost of capital play in a company's investment program, and how do we adapt it when we need to evaluate a specific investment project?

A company's marginal cost of capital (MCC) may increase as additional capital is raised, whereas returns to a company's investment opportunities are generally believed to decrease as the company makes additional investments, as represented by the **investment opportunity schedule** (IOS).[2] We show this relation in Figure 1, graphing the upward-sloping marginal cost of capital schedule against the downward-sloping investment opportunity schedule. In the context of a company's investment decision, the optimal capital budget is that amount of capital raised and invested at which the marginal cost of capital is equal to the marginal return from investing. In other words, the optimal capital budget occurs when the marginal cost of capital intersects with the investment opportunity schedule as seen in Figure 1.

The relation between the MCC and the IOS provides a broad picture of the basic decision-making problem of a company. However, we are often interested in valuing an individual project or even a portion of a company, such as a division

[1] These weights represent the arithmetic average of the three companies' debt proportion and equity proportion, respectively. If instead we chose to use a weighted average, we would calculate the debt proportion as the sum of the debt for all three companies, divided by the sum of the total capital for all three; we would calculate the equity proportion in the same manner. The weighted average proportions are 0.3562 and 0.6438, respectively.

[2] The investment opportunity schedule originates with Fisher's production opportunities [Irving Fisher, *The Theory of Interest* (New York: MacMillan Co.), 1930] and was adapted to capital budgeting by John Hirshleifer ["On the Theory of Optimal Investment Decision," *Journal of Political Economy*, Vol. 66, No. 4 (August 1958), pp. 329–352.]

FIGURE 1 Optimal Investment Decision

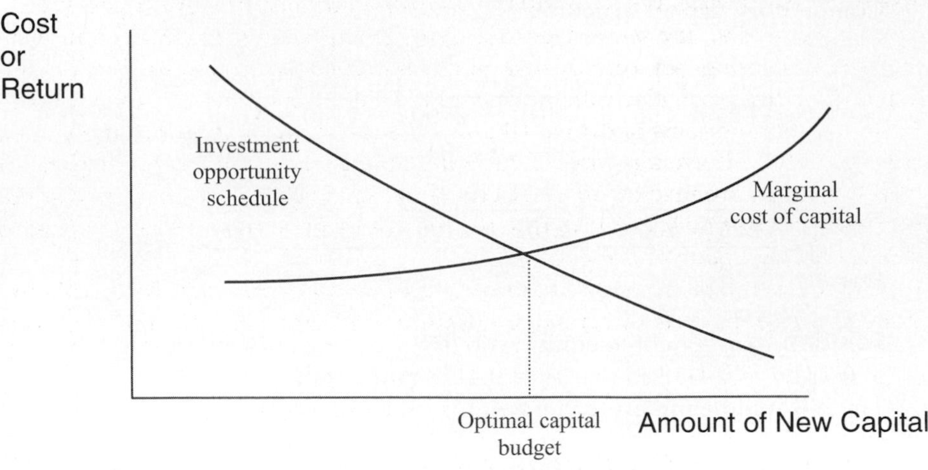

or product line. In these applications, we are interested in the cost of capital for the project, product, or division as opposed to the cost of capital for the company overall. The cost of capital in these applications should reflect the riskiness of the future cash flows of the project, product, or division. For an average-risk project, the opportunity cost of capital is the company's WACC. If the systematic risk of the project is above or below average relative to the company's current portfolio of projects, an upward or downward adjustment, respectively, is made to the company's WACC. Companies may take an *ad hoc* or a systematic approach to making such adjustments. The discussion of a systematic approach is a somewhat advanced topic that we defer to Section 4.1.

The WACC or MCC corresponding to the average risk of the company, adjusted appropriately for the risk of a given project, plays a role in capital-budgeting decision making based on the **net present value (NPV)** of that project. Recall from Reading 44 on capital budgeting that the NPV is the present value of all the project cash flows. It is useful to think of it as the difference between the present value of the cash inflows, discounted at the opportunity cost of capital applicable to the specific project, and the present value of the cash outflows, discounted using that same opportunity cost of capital:

$$\text{NPV} = \text{Present value of inflows} - \text{Present value of outflows}$$

If an investment's NPV is positive, the company should undertake the project. If we choose to use the company's WACC in the calculation of the NPV of a project, we are assuming that the project:

- has the same risk as the average-risk project of the company; and
- will have a constant target capital structure throughout its useful life.[3]

[3] WACC is estimated using fixed proportions of equity and debt. The NPV method assumes a constant required rate of return, whereas a fluctuating capital structure would cause WACC to fluctuate. The importance of this issue is demonstrated by James A. Miles and John R. Ezzell, "The Weighted Average Cost of Capital, Perfect Capital Markets, and Project Life: A Clarification," *Journal of Financial and Quantitative Analysis*, Vol. 15, No. 3 (September 1980), pp. 719–730.

These may not be realistic or appropriate assumptions and are potential drawbacks to using the company's WACC in valuing projects. However, alternative approaches are subject to drawbacks as well, and the approach outlined has wide acceptance.[4]

For the analyst, the second key use of the marginal cost of capital is in security valuation using any one of several discounted cash flow valuation models available.[5] For a particular valuation model, if these cash flows are cash flows to the company's suppliers of capital (that is, free cash flow to the firm), the analyst uses the weighted average cost of capital of the company in the valuation.[6] If these cash flows are strictly those belonging to the company's owners, such as the free cash flow to equity, or dividends, the analyst uses the cost of equity capital to find the present value of these flows.[7]

In the next section, we discuss how an analyst may approach the calculation of the component costs of capital, focusing on debt, preferred stock, and common equity.

COSTS OF THE DIFFERENT SOURCES OF CAPITAL 3

Each source of capital has a different cost because of the differences among the sources, such as seniority, contractual commitments, and potential value as a tax shield. We focus on the costs of three primary sources of capital: debt, preferred equity, and common equity.

3.1 Cost of Debt

The **cost of debt** is the cost of debt financing to a company when it issues a bond or takes out a bank loan. We discuss two methods to estimate the before-tax cost of debt, r_d: the yield-to-maturity approach and debt-rating approach.

3.1.1 Yield-to-Maturity Approach

The **yield to maturity (YTM)** is the annual return that an investor earns on a bond if the investor purchases the bond today and holds it until maturity. In other words, it is the yield, r_d, that equates the present value of the bond's promised payments to its market price:

$$P_0 = \frac{PMT_1}{\left(1 + \frac{r_d}{2}\right)} + \ldots + \frac{PMT_n}{\left(1 + \frac{r_d}{2}\right)^n} + \frac{FV}{\left(1 + \frac{r_d}{2}\right)^n} = \left(\sum_{t=1}^{n} \frac{PMT_i}{\left(1 + \frac{r_d}{2}\right)^t}\right) + \frac{FV}{\left(1 + \frac{r_d}{2}\right)^n} \qquad (45\text{-}2)$$

[4] See Reading 44 on capital budgeting for a discussion.

[5] See John Stowe, Thomas Robinson, Jerald Pinto, and Dennis McLeavey, *Analysis of Equity Investments: Valuation* (AIMR 2002) for a presentation of such models.

[6] **Free cash flow to the firm** (**FCFF**) is the cash flow available to the company's suppliers of capital after all operating expenses (including taxes) have been paid and necessary investments in working capital (e.g., inventory) and fixed capital (e.g., plant and equipment) have been made.

[7] **Free cash flow to equity** (**FCFE**) is the cash flow available to holders of the company's common equity after all operating expenses, interest, and principal payments have been paid and necessary investments in working capital and fixed capital have been made. See John Stowe, Thomas Robinson, Jerald Pinto, and Dennis McLeavey, *Analysis of Equity Investments: Valuation* (AIMR 2002) for more details on FCFF and FCFE and valuation models based on those concepts.

where

P_0	is the current market price of the bond
PMT_t	is the interest payment in period t
r_d	is the yield to maturity[8]
n	is the number of periods remaining to maturity
FV	is the maturity value of the bond

This valuation equation assumes the bond pays semi-annual interest and that any intermediate cash flows (in this case the interest prior to maturity) are reinvested at the rate $r_d/2$.

Example 4 illustrates the calculation of the after-tax cost of debt.

EXAMPLE 4

Calculating the After-Tax Cost of Debt

Valence Industries issues a bond to finance a new project. It offers a 10-year, 5 percent semi-annual coupon bond. Upon issue, the bond sells at \$1,025. What is Valence's before-tax cost of debt? If Valence's marginal tax rate is 35 percent, what is Valence's after-tax cost of debt?

Solution:

Given:

PV	=	\$1,025
FV	=	\$1,000
PMT	=	5 percent of 1,000 ÷ 2 = \$25
n	=	10 × 2 = 20

$$\$1{,}025 = \left(\sum_{t=1}^{20} \frac{\$25}{(1+i)}\right) + \frac{\$1{,}000}{(1+i)^{20}}$$

Use a financial calculator to solve for i, the six-month yield. Because $i = 2.342$ percent, the before-tax cost of debt is $r_d = 2.342$ percent × 2 = 4.684 percent, and Valence's after-tax cost of debt is $r_d(1 - t) = 0.04684(1 - 0.35) = 0.03045$ or 3.045 percent.

3.1.2 Debt-Rating Approach

When a reliable current market price for a company's debt is not available, the **debt-rating approach** can be used to estimate the before-tax cost of debt. Based on a company's debt rating, we estimate the before-tax cost of debt by using the yield on comparably rated bonds for maturities that closely match that of the company's existing debt.

---

[8] r_d is expressed as an annual rate and is divided by the number of payment periods per year. Because most corporate bonds pay semi-annual interest, we divided r_d by 2 in this calculation. The interest payment for each period thus corresponds with the bond's semi-annual coupon payment.

Suppose a company's capital structure includes debt with an average maturity (or duration) of 10 years and the company's marginal tax rate is 35 percent. If the company's rating is AAA and the yield on debt with the same debt rating and similar maturity (or duration) is 4 percent, the company's after-tax cost of debt is[9]

$$r_d = 4 \text{ percent}(1 - 0.35) = 2.6 \text{ percent}$$

A consideration when using this approach is that debt ratings are ratings of the debt issue itself, with the issuer being only one of the considerations. Other factors, such as debt seniority and security, also affect ratings and yields, so care must be taken to consider the likely type of debt to be issued by the company in determining the comparable debt rating and yield. The debt-rating approach is a simple example of pricing on the basis of valuation-relevant characteristics, which in bond markets has been known as evaluated pricing or **matrix pricing**.

3.1.3 Issues in Estimating the Cost of Debt

3.1.3.1 Fixed-Rate Debt versus Floating-Rate Debt Up to now, we have assumed that the interest on debt is a fixed amount each period. We can observe market yields of the company's existing debt or market yields of debt of similar risk in estimating the before-tax cost of debt. However, the company may also issue floating-rate debt in which the interest rate adjusts periodically according to a prescribed index, such as the prime rate or LIBOR, over the life of the instrument.

Estimating the cost of a floating-rate security is difficult because the cost of this form of capital over the long term depends not only on the current yields but also on the future yields. The analyst may use the current term structure of interest rates and term structure theory to assign an average cost to such instruments.

3.1.3.2 Debt with Optionlike Features How should an analyst determine the cost of debt when the company used debt with optionlike features, such as call, conversion, or put provisions? Clearly, options affect the value of debt. For example, a callable bond would have a yield greater than a similar noncallable bond of the same issuer because bondholders want to be compensated for the call risk associated with the bond. In a similar manner, the put feature of a bond, which provides the investor with an option to sell the bond back to the issuer at a predetermined price, has the effect of lowering the yield on a bond below that of a similar nonputable bond.

If the company already has debt outstanding incorporating optionlike features that the analyst believes are representative of the future debt issuance of the company, the analyst may simply use the yield to maturity on such debt in estimating the cost of debt.

If the analyst believes that the company will add or remove option features in future debt issuance, the analyst can make market value adjustments to the current YTM to reflect the value of such additions and/or deletions. The technology for such adjustments is an advanced topic that is outside the scope of this reading.[10]

3.1.3.3 Nonrated Debt If a company does not have any debt outstanding or if the yields on the company's existing debt are not available, the analyst may not always be able to use the yield on similarly rated debt securities. It may be the

[9] Duration is a more precise measure of a bond's interest rate sensitivity than maturity.

[10] See, for example, *Fixed Income Analysis for the Chartered Financial Analyst® Program*, by Frank Fabozzi, for an introduction. Fabozzi discusses the estimation of an option-adjusted spread (OAS) to price the call option feature of a callable bond.

case that the company does not have rated bonds. Though researchers offer approaches for estimating a company's "synthetic" debt rating based on financial ratios, these methods are imprecise because debt ratings incorporate not only financial ratios but also information about the particular bond issue and the issuer that are not captured in financial ratios.

3.1.3.4 Leases A lease is a contractual obligation that can substitute for other forms of borrowing. This is true whether the lease is an operating lease or a capital lease, though only the capital lease is represented as a liability on the company's balance sheet.[11] If the company uses leasing as a source of capital, the cost of these leases should be included in the cost of capital. The cost of this form of borrowing is similar to that of the company's other long-term borrowing.

3.2 Cost of Preferred Stock

The **cost of preferred stock** is the cost that a company has committed to pay preferred stockholders as a preferred dividend when it issues preferred stock. In the case of nonconvertible, noncallable preferred stock that has a fixed dividend rate and no maturity date (**fixed rate perpetual preferred stock**), we can use the formula for the value of a preferred stock:

$$P_p = \frac{D_p}{r_p}$$

where

P_p	is the current preferred stock price per share
D_p	is the preferred stock dividend per share
r_P	is the cost of preferred stock

We can rearrange this equation to solve for the cost of preferred stock:

$$r_p = \frac{D_p}{P_p} \qquad \textbf{(45-3)}$$

Therefore, the cost of preferred stock is the preferred stock's dividend per share divided by the current preferred stock's price per share. Unlike interest on debt, the dividend on preferred stock is not tax-deductible by the company; therefore, there is no adjustment to the cost for taxes.[12]

A preferred stock may have a number of features that affect the yield and hence the cost of preferred stock. These features include a call option, cumulative dividends, participating dividends, adjustable-rate dividends, or convertibil-

[11] In the United States, an operating lease is distinguished from a capital lease in Statement of Financial Accounting Standards No. 13, *Accounting for Leases* (FASB, November 1976). (IAS No. 17 similarly distinguishes between operating and finance leases, another term for capital-type leases.) These two forms of leases are distinguished on the basis of ownership transference, the existence of a bargain purchase option, the term of the lease relative to the economic life of the asset, and the present value of the lease payments relative to the value of the asset. In either case, however, the lease obligation is a form of borrowing, even though it is only in the case of a capital lease that the obligation appears as a liability on the company's balance sheet. The discount rate applied in the valuation of a capital lease is the rate of borrowing at the time of the lease commencement; therefore, it is reasonable to apply the company's long-term borrowing rate when estimating the cost of capital for leasing.

[12] This is not to be confused, however, with the dividends-received deduction, which reduces the effective tax on intercorporate preferred dividends received.

ity into common stock. When estimating a yield based on current yields of the company's preferred stock, we must make appropriate adjustments for the effects of these features on the yield of an issue. For example, if the company has callable, convertible preferred stock outstanding, yet it is expected that the company will issue only noncallable, nonconvertible preferred stock in the future, we would have to either use the current yields on comparable companies' noncallable, nonconvertible preferred stock or estimate the yield on preferred equity using methods outside the scope of this reading.[13]

EXAMPLE 5

Calculating the Cost of Preferred Equity

Alcoa has one class of preferred stock outstanding, a $3.75 cumulative preferred stock, for which there are 546,024 shares outstanding.[14] If the price of this stock is $72, what is the estimate of Alcoa's cost of preferred equity?

Solution: Cost of Alcoa's preferred stock = $3.75/$72.00 = 5.21 percent.

EXAMPLE 6

Choosing the Best Estimate of the Cost of Preferred Equity

Wim Vanistendael is finance director of De Gouden Tulip N.V., a leading Dutch flower producer and distributor. He has been asked by the CEO to calculate the cost of preferred equity and has recently obtained the following information:

- The issue price of preferred stock was €3.5 million and the preferred dividend is 5 percent.
- If the company issued new preferred stock today, the preferred coupon rate would be 6.5 percent.
- The company's marginal tax rate is 30.5 percent.

What is the cost of preferred equity for De Gouden Tulip N.V.?

Solution: If De Gouden Tulip were to issue new preferred stock today, the coupon rate would be close to 6.5 percent. The current terms thus prevail over the past terms when evaluating the actual cost of preferred stock. The cost of preferred stock for De Gouden Tulip is, therefore, 6.5 percent. Because preferred dividends offer no tax shield, there is no adjustment made based upon the marginal tax rate.

---

[13] A method for estimating this yield involves first estimating the **option-adjusted spread** (OAS). For further information on the OAS, see, for example, Frank Fabozzi's *Fixed Income Analysis for the Chartered Financial Analyst® Program.*

[14] Alcoa Annual Report 2004, footnote R, p. 56.

3.3 Cost of Common Equity

The cost of common equity, (r_e), usually referred to simply as the cost of equity, is the rate of return required by a company's common shareholders. A company may increase common equity through the reinvestment of earnings—that is, retained earnings—or through the issuance of new shares of stock.

As we discussed earlier, the estimation of the cost of equity is challenging because of the uncertain nature of the future cash flows in terms of the amount and timing. Commonly used approaches for estimating the cost of equity include the capital asset pricing model, the dividend discount model, and the bond yield plus risk premium method.

3.3.1 Capital Asset Pricing Model Approach

In the capital asset pricing model (CAPM) approach, we use the basic relationship from the capital asset pricing model theory that the expected return on a stock, $E(R_i)$, is the sum of the risk-free rate of interest, R_F, and a premium for bearing the stock's market risk, $\beta(R_M - R_F)$:

$$E(R_i) = R_F + \beta_i[E(R_M) - R_F] \quad \text{(45-4)}$$

where

β_i = the return sensitivity of stock i to changes in the market return
$E(R_M)$ = the expected return on the market
$E(R_M) - R_F$ = the expected market risk premium

A risk-free asset is defined here as an asset that has no default risk. A common proxy for the risk-free rate is the yield on a default-free government debt instrument. In general, the selection of the appropriate risk-free rate should be guided by the duration of projected cash flows. If we are evaluating a project with an estimated useful life of 10 years, we may want to use the rate on the 10-year Treasury bond.

EXAMPLE 7

Using the CAPM to Estimate the Cost of Equity

Valence Industries wants to know its cost of equity. Its CFO believes the risk-free rate is 5 percent, equity risk premium is 7 percent, and Valence's equity beta is 1.5. What is Valence's cost of equity using the CAPM approach?

Solution: Cost of common stock = 5 percent + 1.5(7 percent) = 15.5 percent.

The expected **market risk premium**, or $E(R_M - R_F)$, is the premium that investors demand for investing in a market portfolio relative to the risk-free rate. When using the CAPM to estimate the cost of equity, in practice we typically estimate beta relative to an equity market index. In that case, the market premium estimate we are using is actually an estimate of the **equity risk premium** (ERP).

An alternative to the CAPM to accommodate risks that may not be captured by the **market portfolio** alone is a multifactor model that incorporates factors that may be other sources of **priced risk** (risk for which investors demand compensation for bearing), including **macroeconomic factors** and company-specific factors. In general

$$E(R_i) = R_F + \beta_{i1}(\text{Factor risk premium})_1 + \beta_{i2}(\text{Factor risk premium})_2 + \ldots + \beta_{ij}(\text{Factor risk premium})_j \quad \textbf{(45-5)}$$

where

β_{ij} is stock i's sensitivity to changes in the jth factor
(Factor risk premium)$_j$ is expected risk premium for the jth factor

The basic idea behind these multifactor models is that the CAPM beta may not capture all the risks, especially in a global context, which include inflation, business-cycle, interest rate, exchange rate, and default risks.[15, 16]

There are several ways to estimate the equity risk premium, though there is no general agreement as to the best approach. The three we discuss are the historical equity risk premium approach, the dividend discount model approach, and the survey approach.

The **historical equity risk premium approach** is a well-established approach based on the assumption that the realized equity risk premium observed over a long period of time is a good indicator of the expected equity risk premium. This approach requires compiling historical data to find the average rate of return of a country's market portfolio and the average rate of return for the risk-free rate in that country. For example, an analyst might use the historical returns to the TOPIX Index to estimate the risk premium for Japanese equities. The exceptional bull market observed during the second half of the 1990s, and the bursting of the technology bubble that followed during the years 2000–2002, reminds us that the time period for such estimates should cover complete market cycles.

Elroy Dimson, Paul Marsh, and Mike Staunton conducted an analysis of the equity risk premiums observed in markets located in 16 countries, including the United States, over the period 1900–2002.[17] These researchers found that the annualized U.S. equity risk premium relative to U.S. Treasury bills was 5.3 percent (geometric mean) and 7.2 percent (arithmetic mean). They also found that the annualized U.S. equity risk premium relative to bonds was 4.4 percent (geometric mean) and 6.4 percent (arithmetic mean).[18] Note that the arithmetic mean is

---

[15] An example of the multi-factor model is the three-factor Fama and French model [Eugene Fama and Kenneth French, "The Cross-Section of Expected Stock Returns," *Journal of Finance*, Vol. 47, No. 2 (1992), pp. 427–465], which includes factors for the market, equity capitalization, and the ratio of book value of equity to the market value of equity.

[16] These models are discussed in more detail by Robert F. Bruner, Robert M. Conroy, Wei Li, Elizabeth O'Halloran, and Miquel Palacios Lleras [*Investing in Emerging Markets*, AIMR Research Foundation monograph (August 2003)] and by Eugene F. Fama and Kenneth R. French, "The Capital Asset Pricing Model: Theory and Evidence," *Journal of Economic Perspectives*, Vol. 18, No. 3 (Summer 2004), pp. 3–24.

[17] Elroy Dimson, Paul Marsh, and Mike Staunton, "Global Evidence on the Equity Risk Premium," *Journal of Applied Corporate Finance* (Fall 2003), pp. 27–38.

[18] Jeremy Siegel presents a longer time series of market returns, covering the period from 1802 through 2004, and observes an equity return of 6.82 percent and an equity risk premium in the range of 3.31 to 5.36 percent. See Jeremy J. Siegel, "Perspectives on the Equity Risk Premium," *Financial Analysts Journal*, Vol. 61, No. 6 (November/December 2005), pp. 61–73. The range depends on the method of calculation (compounded or arithmetic) and the benchmark (bonds or bills).

TABLE 1 Equity Risk Premiums Relative to Bonds (1900 to 2001)

	Mean	
Country	**Geometric**	**Arithmetic**
Australia	6.3%	7.9%
Belgium	2.8	4.7
Canada	4.2	5.7
Denmark	1.8	3.1
France	4.6	6.7
Germany	6.3	9.6
Ireland	3.1	4.5
Italy	4.6	8.0
Japan	5.9	10.0
The Netherlands	4.4	6.4
South Africa	5.4	7.1
Spain	2.2	4.1
Sweden	4.9	7.1
Switzerland	2.4	3.9
United Kingdom	4.2	5.5
United States	4.8	6.7
World	4.3	5.4

Note: Germany excludes 1922–23. Switzerland commences in 1911.
Source: Dimson, Marsh, and Staunton (2003).

greater than the geometric mean as a result of the significant volatility of the observed market rate of return and of the observed risk-free rate. Under the assumption of an unchanging distribution of returns through time, the arithmetic mean is the unbiased estimate of the expected single-period equity risk premium, but the geometric mean better reflects growth rate over multiple periods.[19] In Table 1 we provide historical estimates of the equity risk premium for 16 developed markets from Dimson, Marsh, and Staunton's study.

To illustrate the **historical method** as applied in the CAPM, suppose that we use the historical geometric mean for U.S. equity of 4.8 percent to value Citibank Inc. (NYSE: C) as of early January 2006. According to Standard & Poor's, Citibank had a beta of 1.32 at that time. Using the 10-year U.S. Treasury bond yield of 4.38 percent to represent the risk-free rate, the estimate of the cost of equity for Citibank is 4.38 percent + 1.32(4.8 percent) = 10.72 percent.

[19] Aside from the method of averaging (geometric versus arithmetic), estimates of the historical equity risk premium differ depending on the assumed investment horizon (short versus intermediate versus long), whether conditional on some variable or unconditional, whether U.S. or global markets are examined, the source of the data, the period observed, and whether nominal or real returns are estimated.

The historical premium approach has several limitations. One limitation is that the level of risk of the stock index may change over time. Another is that the risk aversion of investors may change over time. And still another limitation is that the estimates are sensitive to the method of estimation and the historical period covered.

EXAMPLE 8

Estimating the Equity Risk Premium Using Historical Rates of Return

Suppose that the arithmetic average T-bond rate observed over the last 100 years is an unbiased estimator for the risk-free rate and amounts to 5.4 percent. Likewise, suppose the arithmetic average of return on the market observed over the last 100 years is an unbiased estimator for the expected return for the market. The average rate of return of the market was 9.3 percent. Calculate the equity risk premium.

Solution: ERP $= \overline{R}_M - \overline{R}_F$ = 9.3 percent − 5.4 percent = 3.9 percent.

A second approach for estimating the equity risk premium is the **dividend discount model based approach** or **implied risk premium approach**, which is implemented using the Gordon growth model (also known as the constant-growth dividend discount model). For developed markets, corporate earnings often meet, at least approximately, the model's assumption of a long-run trend growth rate. We extract the premium by analyzing how the market prices an index. That is, we use the relationship between the value of an index and expected dividends, assuming a constant growth in dividends:

$$P_0 = \frac{D_1}{r_e - g}$$

where P_0 is the current market value of the equity market index, D_1 are the dividends expected next period on the index, r_e is the required rate of return on the market, and g is the expected growth rate of dividends. We solve for the required rate of return on the market as

$$r_e = \frac{D_1}{P_0} + g \qquad \textbf{(45-6)}$$

Therefore, the expected return on the market is the sum of the dividend yield and the growth rate in dividends.[20] The equity risk premium thus is the difference between the expected return on the equity market and the risk-free rate.

Suppose the expected dividend yield on an equity index is 5 percent and the expected growth rate of dividends on the index is 2 percent. The expected return on the market according to the Gordon growth model is

$$E(R_m) = 5 \text{ percent} + 2 \text{ percent} = 7 \text{ percent}$$

A risk-free rate of interest of 3.8 percent implies an equity risk premium of 7 percent − 3.8 percent = 3.2 percent.

[20] We explain Equation 45-6 in more detail in Section 3.3.2.

Another approach to estimate the equity risk premium is quite direct: Ask a panel of finance experts for their estimates and take the mean response. This is the **survey approach**. For example, one set of U.S. surveys found that the expected U.S. equity risk premium over the next 30 years was 5.5 percent to 7 percent forecasting from 2001 as the baseline year and 7.1 percent using 1998 as the baseline year.

Once we have an estimate of the equity risk premium, we fine-tune this estimate for the particular company or project by adjusting it for the specific systematic risk of the project. We adjust for the specific systematic risk by multiplying the market risk premium by beta to arrive at the company's or project's risk premium, which we then add to the risk-free rate to determine the cost of equity within the framework of the CAPM.[21]

3.3.2 Dividend Discount Model Approach

Earlier we used the Gordon growth model to develop an estimate of the equity risk premium for use in the CAPM. We can also use the Gordon growth model directly to obtain an estimate of the cost of equity. To review, the dividend discount model in general states that the **intrinsic value** of a share of stock is the present value of the share's expected future dividends:

$$V_0 = \sum_{t=1}^{\infty}\left(\frac{D_t}{(1 + r_e)^t}\right) = \frac{D_1}{(1 + r_e)} + \frac{D_2}{(1 + r_e)^2} + \ldots$$

where

V_0 is the intrinsic value of a share
D_t is the share's dividend at the end of period t
r_e is the cost of equity

Based on Gordon's constant growth formulation, we assume dividends are expected to grow at a constant rate, g.[22] Therefore, if we assume that price reflects intrinsic value ($V_0 = P_0$), we can rewrite the valuation of the stock as

$$P_0 = \frac{D_1}{r_e - g}$$

We can then rewrite the above equation and estimate the cost of equity as we did for Equation 45-6 in Section 3.3.1:

$$r_e = \frac{D_1}{P_0} + g$$

Therefore, to estimate r_e, we need to estimate the dividend in the next period and the assumed constant dividend growth rate. The current stock price, P_0, is known, and the dividend of the next period, D_1, can be predicted if the

[21] Some researchers argue that the equity risk premium should reflect a country risk premium. For example, a multinational company or project may have a higher cost of capital than a comparable domestic company because of political risk, foreign exchange risk, or higher agency costs. In most cases, this risk is unsystematic and hence does not affect the cost of capital estimate.

[22] Myron J. Gordon, *The Investment, Financing, and Valuation of the Corporation*, Homewood, IL: Irwin, 1962.

company has a stable dividend policy. (The ratio D_1/P_0 may be called the forward annual dividend yield.) The challenge is estimating the growth rate.

There are at least two ways to estimate the growth rate. The first is to use a forecasted growth rate from a published source or vendor. A second is to use a relationship between the growth rate, the retention rate, and the return on equity. In this context, this is often referred to as the **sustainable growth rate** and is interpretable as the rate of dividend (and earnings) growth that can be sustained over time for a given level of return on equity, keeping the capital structure constant and without issuing additional common stock. The relationship is given in Equation 45-7:

$$g = (1 - D/_{EPS})\ ROE \tag{45-7}$$

where D/EPS represents the assumed stable dividend payout ratio and ROE is the historical return on equity. The term (1 − D/EPS) is the company's earnings retention rate.

Consider Citigroup, Inc. Citigroup has an earnings retention rate of 59 percent. As of early January 2006, Citigroup had a forward annual dividend yield of 3.9 percent, a trailing return on equity of approximately 20 percent, but an estimated average return on equity going forward of approximately 16.6 percent. According to Equation 45-7, Citigroup's sustainable growth rate is 0.59(16.6 percent) = 9.79 percent. The dividend discount model estimate of the cost of equity is, therefore, 9.79 percent + 3.9 percent = 13.69 percent.

3.3.3 Bond Yield plus Risk Premium Approach

The **bond yield plus risk premium approach** is based on the fundamental tenet in financial theory that the cost of capital of riskier cash flows is higher than that of less risky cash flows. In this approach, we sum the before-tax cost of debt, r_d, and a risk premium that captures the additional yield on a company's stock relative to its bonds. The estimate is, therefore,

$$r_e = r_d + \text{Risk premium} \tag{45-8}$$

The risk premium compensates for the additional risk of equity compared with debt.[23] Ideally, this risk premium is forward looking, representing the additional risk associated with the stock of the company as compared with the bonds of the same company. However, we often estimate this premium using historical spreads between bond yields and stock yields. In developed country markets, a typical risk premium added is in the range of 3 to 5 percent.

Looking again at Citigroup, as of early January 2006, the yield to maturity of the Citigroup 5.3s bonds maturing in 2016 was approximately 4.95 percent. Adding an arbitrary risk premium of 3.5 percent produces an estimate of the cost of equity of 4.95 + 3.5 = 8.45 percent. This estimate contrasts with the higher estimates of 10.72 percent, under the CAPM approach, and 13.69 percent, under the dividend discount model approach. Such disparities are not uncommon and reflect the difficulty of cost of equity estimation.

[23] This risk premium is not to be confused with the equity risk premium. The equity risk premium is the difference between the cost of equity and the *risk-free rate of interest*. The risk premium in the bond yield plus risk premium approach is the difference between the cost of equity and the *company's cost of debt*.

4 TOPICS IN COST OF CAPITAL ESTIMATION

When calculating a company's weighted average cost of capital (WACC), it is essential to understand the risk factors that have been considered in determining the risk-free rate, the equity risk premium, and beta to ensure a consistent calculation of WACC and avoid the double counting or omission of pertinent risk factors.

4.1 Estimating Beta and Determining a Project Beta

When the analyst uses the CAPM to estimate the cost of equity, he or she must estimate beta. The estimation of beta presents many choices as well as challenges.

One common method of estimating the company's stock beta is to use a market model regression of the company's stock returns (R_i) against market returns (R_m) over T periods:[24]

$$R_{it} = \hat{a} + \hat{b}\, R_{mt} t = 1, 2, \ldots T$$

where $\hat{a}$ is the estimated intercept and $\hat{b}$ is the estimated slope of the regression that is used as an estimate of beta. However, beta estimates are sensitive to the method of estimation and data used. Consider some of the issues:

- *Estimation period.* The estimated beta is sensitive to the length of the estimation period, with beta commonly estimated using data over two to nine years. Selection of the estimation period is a trade-off between data richness captured by longer estimation periods and company-specific changes that are better reflected with shorter estimation periods. In general, longer estimation periods are applied to companies with a long and stable operating history, and shorter estimation periods are used for companies that have undergone significant structural changes in the recent past (such as restructuring, recent acquisition, or divestiture) or changes in financial and operating leverage.
- *Periodicity of the return interval* (e.g., daily, weekly, or monthly). Researchers have observed smaller standard error in beta estimated using smaller return intervals, such as daily returns.[25]
- *Selection of an appropriate market index.* The choice of market index affects the estimate of beta.
- *Use of a smoothing technique.* Some analysts adjust historical betas to reflect the tendency of betas to revert to 1.[26] As an example, the expression $\beta_{i,\text{adj}} = 0.333 + 0.667\beta_i$ adjusts betas above and below 1.0 toward 1.0.
- *Adjustments for small-capitalization stocks.* Small-capitalization stocks have generally exhibited greater risks and greater returns than large-capitalization

---

[24] This equation is commonly referred to as the *market model* and was first introduced by Michael C. Jensen in "The Performance of Mutual Funds in the Period 1945–1964," *Journal of Finance*, Vol. 23, No. 2 (1969), pp. 389–416.

[25] Phillip R. Daves, Michael C. Ehrhardt, and Robert A. Kunkel, "Estimating Systematic Risk: The Choice of Return Interval and Estimation Period," *Journal of Financial and Strategic Decisions*, Vol. 13, No. 1 (Spring 2000), pp. 7–13.

[26] Marshall Blume, "On the Assessment of Risk," *Journal of Finance*, Vol. 26, No. 1, (March 1971), pp. 1–10.

stocks over the long run. Roger Ibbotson, Paul Kaplan, and James Peterson argue that betas for small-capitalization companies be adjusted upward.[27]

Arriving at an estimated beta for publicly traded companies is generally not a problem because of the accessibility of stock return data, the ease of use of estimating beta using simple regression, and the availability of estimated betas on publicly traded companies from financial analysis vendors, such as Barra, Bloomberg, Thompson Financial's Datastream, Reuters, and Value Line. The challenge is to estimate a beta for a company that is not publicly traded or to estimate a beta for a project that is not the average or typical project of a publicly traded company. Estimating a beta in these cases requires proxying for the beta by using the information on the project or company combined with a beta of a publicly traded company.

The beta of a company or project is affected by the systematic components of business risk and by financial risk. Both of these factors affect the uncertainty of the cash flows of the company or project. The **business risk** of a company or project is the risk related to the uncertainty of revenues, referred to as sales risk, and to **operating risk**, which is the risk attributed to the company's operating cost structure. Sales risk is affected by the elasticity of the demand of the product, the cyclicality of the revenues, and the structure of competition in the industry. Operating risk is affected by the relative mix of fixed and variable operating costs: the greater the fixed operating costs, relative to variable operating costs, the greater the uncertainty of income and cash flows from operations.

Financial risk is the uncertainty of net income and net cash flows attributed to the use of financing that has a fixed cost, such as debt and leases. The greater the use of fixed-financing sources of capital, relative to variable sources, the greater the financial risk. In other words, a company that relies heavily on debt financing instead of equity financing is assuming a great deal of financial risk.

How does a financial analyst estimate a beta for a company or project that is not publicly traded? One common method is the **pure-play method**, which requires using a comparable publicly traded company's beta and adjusting it for financial leverage differences.

A **comparable company** is a company that has similar business risk. The reason it is referred to as the *pure-play* method is that one of the easiest ways of identifying a comparable for a project is to find a company in the same industry that is in that *single* line of business. For example, if the analyst is examining a project that involves drug stores, appropriate comparables in the United States may be Walgreens, CVS Corporation, and Rite Aid Corporation.

In estimating a beta in this way, the analyst must make adjustments to account for differing degrees of financial leverage. This requires a process of "unlevering" and "levering" the beta. The beta of the comparable is first "unlevered" by removing the effects of its financial leverage.[28] The unlevered beta is often referred to as the **asset beta** because it reflects the business risk of the assets. Once we determine the unlevered beta, we adjust it for the capital structure of the company or project that is the focus of our analysis. In other words, we "lever" the asset beta to arrive at an estimate of the equity beta for the project or company of interest.

---

[27] Roger G. Ibbotson, Paul D. Kaplan, and James D. Peterson, "Estimates of Small Stock Betas Are Much Too Low," *Journal of Portfolio Management* (Summer 1997), pp. 104–110.

[28] The process of unlevering and levering a beta was developed by Robert S. Hamada ["The Effect of the Firm's Capital Structure on the Systematic Risk of Common Stocks," *Journal of Finance* (May 1972), pp. 435–452] and is based on the capital structure theories of Franco Modigliani and Merton Miller.

For a given company, we can unlever its equity beta to estimate its asset beta. To do this, we must determine the relationship between a company's asset beta and its equity beta. Because the company's risk is shared between creditors and owners, we can represent the company's risk, β_{asset}, as the weighted average of the company's creditors' market risk, β_{debt}, and the market risk of the owners, β_{equity}:

$$\beta_{asset} = \beta_{debt}\, w_d + \beta_{equity}\, w_e$$

or

$$\beta_{asset} = \beta_{debt}\left(\frac{D}{D+E}\right) + \beta_{equity}\left(\frac{E}{D+E}\right)$$

where

E = market value of equity
D = market value of debt
w_d = proportion of debt = $D/D+E$
w_e = proportion of equity = $E/D+E$

But interest on debt is deducted by the company to arrive at taxable income, so the claim that creditors have on the company's assets does not cost the company the full amount but, rather, the after-tax claim; the burden of debt financing is actually less due to interest deductibility. We can represent the asset beta of a company as the weighted average of the betas of debt and equity after considering the effects of the tax-deductibility of interest:

$$\beta_{asset} = \beta_{debt}\frac{(1-t)D}{(1-t)D+E} + \beta_{equity}\frac{E}{(1-t)D+E}$$

where t is the marginal tax rate.

We generally assume that a company's debt does not have market risk, so $\beta_{debt} = 0$. This means that the returns on debt do not vary with the returns on the market, which we generally assume to be true for most large companies. If $\beta_{debt} = 0$, then[29]

$$\beta_{asset} = \beta_{equity}\left[\frac{1}{1+\left((1-t)\frac{D}{E}\right)}\right] \qquad \textbf{(45-9)}$$

Therefore, the market risk of a company's equity is affected by both the asset's market risk, β_{asset}, and a factor representing the nondiversifiable portion of company's financial risk, $[1 + (1-t)^{D}/_{E})]$:

$$\beta_{asset} = \beta_{equity}\left[1+\left((1-t)\frac{D}{E}\right)\right] \qquad \textbf{(45-10)}$$

[29] The first step is $\beta_{asset} = \beta_{equity}\left[\frac{E}{(1-t)D+E}\right]$, which we simplify to arrive at Equation 45-9.

Suppose a company has an equity beta of 1.5, a debt-to-equity ratio of 0.4, and a marginal tax rate of 30 percent. Using Equation 45-9, the company's asset beta is 1.1719:

$$\beta_{asset} = 1.5\left[\frac{1}{1 + ((1 - 0.3)(0.4))}\right] = 1.5[0.7813] = 1.1719$$

In other words, if the company did not have any debt financing, its $\beta_{asset} = \beta_{equity} = 1.1719$; however, the use of debt financing increases its β_{equity} from 1.1719 to 1.5. What would the company's equity beta be if the company's debt-to-equity ratio were 0.5 instead of 0.4? In this case, we apply Equation 45-10, using the debt-to-equity ratio of 0.5:

$$\beta_{equity} = 1.1719\ [1 + ((1-0.3)(0.5))] = 1.5821$$

Therefore, the unlevering calculation produces a measure of market risk for the assets of the company—ignoring the company's capital structure. We use the levering calculation in Equation 45-10 to estimate the market risk of a company given a specific asset risk, marginal tax rate, and capital structure.

We can use the same unlevering and levering calculations to estimate the asset risk and equity risk for a project. We start with the equity beta of the comparable company, which is the levered beta, $\beta_{L,comparable}$, and then convert it into the equivalent asset beta for the unlevered company, $\beta_{U,comparable}$. Once we have the estimate of the unlevered beta, which is the company's asset risk, we then can use the project's capital structure and marginal tax rate to convert this asset beta into an equity beta for the project, $\beta_{L,project}$.

Estimating a Beta Using the Pure-Play Method

Step 1: Select the comparable Determine comparable company or companies. These are companies with similar business risk.

Step 2: Estimate comparable's beta Estimate the equity beta of the comparable company or companies.

Step 3: Unlever the comparable's beta Unlever the beta of the comparable company or companies, removing the financial risk component of the equity beta, leaving the business risk component of the beta.

Step 4: Lever the beta for the project's financial risk Lever the beta of the project by adjusting the asset beta for the financial risk of the project.

We begin by estimating the levered beta of the comparable company, $\beta_{L,comparable}$. Using the capital structure and tax rate of the levered company, we estimate the asset beta for the comparable company, $\beta_{U,comparable}$:

$$\beta_{U,comparable} = \frac{\beta_{L,comparable}}{\left[1 + \left((1 - t_{comparable})\frac{D_{comparable}}{E_{comparable}}\right)\right]} \quad \textbf{(45-11)}$$

We then consider the financial leverage of the project or company and calculate its equity risk, $\beta_{L,project}$:

$$\beta_{L,project} = \beta_{U,comparable}\left[1 + \left((1 - t_{project})\frac{D_{project}}{E_{project}}\right)\right] \quad \textbf{(45-12)}$$

To illustrate the use of these equations, suppose we want to evaluate a project that will be financed with debt and equity in a ratio of 0.4:1 [a debt-to-equity ratio of 0.4, corresponding to approximately 0.4/(0.4 + 1.0) = €0.286 for each euro of capital needed]. We find a comparable company operating in the same line of business as the project. The marginal tax rate for the company sponsoring the project and the comparable company is 35 percent. The comparable company has a beta of 1.2 and a debt-to-equity ratio of 0.125. The unlevered beta of the comparable is 1.1098:

$$\beta_{U,comparable} = \frac{1.2}{[1 + ((1 - 0.35)0.125)]} = 1.1098$$

The levered beta for the project is 1.3983:

$$\beta_{L,project} = 1.1098[1 + ((1 - 0.35)0.4)] = 1.3983$$

We then use the 1.3983 as the beta in our CAPM estimate of the component cost of equity for the project and, combined with the cost of debt in a weighted average, provide an estimate of the cost of capital for the project.[30]

EXAMPLE 9

Inferring an Asset Beta

Suppose that the beta of a publicly traded company's stock is 1.3 and that the market value of equity and debt are, respectively, C$540 million and C$720 million. If the marginal tax rate of this company is 40 percent, what is the asset beta of this company?

Solution:

$$\beta_U = \frac{1.3}{\left[1 + \left((1 - 0.4)\frac{720}{540}\right)\right]} = 0.72$$

[30] In this example, the weights are $w_d = 0.4/1.4 = 0.2857$ and $w_e = 1/1.4 = 0.7143$.

EXAMPLE 10

Calculating a Beta Using the Pure-Play Method

Raymond Cordier is the business development manager of Aerotechnique S.A., a private Belgian subcontractor of aerospace parts. Although Aerotechnique is not listed on the Belgian stock exchange, Cordier needs to evaluate the levered beta for the company. He has access to the following information:

- The average levered and average unlevered betas for the group of comparable companies operating in different European countries are 1.6 and 1.0, respectively.
- Aerotechnique's debt-to-equity ratio, based on market values, is 1.4.
- Aerotechnique's corporate tax rate is 34 percent.

Solution: The beta for Aerotechnique is estimated on the basis of the average unlevered beta extracted from the group of comparable companies. On that basis, and applying the financing structure of Aerotechnique, the estimated beta for Aerotechnique is

$$\beta_{\text{Aerotechnique}} = 1.0\left[1 + \left((1 - 0.34)(1.4)\right)\right] = 1.924$$

EXAMPLE 11

Estimating the Weighted Average Cost of Capital

Georg Schrempp is the CFO of Bayern Chemicals KgaA, a large German manufacturer of industrial, commercial, and consumer chemical products. Bayern Chemicals is privately owned, and its shares are not listed on an exchange. The CFO has appointed Markus Meier, CFA, of Crystal Clear Valuation Advisors, a third-party valuator, to perform a stand-alone valuation of Bayern Chemicals. Meier had access to the following information to calculate Bayern Chemicals' weighted average cost of capital:

- The nominal risk-free rate is represented by the yield on the long-term 10-year German bund, which at the valuation date was 4.5 percent.
- The average long-term historical equity risk premium in Germany is assumed at 5.7 percent.[31]
- Bayern Chemicals' corporate tax rate is 38 percent.
- Bayern Chemicals' target debt-to-equity ratio is 0.7. Bayern is operating at its target debt-to-equity ratio.
- Bayern Chemicals' cost of debt has an estimated spread of 225 basis points over the 10-year bund.
- Table 2 supplies additional information on comparables for Bayern Chemicals.

[31] Dimson, Marsh, and Staunton, *op. cit.*

TABLE 2 Information on Comparables

Comparable Companies	Country	Tax Rate	Market Capitalization in Millions	Net Debt in Millions	D/E	Beta
British Chemicals Ltd.	U.K.	30.0%	4,500	6,000	1.33	1.45
Compagnie Petrochimique S.A.	France	30.3%	9,300	8,700	0.94	0.75
Rotterdam Chemie N.V.	Netherlands	30.5%	7,000	7,900	1.13	1.05
Average					1.13	1.08

Based only on the information given, calculate Bayern Chemicals' WACC.

Solution: To calculate the cost of equity, the first step is to "unlever" the betas of the comparable companies and calculate an average for a company with business risk similar to the average of these companies:

Comparable Companies	Unlevered Beta
British Chemicals Ltd.	0.75
Compagnie Petrochimique S.A.	0.45
Rotterdam Chemie N.V.	0.59
Average[32]	0.60

Levering the average unlevered beta for the peer group average, applying Bayern Chemicals' target debt-to-equity ratio and marginal tax rate, results in a beta of 0.86:

$$\beta_{\text{Bayern Chemical}} = 0.60\,\{1+[(1-0.38)\ 0.7]\} = 0.86$$

The cost of equity of Bayern Chemicals (r_e) can be calculated as follows:

$$r_e = 4.5 \text{ percent} + (0.86)\ (5.7 \text{ percent}) = 9.4 \text{ percent}$$

The weights for the cost of equity and cost of debt may be calculated as follows:

[32] An analyst must apply judgment and experience to determine a representative average for the comparable companies. This example uses a simple average, but in some situations a weighted average based on some factor such as market capitalization may be more appropriate.

$$w_d = \frac{D/E}{\left(\frac{D}{E} + 1\right)} = \frac{0.7}{1.7} = 0.41$$

$$w_e = 1 - w_d = 1 - 0.41 = 0.59$$

The before-tax cost of debt of Bayern Chemicals (r_d) is 6.75 percent:

$$r_d = 4.5 \text{ percent} + 2.25 \text{ percent} = 6.75 \text{ percent.}$$

As a result, Bayern Chemicals' WACC is 7.27 percent:

$$\begin{aligned} \text{WACC} &= [(0.41)\ (0.0675)\ (1 - 0.38)] + [(0.59)\ (0.094)] \\ &= 0.0726 \text{ or } 7.26 \text{ percent.} \end{aligned}$$

4.2 Country Risk

The use of a stock's beta to capture the **country risks** of a project is well supported in empirical studies that examine developed nations. However, beta does not appear to adequately capture country risk for companies in developing nations.[33] A common approach for dealing with this problem is to adjust the cost of equity estimated using the CAPM by adding a country spread to the market risk premium.[34] The country spread is also referred to as a country equity premium.

Perhaps the simplest estimate of the country spread is the **sovereign yield spread**, which is the difference between the government bond yield in that country, denominated in the currency of a developed country, and the Treasury bond yield on a similar maturity bond in the developed country.[35] However, this approach may be too coarse for the purposes of equity risk premium estimation.

Another approach is to calculate the country equity premium as the product of the sovereign yield spread and the ratio of the volatility of the developing country equity market to that of the sovereign bond market denominated in terms of the currency of a developed country:[36]

$$\text{Country equity premium} = \text{Sovereign yield spread}\left[\frac{\text{Annualized standard deviation of equity index}}{\text{Annualized standard deviation of the sovereign bond market in terms of the developed market currency}}\right] \quad \textbf{(45-13)}$$

[33] Campbell R. Harvey, "The International Cost of Capital and Risk Calculator," Duke University working paper (July 2001).

[34] Adding the country spread to the market risk premium for a developing country and then multiplying this sum by the market risk of the project is making the assumption that the country risk premium varies according to market risk. An alternative method calculates the cost of equity as the sum of three terms: (1) the risk-free rate of interest, (2) the product of the beta and the developed market risk premium, and (3) the country risk premium. This latter method assumes that the country risk premium is the same, regardless of the project's market risk.

[35] Jorge O. Mariscal and Rafaelina M. Lee, "The Valuation of Mexican Stocks: An Extension of the Capital Asset Pricing Model," New York: Goldman Sachs (1993).

[36] Aswath Damodaran, "Estimating Equity Risk Premiums," New York University working paper (1999) and Aswath Damodaran, "Measuring Company Exposure to Country Risk: Theory and Practice," New York University working paper (September 2003).

The logic of this calculation is that the sovereign yield spread captures the general risk of the country, which is then adjusted for the volatility of the stock market relative to the bond market. This country equity premium is then used in addition to the equity premium estimated for a project in a developed country. Therefore, if the equity risk premium for a project in a developed country is 4.5 percent and the country equity premium is 3 percent, the total equity risk premium used in the CAPM estimation is 7.5 percent. If the appropriate beta is 1.2 and the risk-free rate of interest is 4 percent, the equity risk premium is

$$\text{Cost of equity} = 0.04 + 1.2(0.045 + 0.03) = 0.13 \text{ or } 13 \text{ percent}$$

EXAMPLE 12

Estimating the Country Equity Premium

Miles Avenaugh, an analyst with the Global Company, is estimating a country equity premium to include in his estimate of the cost of equity capital for Global's investment in Argentina. Avenaugh has researched yields in Argentina and observed that the Argentinean government's 10-year bond is 9.5 percent. A similar maturity U.S. Treasury bond has a yield of 4.5 percent. The annualized standard deviation of the Argentina Merval stock index, a market value index of stocks listed on the Buenos Aires Stock Exchange, during the most recent year is 40 percent. The annualized standard deviation of the Argentina dollar-denominated 10-year government bond over the recent period was 28 percent.

What is the estimated country equity premium for Argentina based on Avenaugh's research?

Solution: Country equity premium $= 0.05\left(\frac{0.40}{0.28}\right) = 0.05(1.4286) =$ 0.0714, or 7.14 percent.

Still another approach is to use country credit ratings to estimate the expected rates of returns for countries that have credit ratings but no equity markets.[37] This method requires estimating reward to credit risk measures for a large sample of countries for which there are both credit ratings and equity markets and then applying this ratio to those countries without equity markets based on the country's credit rating.

4.3 Marginal Cost of Capital Schedule

As we noted in Section 2.3, as a company raises more funds, the costs of the different sources of capital may change, resulting in a change in the weighted average cost of capital for different levels of financing. The result is the marginal cost of capital (MCC) schedule, which we often depict in graphical form as the

[37] Claude Erb, Campbell R. Harvey, and Tadas Viskanta, "Expected Returns and Volatility in 135 Countries," *Journal of Portfolio Management* (Spring 1996), pp. 46–58.

weighted average cost of capital for different amounts of capital raised, as we showed earlier in Figure 1.[38]

Why would the cost of capital change as more capital is raised? One source of a difference in cost depending on the amount of capital raised is that a company may have existing debt with a bond covenant that restricts the company from issuing debt with similar seniority as existing debt. Or, a **debt incurrence test** may restrict a company's ability to incur additional debt at the same seniority based on one or more financial tests or conditions. For example, if a company issues senior debt such that any additional debt at that seniority violates the debt incurrence test of an existing bond covenant, the company may have to issue less senior debt or even equity, which would have a higher cost.

Another source of increasing marginal costs of capital is a deviation from the target capital structure. In the ideal, theoretical world, a company has a target capital structure and goes to the market each period and raises capital in these proportions. However, as a practical matter, companies do not necessarily tap the market in these ideal proportions because of considerations for economies of scale in raising new capital and market conditions. Because of such perceived economies of scale, companies tend to issue new securities such that in any given period, it may deviate from the proportions dictated by any target or optimal capital structure. In other words, these short-run deviations are due to the "lumpiness" of security issuance. As the company experiences deviations from the target capital structure, the marginal cost of capital may increase, reflecting these deviations.

The amount of capital at which the weighted average cost of capital changes—which means that the cost of one of the sources of capital changes—is referred to as a **break point**. The reality of raising capital is that the marginal cost of capital schedule is not as smooth as we depicted in Figure 1 but, rather, is a step-up cost schedule as shown in Figure 2.

FIGURE 2 Marginal Cost of Capital Schedule

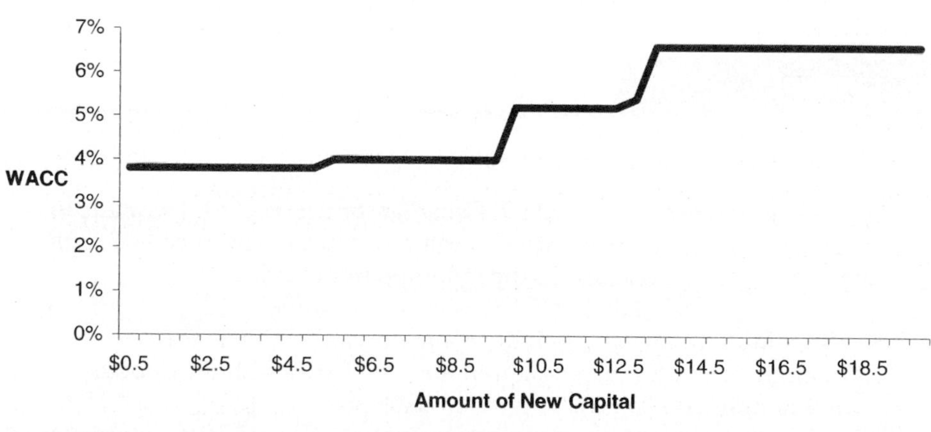

[38] Later in this section, we will discuss cases where a company's WACC may actually decrease as additional capital is raised. For example, if a company financed solely with common equity raises additional capital via debt, then the tax advantages provided by debt will result in a lower WACC under the new capital structure. For this discussion, we are assuming that the company is already operating at or near its optimum balance of debt versus equity.

Consider the case of a company facing the costs of capital given in Table 3.

TABLE 3 Schedule of the Costs of Debt and Equity

Amount of New Debt (in millions)	After-Tax Cost of Debt	Amount of New Equity (in millions)	Cost of Equity
new debt ≤ €2	2.0 percent	new equity ≤ €6	5.0 percent
€2 < new debt ≤ €5	2.5 percent	€6 < new equity ≤ €8	7.0 percent
€5 < new debt	3.0 percent	€8 < new equity	9.0 percent

If the company raises capital according to its target capital structure proportions of 40 percent debt and 60 percent equity, this company faces a marginal cost of capital schedule that is upward sloping, with break points at €5 million, €10 million, €12.5 million, and €13.3 million, as depicted in Figure 2. These break points are determined from the amounts of capital at which the cost changes, calculated as

$$\text{Break point} = \frac{\text{Amount of capital at which the source's cost of capital changes}}{\text{Proportion of new capital raised from the source}} \tag{45-14}$$

For example, the first break point for debt financing is reached with €2 million/0.4 = €5 million of new capital raised. The first break point attributed to a change in equity cost occurs at €6 million/0.6 = €10 million. Example 13 illustrates a marginal cost of capital schedule with break points and also how the WACC figures in the choice of an optimal capital structure.

EXAMPLE 13

Marginal Cost of Capital Schedule

Alan Conlon is the CFO of Allied Canadian Breweries Ltd. He wants to determine the capital structure that will result in the lowest cost of capital for Allied. He has access to the following information:

- The minimum rate at which the company can borrow is the 12-month LIBOR rate plus a premium that varies with the debt-to-capital ratio [D/(D+E)] as given in Table 4.

TABLE 4 Spreads over LIBOR for Alternative Debt-to-Capital Ratios

$\frac{D}{D+E}$	Spread (bps)
Less than 0.40	200
0.40 to 0.49	300
0.50 to 0.59	400
0.60 to 0.69	600
0.70 to 0.79	800
0.80 to 0.89	1,000
0.90 or higher	1,200

- The current 12-month LIBOR is 4.5 percent.
- The market risk premium is 4 percent, and unlevered beta is 0.9.
- The risk-free rate is 4.25 percent.
- The company's tax rate is 36 percent.

1. Determine the WACC for levels of the debt-to-equity ratio given in Table 4.
2. Recommend a target capital structure given that the company is concerned with achieving the lowest possible cost of capital.

Solution to 1: The WACC expressed as a function of the capital structure is shown in Table 5.

TABLE 5 WACC for Alternative Capital Structures

$\frac{D}{D+E}$	β	r_d (percent)	r_e (percent)	WACC (percent)
0.1	0.96	6.5	8.1	7.7
0.2	1.04	6.5	8.4	7.6
0.3	1.15	6.5	8.8	7.4
0.4	1.28	7.5	9.4	7.6
0.5	1.48	8.5	10.2	7.8
0.6	1.76	10.5	11.3	8.6
0.7	2.24	12.5	13.2	9.6
0.8	3.20	14.5	17.1	10.8
0.9	6.08	16.5	28.6	12.4

Solution to 2: The optimal capital structure is 30 percent debt.

4.4 Flotation Costs

When a company raises new capital, it generally seeks the assistance of investment bankers. Investment bankers charge the company a fee based on the size and type of offering. This fee is referred to as the flotation cost. In the case of debt and preferred stock, we do not usually incorporate flotation costs in the estimated cost of capital because the amount of these costs is quite small, often less than 1 percent.[39]

However, with equity issuance, the flotation costs may be substantial, so we should consider these when estimating the cost of external equity capital. For example, Inmoo Lee, Scott Lochhead, Jay Ritter, and Quanshui Zhao observe average flotation costs for new equity in the United States of 7.11 percent.[40] The flotation costs in other countries differ from the U.S. experience: Thomas Bühner and Christoph Kaserer observe flotation costs around 1.65 percent in Germany, Seth Armitage estimates an average issuance cost of 5.78 percent in the United Kingdom, and Christoph Kaserer and Fabian Steiner observe an average cost of 4.53 for Swiss capital offerings.[41] A large part of the differences in costs among these studies is likely attributed to the type of offering; cash underwritten offers, typical in the United States, are generally more expensive than rights offerings, which are common in Europe.

Should we incorporate flotation costs into the cost of capital? There are two views on this topic. One view, which you can find often in textbooks, is to incorporate the flotation costs into the cost of capital. The other view is that flotation costs should not be included in the cost of capital but, rather, incorporated into any valuation analysis as an additional cost of the project.

Consistent with the first view, we can specify flotation costs in monetary terms, as an amount per share or as a percentage of the share price. With flotation costs in monetary terms on a per share basis, F, the cost of external equity is

$$r_e = \left(\frac{D_1}{P_0 - F}\right) + g \qquad \textbf{(45-15)}$$

As a percentage applied against the price per share, the cost of external equity is

$$r_e = \left(\frac{D_1}{P_0(1 - f)}\right) + g \qquad \textbf{(45-16)}$$

where f is the flotation cost as a percentage of the issue price.

Suppose a company has a current dividend of \$2 per share, a current price of \$40 per share, and an expected growth rate of 5 percent. The cost of internally generated equity would be 10.25 percent:

$$r_e = \left(\frac{\$2(1 + 0.05)}{\$40}\right) + 0.05 = 0.0525 + 0.05 = 0.1025\text{, or } 10.25 \text{ percent}$$

---

[39] We can incorporate them for these sources by simply treating the flotation costs as an outlay, hence reducing proceeds from the source.

[40] Inmoo Lee, Scott Lochhead, Jay R. Ritter, and Quanshui Zhao, "The Costs of Raising Capital," *Journal of Financial Research*, Vol. 19 (Spring, 1996), pp. 59–71.

[41] Thomas Bühner and Christoph Kaserer, "External Financing Costs and Economies of Scale in Investment Banking: The Case of Seasoned Equity Offerings in Germany," *European Financial Management*, Vol. 9 (June 2002), pp. 249; Seth Armitage, "The Direct Costs of UK Rights Issues and Open Offers," *European Financial Management*, Vol. 6 (2000), pp. 57–68; Christoph Kaserer and Fabian Steiner, "The Cost of Raising Capital—New Evidence from Seasoned Equity Offerings in Switzerland," Technische Universität München working paper (February 2004).

If the flotation costs are 4 percent of the issuance, the cost of externally generated equity would be slightly higher at 10.469 percent:

$$r_e = \left(\frac{\$2(1 + 0.05)}{\$40(1 - 0.04)}\right) + 0.05 = 0.05469 + 0.05 = 0.1047, \text{ or } 10.47 \text{ percent}$$

The problem with this approach is that the flotation costs are a cash flow at the initiation of the project and affect the value of any project by reducing the initial cash flow. Adjusting the cost of capital for flotation costs is incorrect because by doing so, we are adjusting the present value of the future cash flows by a fixed percentage—in the above example, a difference of 22 basis points, which does not necessarily equate to the present value of the flotation costs.[42]

The alternative and recommended approach is to make the adjustment to the cash flows in the valuation computation. For example, consider a project that requires a €60,000 initial cash outlay and is expected to produce cash flows of €10,000 each year for 10 years. Suppose the company's marginal tax rate is 40 percent and that the before-tax cost of debt is 5 percent. Furthermore, suppose that the company's dividend next period is €1, the current price of the stock is €20, and the expected growth rate is 5 percent so that the cost of equity using the dividend discount model is (€1/€20) + 0.05 = 0.10 or 10 percent. Assume the company will finance the project with 40 percent debt and 60 percent equity. Table 6 summarizes the information on the component costs of capital.

TABLE 6 After-Tax Costs of Debt and Equity

Source of Capital	Amount Raised	Proportion	Marginal After-Tax Cost
Debt	€24,000	0.40	0.05(1 − 0.4) = 0.03
Equity	€36,000	0.60	0.10

The weighted average cost of capital is 7.2 percent calculated as 0.40(3 percent) + 0.60(10 percent). Ignoring flotation costs for the moment, the net present value (NPV) of this project is

$$\text{NPV} = €69{,}591 - €60{,}000 = €9{,}591$$

If the flotation costs are, say, 5 percent of the new equity capital, the flotation costs are €1,800. The net present value considering flotation costs is

$$\text{NPV} = €\ 69{,}591 - €60{,}000 - €1{,}800 = €7{,}791$$

If, instead of considering the flotation costs as part of the cash flows, we adjust the cost of equity, the cost of capital is 7.3578 percent and the NPV is

$$\text{NPV} = €69{,}089 - €60{,}000 = €9{,}089$$

As you can see, we arrive at different assessments of value using these two methods.

[42] This argument is made by John R. Ezzell and R. Burr Porter ["Flotation Costs and the Weighted Average Cost of Capital," *Journal of Financial and Quantitative Analysis*, Vol. 11, No. 3 (September 1976), pp. 403–413]. They argue that the correct treatment is to deduct flotation costs as part of the valuation as one of the initial-period cash flows.

So, if it is preferred to deduct the flotation costs as part of the net present value calculation, why do we see the adjustment in the cost of capital so often in textbooks? The first reason is that it is often difficult to identify particular financing associated with a project. Using the adjustment for the flotation costs in the cost of capital may be useful if specific project financing cannot be identified. Second, by adjusting the cost of capital for the flotation costs, it is easier to demonstrate how costs of financing a company change as a company exhausts internally generated equity (i.e., retained earnings) and switches to externally generated equity (i.e., a new stock issue).

4.5 What Do CFOs Do?

In this reading, we have introduced you to methods that may be used to estimate the cost of capital for a company or a project. What do companies actually use when making investment decisions? In a survey of a large number of U.S. company CFOs, John Graham and Campbell Harvey asked about the methods that companies actually use.[43] Their survey revealed the following:

- The most popular method for estimating the cost of equity is the capital asset pricing model.
- Few companies use the dividend cash flow model to estimate a cost of equity.
- Publicly traded companies are more likely to use the capital asset pricing model than are private companies.
- In evaluating projects, the majority use a single company cost of capital, but a large portion apply some type of risk adjustment for individual projects.

The survey also reveals that the single-factor capital asset pricing model is the most popular method for estimating the cost of equity, though the next most popular methods, respectively, are average stock returns and multifactor return models. The lack of popularity of the dividend discount model indicates that this approach, which was once favored, has lost its following in practice.[44]

In a survey of publicly traded multinational European companies, Franck Bancel and Usha Mittoo provide evidence consistent with the Graham and Harvey survey.[45] They find that over 70 percent of companies use the CAPM to determine the cost of equity; this compares with the 73.5 percent of U.S. companies that use the CAPM. In a survey of both publicly traded and private European companies, Dirk Brounen, Abe de Jong, and Kees Koedijk confirm the result of Graham and Harvey that larger companies are more likely to use the more sophisticated methods, such as CAPM, in estimating the cost of equity.[46]

[43] John Graham and Campbell Harvey, "How Do CFOs Make Capital Budgeting and Capital Structure Decisions," *Journal of Applied Corporate Finance*, Vol. 15, No. 1 (Spring 2002), pp. 8–23.

[44] A survey published in 1982 by Lawrence Gitman and V. Mercurio ["Cost of Capital Techniques Used by Major U.S. Firms: Survey and Analysis of Fortune's 1000," *Financial Management*, Vol. 14, No. 4 (Winter 1982), pp. 21–29] indicated that fewer than 30 percent used the CAPM model in the estimation of the cost of equity.

[45] Franck Bancel and Usha Mittoo, "The Determinants of Capital Structure Choice: A Survey of European Firms," *Financial Management*, Vol. 44, No. 4 (Winter 2004).

[46] Dirk Brounen, Abe de Jong, and Kees Koedijk, "Corporate Finance in Europe: Confronting Theory with Practice," *Financial Management*, Vol. 44, No. 4 (Winter 2004).

Brounen, Jong, and Koedijk find that the popularity of the use of CAPM is less for their sample (ranging from 34 percent to 55.6 percent, depending on the country) than for the other two surveys, which may reflect the inclusion of smaller, private companies in the latter sample.

We learn from the survey evidence that the CAPM is a popular method for estimating the cost of equity capital and that it is used less by smaller, private companies. This latter result is not surprising because of the difficulty in estimating systematic risk in cases in which the company's equity is not publicly traded.

SUMMARY

In this reading, we provided an overview of the techniques used to calculate the cost of capital for companies and projects. We examined the weighted average cost of capital, discussing the methods commonly used to estimate the component costs of capital and the weights applied to these components. The international dimension of the cost of capital, as well as key factors influencing the cost of capital, were also analyzed.

- The weighted average cost of capital is a weighted average of the after-tax marginal costs of each source of capital: $\text{WACC} = w_d r_d (1 - t) + w_p r_p + w_e r_e$.
- An analyst uses the WACC in valuation. For example, the WACC is used to value a project using the net present value method:

$$\text{NPV} = \text{Present value of inflows} - \text{Present value of the outflows}$$

- The before-tax cost of debt is generally estimated by means of one of the two methods: yield to maturity or bond rating.
- The yield-to-maturity method of estimating the before-tax cost of debt uses the familiar bond valuation equation. Assuming semi-annual coupon payments, the equation is

$$P_0 = \frac{PMT_1}{\left(1 + \frac{r_d}{2}\right)} + \ldots + \frac{PMT_n}{\left(1 + \frac{r_d}{2}\right)^n} + \frac{FV}{\left(1 + \frac{r_d}{2}\right)^n} = \left(\sum_{t=1}^{n} \frac{PMT_i}{\left(1 + \frac{r_d}{2}\right)^t}\right) + \frac{FV}{\left(1 + \frac{r_d}{2}\right)^n}$$

  We solve for the six-month yield ($r_d/2$) and then annualize it to arrive at the before-tax cost of debt, r_d.
- Because interest payments are generally tax-deductible, the after-tax cost is the true, effective cost of debt to the company. If a current yield or bond rating is not available, such as in the case of a private company without rated debt or a project, the estimate of the cost of debt becomes more challenging.
- The cost of preferred stock is the preferred stock dividend divided by the current preferred stock price:

$$r_p = \frac{D_p}{P_p}$$

- The cost of equity is the rate of return required by a company's common stockholders. We estimate this cost using the CAPM (or its variants) or the dividend discount method.
- The CAPM is the approach most commonly used to calculate the cost of common stock. The three components needed to calculate the cost of common stock are the risk-free rate, the equity risk premium, and beta:

$$E(R_i) = R_F + \beta_i [E(R_M) - R_F]$$

- When estimating the cost of equity capital using the CAPM when we do not have publicly traded equity, we may be able to use the pure-play method in which we estimate the unlevered beta for a company with similar business risk, β_U,

$$\beta_{U,\text{comparable}} = \frac{\beta_{L,\text{comparable}}}{\left[1 + \left((1 - t_{\text{comparable}}) \frac{D_{\text{comparable}}}{E_{\text{comparable}}}\right)\right]}$$

and then lever this beta to reflect the financial risk of the project or company:

$$\beta_{L,\text{project}} = \beta_{U,\text{comparable}} = \left[1 + \left((1 - t_{\text{project}}) \frac{D_{\text{project}}}{E_{\text{project}}}\right)\right]$$

- It is often the case that country and foreign exchange risk are diversified so that we can use the estimated β in the CAPM analysis. However, in the case in which these risks cannot be diversified away, we can adjust our measure of systematic risk by a country equity premium to reflect this nondiversified risk:

$$\text{Country equity premium} = \text{Sovereign yield spread} \left[\frac{\text{Annualized standard deviation of equity index}}{\text{Annualized standard deviation of the sovereign bond market in terms of the developed market currency}}\right]$$

- The dividend discount model approach is an alternative approach to calculating the cost of equity, whereby the cost of equity is estimated as follows:

$$r_e = \frac{D_1}{P_0} + g$$

- We can estimate the growth rate in the dividend discount model by using published forecasts of analysts or by estimating the sustainable growth rate:

$$g = (1 - D/\text{EPS})\ \text{ROE}$$

- In estimating the cost of equity, an alternative to the CAPM and dividend discount approaches is the bond yield plus risk premium approach. In this approach, we estimate the before-tax cost of debt and add a risk premium that reflects the additional risk associated with the company's equity.
- The marginal cost of capital schedule is a graph plotting the new funds raised by a company on the *x*-axis and the cost of capital on the *y*-axis. The cost of capital is level to the point at which one of the costs of capital changes, such as when the company bumps up against a debt covenant, requiring it to use another form of capital. We calculate a break point using information on when the different sources' costs change and the proportions that the company uses when it raises additional capital:

$$\text{Break point} = \frac{\text{Amount of capital at which the source's cost of capital changes}}{\text{Proportion of new capital raised from the source}}$$

- Flotation costs are costs incurred in the process of raising additional capital. The preferred method of including these costs in the analysis is as an initial cash flow in the valuation analysis.
- Survey evidence tells us that the CAPM method is the most popular method used by companies in estimating the cost of equity. The CAPM is more popular with larger, publicly traded companies, which is understandable considering the additional analyses and assumptions required in estimating systematic risk for a private company or project.

PRACTICE PROBLEMS FOR READING 45

1. The cost of equity is equal to the
   - **A.** expected market return.
   - **B.** rate of return required by stockholders.
   - **C.** cost of retained earnings plus dividends.
   - **D.** risk the company incurs when financing.
2. Which of the following statements is correct?
   - **A.** The appropriate tax rate to use in the adjustment of the before-tax cost of debt to determine the after-tax cost of debt is the average tax rate because interest is deductible against the company's entire taxable income.
   - **B.** For a given company, the after-tax cost of debt is less than both the cost of preferred equity and the cost of common equity.
   - **C.** For a given company, the investment opportunity schedule is upward sloping because as a company invests more in capital projects, the returns from investing increase.
   - **D.** The target capital structure is the average ratio of debt to equity for the most recent fiscal years.
3. Using the dividend discount model, what is the cost of equity capital for Zeller Mining if the company will pay a dividend of C$2.30 next year, has a payout ratio of 30 percent, a return on equity of 15 percent, and a stock price of C$45?
   - **A.** 5.11 percent.
   - **B.** 9.61 percent.
   - **C.** 10.50 percent.
   - **D.** 15.61 percent.
4. Dot.Com has determined that it could issue $1,000 face value bonds with an 8 percent coupon paid semi-annually and a five-year maturity at $900 per bond. If Dot.Com's marginal tax rate is 38 percent, its after-tax cost of debt is *closest* to
   - **A.** 6.2 percent.
   - **B.** 6.4 percent.
   - **C.** 6.6 percent.
   - **D.** 6.8 percent.
5. The cost of debt can be determined using the yield-to-maturity and the bond rating approaches. If the bond rating approach is used, the
   - **A.** coupon is the yield.
   - **B.** yield is based on the interest coverage ratio.
   - **C.** company is rated and the rating can be used to assess the credit default spread of the company's debt.
   - **D.** after-tax cost of the debt is not known.

6. Morgan Insurance Ltd. issued a fixed-rate perpetual preferred stock three years ago and placed it privately with institutional investors. The stock was issued at $25 per share with a $1.75 dividend. If the company were to issue preferred stock today, the yield would be 6.5 percent. The stock's current value is
   - A. $25.00.
   - B. $26.92.
   - C. $37.31.
   - D. $40.18.
7. A financial analyst at Buckco Ltd. wants to compute the company's weighted average cost of capital (WACC) using the dividend discount model. The analyst has gathered the following data:

Before-tax cost of new debt	8 percent
Tax rate	40 percent
Target debt-to-equity ratio	0.8033
Stock price	$30
Next year's dividend	$1.50
Estimated growth rate	7 percent

   Buckco's WACC is *closest* to
   - A. 8 percent.
   - B. 9 percent.
   - C. 12 percent.
   - D. 20 percent.
8. The Gearing Company has an after-tax cost of debt capital of 4 percent, a cost of preferred stock of 8 percent, a cost of equity capital of 10 percent, and a weighted average cost of capital of 7 percent. Gearing intends to maintain its current capital structure as it raises additional capital. In making its capital-budgeting decisions for the average-risk project, the relevant cost of capital is
   - A. 4 percent.
   - B. 7 percent.
   - C. 8 percent.
   - D. 10 percent.
9. Fran McClure of Alba Advisers is estimating the cost of capital of Frontier Corporation as part of her valuation analysis of Frontier. McClure will be using this estimate, along with projected cash flows from Frontier's new projects, to estimate the effect of these new projects on the value of Frontier. McClure has gathered the following information on Frontier Corporation:

	Current Year	Forecasted for Next Year
Book value of debt	\$50	\$50
Market value of debt	\$62	\$63
Book value of shareholders' equity	\$55	\$58
Market value of shareholders' equity	\$210	\$220

The weights that McClure should apply in estimating Frontier's cost of capital for debt and equity are, respectively

A. $w_d = 0.200$; $w_e = 0.800$.

B. $w_d = 0.185$; $w_e = 0.815$.

C. $w_d = 0.223$; $w_e = 0.777$.

D. $w_d = 0.228$; $w_e = 0.772$.

10. Wang Securities had a long-term stable debt-to-equity ratio of 0.65. Recent bank borrowing for expansion into South America raised the ratio to 0.75. The increased leverage has what effect on the asset beta and equity beta of the company?

	Asset Beta	Equity Beta
A.	Same	Higher
B.	Same	Lower
C.	Lower	Higher
D.	Lower	Lower

11. Brandon Wiene is a financial analyst covering the beverage industry. He is evaluating the impact of DEF Beverage's new product line of flavored waters. DEF currently has a debt-to-equity ratio of 0.6. The new product line would be financed with \$50 million of debt and \$100 million of equity. In estimating the valuation impact of this new product line on DEF's value, Wiene has estimated the equity beta and asset beta of comparable companies. In calculating the equity beta for the product line, Wiene is intending to use DEF's existing capital structure when converting the asset beta into a project beta. Which of the following statements is correct?

A. Using DEF's debt-to-equity ratio of 0.6 is appropriate in calculating the new product line's equity beta.

B. Using DEF's debt-to-equity ratio of 0.6 is not appropriate, but rather the debt-to-equity ratio of the new product, 0.5, is appropriate to use in calculating the new product line's equity beta.

C. Wiene should use the new debt-to-equity ratio of DEF that would result from the additional \$50 million debt and \$100 million equity in calculating the new product line's equity beta.

D. Wiene should use the asset beta determined from the analysis of comparables as the equity beta in evaluating the new product line.

12. Trumpit Resorts Company currently has 1.2 million common shares of stock outstanding, and the stock has a beta of 2.2. It also has $10 million face value of bonds that have five years remaining to maturity and 8 percent coupon with semi-annual payments, and are priced to yield 13.65 percent. Trumpit has learned that it can issue new common stock at $10 a share. The current risk-free rate of interest is 3 percent, and the expected market return is 10 percent. If Trumpit issues up to $2.5 million of new bonds, the bonds will be priced at par and have a yield of 13.65 percent; if it issues bonds beyond $2.5 million, the expected yield will be 16 percent. Trumpit's marginal tax rate is 30 percent. If Trumpit raises $7.5 million of new capital while maintaining the same debt-to-equity ratio, its weighted average cost of capital is *closest* to

A. 14.5 percent.

B. 15.5 percent.

C. 16.5 percent.

D. 17.5 percent.

The following information relates to Questions 13–18

Jurgen Knudsen has been hired to provide industry expertise to Henrik Sandell, CFA, an analyst for a pension plan managing a global large-cap fund internally. Sandell is concerned about one of the fund's larger holdings, Swedish auto parts manufacturer Kruspa AB. Kruspa currently operates in 80 countries, with the previous year's global revenues at €5.6 billion. Recently, Kruspa's CFO announced plans for expansion into China. Sandell worries that this expansion will change the company's risk profile and wonders if he should recommend a sale of the position.

Sandell provides Knudsen with the basic information. Kruspa's global annual free cash flow to the firm is €500 million and earnings are €400 million. Sandell estimates that cash flow will level off at a 2 percent rate of growth. Sandell also estimates that Kruspa's after-tax free cash flow to the firm on the China project for next three years is, respectively, €48 million, €52 million, and €54.4 million. Kruspa recently announced a dividend of €4.00 per share of stock. For the initial analysis, Sandell requests that Knudsen ignore possible currency fluctuations. He expects the Chinese plant to sell only to customers within China for the first three years. Knudsen is asked to evaluate Kruspa's planned financing of the required €100 million with a €80 public offering of 10-year debt in Sweden and the remainder with an equity offering.

Additional information:

Equity risk premium, Sweden	4.82 percent
Risk-free rate of interest, Sweden	4.25 percent
Industry debt-to-equity ratio	0.3
Market value of Kruspa's debt	€900 million
Market value of Kruspa's equity	€2.4 billion
Kruspa's equity beta	1.3
Kruspa's before-tax cost of debt	9.25 percent
China credit A2 country risk premium	1.88 percent
Corporate tax rate	37.5 percent
Interest payments each year	Level

13. Using the capital asset pricing model, Kruspa's cost of equity capital for its typical project is *closest* to

A. 7.62 percent.
B. 10.52 percent.
C. 12.40 percent.
D. 14.84 percent.

14. Sandell is interested in the weighted average cost of capital of Kruspa AB prior to its investing in the China project. This weighted average cost of capital (WACC) is *closest* to

A. 7.65 percent.
B. 9.23 percent.
C. 10.17 percent.
D. 10.52 percent.

15. In his estimation of the project's cost of capital, Sandell would like to use the asset beta of Kruspa as a base in his calculations. The estimated asset beta of Kruspa prior to the China project is *closest* to

A. 1.053.
B. 1.110.
C. 1.140.
D. 1.327.

16. Sandell is performing a sensitivity analysis of the effect of the new project on the company's cost of capital. If the China project has the same asset risk as Kruspa, the estimated project beta for the China project, if it is financed 80 percent with debt, is *closest* to

A. 1.053.
B. 1.300.
C. 2.635.
D. 3.686.

17. As part of the sensitivity analysis of the effect of the new project on the company's cost of capital, Sandell is estimating the cost of equity of the China project considering that the China project requires a country equity premium to capture the risk of the project. The cost of equity for the project in this case is *closest* to

A. 9.23 percent.
B. 10.52 percent.
C. 19.91 percent.
D. 28.95 percent.

18. In his report, Sandell would like to discuss the sensitivity of the project's net present value to the estimation of the cost of equity. The China project's net present value calculated using the equity beta without and with the country risk premium are, respectively

A. €26 million and €24 million.
B. €28 million and €25 million.
C. €30 million and €27 million.
D. €32 million and €31 million.

The following information relates to Questions 19–22

Boris Duarte, CFA, covers initial public offerings for Zellweger Analytics, an independent research firm specializing in global small-cap equities. He has been asked to evaluate the upcoming new issue of TagOn, a U.S.-based business intelligence software company. The industry has grown at 26 percent per year for the previous three years. Large companies dominate the market, but sizable "pure-play" companies such as Relevant, Ltd., ABJ, Inc., and Opus Software Pvt. Ltd also compete. Each of these competitors is domiciled in a different country, but they all have shares of stock that trade on the U.S. NASDAQ. The debt ratio of the industry has risen slightly in recent years.

Company	Sales in Millions	Market Value Equity in Billions	Market Value Debt in Millions	Equity Beta	Tax Rate	Share Price
Relevant Ltd.	$752	$3.8	$0.0	1.702	23 percent	$42
ABJ, Inc.	$843	$2.15	$6.5	2.800	23 percent	$24
Opus Software Pvt. Ltd.	$211	$0.972	$13.0	3.400	23 percent	$13

Duarte uses the information from the preliminary prospectus for TagOn's initial offering. The company intends to issue 1 million new shares. In his conversation with the investment bankers for the deal, he concludes the offering price will be between $7 and $12. The current capital structure of TagOn consists of a $2.4 million five-year non-callable bond issue and 1 million common shares. Other information that Duarte has gathered:

Currently outstanding bonds	$2.4 million five-year bonds, coupon of 12.5 percent, with a market value of $2.156 million
Risk-free rate of interest	5.25 percent
Estimated equity risk premium	7 percent
Tax rate	23 percent

19. The asset betas for Relevant, ABJ, and Opus, respectively, are
- **A.** 1.70, 2.52, 2.73.
- **B.** 1.70, 2.79, 3.37.
- **C.** 1.70, 2.81, 3.44.
- **D.** 2.634 for each.

20. The weighted average asset beta for the pure players in this industry, Relevant, ABJ, and Opus, weighted by market value is *closest* to
- **A.** 1.37.
- **B.** 1.67.
- **C.** 1.97.
- **D.** 2.27.

21. Using the capital asset pricing model, the cost of equity capital for a company in this industry with a debt-to-equity ratio of 0.01 and a marginal tax rate of 23 percent is *closest* to

A. 17 percent.
B. 21 percent.
C. 24 percent.
D. 31 percent.

22. The marginal cost of capital for TagOn, based on the average asset beta for the industry and assuming that new stock can be issued at $8 per share, is *closest* to

A. 20.0 percent.
B. 20.5 percent.
C. 21.0 percent.
D. 21.5 percent.

2005 exam

23. Two years ago, a company issued $20 million in long-term bonds at par value with a coupon rate of 9 percent. The company has decided to issue an additional $20 million in bonds and expects the new issue to be priced at par value with a coupon rate of 7 percent. The company has no other debt outstanding and has a tax rate of 40 percent. To compute the company's weighted average cost of capital, the appropriate after-tax cost of debt is *closest* to

A. 3.6%.
B. 4.2%.
C. 4.8%.
D. 5.4%.

2005 exam

24. An analyst gathered the following information about a company and the market:

Current market price per share of common stock	$28.00
Most recent dividend per share paid on common stock (D_0)	$2.00
Expected dividend payout rate	40%
Expected return on equity (ROE)	15%
Beta for the common stock	1.3
Expected rate of return on the market portfolio	13%
Risk-free rate of return	4%

Using the discounted cash flow (DCF) approach, the cost of retained earnings for the company is *closest* to

A. 13.6%.
B. 15.7%.
C. 16.1%.
D. 16.8%.

25. An analyst gathered the following information about a company and the market:

2005 exam

Current market price per share of common stock	$28.00
Most recent dividend per share paid on common stock (D_0)	$2.00
Expected dividend payout rate	40%
Expected return on equity (ROE)	15%
Beta for the common stock	1.3
Expected rate of return on the market portfolio	13%
Risk-free rate of return	4%

Using the Capital Asset Pricing Model (CAPM) approach, the cost of retained earnings for the company is *closest* to

A. 13.6%.

B. 15.7%.

C. 16.1%.

D. 16.8%.

26. An analyst gathered the following information about a private company and its publicly-traded competitor:

Comparable Companies	Tax Rate	Debt/Equity	Equity Beta
Private company	30.0%	1.00	N.A.
Public company	35.0%	0.90	1.75

Using the pure-play method, the estimated equity beta for the private company is *closest* to:

A. 1.029.

B. 1.104.

C. 1.877.

D. 2.774.

27. An analyst gathered the following information about the capital markets in the U.S. and in Paragon, a developing country.

Selected Market Information	
Yield on U.S. 10-year Treasury bond	4.5%
Yield on Paragon 10-year government bond	10.5%
Annualized standard deviation of Paragon stock index	35.0%
Annualized standard deviation of Paragon dollar-denominated government bond	25.0%

Based on the analyst's data, the estimated country equity premium for Paragon is *closest* to

A. 2.10%.

B. 4.29%.

C. 6.00%.

D. 8.40%.

WORKING CAPITAL MANAGEMENT

by Edgar A. Norton, Jr., Kenneth L. Parkinson, and Pamela P. Peterson

READING

46

LEARNING OUTCOMES

The candidate should be able to:

a. calculate and interpret liquidity measures using selected financial ratios for a company and compare the company with peer companies;

b. evaluate overall working capital effectiveness of a company, using the operating and cash conversion cycles, and compare the company's effectiveness with other peer companies;

c. classify the components of a cash forecast and prepare a cash forecast, given estimates of revenues, expenses, and other items;

d. identify and evaluate the necessary tools to use in managing a company's net daily cash position;

e. compute and interpret comparable yields on various securities, compare portfolio returns against a standard benchmark, and evaluate a company's short-term investment policy guidelines;

f. evaluate the performance of a company's accounts receivable, inventory management, and accounts payable functions against historical figures and comparable peer company values;

g. evaluate the choices of short-term funding available to a company and recommend a financing method.

INTRODUCTION 1

The focus of this reading is on the short-term aspects of corporate finance activities collectively referred to as **working capital management**. The goal of effective working capital management is to ensure that a company has adequate ready access to the funds necessary for day-to-day operating expenses, while at the same time making sure that the company's assets are invested in the most productive way. Achieving this goal requires a balancing of concerns. Insufficient access to cash could ultimately lead to severe restructuring of a company by selling off assets, reorganization via bankruptcy proceedings, or final liquidation of the company. On the other hand, excessive investment in cash and liquid assets may not be the best use of company resources.

Effective working capital management encompasses several aspects of short-term finance: maintaining adequate levels of cash, converting short-term assets (i.e., accounts receivable and inventory) into cash, and controlling outgoing payments to vendors, employees, and others. To do this successfully, companies invest short-term funds in working capital portfolios of short-dated, highly liquid securities, or they maintain credit reserves in the form of bank lines of credit or access to financing by issuing commercial paper or other money market instruments.

Working capital management is a broad-based function. Effective execution requires managing and coordinating several tasks within the company, including managing short-term investments, granting credit to customers and collecting on this credit, managing inventory, and managing payables. Effective working capital management also requires reliable cash forecasts, as well as current and accurate information on transactions and bank balances.

Both internal and external factors influence working capital needs; we summarize them in Exhibit 1.

EXHIBIT 1 Internal and External Factors That Affect Working Capital Needs

Internal Factors	External Factors
▶ Company size and growth rates	▶ Banking services
▶ Organizational structure	▶ Interest rates
▶ Sophistication of working capital management	▶ New technologies and new products
▶ Borrowing and investing positions/activities/capacities	▶ The economy
	▶ Competitors

The scope of working capital management includes transactions, relations, analyses, and focus:

- Transactions include payments for trade, financing, and investment.
- Relations with financial institutions and trading partners must be maintained to ensure that the transactions work effectively.
- Analyses of working capital management activities are required so that appropriate strategies can be formulated and implemented.

- Focus requires that organizations of all sizes today must have a global viewpoint with strong emphasis on liquidity.

In this reading, we examine the different types of working capital and the management issues associated with each. We also look at methods of evaluating the effectiveness of working capital management.

MANAGING AND MEASURING LIQUIDITY 2

Liquidity is the extent to which a company is able to meet its short-term obligations using assets that can be readily transformed into cash. When we evaluate the liquidity of an asset, we focus on two dimensions: the type of asset and the speed at which the asset can be converted to cash, either by sale or financing. Unlike many aspects of corporate finance, corporate liquidity management does not involve a great deal of theory or generally accepted principles. For companies that have the luxury of large excesses of cash, liquidity is typically taken for granted, and the focus is on putting the excess liquidity to its most productive use. On the other hand, when a company faces tighter financial situations, it is important to have effective liquidity management to ensure solvency. Unfortunately, this recognition comes too late for some companies, with bankruptcy and possible liquidation representing the company's final choice.

2.1 Defining Liquidity Management

Liquidity management refers to the ability of an organization to generate cash when and where it is needed. Liquidity refers to the resources available for an entity to tap into cash balances and to convert other assets or extend other liabilities into cash for use in keeping the entity solvent (i.e., being able to pay bills and continue in operation). For the most part, we associate liquidity with short-term assets and liabilities, yet longer-term assets can be converted into cash to provide liquidity. In addition, longer-term liabilities can also be renegotiated to reduce the drain on cash, thereby providing liquidity by preserving the limited supply of cash. Of course, the last two methods may come at a price as they tend to reduce the company's overall financial strength.

The challenges of managing liquidity include developing, implementing, and maintaining a liquidity policy. To do this effectively, a company must manage all of its key sources of liquidity efficiently. These key sources may vary from company to company, but they generally include the primary sources of liquidity, such as cash balances, and secondary sources of liquidity, such as selling assets.

2.1.1 Primary Sources of Liquidity

Primary sources of liquidity represent the most readily accessible resources available. They may be held as cash or as near-cash securities. Primary sources include:

- Ready cash balances, which is cash available in bank accounts, resulting from payment collections, investment income, liquidation of near-cash securities (i.e., those with maturities of less than 90 days), and other cash flows.

- Short-term funds, which may include items such as trade credit, bank lines of credit, and short-term investment portfolios.
- Cash flow management, which is the company's effectiveness in its cash management system and practices, and the degree of decentralization of the collections or payments processes. The more decentralized the system of collections, for example, the more likely the company will be to have cash tied up in the system and not available for use.

These sources represent liquidity that is typical for most companies. They represent funds that are readily accessible at relatively low cost.

2.1.2 Secondary Sources of Liquidity

The main difference between the primary and secondary sources of liquidity is that using a primary source is not likely to affect the normal operations of the company, whereas using a secondary source may result in a change in the company's financial and operating positions. Secondary sources include:

- negotiating debt contracts, relieving pressures from high interest payments or principal repayments;
- liquidating assets, which depends on the degree to which short-term and/or long-term assets can be liquidated and converted into cash without substantial loss in value; and
- filing for bankruptcy protection and reorganization.

Use of secondary sources may signal a company's deteriorating financial health and provide liquidity at a high price—the cost of giving up a company asset to produce emergency cash. The last source, reorganization through bankruptcy, may also be considered a liquidity tool because a company under bankruptcy protection that generates operating cash will be liquid and generally able to continue business operations until a restructuring has been devised and approved.

2.1.3 Drags and Pulls on Liquidity

Cash flow transactions—that is, cash receipts and disbursements—have significant effects on a company's liquidity position. We refer to these effects as drags and pulls on liquidity. A **drag on liquidity** is when receipts lag, creating pressure from the decreased available funds; a **pull on liquidity** is when disbursements are paid too quickly or trade credit availability is limited, requiring companies to expend funds before they receive funds from sales that could cover the liability.

Major drags on receipts involve pressures from credit management and deterioration in other assets and include:

- *Uncollected receivables.* The longer these are outstanding, the greater the risk that they will not be collected at all. They are indicated by the large number of days of receivables and high levels of bad debt expenses. Just as the drags on receipts may cause increased pressures on working capital, pulls on outgoing payments may have similar effects.
- *Obsolete inventory.* If inventory stands unused for long periods, it may be an indication that it is no longer usable. Slow inventory turnover ratios can also indicate obsolete inventory. Once identified, obsolete inventory should be attended to as soon as possible in order to minimize storage and other costs.

- *Tight credit.* When economic conditions make capital scarcer, short-term debt becomes more expensive to arrange and use. Attempting to smooth out peak borrowings can help blunt the impact of tight credit as can improving the company's collections.

In many cases, drags may be alleviated by stricter enforcement of credit and collection practices.[1]

However, managing the cash outflows may be as important as managing the inflows. If suppliers and other vendors who offer credit terms perceive a weakened financial position or are unfamiliar with a company, they may restrict payment terms so much that the company's liquidity reserves are stretched thin. Major pulls on payments include:

- *Making payments early.* By paying vendors, employees, or others before the due dates, companies forgo the use of funds. Effective payment management means not making early payments. Payables managers typically hold payments until they can be made by the due date.
- *Reduced credit limits.* If a company has a history of making late payments, suppliers may cut the amount of credit they will allow to be outstanding at any time, which can squeeze the company's liquidity. Some companies try to extend payment periods as long as possible, disregarding the possible impact of reduced credit limits.
- *Limits on short-term lines of credit.* If a company's bank reduces the line of credit it offers the company, a liquidity squeeze may result. Credit line restrictions may be government-mandated, market-related, or simply company-specific. Many companies try to avert this situation by establishing credit lines far in excess of what they are likely to need. This "over-banking" approach is often commonplace in emerging economies or even in more-developed countries where the banking system is not sound and the economy is shaky.
- *Low liquidity positions.* Many companies face chronic liquidity shortages, often because of their particular industry or from their weaker financial position. The major remedy for this situation is, of course, to improve the company's financial position, or else the company will be heavily affected by interest rates and credit availability. Most companies facing this situation have to deal with secured borrowing to obtain any working capital funds. Therefore, it is important for these companies to identify assets that can be used to help support the company's short-term borrowing activities.

It is critical that these drags and pulls be identified as soon as possible, often when they have not yet happened or have just arisen.

2.2 Measuring Liquidity

Liquidity contributes to a company's creditworthiness. **Creditworthiness** is the perceived ability of the borrower to pay what is owed on the borrowing in a

[1] In a recent survey of CFOs, companies have become more efficient in working capital management, with U.S. companies in 2005 reducing their investment in working capital by 2.5 percent from 2004 levels and European companies reducing their investment by 3.3 percent (REL 2005 CFO Survey, www.relconsult.com/CFO).

timely manner and represents the ability of a company to withstand adverse impacts on its cash flows. Creditworthiness allows the company to obtain lower borrowing costs and better terms for trade credit and contributes to the company's investment flexibility, enabling it to exploit profitable opportunities.

The less liquid the company, the greater the risk it will suffer financial distress or, in the extreme case, insolvency or bankruptcy. Because debt obligations are paid with cash, the company's cash flows ultimately determine solvency. The immediate source of funds for paying bills is cash on hand, proceeds from the sale of marketable securities, or the collection of accounts receivable. Additional liquidity also comes from inventory that can be sold and thus converted into cash either directly through cash sales or indirectly through credit sales (i.e., accounts receivable).

There is, however, some point at which a company may have too much invested in low-and non-earning assets. Cash, marketable securities, accounts receivable, and inventory represent a company's liquidity. However, these investments are low earning relative to the long-term, capital investment opportunities that companies may have available.

Various financial ratios can be used to assess a company's liquidity as well as its management of assets over time. Here we will look at some of these ratios in a little more detail.

We calculate **liquidity ratios** to measure a company's ability to meet short-term obligations to creditors as they mature or come due. This form of liquidity analysis focuses on the relationship between current assets and current liabilities and the rapidity with which receivables and inventory can be converted into cash during normal business operations.

In short-term financial management, a great deal of emphasis is placed on the levels of and changes in current assets and liabilities. The two most common measurements are the current ratio and the quick ratio. The **current ratio** is the ratio of current assets to current liabilities:

$$\text{Current ratio} = \frac{\text{Current assets}}{\text{Current liabilities}}$$

The **quick ratio** (also known as the **acid-test ratio**) is the ratio of the quick assets to current liabilities. **Quick assets** are those assets that can be most readily converted to cash. In most situations, the least liquid of the current assets is inventory. Hence, we typically exclude inventory when calculating the quick ratio:

$$\text{Quick ratio} = \frac{\text{Cash} + \text{Short-term marketable investments} + \text{Receivables}}{\text{Current liabilities}}$$

The greater the current ratio or the quick ratio (that is, the greater the potential ability to cover current liabilities), the higher a company's liquidity. Whether a given current or quick ratio is good or bad, however, depends on a number of factors, including the trend in these ratios, the comparability of these ratios with competitors, and the available opportunities in more-profitable, long-lived, capital investments.

In addition to looking at the relations among these balance sheet accounts, we can also form ratios that measure how well key current assets are managed over time. The key ratios for asset management are turnover ratios. For example, the **accounts receivable turnover** is the ratio of sales on credit to the average balance in accounts receivable:[2]

$$\text{Accounts receivable turnover} = \frac{\text{Credit sales}}{\text{Average receivables}}$$

This ratio is a measure of how many times, on average, accounts receivable are created by credit sales and collected on during the fiscal period. As another example, the **inventory turnover** is the ratio of the cost of goods sold to the balance in inventory:

$$\text{Inventory turnover} = \frac{\text{Cost of goods sold}}{\text{Average inventory}}$$

This ratio is a measure of how many times, on average, inventory is created or acquired and sold during the fiscal period.

Another perspective on the activity within the **current accounts** is to estimate the number of days of the current asset or liability that are on hand. For example, the **number of days of receivables**, also referred to as the **day's sales outstanding** and days in receivables, gives us an idea of the management of the extension and collection of credit to customers:

$$\text{Number of days of receivables} = \frac{\text{Accounts receivable}}{\text{Average day's sales on credit}} = \frac{\text{Accounts receivable}}{\text{Sales on credit} / 365}$$

For example, if this number of days is 35.5, this tells us that it takes, on average, 35.5 days to collect on the credit accounts. Whether this is good or bad depends on credit terms that are offered to customers and the relation between sales and the extension of credit, which is often dictated by industry customs and competitive pressures.

The **number of days of inventory** gives us an indication of how well the inventory acquisition, process, and distribution is managed:

$$\text{Number of days of inventory} = \frac{\text{Inventory}}{\text{Average day's cost of goods sold}} = \frac{\text{Inventory}}{\text{Cost of goods sold} / 365}$$

---

[2] You will notice that we use credit sales instead of total revenue; the difference lies in the context. Within the context of working capital management, the corporate financial analyst would have access to details regarding the company's credit versus cash sales. For some companies, sales may be for cash or be some combination of cash sales and credit sales. For the analyst who is looking at the company without benefit of internal information regarding how much of sales is in the form of credit sales, an approximation is generally used based on industry norms for credit practices.

The number of days of inventory, also known as the average inventory period, day's sales in ending inventory, and the inventory holding period, is the length of time, on average, that the inventory remains within the company during the fiscal period. We expect variation in the number of days of inventory among industries because of differences in the production cycle of different types of inventory. For example, we expect a grocery store to have a lower number of days inventory than, say, an aircraft manufacturer.

We can also look at the disbursement side of cash flows with the **number of days of payables**, which provides a measure of how long it takes the company to pay its own suppliers:

$$\text{Number of days of payables} = \frac{\text{Accounts payable}}{\text{Average day's purchases}} = \frac{\text{Accounts payable}}{\text{Purchases} / 365}$$

The number of days of payables is also referred to as the day's payables outstanding and the average days payable. Purchases are not an item on published financial statements, so if you are evaluating a company's payables, you can estimate the purchases by using what you know about the company's cost of goods sold and beginning and ending balances in inventory.[3]

Each of these turnover ratios and numbers of days helps tell a story of how the company is managing its liquid assets. Like all ratios, the numbers themselves do not indicate much, but when we put these together with trends, information on the company's profitability, and information about competitors, we develop a good understanding of a company's performance.[4]

Some of the major applications of this type of analysis include performance evaluation, monitoring, creditworthiness, and financial projections. But ratios are useful only when they can be compared. The comparison should be done in two ways—comparisons over time for the same company and over time for the company compared with its peer group. Peer groups can include competitors from the same industries as the company as well as other companies with comparable size and financial situations.

Consider Wal-Mart Stores, Inc. We can see the change in the current ratio and quick ratio over the fiscal years 1992 through 2005 in Exhibit 2, Panel A. Here, we see that the current ratio has declined, yet the quick ratio has increased slightly. We can see what is driving these trends in Panel B of this exhibit. One driver is the efficiency in the management of inventory, which results in holding on to inventory fewer days, as indicated by the downward trend in the number of days of inventory. Putting it in perspective, this trend may be because of, in part, the product shift when Wal-Mart Stores increased its presence in the grocery line of business. Another driver is the increasing number of days of payables, which means that company is taking longer to pay what it owes suppliers.

---

[3] We know that Beginning inventory + Purchases − Cost of good sold = Ending inventory. Therefore, if we know the inventory balances (from the balance sheet) and the cost of goods sold (from the income statement), we can determine the purchases: Purchases = Cost of goods sold + Ending inventory − Beginning inventory.

[4] For example, if we see a small number of days of inventory, it could mean that the company is managing its production very efficiently or it could mean that the company is at significant risk of a shortage of inventory. We don't know more until we look at what is needed or usual for companies in the industry, trends in turnover for the company, and the company's profitability in relation to the number of days of inventory.

EXHIBIT 2 Liquidity Analysis of Wal-Mart Stores

Panel A: Current and Quick Ratios, 1992–2005

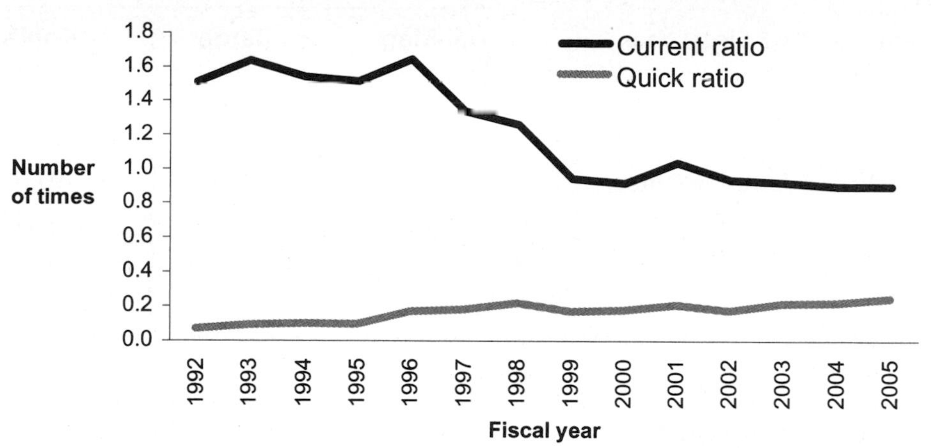

Panel B: Number of Days of Inventory and Number of Days of Payables

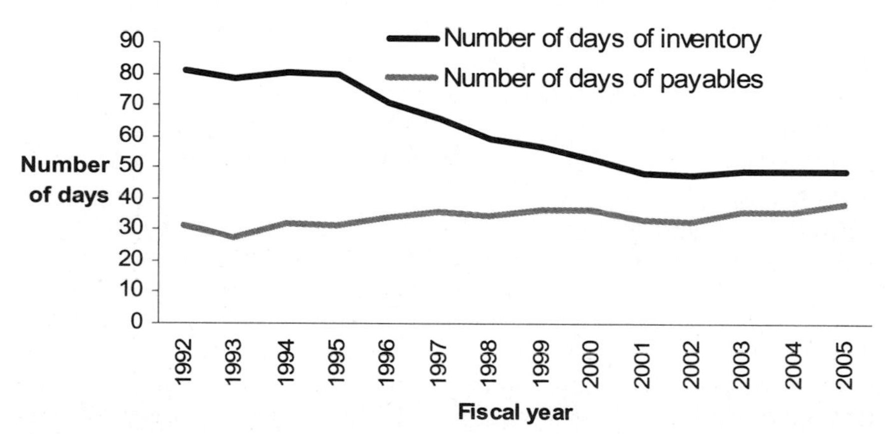

Source: Wal-Mart Stores, Inc., 10-K filings, various years.

Comparing Wal-Mart with Target Inc. and Kohl's in the 2005 fiscal year, as shown in Exhibit 3, we see differences among these three competitors. These differences may be explained, in part, by the different product mixes (e.g., Wal-Mart has more sales from grocery lines than the others), as well as different inventory management systems and different inventory suppliers. The different need for liquidity may also be explained, in part, by the different operating cycles of the companies.

EXHIBIT 3 Liquidity Ratios among Discount Retailers

Ratio for 2005 Fiscal Year	Company		
	Wal-Mart	Target	Kohl's
Current ratio	0.9	1.5	2.4
Quick ratio	0.2	0.9	1.2
Number of days of inventory	48.9	61.0	94.5
Number of days of payables	38.1	64.7	33.9

Source: Company 10-K filings with Securities and Exchange Commission for fiscal year 2005.

EXAMPLE 1

Measuring Liquidity

Given the following ratios, how well has the company been managing its liquidity for the past two years?

Ratio	Current Year		Past Year	
	Company	Industry	Company	Industry
Current ratio	1.9	2.5	1.1	2.3
Quick ratio	0.7	1.0	0.4	0.9
Number of days of receivables	39.0	34.0	44.0	32.5
Number of days of inventory	41.0	30.3	45.0	27.4
Number of days of payables	34.3	36.0	29.4	35.5

Solution: The ratios should be compared in two ways—over time (there would typically be more than two years' worth of data) and against the industry averages. In all ratios shown here, the current year shows improvement over the previous year in terms of increased liquidity. In each case, however, the company remains behind the industry average in terms of liquidity. A brief snapshot such as this example could be the starting point to initiate or encourage more improvements with the goal of reaching or beating the industry standards.

We can combine the number of days of inventory, number of days of receivables, and number of days of payables to get a sense of the company's operating cycle and net operating cycle. The **operating cycle** is a measure of the time needed to convert raw materials into cash from a sale. It consists of the number of days of inventory and the number of days of receivables:

$$\text{Operating cycle} = \frac{\text{Number of days}}{\text{of inventory}} + \frac{\text{Number of days}}{\text{of receivables}}$$

The operating cycle does not take everything into account, however, because the available cash flow is increased by deferring payment to suppliers. This deferral is considered in the **net operating cycle**, also called the **cash conversion cycle**. The net operating cycle is a measure of the time from paying suppliers for materials to collecting cash from the subsequent sale of goods produced from these supplies. It consists of the operating cycle minus the number of days of payables:

$$\text{Net operating cycle} = \begin{matrix}\text{Number of days}\\\text{of inventory}\end{matrix} + \begin{matrix}\text{Number of days}\\\text{of receivables}\end{matrix} - \begin{matrix}\text{Number of days}\\\text{of payables}\end{matrix}$$

In general, the shorter these cycles the greater a company's cash-generating ability and the less its need for liquid assets or outside finance. For many companies, the cash conversion cycle represents a period of time that requires financing—that is, the company offsets some of the financing need by deferring payments through payables terms, but the remainder must be financed.

MANAGING THE CASH POSITION

3

Although the mix or magnitude of data items may change from day to day, the goal is the same: ensuring that the net cash position is not negative. Ideally, the company's daily cash inflows and outflows would be equal, but this is rarely the case. Without the reliability of matching these flows, companies must take other steps to ensure that the flows net out each day. Most companies try to avoid negative balances because the cost of garnering daily funds by issuing debt or by drawing on bank overdraft facilities is very costly, although the cost of maintaining a small short-term investment portfolio, in terms of an opportunity cost, is regarded as an acceptable cost of doing business.

In addition, it is difficult to borrow the exact amount needed, so many companies borrow a little extra to be safe and invest any small excesses overnight at lower rates than if they could invest them earlier or in securities with higher rates. To manage the cash position effectively, the treasury function, which is usually responsible for this activity, must gather information from various sources at all times during the day, making decisions based on the latest information.

Several critical factors help determine how a company can establish an efficient cash flow system. In most cases, the central treasury function may not be able to dictate how the company collects from customers or pays its vendors. What it can do, however, is use the best services and techniques associated with the company's payment configuration.

As an example of a typical cycle of cash management information that occurs daily, consider the process outlined in Exhibit 4. This hypothetical schedule shows how important it is to have an efficient, smooth-flowing information system that can meet the time requirements.

EXHIBIT 4 An Example of the Daily Cycle of Cash Management

Information from bank reporting systems is gathered and analyzed.	*Morning*

The cash manager receives information from company sources.	

The cash manager receives updates from the company's bank(s) on current-day transactions.	

The cash management staff is arranging short-term investments and/or loans, as necessary, through broker–dealers from their banks or investment banks.	

The cash management staff makes funds transfers.	*Midday*

The cash movements for the day are completed or are scheduled for completion, and the company's cash position is finalized.	
↓	
Necessary paperwork for all transactions is completed. Also, the running cash worksheet is updated and set for the next business day.	*Close of the business day*

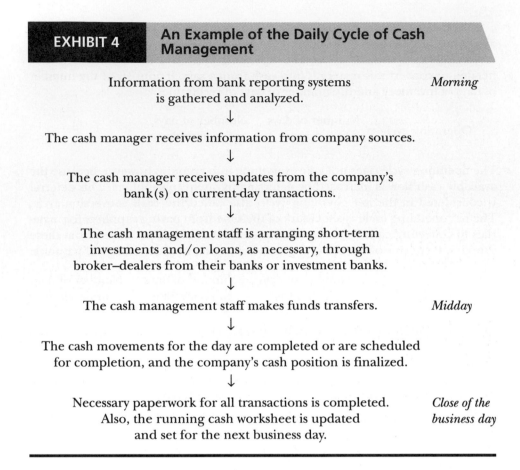

3.1 Forecasting Short-Term Cash Flows

Forecasting cash flows is necessary to allow effective management of working **capital accounts**. For cash forecasting to be effective, it has to be relatively precise. However, a forecast that is precise may not be *accurate.* There are many factors that are outside of the company's control, such as the general economy, unexpected raw material shortages, and changing interest rates. The uncertainty in forecasting encourages companies to maintain some minimum level of cash on hand as a buffer.

3.1.1 Minimum Cash Balances

Most companies want a cash buffer as protection from unexpected cash needs or to provide the financial flexibility to take advantage of attractive opportunities, such as procuring raw material inventory at a discount. This buffer is often expressed as a minimum desired cash balance. The size of this buffer depends on several influences, including the variation in the levels of the company's cash inflows and outflows, the company's ability to access other liquidity sources, and the company's ability to access borrowing facilities with little lead time.

3.1.2 Identifying Typical Cash Flows

Having an accurate forecast can help a financial manager make better use of the company's financial history. Many product lines, especially those that are not in high-growth stages but rather are in steadier, mature stages, will have similar cash flows from year to year or season to season. If an extensive database has been established, it will be possible to draw reasonable projections for the current period or longer.

Even in cases of heavy growth through mergers and acquisitions, companies should try to transfer the acquired company's cash flow history to be used as a starting point for consolidating the new operation into the rest of the company. The cash manager must identify cash flow elements to build a reliable forecast. These elements are not difficult to identify in general terms, but it is much harder to define them more specifically to be able to collect data regularly.

The cash elements that comprise a total forecast vary from company to company. However, it is good practice to identify the elements that pertain to any one individual company. Exhibit 5 shows typical elements arranged as inflows and outflows. It may be more useful to try to arrange the elements in this manner—i.e., show matching elements by the direction of their flow (in or out). In most cases, a company's data elements can be arranged this way to facilitate data gathering, reviewing variances, and presenting final reports to management and other cash users or providers.

EXHIBIT 5 Examples of Cash Inflows and Outflows

Inflows	Outflows
▶ Receipts from operations, broken down by operating unit, departments, etc.	▶ Payables and payroll disbursements, broken down by operating unit, departments, etc.
▶ Funds transfers from subsidiaries, joint ventures, third parties	▶ Funds transfers to subsidiaries
▶ Maturing investments	▶ Investments made
▶ Debt proceeds (short and long term)	▶ Debt repayments
▶ Other income items (interest, etc.)	▶ Interest and dividend payments
▶ Tax refunds	▶ Tax payments

These elements should reflect real cash flows, excluding such items as depreciation or accruals that are paid at a later date (these should be included when they are to be paid).

3.1.3 Cash Forecasting Systems

Cash forecasting should be structured as a system in order to be effective, and to do this, several aspects of the forecast must be considered. We provide some examples of these aspects in Exhibit 6, which highlights each aspect for three different forecast horizons. In some cases, one aspect may be more important than others. For instance, if daily cash is being handled fairly easily, it may be more critical to spend time and resources to ensure that the medium-term forecasting part of the overall system is functioning at the highest levels of reliability. In addition, some factors, such as format or time horizon, should not be changed arbitrarily because change may affect their accuracy and reliability levels.

EXHIBIT 6 Examples of Cash Forecasting Aspects over Different Forecast Horizons

	Short Term	Medium Term	Long Term
Data frequency	Daily/weekly for 4–6 weeks	Monthly for one year	Annually for 3–5 years
Format	Receipts and disbursements	Receipts and disbursements	Projected financial statements
Techniques	Simple projections	Projection models and averages	Statistical models
Accuracy	Very high	Moderate	Lowest
Reliability	Very high	Fairly high	Not as high
Uses	Daily cash management	Planning financial transactions	Long-range financial position

3.2 Monitoring Cash Uses and Levels

Another facet of cash forecasting is monitoring and control. Managing the cash position essentially means keeping a "running score" on daily cash flows. Monitoring daily cash flows is a key aspect of a company's cash forecasting system in that the financial manager in charge of managing the cash position must know the company's cash balance in the bank on virtually a real-time basis. However, it really is not *forecasting* as such, because most of the transactions are actually known; the challenge lies in the collection of this known information in time to do something with that information. For example, receiving information about a deposit too late to transfer the funds renders the information valueless.

To receive the appropriate information on a timely basis, information should be gathered from principal users and providers of cash, supplemented by short-term cash projections in days or even throughout the current day. The minimum level of cash available is estimated in advance, adjusted for known funds transfers, seasonality, or other factors, and is used as a **target balance** figure for each bank. Note that most companies use one major bank as their lead bank (or concentration bank) and control the balances for the bank through one main concentration account, with the target balance applied to the main account. For larger companies, more than one concentration bank is possible, but managing the cash positions in multiple concentration banks quickly makes the system complex and requires an efficient information processing system.

For most companies, it is necessary to manage a cash position with the assistance of short-term investments and borrowings. These short-term liquidity sources help counter the excesses and deficits that typically occur in a company's cash flow. The short-term investments are usually kept in a portfolio that is very liquid, with short maturities. In this way, funds are available whenever they are needed, but the company gives up the extra yield that might have been earned if the investments were made for longer periods of time or with securities with less liquidity. Short-term borrowing is for very short periods of time, but a borrower may find more economies in borrowing for regular periods, such as thirty days, to reduce the number of transactions and associated paperwork. Also, by extending the borrowing period, companies can usually obtain better rates and availabilities of funds than if they continually borrow very short maturities.

Many companies face predictable peaks and valleys in their business throughout the year. For instance, manufacturers of consumer electronics products achieve the bulk of their sales during the holiday shopping season (from late November through the end of the year), which means that they have build-up of products that are shipped well before they receive payment. Thus, they have to finance this inventory roll-out before they receive any cash. During this period, they are likely to use up most or all of the temporary excess funds they set aside or to tap into the credit lines they arranged for this purpose. When sales roll in during the busy shopping season, they use the proceeds to pay down the borrowing and then invest any excess.

Other influencing factors on a company's cash needs may be associated with non-operating activities, such as major capital expenditure programs, mergers and acquisitions, sales or disposition of company assets, and the timing of long-term financial transactions, such as bond issues, private placements of debt or equity, and equity issues.

Predicting the peak need caused by seasonality or other non-operating activities is important if the company is going to have to borrow funds to cover the need. If a company sets aside too much, it will incur excess costs that are unjustified. If it sets aside too little, it will have to pay a penalty to raise funds quickly. Either case is a costly error. A reliable forecast can help avoid this situation.

INVESTING SHORT-TERM FUNDS 4

Short-term investments represent a temporary store of funds that are not necessarily needed in a company's daily transactions. If a substantial portion of a company's working capital portfolio is not needed for short-term transactions, it should be separated from a working capital portfolio and placed in a longer-term portfolio. Such longer-term portfolios are often handled by another area or are handled by an outside money manager under the company's supervision. In this way, the risks, maturities, and portfolio management of longer-term portfolios can be managed independently of the working capital portfolio.

Short-term working capital portfolios consist of securities that are highly liquid, less risky, and shorter in maturity than other types of investment portfolios. Thus, a company's working capital portfolio may consist of short-term debt securities, such as short-term U.S. government securities and short-term bank and corporate obligations. This type of portfolio changes almost constantly, as cash is needed or more excess cash is available for investments.

4.1 Short-Term Investment Instruments

We describe examples of the major instruments for short-term investments in Exhibit 7. The relative amounts of each security can vary from one company to another, depending on the company's risk tolerance and how quickly the invested funds will be needed.

EXHIBIT 7 Examples of Short-Term Investment Instruments

Instruments	Typical Maturities	Features	Risks
U.S. Treasury Bills (T-bills)	13, 26, and 52 weeks	▶ Obligations of U.S. government (guaranteed), issued at a discount ▶ Active secondary market ▶ Lowest rates for traded securities	Virtually no risk

(Exhibit continued on next page . . .)

EXHIBIT 7 (continued)

Instruments	Typical Maturities	Features	Risks
Federal agency securities	5–30 days	▶ Obligations of U.S. federal agencies (e.g., Fannie Mae, Federal Home Loan Board) issued as interest-bearing ▶ Slightly higher yields than T-bills	Slight liquidity risk; insignificant credit risk
Bank certificates of deposit (CDs)	14–365 days	▶ Bank obligations, issued interest-bearing in $100,000 increments ▶ "Yankee" CDs offer slightly higher yields	Credit and liquidity risk (depending on bank's credit)
Banker's acceptances (BAs)	30–180 days	▶ Bank obligations for trade transactions (usually foreign), issued at a discount ▶ Investor protected by underlying company and trade flow itself ▶ Small secondary market	Credit and liquidity risk (depending on bank's credit)
Eurodollar time deposits	1–180 days	▶ Time deposit with bank off-shore (outside United States, such as Bahamas) ▶ Can be CD or straight time deposit (TD) ▶ Interest-bearing investment ▶ Small secondary market for CDs, but not TDs	Credit risk (depending on bank) Very high liquidity risk for TDs
Bank sweep services	1 day	▶ Service offered by banks that essentially provides interest on checking account balance (usually over a minimum level) ▶ Large number of sweeps are for overnight	Credit and liquidity risk (depending on bank)
Repurchase agreements (Repos)	1 day +	▶ Sale of securities with the agreement of the dealer (seller) to buy them back at a future time ▶ Typically over-collateralized at 102 percent ▶ Often done for very short maturities (< 1 week)	Credit and liquidity risk (depending on dealer)
Commercial paper (CP)	1–270 days	▶ Unsecured obligations of corporations and financial institutions, issued at discount ▶ Secondary market for large issuers ▶ CP issuers obtain short-term credit ratings	Credit and liquidity risk (depending on credit rating)
Mutual funds and money market mutual funds	Varies	▶ Money market mutual funds commonly used by smaller businesses ▶ Low yields but high liquidity for money market funds; mutual fund liquidity dependent on underlying securities in fund ▶ Can be linked with bank sweep arrangement	Credit and liquidity risk (depending on fund manager)

(Exhibit continued on next page . . .)

EXHIBIT 7 (continued)

Instruments	Typical Maturities	Features	Risks
Tax-advantaged securities	7, 28, 35, 40, and 90 days	▶ Preferred stock in many forms, including adjustable rate preferred stocks (ARPs), auction rate preferred stocks (AURPs), and convertible adjustable preferred stocks (CAPs) ▶ Dutch auction often used to set rate ▶ Offer higher yields	Credit and liquidity risk (depending on issuer's credit)

4.1.1 *Computing Yields on Short-Term Investments*

Some securities, such as T-bills and banker's acceptances, are issued at a discount. Thus, the investor invests less than the face value of the security and receives the face value back at maturity. For instance, a \$1 million security that pays 5 percent in interest with one month remaining to maturity would be purchased at:

$$\text{Purchase price} = \$1{,}000{,}000 - [(0.05)(1/12)(\$1{,}000{,}000)] = \$995{,}833.33$$
$$\text{Proceeds (face value)} = \$1{,}000{,}000$$

The difference between the purchase price and the face value, \$4,166.67, is the **discount interest**.

Interest-bearing securities differ from discounted securities in that the investor pays the face amount and receives back that same face amount plus the interest on the security. For example, a 5 percent, 30-day, \$1 million security would return \$1 million face value plus interest earned:

$$\text{Purchase price (face value)} = \$1{,}000{,}000$$
$$\text{Proceeds} = \$1{,}000{,}000 + [(0.05)(1/12)(\$1{,}000{,}000)] = \$1{,}004{,}166.67$$

Rates on securities may be quoted as nominal rates or as yields. A **nominal rate** is a rate of interest based on the security's face value. In the previous two examples, the nominal rate in each instance was 5 percent. A **yield**, on the other hand, is the actual return on the investment if it is held to maturity. For example, if you buy the discount security for \$995,833.33 and hold it for one month until it matures for \$1 million, your yield on this investment is

$$\text{Yield} = \left(\frac{\$1{,}000{,}000 - 995{,}833.33}{995{,}833.33}\right)(12) = (0.004184)(12) = 5.0209\%$$

where the second factor, 12, annualizes the monthly yield of 0.4184 percent. The factor that is used to annualize the yield depends on the type of security and the traditions for quoting yields. For example, the **money market yield** is typically annualized using the ratio of 360 to the number of days to maturity:

$$\text{Money market yield} = \left(\frac{\text{Face value} - \text{Purchase price}}{\text{Purchase price}}\right)\left(\frac{360}{\text{Number of days to maturity}}\right)$$

On the other hand, the **bond equivalent yield** is typically annualized using the ratio of 365 to the number of days to maturity:

$$\text{Bond equivalent yield} = \left(\frac{\text{Face value} - \text{Purchase price}}{\text{Purchase price}}\right)\left(\frac{365}{\text{Number of days to maturity}}\right)$$

One source of confusion is that the yield on U.S. T-bills may be quoted on the basis of the discount basis or the bond equivalent basis (also referred to as the investment yield basis). The yield on a T-bill using the discount basis is calculated using the face value as the basis for the yield and then using a 360-day year:

$$\text{Discount-basis yield} = \left(\frac{\text{Face value} - \text{Purchase price}}{\text{Face value}}\right)\left(\frac{360}{\text{Number of days to maturity}}\right)$$

Although the relevant yield for investment decision purposes is the bond equivalent yield, it is important to understand the discount basis because it is often quoted in the context of these securities.

EXAMPLE 2

Computing Investment Yields

For a 91-day $100,000 U.S. T-bill sold at a discounted rate of 7.91 percent, calculate the following:

1. Money market yield
2. Bond equivalent yield

Purchase price = $100,000 − [(.0791)(91/360)($100,000)] = $98,000.53

Solution to 1: Money market yield = [1,999.47/98,000.53] × [360/91] = 8.07 percent

Solution to 2: Bond equivalent yield = [1,999.47/98,000.53] × [365/91] = 8.18 percent

4.1.2 Investment Risks

Investors face several types of risks. We list a number of these in Exhibit 8. In this exhibit, we list the types of risk—credit, market, liquidity, and foreign exchange—and the attributes and safety measures associated with each type. The attributes describe the conditions that contribute to the type of risk, and the safety measures describe the steps that investors usually take to prevent losses from the risk. With the exception of foreign exchange risk, the key safety measures taken are to shift to "safety" (i.e., government securities, such as U.S. T-bills) or to shorten maturities so that securities will mature quicker, allowing an investor to shift funds to a safer type of security.

EXHIBIT 8 Types of Investment Risks and Safety Measures

Type of Risk	Key Attributes	Safety Measures
Credit (or default)	▶ Issuer may default ▶ Issuer could be adversely affected by economy, market ▶ Little secondary market	▶ Minimize amount ▶ Keep maturities short ▶ Watch for "questionable" names ▶ Emphasize government securities
Market (or interest rate)	▶ Price or rate changes may adversely affect return ▶ There is no market to sell the maturity to, or there is only a small secondary market	▶ Keep maturities short ▶ Keep portfolio diverse in terms of maturity, issuers
Liquidity	▶ Security is difficult or impossible to (re)sell ▶ Security must be held to maturity and cannot be liquidated until then	▶ Stick with government securities ▶ Look for good secondary market ▶ Keep maturities short
Foreign exchange	▶ Adverse general market movement against your currency	▶ Hedge regularly ▶ Keep most in your currency and domestic market (avoid foreign exchange)

4.2 Strategies

Short-term investment strategies are fairly simple because the securities in a working capital portfolio are limited in type and are much shorter in maturity than a longer-term portfolio. Most short-term investors seek "reasonable" returns and do not want to take on substantial risk. Short-term investment strategies can be grouped into two types: passive and active. A **passive strategy** is characterized by one or two decision rules for making daily investments, whereas an **active strategy** involves constant monitoring and may involve matching, mismatching, or laddering strategies.

Passive strategies are less aggressive than active ones and place top priority on safety and liquidity. Yet, passive strategies do not have to offer poor returns, especially if companies have reliable cash forecasts. Often, companies with good cash forecasts can combine a passive strategy with an active matching strategy to enhance the yield of a working capital portfolio without taking on substantially greater risks.

The major problem associated with passive strategies is complacency, which can cause the company to roll over the portfolio mechanically, with little attention paid to yields and more focus on simply reinvesting funds as they mature. Passive strategies must be monitored, and the yield from investment portfolios should be benchmarked regularly against a suitable standard, such as a T-bill with comparable maturity.

Active strategies require more daily involvement and possibly a wider choice of investments. Although investments are rolled over with an active strategy, just as they are with a passive strategy, this type of strategy calls for more shopping around, better forecasts, and a more flexible investment policy/guideline.

Active strategies can include intentional matching or mismatching the timing of cash outflows with investment maturities. A **matching strategy** is the more conservative of the two and uses many of the same investment types as are used with passive strategies. A **mismatching strategy** is riskier and requires very accurate and reliable cash forecasts. These strategies usually use securities that are more liquid, such as T-bills, so that securities can be liquidated if adverse market conditions arise. Mismatching strategies may also be accomplished using derivatives, which may pose additional risks to a company unaccustomed to buying and selling derivatives.

A **laddering strategy** is another form of active strategy, which entails scheduling maturities on a systematic basis within the investment portfolio such that investments are spread out equally over the term of the ladder. A laddering strategy falls somewhere between a matching and a passive strategy. Laddering strategies have been used effectively in managing longer-term investment portfolios, but laddering also should be an effective short-term strategy.

Managing a working capital portfolio involves handling and safeguarding assets of the company. Accordingly, companies with investment portfolios should have a formal, written policy/guideline that protects the company and the investment managers. Investment policy/guidelines should not be very lengthy, especially because they must be understood by the company's investment managers and communicated to the company's investment dealers.

Although the investment policy/guideline should be customized for an individual company, the basic structure of such a policy is provided in Exhibit 9.

EXHIBIT 9 Sample Format of an Investment Policy

Purpose List and explain the reasons that the portfolio exists and also describe the general attributes of the portfolio, such as a summary of the strategy that will be used and the general types of securities that are acceptable investments.

Authorities Identify the executives who oversee the portfolio managers who make the investments that compose the portfolio and the outside managers that could be used and how they would be managed. Also describe procedures that must be performed if the policy is not followed.

(Exhibit continued on next page . . .)

EXHIBIT 9 (continued)

Limitations and/or restrictions	Describe, in general terms, the types of investments that should be considered for inclusion in the portfolio. The list should not consist of specific securities; it should describe the general *types* of securities, such as commercial paper, U.S. T-bills, or bank CDs. In this manner, the policy retains more flexibility than if specific issuers or securities are listed. In the latter case, the policy would require change every time an issuer was no longer issuing any securities. This section should also include any restrictions as to the relative amount of each security that is allowable in the overall portfolio. This section may also include procedures when a maximum has been exceeded or must be exceeded under special circumstances, such as when the portfolio is temporarily inflated prior to using the funds for an acquisition or other long-term use.
Quality	May be in a separate section or may be included with the previous one. Investments with working capital funds must be safe, so many companies include credit standards for potential investments in their policy statements. Reference may be made to long-term ratings or, more frequently, to short-term credit ratings. The ratings cited are usually those from the major rating agencies: Standard & Poor's and Moody's.
Other items	Other items are sometimes included in a policy/guideline, such as statements that require the portfolio to be included in the financial audit or that regular reports will be generated by the investment manager. Some companies also define the types of securities that are "eligible," but this does not seem necessary if the policy is well written.

EXAMPLE 3

Evaluating an Investment Policy

A sample investment policy is shown below. Review the client's investment policy, considering the basic investment policy structure shown in Exhibit 9. The average portfolio size is $100 million, with no significant peaks or valleys throughout the year. After reviewing the policy, answer the following questions:

1. Is the policy an effective one?
2. What shortcomings or potential problem areas, if any, does it have?
3. How would you change this policy, if at all?

Working Capital Portfolio Investment Policy/Guidelines

- Purpose: This is a working capital portfolio with emphasis on safety and liquidity. We will sacrifice return for either of these two goals.

- Authorities: The treasurer, with agreement from the CFO, will be in charge of managing short-term investments. Authority and control to execute can be delegated by the treasurer or CFO to another treasury manager if documented.
- Maximum maturity: Securities may not be made for longer than three (3) years.
- Types/amounts of investments permitted: no more than 10 percent of the portfolio or $50 million with any issuer, subject to the credit limitation that any eligible issuer must be rated A-1, P-1 by Standard & Poor's and Moody's.
- Repurchase agreements must be equal to, or preferably exceed, the PSA Standard Investment Agreement, which requires 102 percent collateral for repurchases.
- All investments must be held in safekeeping by XYZ Bank.
- The investment manager can execute exception transactions but must document them in writing.

Solution to 1: The policy is fairly effective in that it tries to provide simple, understandable rules. It calls for credit quality, limits the possible position with any single issuer, accepts market standards (such as the PSA), and calls for safekeeping. It also has an exception procedure that is straightforward.

Solution to 2: The credit ratings may be too restrictive. Many investment securities may not be rated by both S&P and Moody's, which is implied, if not stated, in the policy. Also, the 10 percent limitation apparently is to be applied to all securities. However, most investment managers do not consider securities issued by governmental agencies or the government itself to be so risky that a limitation needs to be applied.

Solution to 3: The words "or equivalent" should be added to the credit quality of the types of investments. Also, there should be no limitation to highly rated governmental securities, such as U.S. Treasury-bills and the equivalent from the major developed countries. A credit rating reference could be applied to determine eligible governmental securities.

4.3 Evaluating Short-Term Funds Management

Tracking tools can range from simple spreadsheets to more expensive treasury workstations. If both portfolios are not too large or diversified, a spreadsheet may be sufficient to be able to compare effective yields and borrowing costs on an ongoing basis and to generate periodic performance reports.

Investment returns should be expressed as bond equivalent yields, to allow comparability among investment alternatives. In addition, the overall portfolio return should be weighted according to the currency size of the investment. We provide an abbreviated example of a portfolio report in Exhibit 10. The report provides the weighted average returns of the different investments. The yields are all calculated on a bond equivalent yield basis.

EXHIBIT 10 Short-Term Investment Portfolio Report

Security/Loan	Dealer/Bank	€ Amt (000)	Weight	Yield	Maturity
U.S. T-bills	ABC Bank	23,575	39.8%	3.50%	90 days
Finco CP	XYZ Co.	20,084	33.9%	4.65%	45 days
Megabank CD	Megabank	15,560	26.3%	5.05%	30 days
Weighted average yield from investments				**4.30%**	
Short-term benchmark rate[a]				**4.25%**	

[a] Benchmark rate = independent source, such as synthetic portfolio maintained independently or rate provided by third party, such as a money manager or other empirical source (e.g., a financial institution, trade association, or central bank).

MANAGING ACCOUNTS RECEIVABLE 5

Credit accounts vary by type of customer and the industry, and granting credit involves a tradeoff between increasing sales and uncollectible accounts. There are three primary activities in accounts receivable management: granting credit and processing transactions, monitoring credit balances, and measuring performance of the credit function.

Processing accounts receivable transactions requires recording credit sales to create a record and posting customer payments—or at least monitoring the posting—to the accounts receivable account by applying the payment against the customer's outstanding credit balance. Monitoring the outstanding accounts receivable requires a regular reporting of outstanding receivable balances and notifying the collection managers of past due situations. Monitoring is an ongoing activity. Measuring the performance of the credit functions entails preparing and distributing key performance measurement reports, including an account receivable aging schedule and day's sales outstanding reports.

Essentially, the accounts receivable management function is a go-between for the credit manager, treasury manager, and accounting manager. This role is an important one because it can slow up the recording of payments, which may, in turn, prevent customers from purchasing more of the company's products or, worse yet, could prevent the treasury manager from depositing the check and converting the check to available funds.

The accounts receivable management function is also considered to be a derivative activity from credit granting because it helps in providing information needed by the credit management function. It depends on the source of the sale for its records, on the credit manager for additional information on the status of the accounts receivable record, and possibly on the treasury manager to establish an efficient system of getting the payment information to the accounts receivable manager for cash application (e.g., from a bank lockbox).

The goals for the accounts receivable management system include the following:

- efficient processing and maintaining accurate, up-to-date records that are available to credit managers and other interested parties as soon as possible after payments have been received;
- control of accounts receivable and ensuring that accounts receivable records are current and that no unauthorized entry into the accounts receivable file has occurred;
- collection on accounts and coordination with the treasury management function;
- coordination and notification with the credit managers frequently; and
- preparation of regular performance measurement reports.

Companies may achieve scale economies by centralizing the accounts receivable function by using a captive finance subsidiary.[5] A **captive finance subsidiary** is a wholly owned subsidiary of the company that is established to provide financing of the sales of the parent company.

One of the challenges in accounts receivable management is monitoring receivables and collecting on accounts. Many companies resort to outsourcing the accounts receivable function, primarily to increase the collection on accounts, provide credit evaluation services, and to apply the most recent technology.[6] Also, some companies may invest in credit insurance, which reduces the risk of bad debts and shifts some of the evaluation of creditworthiness to the insurer.

5.1 Key Elements of the Trade Credit Granting Process

Credit management is an integral part of the collection process. It sets the framework for sales in that it can restrict sales by rejecting credit or expand it by loosening acceptance criteria. It also links the collection and cash application processes and has a profound effect on the method of collection as well. In addition, credit management techniques incorporate fundamental financial analysis methods in setting credit policy, granting credit, and managing existing credit customers.

A weak, ineffective credit management function may enhance sales, but many of those sales may become bad debts. On the other hand, a strong, active credit management function can work in tandem with sales and marketing on one side and accounting and treasury on the other. To establish an effective credit management function a company must have a well-conceived strategy customized to the company's needs and reflecting the company's goals.

Credit management policies are usually established as a set of basic guidelines to be used by credit managers. A company's credit policy sets the boundaries for the credit management function. It lays out procedures as part of the policy and offers guidance for each typical situation. The policy shows the steps in the granting process and provides decision rules for specific situations. The

---

[5] As pointed out by Shehzad L. Mian and Clifford W. Smith ["Accounts Receivable Management Policy: Theory and evidence," *Journal of Finance*, vol. 47, no. 1 (March 1992) pp. 169–200], companies that have highly variable accounts receivable (for example., from seasonality) may find the use of a captive finance subsidiary attractive because it may allow the subsidiary's debt indentures to differ from those of the parent company.

[6] Martin Hall, "A/R Outsourcing: Coming of Age in the New Millennium," *Business Credit* (February 2003), pp. 1–2.

policy can also influence the sales level by making it easy or difficult for customers to buy on credit.

Customers may start out with one type of credit account that is restrictive, such as cash on delivery, and may eventually demonstrate that they are regular payers and can be given open book credit accounts.

The major types of credit accounts include the following:

- open book, which is the most common for company to company;
- documentary, with or without lines of credit, most common for cross-border transactions;
- installment credit, with regular timed payments; and
- revolving credit.

The types of credit terms offered vary by type of customer, the relative financial strength of the customer, and the type of credit terms the competition is offering. The different forms of terms of credit other than cash, which generally implies 7 to 10 days, include the following:

- **Ordinary terms**. Terms are set forth in a standard format—*net t* or d/t_1 *net* t_2, where t in the first example refers to the length of time a customer has to pay the invoice before becoming past due. In the second example, t_1 is the time period for taking discounts, and t_2 is the same as t in the first example. For example, *net 60* means that the full amount of the invoice is due in 60 days. Most trade credit customers will take the full 60 days. Terms of *1/10 net 30* mean that the customer can take a 1 percent discount if the invoice is paid within 10 days or else pay the full amount of the invoice by 30 days from the invoice date.
- **Cash before delivery (CBD)** terms require that the amount of the invoice must be paid in advance before delivery will be scheduled. Checks must clear before any shipment is made.
- **Cash on delivery (COD)** terms require that payment must be made (usually in the form of a bank check) when the product is delivered; otherwise, no delivery will be made.
- **Bill-to-bill**. These terms require that each prior bill must be paid before new shipments are possible.
- **Monthly billing**. These terms require payment monthly. They have a different format; for example, *2/10th Prox net 30th* means that the customer can take a 2 percent discount if it pays within the first 10 days of the next month or else it must pay the full amount of the invoice by the 30th day of the next month.

Credit managers may evaluate customers' creditworthiness using a credit scoring model. A **credit scoring model** is a statistical model used to classify borrowers according to creditworthiness. These models were first designed for assisting in making consumer credit decisions. Major credit card issuers needed a tool they could use to make mass credit decisions. It was also used for small business loans after many larger banks discovered that their costs of reviewing and deciding whether to grant loans were such that they could not efficiently make loans of the smaller sizes required by smaller businesses. To overcome this problem, they adopted credit scoring models.

Credit scoring models offer an opportunity for a company to make fast decisions on the basis of simple data, not requiring a great deal of paperwork. The scoring models give greater weight to such factors as:

- ready cash (e.g., high checking account balances);
- organization type, with corporations rated higher than sole proprietorships or partnership; and
- being current in supplier payments, as indicated by financial services such as Dun & Bradstreet.

The models penalize the potential borrower for:

- prior late payment behavior or defaults: payment patterns are habitual;
- heavy use of personal credit cards: no reserves or reduced reserves available;
- previous *personal* bankruptcy or tax liens: carries over from person to company; and
- high-risk categories: food services, hospitality industries.

Credit scoring can also be used to predict late payers.

5.2 Managing Customers' Receipts

Cash collections systems are a function of the types of customers a company has and the methods of payment that the customers use. For instance, if a company's sales are made at retail locations, it cannot take advantage of the benefits offered by bank lockbox services. Instead, it must deal with organizing and controlling local deposits and concentrating these deposits efficiently and economically. On the other hand, if a company manufactures and sells products to other businesses, it can use a bank lockbox services to expedite processing and clearing of check payments.

We illustrate a typical network for a company with both electronic and check payments in Exhibit 11. Checks from one type of customer are directed to a bank lockbox, while electronic payments from another type of customer are transmitted via **electronic funds transfer (EFT)** through one of the available networks, such as the **Automated Clearing House (ACH)** system or the **Giro system**. The ACH system is an electronic payment network available to businesses, individuals, and financial institutions in the United States, U.S. Territories, and Canada. The Giro systems are postal-based systems in Europe and elsewhere.

In most cases, the best practice for collections involves the establishment of a system that accelerates payments as well as their information content, such as the customer's name and identification number and which invoices are being paid. From the collecting company's point of view, the way to achieve this best practice is to establish an electronic collection network. This can apply to either retail or wholesale companies.

Retail payments can be made by credit/debit cards or electronic checks, which are converted to electronic debits or digitized images, or by direct debit. These payments clear electronically and can be facilitated through **point of sale (POS)** systems, which are systems that capture the transaction data at the physical location in which the sale is made. A **direct debit program** is an arrangement whereby the customer authorizes a debit to a demand account and is used by companies—such as utilities, telecommunications service providers, cable companies, insurance companies, and credit card companies—to collect routine payments for services.

EXHIBIT 11 Cash Collections and Concentration

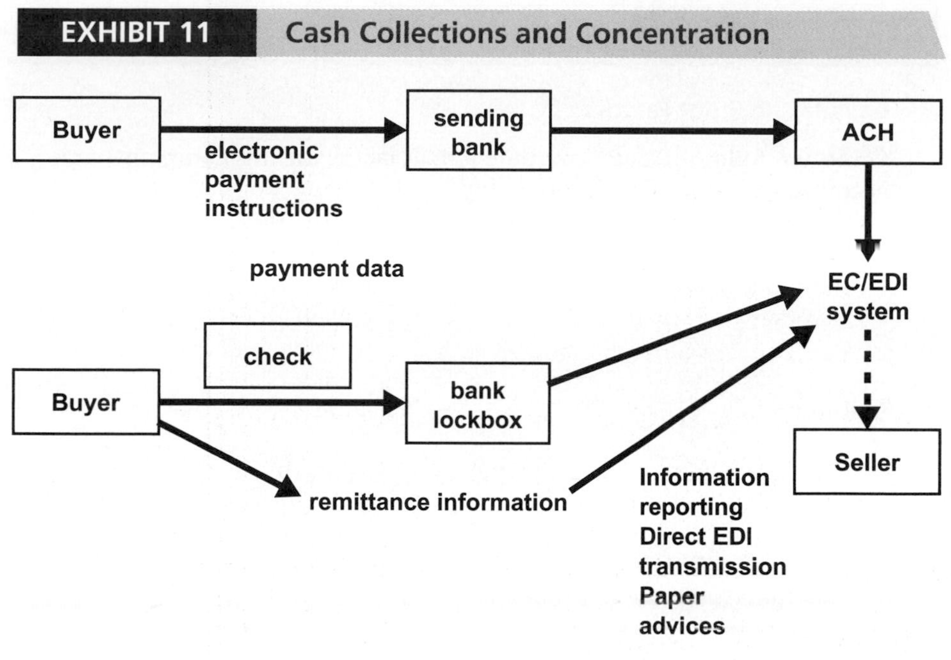

If payments cannot be converted to electronic payments, the next best practice is to use a bank lockbox service. A **lockbox system** is coordinated with the banking institution in which customer payments are mailed to a post office box and the banking institution retrieves and deposits these payments several times a day, enabling the company to have use of the fund sooner than in a centralized system in which customer payments are sent to the company. An acceptable bank lockbox arrangement is one in which the checks deposited today are available tomorrow or the next business day. This one-day availability lays the groundwork for best practices in cash concentration.

A good performance measure for check deposits is a calculated **float factor**. The **float** in this context is the amount of money that is in transit between payments made by customers and the funds that are usable by the company. We compute the float factor by dividing the average daily deposit in dollars into the average daily float:[7]

$$\text{Float factor} = \frac{\text{Average daily float}}{\text{Average daily deposit}} = \frac{\text{Average daily float}}{\text{Total amount of checks deposited/Number of days}}$$

This calculation gives the average number of days it took deposited checks to clear. If the float factor is very small (e.g., less than 1.0), it is probably worthwhile to investigate further to determine whether same-day wire transfers from the depository account are warranted, assuming the depository account is with a bank other than the company's lead bank. The float factor only measures how long it takes for checks to clear, not how long it takes to receive the checks, deposit them, and then have them clear. However, it is still very useful and can be computed easily for any depository accounts.

[7] We determine the average daily float from an analysis of cash accounts.

EXAMPLE 4

Calculating Float Factors

Given the following data, compute a float factor for this company bank account.

Total deposits for the month:	\$3,360,900
Number of days in month:	30 days
Average daily float:	\$154,040

Solution:

Average daily deposit = (\$3,360,900)/30 = \$112,030

Float factor = Average daily float/Average daily deposit = \$154,040/\$112,010 = 1.375

Cash concentration involves two major activities: consolidating deposits and moving funds between company accounts or to outside points. The best practice for cash concentration may be different for consolidating deposits than for moving funds, depending on the timing required and the availability of the funds being transferred.

For bank lockbox concentration, assuming that the checks clear in one business day (on average), the concentration technique of choice is the electronic funds transfer method. In this method, bank lockbox personnel call in the deposit via a reporting service or directly to the concentration bank. The concentration bank creates an electronic funds transfer debit that clears overnight, giving the company available funds in its concentration account. This system can be set up to run with or without intervention by the company's cash manager. In most cases, the best practice does not involve any intervention.

Electronic funds transfers offer distinct advantages to companies that use them for concentration of funds. First, they are substantially cheaper than the alternative, the wire transfer. In addition, they are reliable in that the transfer can be made part of a routine that can be performed daily without exception. Even small payments that would not be economical to transfer out by wire can be transferred economically by electronic funds transfer.

5.3 Evaluating Accounts Receivable Management

There are numerous ways of measuring accounts receivable performance. Most of them deal with how effectively outstanding accounts receivable items can be converted into cash. Measures can be derived from general financial reports as well as more detailed internal financial records.

Many measures, such as number of days of receivables, can be calculated easily from financial statements. The standard number of days of receivables evaluates the total receivables outstanding but does not consider the age distribution within this outstanding balance.

5.3.1 Accounts Receivable Aging Schedule

One key report that accounts receivable managers should use is the **aging schedule**, which is a breakdown of the accounts into categories of days outstanding. We provide an example of an aging schedule in Exhibit 12, Panel A. As you can see

EXHIBIT 12 An Accounts Receivable Aging Schedule

Panel A: The Aging Schedule

($ millions)	January	February	March	April
Sales	530	450	560	680
Total accounts receivable	600	560	650	720
Current (1–30 days old)	330	290	360	280
1–30 days past due	90	120	160	250
31–60 days past due	80	60	60	110
61–90 days past due	70	50	40	50
>90 days past due	30	40	30	30

Aging Expressed as Percent	January	February	March	April
Current (1–30 days old)	55.0%	51.8%	55.4%	38.9%
1–30 days past due	15.0%	21.4%	24.6%	34.7%
31–60 days past due	13.3%	10.7%	9.2%	15.3%
61–90 days past due	11.7%	8.9%	6.2%	6.9%
>90 days past due	5.0%	7.1%	4.6%	4.2%

Panel B: Calculation of the Weighted Average Collection Period

	March			April		
Aging Group	Collection Days[a]	Weight[b]	Weighted Days[c]	Collection Days	Weight	Weighted Days
Current (1–30 days)	20	55.4%	11.1	29	38.9%	11.3
31–60 days	48	24.6%	11.8	55	34.7%	19.1
61–90 days	80	9.2%	7.4	88	15.3%	13.5
91–120 days	110	6.2%	6.8	115	6.9%	7.9
121+ days	130	4.6%	6.0	145	4.2%	6.1
Weighted average collection days[d]			43.0			57.9

[a] The average days for collecting receivables in each grouping.
[b] The weighting from the aging schedule.
[c] This figure, expressed in days, is the product of the previous two columns.
[d] The sum of each grouping's product equals the overall days.

in this example, the report shows the total sales and receivables for each reporting period (typically 30 days). It is handier to convert the aging schedule to percentages, as we show in this exhibit. Note that in the exhibit, it is easy to spot a change in April's aging: Accounts receivable have not been collected and converted to cash as rapidly as in previous months. In this case, the April change should be scrutinized. For example, the extension of credit terms may have been increased as part of a special program. This change could also signal a change in payments by the company's customers.

5.3.2 The Number of Days of Receivables

The number of days of receivables gives us the overall picture of accounts receivable collection. We can compare the number of days with the credit policy to give us an idea of how well the company is collecting on its accounts, relative to the terms that it grants credit. But we can take this a step further by calculating a weighted average of the collection period, or weighted average day's sales outstanding. By focusing on the time it takes to collect receivables, the weighted average collection period is a good measure of how long it is taking to collect from the company's customers regardless of the sales level or the changes in sales.

The calculation of the weighted average collection period requires data on the number of days it takes to collect accounts of each age grouping. For example, we could group receivables in regular increments, such as 30-day periods, and then weight the collection period in each group by the monetary amount of accounts in the group.

Using the data provided in Exhibit 12, Panel A, it is possible to compute number of days of receivables for March and April, as shown in Panel B of this exhibit. As you can see in this example, we can get a better idea of why the number of days of receivables changed from one month to the next. The weighted average collection days increased from March to April, primarily because of the large representation in receivable accounts in the 31–60 and 61–90 day ranges, which made up only 24.6 percent + 9.2 percent = 33.8 percent of accounts in March, but 50 percent of accounts in April.

The primary drawback to this measure is that it requires more information than number of days of receivables, and this information is not readily available, especially for comparisons among companies.

6 MANAGING INVENTORY

The primary goal for an inventory system is to maintain the level of inventory so that production management and sales management can make and sell the company's products without more than necessary invested in this asset. Like cash and accounts receivable management, inventory management involves balancing: having sufficient inventory, but not too much.

Inventory is a current asset that is created by purchasing, paid by accounts payable, and funded by the treasury. The investment in inventory does not produce cash until it is sold or otherwise disposed of. Excessive levels of inventory can possibly overstate the value of inventory because the more that is on hand, the greater the potential for obsolete inventory, which can be sold off, but at a discount. Shortages of inventory result in lost sales.

The amount of inventory that a company holds or feels it has to hold creates a financial requirement for the company. If the company's product lines are more diverse or if its production processes are more involved in using inventory to make final products and then store the products, the company may have a significant financial investment in inventory.

The investment in inventory has been quite staggering for many companies, which has caused them to look for new inventory management techniques. New techniques in inventory control, aided by improved technology, have enabled substantial reduction of the inventory levels a company must maintain and still be able to make products and have them available for sale as needed. For instance, newer just-in-time approaches to inventory management have lowered required inventory balances and cemented major trading partner relationships.

The motives for holding inventory, which dictate how much inventory will be held and, in turn, how much working capital will be tied up in inventory, are very similar to the need for holding cash. The major motives include the transactions motive, the precautionary motives, and the speculative motive.

The **transactions motive** reflects the need for inventory as part of the routine production–sales cycle. Inventory need is equal to the planned manufacturing activity, and the approach to inventory will be dictated by the manufacturing plan.

Precautionary stocks also may be desirable to avoid any **stock-out losses**, which are profits lost from not having sufficient inventory on hand to satisfy demand. Managing inventory well means keeping extra inventory, especially if it could become obsolete quickly, at a minimum. To do this, a company must have a reliable forecast and a flexible inventory approach. In addition, many companies that do not have a reliable forecast maintain a reserve as a precaution for shortfalls in the plan. Of course, how much stock is determined by the lead time for additional inventory purchases, the length of time it takes to deliver final products to the market, and how much can be spent on extra inventory.

In certain industries, managers may acquire inventory for speculative reasons, such as ensuring the availability and pricing of inventory. Inventory managers working together with purchasing managers can benefit from out-of-the-ordinary purchases. For instance, if a publisher is certain that paper costs will be increasing for the next year, it can buy more paper in the current year and store it for future use. This decision assumes that the storage costs are not greater than the savings.

Companies usually attempt to strike a balance in managing their inventory levels. Overinvestment can result in liquidity squeezes or related problems with an increase in debt without an increase in cash. Overinvestment can also lead to the misuse of facilities as more storage is required for the built-up inventory. Having large amounts of inventory on hand can result in losses from shrinkage, spoilage, and so on. Finally, overinvestment can reduce the company's competitiveness as it may not be able to match pricing because of its large inventory costs.

On the other hand, underinvestment in inventory can create problems from losing customers who could not purchase a product, or gaining their ill-will from long delays in delivery. Plant shutdowns and expensive special runs can also be costly. Finally, a risk with underinvestment is the company's inability to avoid price increases by suppliers.

6.1 Approaches to Managing Levels of Inventory

To control inventory costs, a company should adopt the appropriate approach for its inventory. The two basic approaches are the economic order quantity and just-in-time.

Many companies use the classical approach, **economic order quantity–reorder point (EOQ–ROP)**, at least for some portion of their inventory. This method is based on expected demand and the predictability of demand, and it requires determining the level of inventory at which new inventory is ordered. This ordering point is determined based on the costs of ordering and carrying inventory, such that the total cost associated with inventory is minimized. The demand and lead times determine the inventory level. For EOQ–ROP to work well, there must be a reliable short-term forecast. Often, a company may use EOQ–ROP for smaller items that have low unit costs.

Use of the EOQ–ROP method may involve safety stocks and anticipation stocks. A **safety stock** is a level of inventory beyond anticipated needs that provides a cushion in the event that it takes longer to replenish inventory than expected or in the case of greater than expected demand. A company may consider the number of days of inventory on hand and the lead time in replenishing stock in determining the appropriate level of the safety stock. An **anticipation stock** is inventory in excess of that needed for anticipated demand, which may fluctuate with the company's sales or production seasonality. We illustrate the EOQ–ROP method in Exhibit 13.

EXHIBIT 13 EOQ–ROP Inventory Method

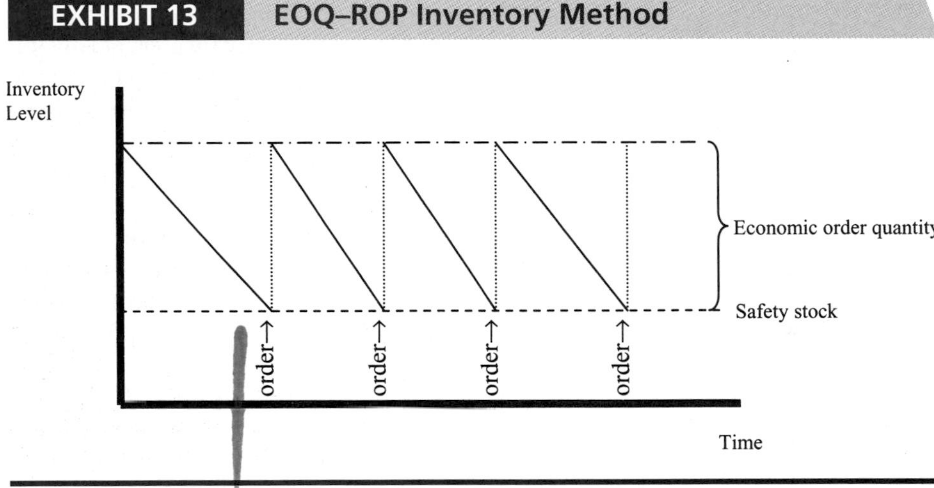

The **just-in-time (JIT) method** is a system that minimizes in-process inventory stocks—raw materials and in production—by evaluating the entire system of the delivery of materials and production. Materials are ordered, for example, at a point at which current stocks of material reach a reorder point, a point determined primarily by historical demand. Materials or **manufacturing resource planning (MRP)** systems incorporate production planning into inventory management. The analysis of production and materials needed for production are incorporated into an analysis that provides both a materials acquisition schedule and a production schedule. Combining the JIT and MRP methods can provide a broader base for integrating inventory into the company's supply chain management and effectively reduce inventory levels.[8]

[8] More-recent innovations have integrated cash management and inventory management. For example, the moment a customer orders and pays for a computer with Dell Corporation, the production process begins. This efficiency results in a negative operating cycle; that is, Dell Corporation is collecting on accounts as it invests in the inventory production. Because it uses trade credit for its supplies, it has little need for working capital.

In most instances, companies will have several types of inventory that can be managed effectively using one or more of these approaches. Obviously, a company should select the method that allows the most cost-beneficial investment in inventory.

6.2 Inventory Costs

There are several component costs of inventory. Some components represent opportunity costs, whereas others may be real costs. The component costs include:

- *Ordering.* Procurement or replenishment costs, both of which may be fixed or variable. These costs depend on the number of orders placed. Examples: freight, labor and handling, paperwork, machine setup.
- *Carrying.* Financing and holding costs, which are opportunity or real costs. These costs depend on average inventory levels and the type of goods. Examples: storage, capital costs, obsolescence, insurance, and taxes.
- *Stock-out.* Opportunity or real costs, which are affected by level of inventory, item mix, processing time versus term of sale. These costs might vary greatly depending on how they are estimated. Examples: lost sales, back-order costs, substitution costs.
- *Policy.* Costs of gathering data and general operating costs, which may be real costs or "soft" costs. These costs depend on inventory mix and complexity. Examples: data processing, labor charges, overtime, training.

6.3 Evaluating Inventory Management

The most common way to measure the company's investment in inventory and evaluate its inventory management is to compute the inventory turnover ratio and the number of days of inventory. The inventory turnover is a rough measure, but it is simple to calculate and compare with other standards or past history. Inventory turnover will vary among industries, as you can see in Exhibit 14, which provides a calculated inventory turnover and number of days of inventory for various industries.

Further, the inventory turnover may differ among companies within an industry because of different product mixes. For example, in fiscal year 2005, Wal-Mart Stores had an inventory turnover of 7.5 times compared with Target's 5.7 times. This difference may be because of Wal-Mart's greater foothold in the higher turnover grocery business, as compared with Target.

Although the analysis of trends is important, care should be taken when interpreting changes. For example, a decrease in the inventory turnover may mean that more inventory is on hand and is not moving through manufacturing and being sold. On the other hand, a decrease in inventory turnover may indicate a change in the company's product mix, or it may mean that the company is reducing its risk of inventory stock-outs.

EXHIBIT 14 Inventory Turnover and Number of Days of Inventory for U.S. Corporations in Different Industries, 2002

Industry	Inventory Turnover (times)	Number of Days of Inventory
Apparel manufacturing	4.9	74.0
Chemical manufacturing	5.7	64.4
Electronics and appliances stores	7.3	50.2
Food manufacturing	8.1	44.9
Food, beverage, and liquor stores	11.2	32.7
Machinery manufacturing	5.6	65.2
Mining	10.4	35.2
Motor vehicle dealers and parts dealers	5.6	65.2
Paper manufacturing	6.8	53.8
Transportation equipment manufacturing	9.7	37.7

Source: Statistics of Income, 2002, Corporation Returns with Net Income, Table 7, www.irs.gov.

EXAMPLE 5

Financial Impact of Inventory Methods

If a company's inventory turnover ratio is 6.1 times (annually) and the industry average number of days of inventory is 52 days, how does the company compare with the industry average?

Solution: Convert the turnover ratio to a number of days of inventory:

Number of days of inventory = 365/Inventory turnover = 365/6.1 = 59.84 days

Comparing this answer with the industry average, 52.0 days, it appears that the company's inventory turnover is slower than the industry average.

7

MANAGING ACCOUNTS PAYABLE

Accounts payable are amounts due suppliers of goods and services that have not been paid. They arise from **trade credit**, which is a spontaneous form of credit in which a purchaser of the goods or service is, effectively, financing its purchase by delaying the date on which payment is made. Trade credit may involve a delay of payment, with a discount for early payment. The terms of the latter form of credit are generally stated in the discount form: A discount from the purchase price is allowed if payment is received within a specified number of days; otherwise the full amount is due by a specified date. For example, the terms "2/10, net 30" indicate that a 2 percent discount is available if the account is paid within 10 days; otherwise the full amount is due by the 30th day. The terms will differ among industries, influenced by tradition within the industry, terms of competitors, and current interest rates.

A key working capital link is the purchasing–inventory–payables process. This process is concerned with the procurement of goods—finished or not—that become the company's items for sale. Handled efficiently, the process minimizes excess funds "in the pipeline." Handled inefficiently, the process can create a severe drain on a company's liquidity, tying up funds and reducing the company's financial reserves.

Inefficiencies may arise in managing purchasing, inventory, and payables. Each area has to be organized and efficiently linked with the other areas. Purchasing can often influence how payments are to be made and the terms of credit. Here again, purchasing management needs to be kept informed as to the types of payment mechanisms the company can handle to avoid agreeing with suppliers to make payments in a medium that the company does not yet support.

The effective management of accounts payable is an important working capital management activity because inefficient payables management may result in opportunity costs from payments made too early, lost opportunities to take advantage of trade discounts, and failure to use the benefits of technologies offered by e-commerce and other web-based activities.

Accounts payable is the final step in the procurement cycle because it combines the paperwork, approvals, and disbursements of funds. An effective accounts payable function helps integrate the components of the cycle and does not require the uneconomical outlay of the company's funds until the outlay is due.

A company may not believe that it needs a formal guideline or policy to manage the function well. However, there must be some method to ensure that payables practices are organized, consistent, and cost-effective. For example, if payables management is decentralized and more than one operating entity deals with the same supplier, the credit terms offered to each entity should be the same unless there are special circumstances, such as volume constraints, that warrant different terms. To handle payables effectively, a company needs rules to ensure that company assets are not being depleted unnecessarily.

There are several factors that a company should consider as guidelines for effectively managing its accounts payable, including:

- *Financial organization's centralization.* The degree to which the company's core financial function is centralized or decentralized affects how tightly payables can be controlled.
- *Number, size, and location of vendors.* The composition of the company's supply chain and how dependent the company is on its trading partners (and vice versa) determines how sophisticated a payables system it needs.
- *Trade credit and cost of borrowing or alternative cost.* The importance of credit to the company and its ability to evaluate trade credit opportunities, such as trade discounts, encourages standardized payables procedures and enhanced information management throughout the company.
- *Control of disbursement float.* Many companies still pay suppliers by check and create **disbursement float**—the amount of time between check issuance and a check's clearing back against the company's account. This float has value to many companies because it allows them to use their funds longer

than if they had to fund their checking account on the day the checks were mailed.

- *Inventory management.* Newer inventory control techniques, such as MRP and JIT, increase the number of payments that must be processed by accounts payable. Many older systems cannot accommodate this extra volume, so newer management techniques and systems are required.
- *E-commerce and electronic data interchange (EDI).* Global developments to use the internet and other direct connections between customer and supplier are revolutionizing the supply chain for many companies. Because payments for many of these activities should be considered as part of the overall process, many companies have determined that paying electronically offers a more efficient, cost-effective alternative to checks, which only are more valuable when the disbursement float value is large and interest rates (which provide value to float) are also high.

Stretching payables, also known as pushing on payables when it stretches beyond the due date, is sometimes done by corporate cash managers and other financial managers.[9] Stretching payables is taking advantage of vendor grace periods. The evaluation of payables stretching opportunities is fairly straightforward. The number of additional days that payments can be extended or stretched is determined and valued by applying the company's opportunity cost for the additional days times the amount of the payable.

For example, if a payable that averaged \$100,000 can be stretched for an additional seven days, the company gains an additional seven days' use of the funds. This opportunity can be valued by multiplying the amount, \$100,000, by the company's opportunity cost for short-term funds. For example, if the company's estimated cost for short-term funds is 8 percent annually (0.02191 percent daily), then the value of stretching a \$100,000 payment for seven days is \$153.42. The values for each opportunity (throughout a year's activity) can be valued in this way to determine the overall benefit, which can then be weighed against the costs (both financial and nonfinancial ones).

There are basically two countering forces: paying too early is costly unless the company can take advantage of discounts, and paying late affects the company's perceived creditworthiness.

7.1 The Economics of Taking a Trade Discount

One key activity that companies should review from time to time is the evaluation of trade discounts. Trade discounts should be evaluated using the formula shown below, which computes the implicit rate (of return) that is represented by the trade discount offer; that is, it is the equivalent return to the customer of an alternative investment.

The implicit rate is calculated as follows:

$$\text{Cost of trade credit} = \left(1 + \frac{\text{Discount}}{1 - \text{Discount}}\right)^{\left(365 \Big/ \text{Number of days beyond discount period}\right)} - 1 \qquad \textbf{(46-1)}$$

The cost of funds during the discount period is 0 percent, so it is beneficial for the customer to pay close to the end of the discount period. Once the discount period ends, the cost of the credit to the customer jumps up and then

[9] Keep in mind that stretching payments beyond their due dates might be considered unethical and may draw retaliation from suppliers in the form of tighter credit terms in the future.

declines as the net day is approached. For example, if the terms are 2/10, net 30, which means that there is a 2 percent discount for paying within 10 days and the net amount is due by the 30th day, the cost of trade credit is 109 percent if the credit is paid on the 20th day, but it is only 44.6 percent if paid on the 30th day.

If the customer's cost of funds or short-term investment rate is less than the calculated rate, the discount offers a better return or incremental return over the company's short-term borrowing rate.

EXAMPLE 6

Evaluating Trade Discounts

Compute the cost of trade credit if terms are 1/10, net 30 and the account is paid on:

- the 20th day
- the 30th day

Solution:

$$\text{Cost of trade credit if paid on day 20} = \left(1 + \frac{0.01}{1 - 0.01}\right)^{(365/10)} - 1$$
$$= 44.32 \text{ percent}$$

$$\text{Cost of trade credit if paid on day 30} = \left(1 + \frac{0.01}{1 - 0.01}\right)^{(365/20)} - 1$$
$$= 20.13 \text{ percent}$$

As you can see, the cost of the credits is much lower when the company pays on the net day than any day prior to the net day.

7.2 Managing Cash Disbursements

Handling cash disbursements effectively is a common goal for most companies. To accomplish this, companies use best practices that include the ability to delay funding bank accounts until the day checks clear, to erect safeguards against check fraud, to pay electronically when it is cost-effective to do so, and to manage bank charges for disbursement services. Best practices in cash disbursements, like check collections, depend on the nature of the payments—i.e., whether they are made electronically or by check.

Banks offer controlled disbursement services to optimize the funding of checks on the same day they clear against the company's account. When combined with a positive pay service, which provides a filter against check fraud, this method provides the best practice in handling paper-based (check) disbursements.

7.3 Evaluating Accounts Payable Management

The number of days of payables, which is also referred to as the average age of payables, is a useful measure in evaluating a company's credit extension and collection.

If the accounts payable balance from the company's balance sheet is €450 million and the amount of purchases is €4,100 million, the number of days of payables is

$$\text{Number of days of payables} = \frac{\text{Accounts payable}}{\text{Average day's purchases}} = \frac{450}{4100\ /\ 365} = 41.06 \text{ days}$$

Comparing the number of days of payables with the credit terms under which credit was granted to the company is important; paying sooner than necessary is costly in terms of the cost of credit, and paying later than the net day is costly in terms of relations with suppliers.

In some cases, treasurers will manage the company's payables closely, comparing the number of days of payables with the number of days of inventory because in some industries these two numbers of days are similar to one another.

8 MANAGING SHORT-TERM FINANCING

An overall short-term financial strategy should focus on ensuring that the company maintains a sound liquidity position. It should also reflect the degree of risk the company believes can be managed without affecting the company's stability. It is common to consider short-term financial strategies as applying mostly to investments. However, they should include other financial activities as well. In many cases, a company will only be an investor or borrower, but it is common for large multinational corporations to have both short-term investments and short-term borrowing.

A short-term policy should include guidelines for managing investment, borrowing, foreign exchange, and risk management activities and should encompass all the company's operations, including foreign subsidiaries and other domestic subsidiaries that are self-financing. These guidelines accomplish several things.

Too often companies do not explore their options sufficiently, and as a result, they do not take advantage of cost savings that some forms of borrowing offer. This lack of awareness usually indicates that a company's treasurer may not be familiar with the common forms of short-term borrowing and has not factored them into an effective borrowing strategy.

8.1 Sources of Short-Term Financing

The main types of short-term borrowing alternatives that borrowers should consider include bank sources as well as money market sources. The main types of bank short-term borrowing include uncommitted and committed bank lines of credit and revolving credit agreements ("revolvers"). The latter two types can be unsecured or secured, depending on the company's financial strength and the general credit situation, which may vary from country to country. Two of these types—uncommitted lines and revolvers—are more common in the United States, whereas regular lines are more common in other parts of the world. We provide examples of several types of short-term borrowing options in Exhibit 15, with bank sources in Panel A of this exhibit and nonbank sources in Panel B. In this exhibit, we provide the primary features for each type of borrowing, including the typical users, source(s) for the alternative, the base rate for computing interest, type of compensation required, and any other comments.

EXHIBIT 15 Short-Term Financing Instruments

Panel A: Bank Sources

Source/Type	Users	Rate Base	Compensation	Other
Uncommitted line	Large corporations	Prime (U.S.) or base rate (other countries), money market, LIBOR +	None	Mainly in U.S.; limited reliability
Regular line	All sizes		Commitment fee	Common everywhere
Overdraft line	All sizes		Commitment fee	Mainly outside U.S.
Revolving credit agreement	Larger corporations		Commitment fee + extra fees	Strongest form (primarily in U.S.)
Collateralized loan	Small, weak borrowers	Base+	Collateral	Common everywhere
Discounted receivables	Large companies	Varies	Extra fees	More overseas, but some in U.S.
Banker's acceptances	International companies	Spread over commercial paper	None	Small volume
Factoring	Smaller	Prime++	Service fees	Special industries

Panel B: Nonbank Sources

Source/Type	Users	Rate Base	Compensation	Other
Nonbank finance companies	Small, weak borrowers	Prime+++	Service fees	Weak credits
Commercial paper	Largest corporations	Money market sets rate	Backup line of credit, commissions+	Lowest rates for short-term funds

Uncommitted lines of credit are, as the name suggests, the weakest form of bank borrowing. A bank may offer an uncommitted line of credit for an extended period of time, but it reserves the right to refuse to honor any request for use of the line. In other words, an uncommitted line is very unstable and is only as good as the bank's desire to offer it. Therefore, companies should not rely very much on uncommitted lines. In fact, banks will not "officially" acknowledge that an uncommitted line is usable, which means that uncommitted lines cannot be shown as a financial reserve in a footnote to the company's financial statements. The primary attraction of uncommitted lines is that they do not require any compensation other than interest.

Committed lines of credit are the form of bank line of credit that most companies refer to as regular lines of credit. They are stronger than uncommitted because of the bank's formal commitment, which can be verified through an acknowledgment letter as part of the annual financial audit and can be footnoted in the company's annual report. These lines of credit are in effect for 364 days (one day short of a full year). This effectively makes sure that they are short-term liabilities, usually classified as notes payable or the equivalent, on the financial statements.

Regular lines are unsecured and are pre-payable without any penalties. The borrowing rate is a negotiated item. The most common interest rates negotiated are borrowing at the bank's prime rate or at a money market rate plus a spread. The most common money market rate is an offshore rate—the **London Interbank Offered Rate (LIBOR)**, which is a Eurodollar rate—plus a spread. The spread varies depending on the borrower's creditworthiness. Regular lines, unlike uncommitted lines, require compensation, usually in the form of a commitment fee. The fee is typically a fractional percent (e.g., ½ percent) of the full amount or the unused amount of the line, depending on bank–company negotiations.

Revolving credit agreements, which are often referred to as revolvers, are the strongest form of short-term bank borrowing facilities. They have formal legal agreements that define the aspects of the agreement. These agreements are similar to regular lines with respect to borrowing rates, compensation, and being unsecured. Revolvers differ in that they are in effect for multiple years (e.g., 3–5 years) and may have optional medium-term loan features. In addition, they are often done for much larger amounts than a regular line, and these larger amounts are spread out among more than one bank.

For companies with weak financial positions, such as those facing financial distress or that have deteriorated profitability, and many smaller companies that do not have sufficient capital, banks or other lenders (see nonbank sources in Exhibit 15) require that the company (or individual for much smaller companies) provide collateral in the form of an asset, such as a fixed asset that the company owns or high-quality receivables and inventory. These assets are pledged against the loans, and banks or other lenders file a lien against them with the state in which the loan is made. This lien becomes part of the borrower's financial record and is shown on its credit report.

8.2 Short-Term Borrowing Approaches

Given the various forms of short-term borrowing, it is essential that a borrower have a planned strategy before getting stuck in an uneconomical situation. Many borrowing companies spend too little time establishing a sound strategy for their short-term borrowing beyond making sure that they are able to borrow at all, from any source.

The major objectives of a short-term borrowing strategy include the following:

- Ensuring that there is sufficient capacity to handle peak cash needs.
- Maintaining sufficient sources of credit to be able to fund ongoing cash needs.
- Ensuring that rates obtained are cost-effective and do not substantially exceed market averages.

In addition, there are several factors that borrowers should consider as part of their short-term borrowing strategies, including the following:

- *Size and creditworthiness.* There is no doubt that the size of the borrower dictates the options available. Larger companies can take advantage of economies of scale to access commercial paper, banker's acceptances, and so on. The size of the borrower often reflects a manufacturing company's need for short-term financing. The size of lender is also an important criterion, as larger banks have higher house or legal lending limits. Creditworthiness of the borrower will determine the rate, compensation, or even whether the loan will be made at all.
- *Sufficient access.* Borrowers should diversify to have adequate alternatives and not be too reliant on one lender or form of lending if the amount of their lending is very large. Even so, it is typical for borrowers to use one

alternative primarily, but often with more than one provider. Borrowers should be ready to go to other sources and know how to. Borrowers should not stay too long with just one source or with lowest rates. Many borrowers are usually prepared to trade off rates (somewhat) for certainty.

- *Flexibility of borrowing options.* Flexibility means the ability to manage maturities efficiently; that is, there should not be any "big" days, when significant amounts of loans mature. To do this successfully, borrowers need active maturity management, awareness of the market conditions (e.g., knowing when the market or certain maturities should be avoided), and the ability to prepay loans when unexpected cash receipts happen.

Borrowing strategies, like investment strategies, can be either passive or active. Passive strategies usually involve minimal activity with one source or type of borrowing and with little (if any) planning. This "take what you can get" strategy is often reactive in responding to immediate needs or "panic attacks." Passive strategies are characterized by steady, often routine rollovers of borrowings for the same amount of funds each time, without much comparison shopping. Passive strategies may also arise when borrowing is restricted, such as instances where borrowers are limited to one or two lenders by agreement (e.g., in a secured loan arrangement).

Active strategies are usually more flexible, reflecting planning, reliable forecasting, and seeking the best deal. With active strategies, borrowers are more in control and do not fall into the rollover "trap" that is possible with passive strategies.

Many active strategies are matching strategies. Matching borrowing strategies function in a manner similar to matching investment strategies—loans are scheduled to mature when large cash receipts are expected. These receipts can pay back the loan, so the company does not have to invest the funds at potentially lower rates than the borrowing cost, thereby creating unnecessary costs.

8.3 Asset-Based Loans

Many companies that do not have the credit quality sufficient to qualify for unsecured bank loans may borrow from financial institutions by arranging for a secured loan, where the loan is secured using assets of the company. These secured loans are often referred to as **asset-based loans**. Often the assets used in short-term secured loans are the current assets of receivables and inventory. Unlike the collateral that may be used in longer-term borrowing, asset-based loans secured by accounts receivable and inventory present a challenge for the lender because the cash flows from accounts receivable depend on the amount and timing of collections and are influenced by the business risk of the company and its customers.

Lenders of these short-term asset-based loans are protected by the existence of the collateral and by provisions in the law that may provide them with a blanket lien on current and future assets of the company. The downside of a blanket lien is that even if the asset-based loan was secured by, say, accounts receivable, the lender may have a legal interest in other assets of the company until the loan is repaid.

Besides using working capital as the security for a loan, a company can use other means to generate cash flow from these working capital accounts. For example, a company can use its accounts receivable to generate cash flow through the **assignment of accounts receivable**, which is the use of these receivables as collateral for a loan, or a company can **factor** its accounts receivable, which is selling the receivables to the factor. In an assignment arrangement, the company remains responsible for the collection of the accounts, whereas in a factoring arrangement the company is shifting the credit granting and collection process to the factor. The cost of this credit depends on the credit quality of the accounts and the costs of collection.

Like accounts receivables, inventory may be a source of cash flow through the use of the inventory as collateral, with different types of arrangements possible:

- An **inventory blanket lien**, in which the lender has a claim on some or all of the company's inventory, but the company can sell the inventory in the ordinary course of business.
- A **trust receipt arrangement**, in which the lender requires the company to certify that the goods are segregated and held in trust, with proceeds of any sale remitted to the lender immediately.
- A **warehouse receipt arrangement** is similar to the trust receipt arrangement, but there is a third party (i.e., a warehouse company) that supervises the inventory.

The cost of asset-based loans security by inventory depends on the length of time it takes to sell the goods.

8.4 Computing the Costs of Borrowing

In carrying out a sound short-term borrowing strategy, one of the key decisions is selecting the most cost-effective form of short-term loan. However, this selection is often not a simple task, because each of the major forms has to be adjusted to be on a common basis for comparability. The fundamental rule is to compute the total cost of the form of borrowing and divide that number by the total amount of loan you received (i.e., net proceeds), adjusted for any discounting or compensating balances.

For example, in the case of a line of credit that requires a commitment fee,[10] the cost of the line of credit is

$$\text{Cost} = \frac{\text{Interest} + \text{Commitment fee}}{\text{Loan amount}}$$

On the other hand, if the interest rate is stated as "all inclusive" such that the amount borrowed includes the interest, as may be the case in a banker's acceptance, the interest is compared with the net proceeds when determining the cost:

$$\text{Cost} = \frac{\text{Interest}}{\text{Net proceeds}} = \frac{\text{Interest}}{\text{Loan amount} - \text{Interest}}$$

If there are dealer's fees and other fees, the expenses beyond the interest must be considered when determining the cost. For example, if a borrowing involves a dealer's fee and a backup fee and is quoted as all inclusive, the cost is

$$\text{Cost} = \frac{\text{Interest} + \text{Dealer's commission} + \text{Backup costs}}{\text{Loan amount} - \text{Interest}}$$

The key is to compare the interest and fees paid with the net proceeds of the loan. If the loan is for a period less than a year, then we annualize accordingly.

[10] A commitment fee is a fee paid to the lender in return for the legal commitment to lend funds in the future.

EXAMPLE 7

Computing the Effective Cost of Short-Term Borrowing Alternatives

You are asked to select one of the following choices as the best offer for borrowing $5,000,000 for one month:

1. Drawing down on a line of credit at 6.5 percent with a 1/2 percent commitment fee on the full amount.
2. A banker's acceptance at 6.75 percent, an all-inclusive rate.
3. Commercial paper at 6.15 percent with a dealer's commission of 1/8 percent and a backup line cost of 1/4 percent, both of which would be assessed on the $5 million of commercial paper issued.

Solution:

Line of credit cost:

$$\text{Line cost} = \frac{\text{Interest} + \text{commitment fee}}{\text{Usable loan amount}} \times 12$$

$$= \frac{(0.065 \times \$5{,}000{,}000 \times 1/12) + (0.005 \times \$5{,}000{,}000 \times 1/12)}{\$5{,}000{,}000} \times 12$$

$$= \frac{\$27{,}083.33 + 2{,}083.33}{\$5{,}000{,}000} \times 12 = 0.07 \text{ or } 7 \text{ percent}$$

Banker's acceptance cost:

$$\text{BA cost} = \frac{\text{Interest}}{\text{Net proceeds}} \times 12$$

$$= \frac{0.0675 \times \$5{,}000{,}000 \times 1/12}{\$5{,}000{,}000 - (0.0675 \times \$5{,}000{,}000 \times 1/12)} \times 12$$

$$= \frac{\$28{,}125}{\$4{,}971{,}875} \times 12 = 0.0679 \text{ or } 6.79 \text{ percent}$$

Commercial paper cost (quoted as nominal rate at a discount):

CP cost

$$= \frac{\text{Interest} + \text{Dealer's commissions} + \text{Back-up costs}}{\text{Net proceeds}} \times 12$$

$$= \frac{(0.0615 \times \$5{,}000{,}000 \times 1/12) + (0.00125 \times \$5{,}000{,}000 \times 1/12) + (0.0025 \times \$5{,}000{,}000 \times 1/12)}{\$5{,}000{,}000 - (0.0615 \times \$5{,}000{,}000 \times 1/12)} \times 12$$

$$= \frac{\$25{,}625 + 520.83 + 1041.67}{\$5{,}000{,}000 - 25{,}625} \times 12 = 0.0656 \text{ or } 6.56 \text{ percent}$$

We have simplified this cost analysis by assuming a loan for one month, using a factor of 1/12 to determine the interest and a factor of 12 to annualize. For specific arrangements for which the cost is determined using a 365-day or 360-day year, the appropriate adjustment would be required.

As the results show, the commercial paper alternative comes out with the lowest effective cost, and the line of credit has the highest effective cost. The commitment fee that was payable on the full line added more additional costs than the additional fees and discounting effects added in the other two options.

Line cost	7.00 percent
Banker's acceptance cost	6.79 percent
Commercial paper cost	6.56 percent

SUMMARY

In this reading, we considered a key aspect of financial management: the management of a company's working capital. This aspect of finance is a critical one in that it ensures, if done effectively, that the company will stay solvent and remain in business. If done improperly, the results can be disastrous for the company.

Working capital management covers a wide range of activities, most of which are focused on or involve the company's cash levels. Competing uses for the company's cash, which is often a scarce resource, create the need for an efficient method of handling the short-term financing of company activities.

Major points that were covered in this reading:

- Understanding how to evaluate a company's liquidity position.
- Calculating and interpreting operating and cash conversion cycles.
- Evaluating overall working capital effectiveness of a company and comparing it with other peer companies.
- Identifying the components of a cash forecast to be able to prepare a short-term (i.e., up to one year) cash forecast.
- Understanding the common types of short-term investments, and computing comparable yields on securities.
- Measuring the performance of a company's accounts receivable function.
- Measuring the financial performance of a company's inventory management function.
- Measuring the performance of a company's accounts payable function.
- Evaluating the short-term financing choices available to a company and recommending a financing method.

Working capital management is an integral part of the financial management of a company because many short-term activities have effects on long-term financial decisions. Having an effective short-term financial strategy, for example, allows a company to plan ahead with the confidence that its short-term concerns are being handled properly. Perhaps unlike other areas of finance, short-term finance has more qualitative features, making each company's case somewhat different from another's. This unique nature, combined with the short time frame associated with this aspect of finance, makes short-term finance a dynamic, challenging activity.

PRACTICE PROBLEMS FOR READING 46

1. Suppose a company has a current ratio of 2.5 times and a quick ratio of 1.5 times. If the company's current liabilities are €100 million, the amount of inventory is closest to
   A. €50 million.
   B. €100 million.
   C. €150 million.
   D. €200 million.

2. Given the following financial statement data, calculate the operating cycle for this company.

	In Millions
Credit sales	$25,000
Cost of goods sold	$20,000
Accounts receivable	$2,500
Inventory – Beginning balance	$2,000
Inventory – Ending balance	$2,300
Accounts payable	$1,700

   The operating cycle for this company is closest to
   A. 36.5 days.
   B. 42.0 days.
   C. 47.9 days.
   D. 78.5 days.

3. Given the following financial statement data, calculate the net operating cycle for this company.

	In Millions
Credit sales	$40,000
Cost of goods sold	$30,000
Accounts receivable	$3,000
Inventory – Beginning balance	$1,500
Inventory – Ending balance	$2,000
Accounts payable	$4,000

The net operating cycle of this company is closest to

A. 3.8 days.
B. 24.3 days.
C. 27.4 days.
D. 51.7 days.

4. The bond equivalent yield for a 182-day U.S. Treasury bill that has a price of $9,725 per $10,000 face value is closest to

A. 5.41 percent.
B. 5.53 percent.
C. 5.67 percent.
D. 5.79 percent.

5. A company increasing its credit terms for customers from 1/10, net 30 to 1/10, net 60 will likely experience

A. an increase in cash on hand.
B. an increase in the average collection period.
C. higher net income.
D. a higher level of uncollectible accounts.

6. Suppose a company uses trade credit with the terms of 2/10, net 50. If the company pays its account on the 50th day, the effective borrowing cost of skipping the discount on day 10 is closest to

A. 14.6 percent.
B. 14.9 percent.
C. 15.0 percent.
D. 20.2 percent.

7. William Jones is evaluating three possible means of borrowing $1 million for one month:

- Drawing down on a line of credit at 7.2 percent with a 1/2 percent commitment fee on the full amount with no compensating balances.
- A banker's acceptance at 7.1 percent, an all-inclusive rate.
- Commercial paper at 6.9 percent with a dealer's commission of 1/4 percent and a backup line cost of 1/3 percent, both of which would be assessed on the $1 million of commercial paper issued.

Which of these forms of borrowing results in the lowest cost of credit?

A. Line of credit.
B. Banker's acceptance.
C. Commercial paper.
D. All three forms have identical costs of borrowing.

The following information relates to Questions 8–12

Mary Gonzales is evaluating companies in the office supply industry and has compiled the following information:

	20X1		20X2	
Company	**Credit Sales**	**Average Receivables Balance**	**Credit Sales**	**Average Receivables Balance**
A	\$5.0 million	\$1.0 million	\$6.0 million	\$1.2 million
B	\$3.0 million	\$1.2 million	\$4.0 million	\$1.5 million
C	\$2.5 million	\$0.8 million	\$3.0 million	\$1.0 million
D	\$0.5 million	\$0.1 million	\$0.6 million	\$0.2 million
Industry	\$25.0 million	\$5.0 million	\$28.0 million	\$5.4 million

8. Which of the companies had the highest number of days of receivables for the year 20X1?
   A. Company A.
   B. Company B.
   C. Company C.
   D. Company D.

9. Which of the companies has the lowest accounts receivable turnover in the year 20X2?
   A. Company A.
   B. Company B.
   C. Company C.
   D. Company D.

10. The industry average receivables collection period
   A. increased from 20X1 to 20X2.
   B. decreased from 20X1 to 20X2.
   C. did not change from 20X1 to 20X2.
   D. increased along with the increase in the industry accounts receivable turnover.

11. Which of the companies reduced the average time it took to collect on accounts receivable from 20X1 to 20X2?
   A. Company A.
   B. Company B.
   C. Company C.
   D. Company D.

12. Gonzales determined that Company A had an operating cycle of 100 days in 20X2, whereas Company D had an operating cycle of 145 days for the same fiscal year. This means that

A. Company D's inventory turnover is less than that of Company A.

B. Company D's inventory turnover is greater than that of Company A.

C. Company D's cash conversion cycle is shorter than that of Company A.

D. Company D's cash conversion cycle is longer than that of Company A.

FINANCIAL STATEMENT ANALYSIS

by Pamela P. Peterson

READING 47

LEARNING OUTCOMES

The candidate should be able to:

a. calculate, interpret, and discuss the DuPont expression and extended DuPont expression for a company's return on equity and demonstrate its use in corporate analysis;

b. demonstrate the use of pro forma income and balance sheet statements.

INTRODUCTION 1

The financial analysis of a company is a process of selecting, evaluating, and interpreting financial data, along with other pertinent information, in order to formulate an assessment of the company's present and future financial condition and performance. We can use financial analysis to evaluate the efficiency of a company's operations, its ability to manage expenses, the effectiveness of its credit policies, and its creditworthiness, among other things.

The analyst draws the data needed in financial analysis from many sources. The primary source of these data is the company itself, through its annual and quarterly reports and other required disclosures. The annual report comprises the income statement, the balance sheet, the statement of cash flows, and the statement of shareholders' equity, as well as footnotes to these statements and management's discussion and analysis.

This reading will focus on two indispensable tools that are used by analysts to make sense of financial data and to gauge a company's performance and value: DuPont analysis and pro forma analysis.

2 DUPONT ANALYSIS

DuPont analysis was developed by E.I. du Pont de Nemours in 1919 as a way to better understand return ratios and why they change over time.[1] The bases for this approach are the linkages made through financial ratios between the balance sheet and the income statement. We can better understand a company's returns over time or its returns in comparison with its competitors by breaking returns into their components. This approach began as an analysis of the elements in the return on assets. For example,

$$\text{Return on assets} = \frac{\text{Net income}}{\text{Average total assets}} = \frac{\text{Net income}}{\text{Revenues}} \times \frac{\text{Revenues}}{\text{Average total assets}}$$

or

$$\text{Return on assets} = \text{Net profit margin} \times \text{Total asset turnover}$$

This breakdown of a return on assets into a two-component model is the simplest form of the DuPont approach.[2] The approach to breaking down return ratios was originally depicted as the DuPont Triangle, shown in Exhibit 1, with the return on assets at the top of the triangle and the profit margin and total asset turnover at the bottom.

EXHIBIT 1 The DuPont Triangle

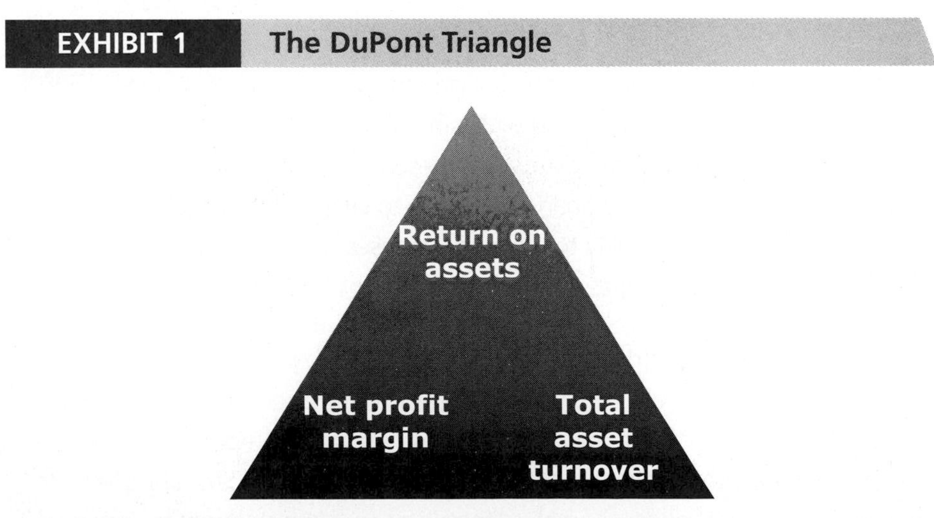

[1] American Management Association, "Executive Committee Control Charts," *AMA Management Bulletin*, no. 6 (1960):22. This system is consistent with the logic set forth by Alfred Marshall in his *Elements of Economics of Industry* (MacMillan and Co., 1892), book 2, chapter 12, sections 3 and 4.

[2] An easy way to remember the DuPont system is to keep in mind that cross-cancellation of terms produces the desired return. For example,

$$\text{Return on assets} = \frac{\text{Net income}}{\text{Average total assets}} = \frac{\text{Net income}}{\cancel{\text{Revenues}}} \times \frac{\cancel{\text{Revenues}}}{\text{Average total assets}}$$

For example, using the financial data found in Exhibit 2, we can calculate that for the fiscal year 2004, Office Depot, Inc., had a return on assets of 4.95 percent. We can use the DuPont approach to look at the components of this return, with dollar amounts in millions:[3]

$$\text{Return on assets} = \frac{\text{Net income}}{\text{Revenues}} \times \frac{\text{Revenues}}{\text{Average total assets}}$$

$$\frac{\$335}{\$6{,}767} = \frac{\$335}{\$13{,}565} \times \frac{\$13{,}565}{\$6{,}767}$$

$$4.95\% = 2.47\% \times 2.00$$

EXHIBIT 2 Financial Data for Office Depot, Inc.

Office Depot, Inc.
Consolidated Balance Sheet
(millions of dollars)

	2003	2004
Assets		
Cash and cash equivalent	$ 791	$ 794
Investment securities	100	161
Accounts receivable	1,112	1,304
Inventories	1,336	1,409
Deferred income taxes	170	133
Prepaid expenses and other current assets	68	115
Total current assets	$ 3,577	$ 3,916
Net property, plants, and equipment	$ 1,294	$ 1,463
Goodwill	1,004	1,050
Other assets	320	338
Total Assets	$ 6,195	$ 6,767
Liabilities and Stockholders' Equity		
Accounts payable	$ 1,323	$ 1,650
Accrued and other liabilities	814	820
Taxes payable	129	133
Current maturities of long-term debt	13	15
Total current liabilities	$ 2,279	$ 2,618
Deferred income taxes	$ 340	$ 342
Long-term debt	829	584
Total liabilities	$ 3,448	$ 3,544

(Exhibit continued on next page . . .)

[3] *Source:* Office Depot, 2004 annual report for fiscal year ending 25 December 2004.

EXHIBIT 2 (continued)

Common shareholders' equity	$ 489	$ 630
Retained earnings	2,258	2,593
Total shareholders' equity	$ 2,747	$ 3,223
Total liabilities and shareholders' equity	$ 6,195	$ 6,767

Office Depot, Inc.
Consolidated Statement of Earnings
(millions of dollars)

	2003	2004
Sales	$12,359	$13,565
Cost of sales	8,484	9,309
Gross profit	$ 3,875	$ 4,256
Selling, general, and administrative expenses	3,409	3,726
Operating income	$ 466	$ 530
Interest expense and other nonoperating expenses	25	69
Earnings before income taxes	$ 441	$ 461
Income tax	142	126
Earnings after income taxes	$ 299	$ 335
Cumulative effect of accounting change	(26)	0
Net earnings	$ 273	$ 335

Note: Fiscal year ending 25 December.
Source: Office Depot, Inc., 10-K.

Using the two-component breakdown, we can also use the DuPont approach to compare Office Depot's return on assets for 2003 and 2004 and examine why the return changed from 4.41 percent in 2003 to 4.95 percent in 2004:

$$\text{Return on assets} = \frac{\text{Net income}}{\text{Revenues}} \times \frac{\text{Revenues}}{\text{Average total assets}}$$

$$\frac{\$273}{\$6{,}195} = \frac{\$273}{\$12{,}359} \times \frac{\$12{,}359}{\$6{,}195}$$

$$4.41\% = 2.21\% \times 1.99$$

Comparing the breakdowns from 2003, we see that we can attribute the increase in the return on assets to the increase in the net profit margin from 2.21 percent to 2.47 percent. Taking a look over a longer span of time, 1991–2004, as shown in Exhibit 3, we see that the primary driver of Office Depot's return on assets over time is its net profit margin. In 2000, for example, the return on assets declined, along with the net profit margin, despite an increasing total asset turnover. This observation tells us that to understand changes in return, we need to better understand what drives Office Depot's net profit margin.

EXHIBIT 3 Return on Assets for Office Depot for Fiscal Years 1991–2004

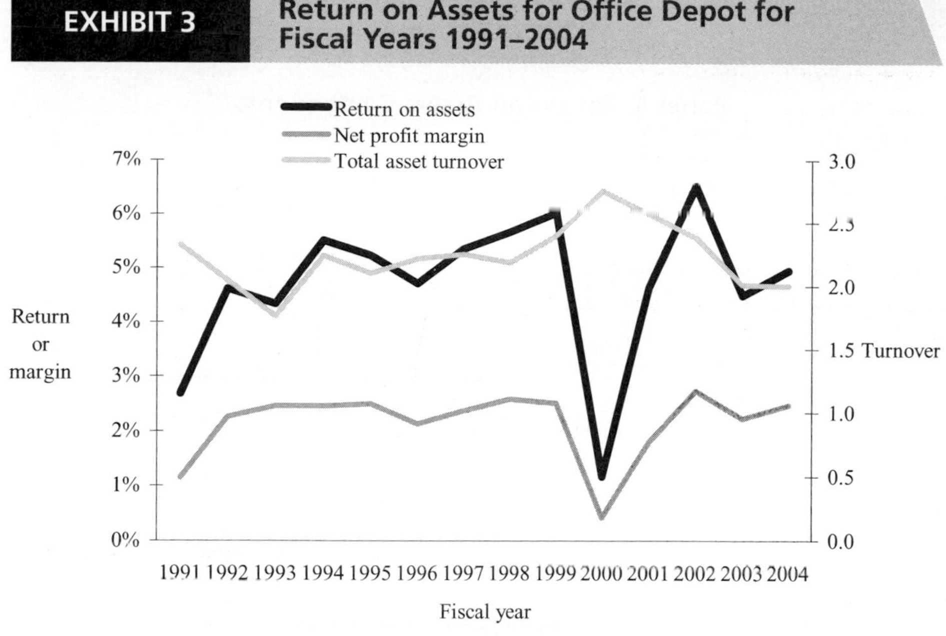

Source: The Office Depot, Inc., annual reports, various years.

We can also compare one company with another using the DuPont approach. Consider Office Depot's competitor Staples, Inc. In 2004, Staples had revenues of \$14,448 million, net income of \$708 million, and total assets of \$7,071 million. Its return on assets for 2004 was higher than Office Depot's—10.01 percent versus 4.95 percent—due to its higher net profit margin:

$$\text{Return on assets} = \frac{\text{Net income}}{\text{Revenues}} \times \frac{\text{Revenues}}{\text{Average total assets}}$$

$$\frac{\$708}{\$7{,}071} = \frac{\$708}{\$14{,}448} \times \frac{\$14{,}448}{\$7{,}071}$$

$$10.01\% = 4.90\% \times 2.04$$

The key to understanding Office Depot's return on assets, both in comparison with itself over time and in comparison with competitors, is the net profit margin. We can gain a better understanding of the net profit margin by breaking this ratio into three components: the operating profit margin, the effect of nonoperating expenses (or nonoperating income), and the tax effect. Exhibit 4 shows this finer breakdown, with return on assets broken down into the four components of total asset turnover, the operating profit margin, the effect of nonoperating items, and the tax effect in Panel A. Panel B of this exhibit provides the two-component and four-component DuPont models for Office Depot's return on assets for 2004.

EXHIBIT 4 **Two-Component and Four-Component DuPont Models of the Return on Assets**

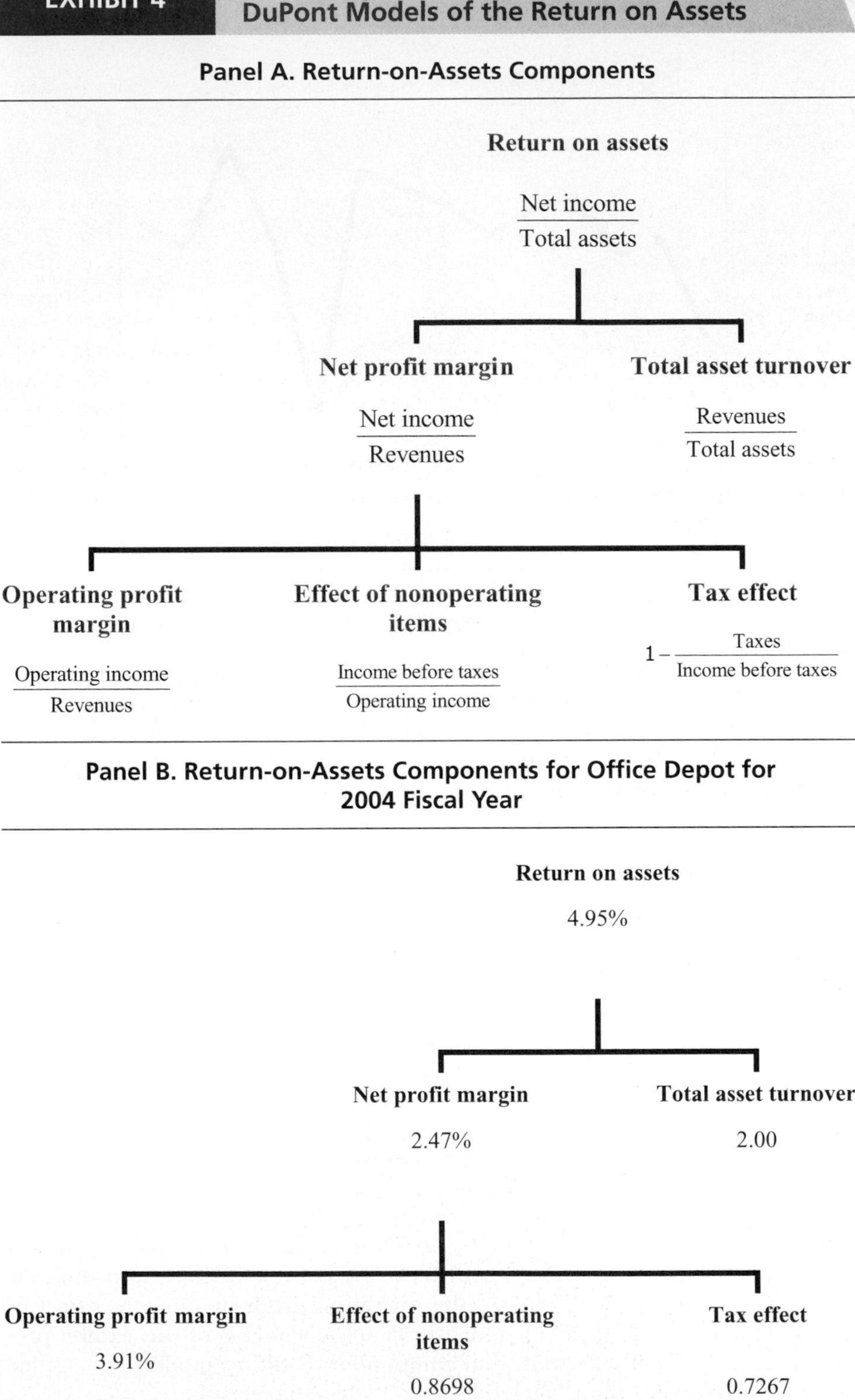

The effect of nonoperating items reflects everything in the company's income statement between its operating income and its earnings before taxes. If the company has net nonoperating expense, the ratio of income before tax to operating income is less than 1.0; on the other hand, if the company has net nonoperating income, this ratio is greater than 1.0. The effect of nonoperating items is often referred to as the *interest effect* or *interest burden* because for many companies the interest expense is the primary nonoperating expense. Companies with higher interest expense have lower ratios of income before taxes to operating income, whereas companies with larger nonoperating income have higher ratios of income before taxes to operating income. In the case of Office Depot in 2004, its nonoperating net expenses are 13.02 percent of its operating income.

The tax effect is one minus the ratio of taxes to income before taxes, or 1 − (Taxes/Income before taxes). The complement of the tax effect is the average *tax burden,* which is the ratio of taxes to income before taxes. For Office Depot, the tax effect ratio is 0.7267; therefore, its average tax rate for 2004 is 1 − 0.7267 = 27.33 percent.

So far, we have seen how the return on assets can be broken down into two or four components. Similarly, we can represent the return on shareholders' equity as a three-component DuPont model:

$$\text{Return on equity} = \frac{\text{Net income}}{\text{Average shareholders' equity}} = \frac{\text{Net income}}{\text{Revenues}} \times \frac{\text{Revenues}}{\text{Average total assets}} \times \frac{\text{Average total assets}}{\text{Average shareholders' equity}}$$

Extending this model to include the net profit margin in components as we did previously, we can produce a five-component DuPont model, as illustrated in the corresponding expanded DuPont Triangle in Exhibit 5.

EXHIBIT 5 The Five-Component DuPont Triangle

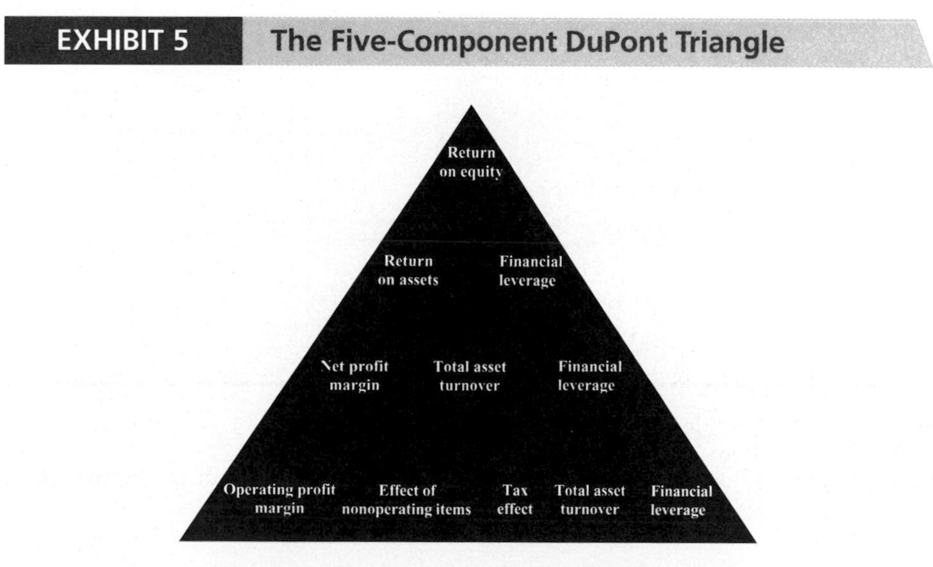

For example, we can use the five-component DuPont model for Office Depot's return on equity, as Panel A of Exhibit 6 shows.

EXHIBIT 6 Five-Component DuPont Model

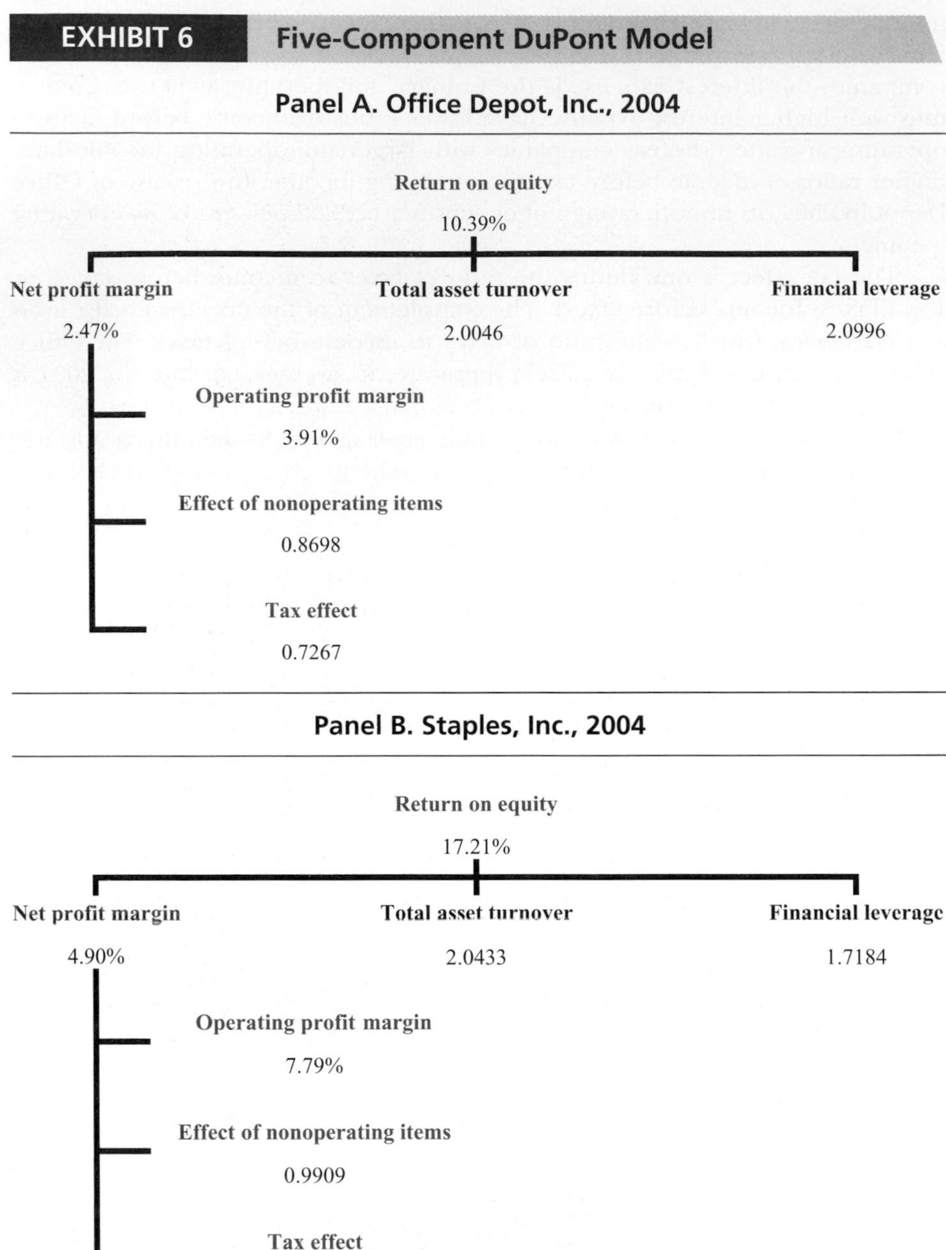

Using the breakdown in Panel A, we can show that the product of the five components is the return on equity:

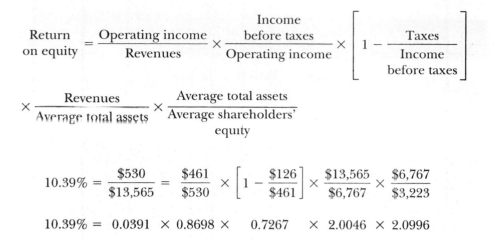

$$\text{Return on equity} = \frac{\text{Operating income}}{\text{Revenues}} \times \frac{\text{Income before taxes}}{\text{Operating income}} \times \left[1 - \frac{\text{Taxes}}{\text{Income before taxes}}\right]$$

$$\times \frac{\text{Revenues}}{\text{Average total assets}} \times \frac{\text{Average total assets}}{\text{Average shareholders' equity}}$$

$$10.39\% = \frac{\$530}{\$13{,}565} = \frac{\$461}{\$530} \times \left[1 - \frac{\$126}{\$461}\right] \times \frac{\$13{,}565}{\$6{,}767} \times \frac{\$6{,}767}{\$3{,}223}$$

$$10.39\% = 0.0391 \times 0.8698 \times 0.7267 \times 2.0046 \times 2.0996$$

We can also compare these components with competitors' components to understand the differences among the companies' financial condition and performance that produce different returns on equity. For example, Staples in 2004 has a higher return on equity than Office Depot, 17.21 percent versus 10.39 percent. We can take a closer look at the differences by comparing Office Depot's five-component DuPont model with Staples' five-component model, as shown in Panel B of Exhibit 6. Here, we see that although the total asset turnover is similar for the two companies, the companies differ primarily in two ways:

1. The management of operating costs, as reflected in the operating profit margin, with Staples able to generate greater operating profits per dollar of revenues.
2. The financing decisions, with Office Depot slightly more reliant on debt financing. This reliance affects not only the financial leverage but also the interest expense that influences the net profit margin.

Another use of DuPont analysis is to diagnose the source of change in returns on equity over time. Consider Kmart during the years leading up to and including its bankruptcy filing in January 2002. What was the source of Kmart's woes? A company's financial difficulties usually have more than one source, but the DuPont approach allows us to get some idea of what led to Kmart's challenges.

We can see in Panel A of Exhibit 7 that Kmart's return on equity was negative in several years and that Kmart was unable to provide consistent, positive returns to its shareholders. Looking more closely at the components of the return on equity, we get a clearer picture of the elements that led toward Kmart's bankruptcy. In Panel B, we see that the financial leverage ratio is relatively consistent, with the exception of the year ending around the bankruptcy filing. We can see that Kmart had total assets that were twice its equity throughout the 1990–2000 period. In other words, its debt-to-equity ratio was around 1.0, and its use of debt financing did not change much in the 10 years leading up to bankruptcy. Looking at Kmart's total asset turnover in Panel C, we see that the turnover in fact rose slightly over the 10 years leading up to bankruptcy. The company's net profit margin, as shown in Panel D, is evidently the source of the problem. The changing net profit margin—and hence Kmart's inability to manage its expenses—appears to have been a strong influence on Kmart's return on equity.

EXHIBIT 7 DuPont Analysis of Kmart's Return on Assets Leading Up to Bankruptcy in 2002

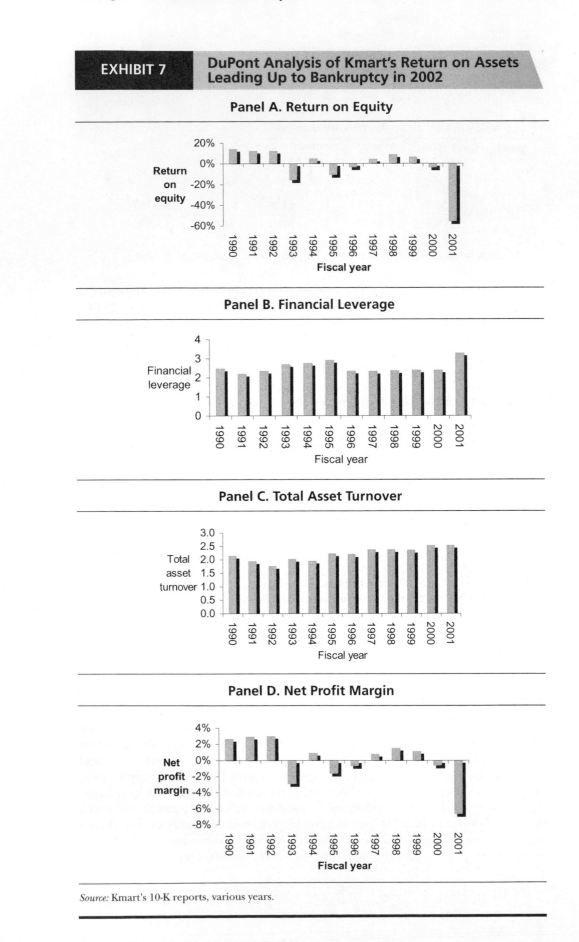

Panel A. Return on Equity

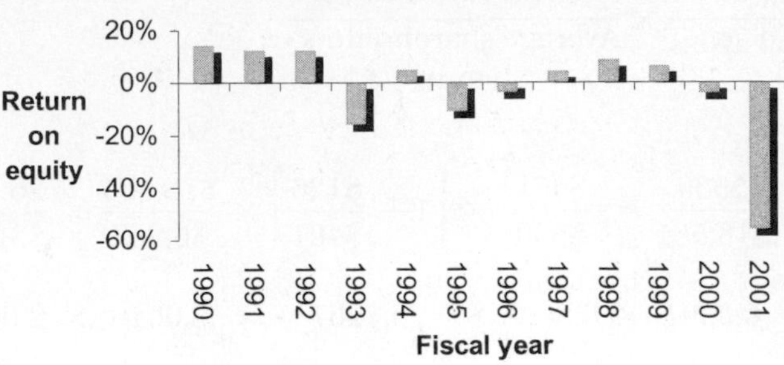

Panel B. Financial Leverage

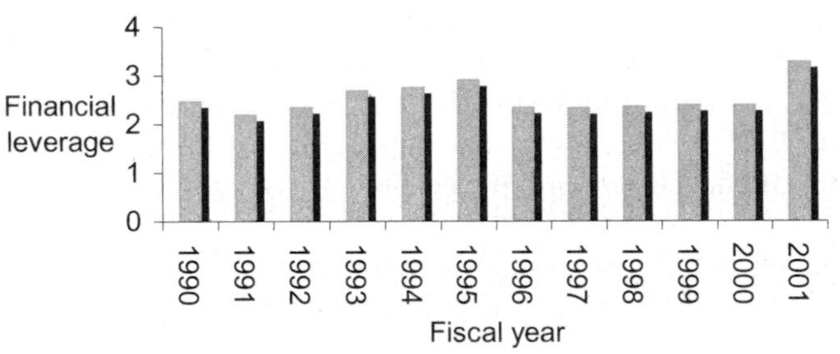

Panel C. Total Asset Turnover

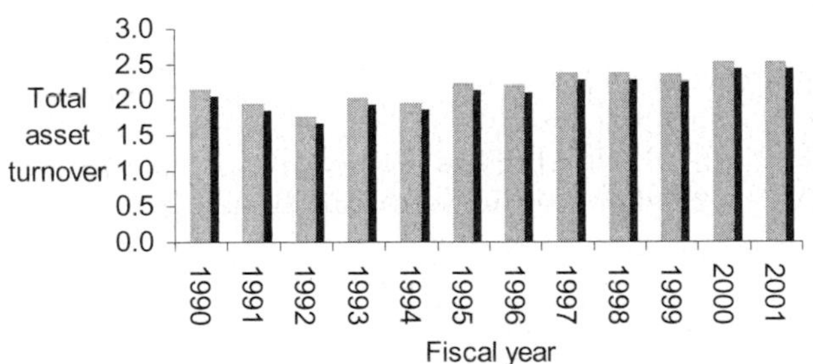

Panel D. Net Profit Margin

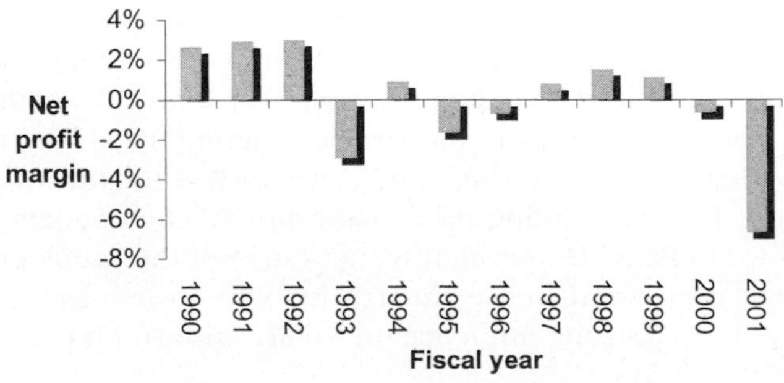

Source: Kmart's 10-K reports, various years.

What does this all mean? What we surmise from this analysis is that Kmart's difficulties are related to the management of expenses rather than the deployment and use of its assets or its assumption of financial risk. If we wanted a more detailed picture, we would:

- break the net profit margin into its components—the operating profit margin, the interest burden, and the tax burden—as we did for Office Depot and Staples, to see why the net profit margin changed over time; and
- compare the trends in these components with those of Kmart's major competitors during this period, namely, Wal-Mart Stores and Target Corporation.

PRO FORMA ANALYSIS 2

We use common-size statements and financial ratios to gauge the company's financial condition and performance over recent fiscal periods. These analyses are useful in the assessment of what the company has done in the past and what trends and patterns may continue into the future. We can get an even stronger sense of a company's future by constructing pro forma statements, based both on relationships that existed in the recent past and on anticipated events and changes.[4] Pro forma statements are income statements and balance sheets based on projections. We often make these projections by using relations that we estimate from the recent past, forecasting revenues, and then using these forecasted revenues in conjunction with the past relations to develop a picture of the company's future.

If we simply take a company's current balance sheet and income statement and make the bold assumptions that all elements vary with sales and that the company will continue to grow at a rate similar to its most recent past growth rate, we can generate pro forma income statements and balance sheets quite easily. For example, using Procter & Gamble and assuming the same growth in revenues in 2005 as in 2004, the pro forma income statement for 2005 is as follows:

Fiscal Year Ending 30 June	Actual 2004 in Millions	Projected Percent of Sales	Pro Forma 2005 in Millions
Sales	$51,407	100.0	$60,924
Cost of sales	25,076	48.8	29,718
Gross profit	$26,331	51.2	$31,206
Selling, general, and administrative expenses	16,504	32.1	19,559
Operating income	$ 9,827	19.1	$11,647
Interest expense	629	1.2	745
Other nonoperating income, net	152	0.3	180
Earnings before income taxes	$ 9,350	18.2	$11,082
Income tax	2,869	5.6	3,400
Net income	$ 6,481	12.6	$ 7,682

[4] *Pro forma statements* should not be confused with pro forma financial information released by companies in disclosures regarding financial performance. In the former use of the term *pro forma*, we are referring to projections or predictions of future results and conditions; in the latter case, the term *pro forma* is used to indicate reported results that are not calculated in conformity with generally accepted accounting principles.

How far did we miss in our projections? We predicted $7.682 billion in net income, yet the actual net income for 2005 was $7.257 billion. As you can see, we were off by approximately $425 million:

Fiscal Year Ending 30 June	Projected Percent of Sales	Pro Forma 2005 in Millions	Actual Percent of Sales	Actual 2005 in Millions
Sales	100.0	$60,924	100.0	$56,741
Cost of sales	48.8	29,718	49.0	27,804
Gross profit	51.2	$31,206	51.0	$28,937
Selling, general, and administrative expenses	32.1	19,559	31.7	18,010
Operating income	19.1	$11,647	19.3	$10,927
Interest expense	1.2	745	1.5	834
Other nonoperating income, net	0.3	180	0.6	346
Earnings before income taxes	18.2	$11,082	18.4	$10,439
Income tax	5.6	3,400	5.6	3,182
Net income	12.6	$ 7,682	12.8	$ 7,257

EXHIBIT 8 Pro Forma Analysis

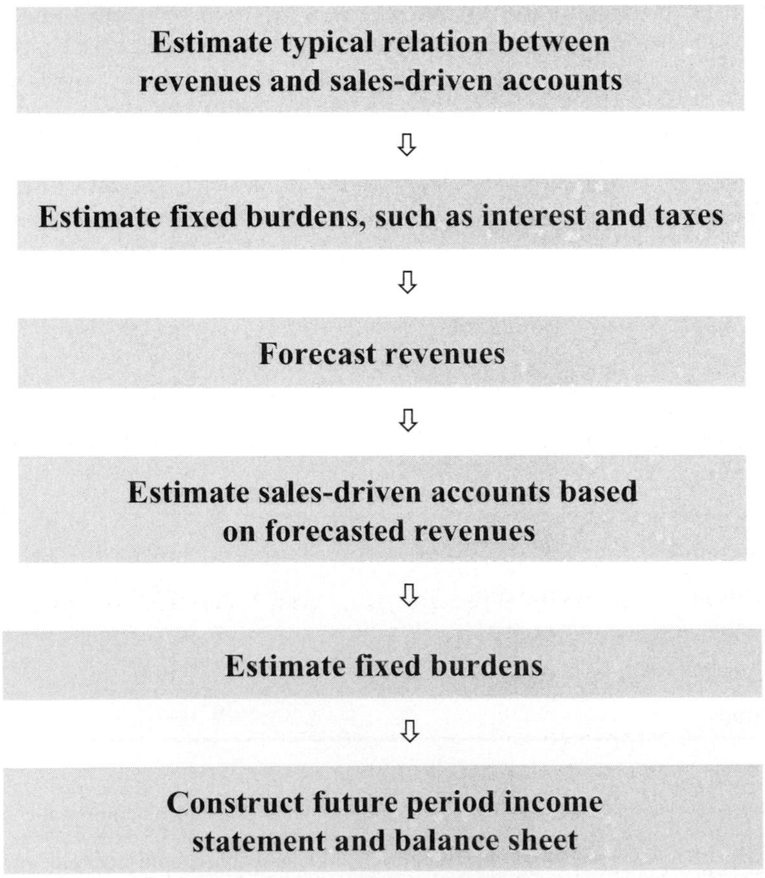

Estimate typical relation between revenues and sales-driven accounts

⇩

Estimate fixed burdens, such as interest and taxes

⇩

Forecast revenues

⇩

Estimate sales-driven accounts based on forecasted revenues

⇩

Estimate fixed burdens

⇩

Construct future period income statement and balance sheet

Why did we miss the mark? The projected percentages of sales were actually quite close to the actual percentages of sales, with the primary exception being "other nonoperating income, net," which is difficult to predict for most companies. We also missed slightly in terms of revenue growth. Using 2004 revenue growth of 18.5 percent, we predicted sales of roughly $60.9 billion. Actual revenue growth was lower, at 10.4 percent.

As you can see in this example, it is important to produce a good prediction of revenue growth, as well as refinement in terms of how other income and expenses vary with sales. We can develop more accurate forecasts by determining which accounts in the income statement and balance sheet tend to vary with revenues and which do not. For example, interest expense and nonoperating income and expenses do not tend to vary with revenues but rather are driven by other factors. Exhibit 8 outlines the process of considering both sales-driven and non-sales-driven accounts in the development of pro forma statements.

For purposes of demonstrating this process, we will use the statements for Imaginaire, a fictitious company:[5]

Imaginaire Company Income Statement, Year 0 (in millions)		**Imaginaire Company Balance Sheet, End of Year 0 (in millions)**	
Sales revenues	€1,000.0	Current assets	€ 600.0
Cost of goods sold	600.0	Net plant and equipment	1,000.0
Gross profit	€ 400.0	Total assets	€1,600.0
Selling, general, and administrative expenses	100.0		
Operating income	€ 300.0	Current liabilities	€ 250.0
Interest expense	32.0	Long-term debt	400.0
Earnings before taxes	€ 268.0	Common stock and paid-in capital	25.0
Taxes	93.8	Retained earnings	925.0
Net income	€ 174.2	Total liabilities and equity	€1,600.0
Dividends	€ 87.1		

2.1 Estimating the Sales-Driven Relations

There are several accounts that tend to vary with the revenues of a business. In other words, the relation between these accounts and revenues is relatively fixed over time. In general, these sales-driven accounts include the cost of goods sold; selling, general, and administrative expenses; and the working capital accounts included in current assets and current liabilities.

In the case of the Imaginaire Company, we calculate the following:

Cost of goods sold as a percentage of sales	60%
Operating expenses as a percentage of sales	10%
Current assets as a percentage of sales	60%
Current liabilities as a percentage of sales	25%

[5] Note that at various points throughout our Imaginaire example, the calculations may vary slightly due to rounding. For this example, calculations were completed with a spreadsheet.

As a real-world example, Exhibit 9 shows the sales-driven relations for Wal-Mart Stores. The cost of goods sold as a percentage of sales has been rather constant at about 79 percent during the past 15 years. Operating expenses, including selling, general, and administrative expenses, have been approximately 16 percent of sales. When making projections involving Wal-Mart Stores, we can be fairly confident that the sales-driven costs of sales and operations are relatively constant.

If we look at Wal-Mart's current assets and current liabilities, we see that while these may be sales-driven, there is some variability in the percentages. The current assets range from 12.5 percent to 19 percent of sales, whereas the current liabilities range from 10.4 percent to 15.6 percent of sales. However, the last five years' percentages are rather constant for both accounts, providing a reasonable estimation of current assets of approximately 13.5 percent of sales and current liabilities of approximately 15 percent of sales.

EXHIBIT 9 Sales-Driven Accounts for Wal-Mart Stores, 1990–2004

Panel A. Sales-Driven Income Statement Accounts

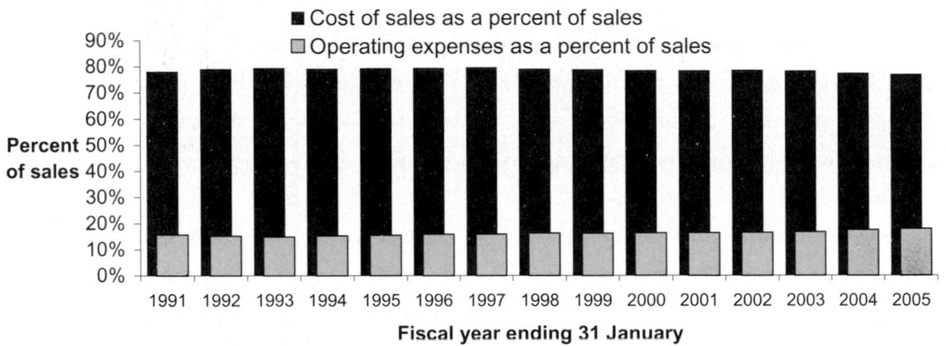

Panel B. Sales-Driven Balance Sheet Accounts

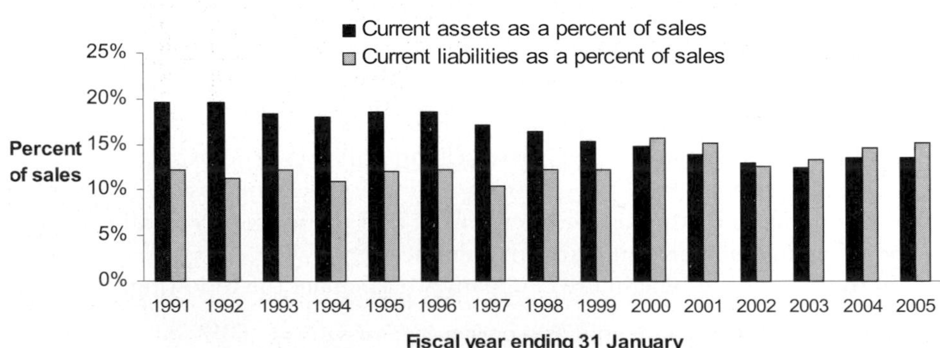

Source: Wal-Mart Stores annual reports, various years.

2.2 Estimating the Fixed Burdens

The fixed burdens are primarily interest and taxes. If we make the assumption that tax rates will not change in the near future, we can look at the company's recent experience with taxes to assess the tax burden. In the case of the Imaginaire Company, the tax rate is 35 percent. In most cases, the tax burden is constant unless a change occurs in the federal corporate tax structure. If tax rates are expected to change, this estimate can be adjusted accordingly.

The interest burden is a function of the company's capital structure. In making our forecasts, we must make an assumption about the company's capital structure in the future and then work from there to determine the interest burden. If we assume that the capital structure will not change, we look at the interest burden in the past to make our projections for the future.

2.3 Forecasting Revenues

We can forecast future revenues a number of ways. We already saw that if we simply use the most recent year's revenue growth for Procter & Gamble, we wind up with a significant forecast error for 2005. If we forecast revenues into the future using the average growth rate of 5.43 percent over the period 1994–2004, we predict revenues of $54,198 million for the fiscal year ending 30 June 2005.[6] On the other hand, if we use a time-series **linear regression** to forecast revenues, we predict revenues of $47,841 million in 2005.[7] The actual revenues for 2005 were $56,741 million. In other words, whether relying on the average growth rate to continue for the following year or extrapolating a **linear trend**, we would have underforecasted revenues. Why are we off?

Strictly using forecasts from prior periods does not take into account the other factors that affect revenues. For example, recent acquisitions and divestitures can change the product mix, affecting the predictability of the different segments' revenues.

In predicting revenues, we want to consider not only the path that revenues have taken in the past but also company-specific, market, and economic events that may affect future revenues. If the company provides consistent segment data, we can often track trends in these segments to develop the forecasts for the company as a whole.

2.4 Constructing Pro Forma Statements

We construct the financial statements based on the sales-driven estimates and the interest and tax burdens. If all accounts vary with sales, the projections that we provide in the pro forma statements are simple: We extrapolate forward in time using the percentages, typically using the components we determined in our common-size analysis. But not all accounts vary with sales, so we will encounter a residual that we need to resolve.

When we make predictions for both the sales-driven accounts and the fixed burdens, we will inevitably encounter either a financing deficiency or a surplus. We must then make an assumption regarding how we expect the company to deal with this residual. Will the company finance expansion with debt? Equity?

[6] The growth rate of revenues varied widely between 1994 and 2004, from −1.77 percent in 2001 to 18.51 percent in 2004.

[7] We estimate the linear regression based on the 11 years of revenues, 1994 through 2004, against time, forecasting the following year's revenues as $29,301 + $1,545(12) = $47,841.

Both? When funds are available in excess of operating needs, will they be used to pay down debt? Repurchase stock? Both? In other words, we need to make an assumption about the company's capital structure decisions. To see how this question plays out, we will forecast one year ahead for the Imaginaire Company. If we assume that revenues will grow at 5 percent, the predicted net income one year ahead, assuming no changes in financing, is €184 million:

Imaginaire Company
Income Statement (in millions)

	Year 0	One Year Ahead	
Sales revenues	€1,000.0	€1,050.0	← Growth at 5 percent
Cost of goods sold	600.0	630.0	← 60 percent of revenues
Gross profit	€ 400.0	€ 420.0	← Sales revenues less cost of goods sold
Selling, general, and admin. expenses	100.0	105.0	← 10 percent of revenues
Operating income	€ 300.0	€ 315.0	← Gross profit less operating expenses
Interest expense	32.0	32.0	← 8 percent of long-term debt
Earnings before taxes	€ 268.0	€ 283.0	← Operating income less interest expense
Taxes	93.8	99.1	← 35 percent of earnings before taxes
Net income	€ 174.2	€ 184.0	← Earnings before taxes less taxes
Dividends	€ 87.1	€ 92.0	← Assume dividend payout ratio of 50 percent

We then carry the income statement information into our forecast for the next year's balance sheet:

Imaginaire Company
Balance Sheet, End of Year (in millions)

	Year 0	One Year Ahead	
Current assets	€ 600.0	€ 630.0	← 60 percent of revenues
Net plant and equipment	1,000.0	1,050.0	← 100 percent of revenues
Total assets	€1,600.0	€1,680.0	
Current liabilities	€ 250.0	€262.5	← 25 percent of revenues
Long-term debt	400.0	400.0	← Assume no change
Common stock and paid-in capital	25.0	25.0	← Assume no change
Retained earnings	925.0	1,017.0	← Retained earnings in Year 0, plus net income, less dividends
Total shareholders' equity	950.0	1,042.0	
Total financing	€1,600.0	€1,704.5	← Sum of projected liabilities and equity
Total assets		1,680.0	
Financing surplus (or deficiency)		€ 24.5	← Difference between financing and assets

Whenever we make projections with a combination of percentages of sales and fixed burdens, we are likely to need a "plug" item to balance the accounts. In this case, we see that there is a financing surplus of €24.5 million, which means that the company can pay down debt, repurchase equity, or increase dividends by €24.5 million. If we assume that the company's capital structure does not change, we assume that the €24.5 million is spread proportionately between debt and equity. But now we have another issue: If debt changes, there are consequences for the interest expense, taxes, net income, and equity. In other words, the adjustment is not a simple one but rather one that requires iterations until the appropriate solution is determined.

For example, if we assume that Imaginaire will make adjustments only in debt, then the pro forma financial statements are as follows:

Imaginaire Company
Income Statement (in millions)

	Year 0	One Year Ahead	
Sales revenues	€1,000.0	€1,050.0	← Growth at 5 percent
Cost of goods sold	600.0	630.0	← 60 percent of revenues
Gross profit	€ 400.0	€ 420.0	← Sales revenues less cost of goods sold
Selling, general, and admin. expenses	100.0	105.0	← 10 percent of revenues
Operating income	€ 300.0	€ 315.0	← Gross profit less operating expenses
Interest expense	32.0	30.0	← 8 percent of long-term debt (originally €400 million, now €375.5 million)
Earnings before taxes	€ 268.0	€ 285.0	← Operating income less interest expense
Taxes	93.8	99.7	← 35 percent of earnings before taxes
Net income	€ 174.2	€ 185.2	← Earnings before taxes less taxes
Dividends	€ 87.1	€ 92.6	← Assume dividend payout ratio of 50 percent

Imaginaire Company
Balance Sheet, End of Year (in millions)

	Year 0	One Year Ahead	
Current assets	€ 600.0	€ 630.0	← 60 percent of revenues
Net plant and equipment	1,000.0	1,050.0	← 100 percent of revenues
Total assets	€1,600.0	€1,680.0	
Current liabilities	€ 250.0	€ 262.5	← 25 percent of revenues
Long-term debt	400.0	375.5	← Financing surplus applied toward debt
Common stock and paid-in capital	25.0	25.0	← Assume no change
Retained earnings	925.0	1,017.6	← Retained earnings in Year 0, plus net income, less dividends
Total liabilities and equity	€1,600.0	€1,608.6	

With one iteration, we have reduced the financing surplus to €0.6 million. Additional iterations would eventually reduce the surplus (or deficit) to the point where it would be small enough to eliminate through rounding. For example, a second iteration would reduce long-term debt to €374.9 million and reduce the surplus to €328.00.

If we were instead to make the assumption that the company will maintain its current relation between total debt and equity, the pro forma statements would be slightly different:

Imaginaire Company
Income Statement (in millions)

	Year 0	One Year Ahead	
Sales revenues	€1,000.0	€1,050.0	← Growth at 5 percent
Cost of goods sold	600.0	630.0	← 60 percent of revenues
Gross profit	€ 400.0	€ 420.0	← Sales revenues less cost of goods sold
Selling, general, and admin. expenses	100.0	105.0	← 10 percent of revenues
Operating income	€ 300.0	€ 315.0	← Gross profit less operating expenses
Interest expense	32.0	33.6	← 8 percent of long-term debt (now €420.0 million)
Earnings before taxes	€ 268.0	€ 281.4	← Operating income less interest expense
Taxes	93.8	98.5	← 35 percent of earnings before taxes
Net income	€ 174.2	€ 182.9	← Earnings before taxes less taxes
Dividends	€ 87.1	€ 91.5	← Assume dividend payout ratio of 50 percent

Imaginaire Company
Balance Sheet, End of Year (in millions)

	Year 0	One Year Ahead	
Current assets	€ 600.0	€ 630.0	← 60 percent of revenues
Net plant and equipment	1,000.0	1,050.0	← 100 percent of revenues
Total assets	€1,600.0	€1,680.0	
Current liabilities	€ 250.0	€262.5	← 25 percent of revenues
Long-term debt	400.0	420.0	← Debt increased by €20 million to maintain the same capital structure
Common stock and paid-in capital	25.0	25.0	← Assume no change
Treasury stock		(44.0)	← Repurchased shares
Retained earnings	925.0	1,016.5	← Retained earnings in Year 0, plus net income, less dividends
Total liabilities and equity	€1,600.0	€1,608.0	

Retained earnings for one year ahead were found by adding net income less dividends to retained earnings in Year 0. If the common stock and paid-in capital account remains at €25.0 million, then a Treasury stock purchase of €44.0 million is required to eliminate the financing surplus. A repurchase of shares creates a Treasury stock contra-equity account, which results in a reduction of the company's reported equity.

As you can see, generating pro forma statements requires a reliance on assumptions about the growth in revenues, which items in the balance sheet and income statement tend to vary with revenues, and how the company will deal with financing shortfalls or surpluses. Divergences from these assumptions can have a dramatic impact on overall results. Thus, great care should be taken to ensure that pro forma assumptions are as realistic as possible.

SUMMARY

A challenge that we face in financial analysis is making sense of the wealth of information that is available about a company and the industry in which it operates. Companies provide shareholders and investors with quarterly and annual financial statements, as well as numerous other financial releases. We can use tools, such as the DuPont model, to help understand where a company has been. We then apply these relationships in pro forma analysis, forecasting the company's income statements and balance sheets for future periods, to see how the company's performance is likely to evolve.

PRACTICE PROBLEMS FOR READING 47

1. DuPont analysis involves breaking return-on-assets ratios into their
   A. profit components.
   B. marginal and average components.
   C. operating and financing components.
   D. profit margin and turnover components.
2. The DuPont system allows us to break down the return on equity into
   A. return on assets and the financial leverage ratio.
   B. profit margin, the tax retention ratio, and inventory turnover.
   C. operating return on assets, the tax burden, and the interest burden.
   D. gross profit margin, total asset turnover, and the debt-to-equity ratio.
3. If a company's net profit margin is −5 percent, its total asset turnover is 1.5 times, and its financial leverage ratio is 1.2 times, its return on equity is *closest* to
   A. −9.0 percent.
   B. −7.5 percent.
   C. −3.2 percent.
   D. 1.8 percent.

Use the information in the following table to answer Questions 4–5

LaPearla Company Income Statement for Year 2005 (in millions)		LaPearla Company Balance Sheet, End of Year 2005 (in millions)	
Revenues	€10,000	Current assets	€ 2,000
Cost of goods sold	5,500	Net plant and equipment	18,000
Gross profit	€ 4,500	Total assets	€20,000
Selling, general, and administrative expenses	800		
Operating income	€ 3,700	Current liabilities	€ 1,000
Interest expense	500	Long-term debt	5,000
Earnings before taxes	€ 3,200	Common stock and paid-in capital	500
Taxes	960	Retained earnings	13,500
Net income	€ 2,240	Total liabilities and equity	€20,000

4. Suppose that LaPearla's revenues are expected to grow at a rate of 10 percent and all elements of the income statement and balance sheet are sales-driven except for the tax burden, which remains at 30 percent. LaPearla's pro forma net income for 2006 is *closest* to
   A. €2.2 billion.
   B. €2.5 billion.
   C. €2.8 billion.
   D. €3.0 billion.

5. If LaPearla's long-term debt and paid-in capital accounts remain at their 2005 levels, the tax rate remains at the 2005 rate, and all other income statement and balance sheet accounts are sales-driven with an expected growth rate of revenues of 10 percent, in 2006 LaPearla will have a financing
   A. deficiency if it pays no dividends.
   B. surplus if it pays out all income in dividends.
   C. surplus if it pays out 50 percent of its net income in dividends.
   D. deficiency if it pays out 50 percent of its net income in dividends.

THE CORPORATE GOVERNANCE OF LISTED COMPANIES: A MANUAL FOR INVESTORS

READING 48

LEARNING OUTCOMES

The candidate should be able to:

a. define and describe corporate governance;

b. discuss and critique characteristics and practices related to board and committee independence, experience, compensation, external consultants, and frequency of elections, and determine whether they are supportive of shareowner protection;

c. describe board independence and explain the importance of independent board members in corporate governance;

d. identify factors that indicate a board and its members possess the experience required to govern the company for the benefit of its shareowners;

e. explain the provisions that should be included in a strong corporate code of ethics and the implications of a weak code of ethics with regard to related-party transactions and personal use of company assets;

f. state the key areas of responsibility for which board committees are typically created, and explain the criteria for assessing whether each committee is able to adequately represent shareowner interests;

g. evaluate, from a shareowner's perspective, company policies related to voting rules, shareowner-sponsored proposals, common stock classes, and takeover defenses.

The Purpose of This Manual

Some of the most spectacular corporate collapses and losses in recent memory have highlighted the role that corporate governance practices play in maintaining viable entities, and safeguarding Investors' interests. The governance failures at Enron, Parmalat and others since 2001 are harsh examples of the risks posed by corporate governance breakdowns. Losses of tens of billions of dollars of Investors' capital proved that the existing set of corporate checks and balances on insiders' activities could not protect Shareowners from the misplaced priorities of Board Members and the manipulation and misappropriation of Company resources by management and other groups that exercised significant and improper influence over the Company's affairs.

Thus, it is with the goal of educating and empowering **the Investor** that this manual endeavors to provide Investors a way of assessing a Company's corporate governance policies, and the associated risks. It is our hope that all Investors—be they existing Shareowners, potential Investors, or analysts—can use this information as part of their analyses and valuations, in light of their particular investment perspectives, objectives, and risk-tolerance levels, to evaluate a Company. In particular, we hope that use of this manual will help Investors better recognize, understand and analyze how corporate governance may affect the value of their investments, and thus help them in making more informed investment decisions.

In response to wide-ranging effects of recent corporate failures on the global markets, many countries, industry groups and other constituencies have proposed or created new or amended corporate governance codes. Many of these codes seek to establish internal controls or set an ethical tone that focus on Investors' interests. While these government-mandated and voluntary industry codes may help to restore a degree of Investor confidence in the markets, they provide only part of the answer. Investors also must take the initiative to evaluate the presence—or absence—of corporate governance safeguards of Companies in which they invest, as well as their corporate cultures.

To this end, the CFA Centre for Financial Market Integrity ("CFA Centre"), through the work of its Global Corporate Governance Task Force, has prepared this manual. While suggesting issues for Investors to consider, the manual does not provide a set of best practices, nor attempt to decide what corporate governance structures are best for Investors. Instead, its purpose is to alert Investors to the primary corporate governance issues and risks affecting Companies, and to highlight some of the factors they should consider. It will evolve over time as listed Companies and financial markets change, and will serve as a starting point from which the CFA Centre can address revisions to this manual necessitated by such change.

Issuers of financial securities may also find this manual useful as a reference tool for determining what corporate governance issues are important to Investors. We hope that this manual will raise awareness of their governance standards within the investment community.

The Importance of Corporate Governance to Investors

For corporate governance structures to work effectively, Shareowners must be active and prudent in the use of their rights. In this way, Shareowners must act like owners and continue to exercise the rights available to them. Benjamin Graham and David Dodd stated in the 1930s that:

> *The choice of a common stock is a single act, its ownership is a continuing process. Certainly there is just as much reason to exercise care and judgment in being a shareholder as in becoming one.*[1]

A number of studies published in recent years have shown a strong link between good corporate governance and strong profitability and investment performance measures. For example, a joint study of Institutional Shareholder

[1] Benjamin Graham and David Dodd, *Security Analysis*, 1st ed. (New York: McGraw Hill, 1934).

Services ("ISS") and Georgia State University[2] found that the best-governed Companies—as measured by ISS's Corporate Governance Quotient—had mean returns on investment and equity that were 18.7% and 23.8% better, respectively, than those of poorly governed companies during the year reviewed. Research carried out by employees of the California Public Employees Retirement System ("CalPERS") on the effects of the system's "Focus List" suggests that efforts by investment funds to improve the governance of Companies which are considered poorly governed also produces good returns in excess of market performance.[3]

On this basis, one would expect Investors to reward Companies that have superior governance with higher valuations. Indeed, a study of U.S. markets by Paul Gompers of Harvard University and colleagues from Harvard and the University of Pennsylvania[4] found that portfolios of Companies with strong shareowner-rights protections outperformed portfolios of Companies with weaker protections by 8.5% per year. A similar study in Europe found annual disparities of 3.0%.[5] Another study establishing and testing a governance rating system in the German market for the period from March 1998 to February 2002 shows that a portfolio consisting of the best governed Companies outperformed a portfolio of the worst governed Companies by a statistically significant average of 2.33% per month.[6]

This phenomenon is neither new nor limited to developed markets. Even before the collapse of Enron, Amar Gill, an analyst in Malaysia, found that Investors in emerging markets experienced higher investment returns from Companies with good governance.[7] Of the 100 largest emerging markets Companies his firm followed, those with the best governance—based on management discipline, transparency, Independence, accountability, responsibility, fairness and social responsibility—generated five-year returns well above average.[8]

The conclusion is that good corporate governance leads to better results for Companies and for Investors. Corporate governance, therefore, is a factor that Investors cannot ignore but should consider in seeking the best possible results for themselves or their clients.

---

[2] Brown, Lawrence D., and Caylor, Marcus, "Corporate Governance Study: The Correlation between Corporate Governance and Company Performance," Institutional Shareholder Services (2004).

[3] Anson, Mark, Ted White, and Ho Ho, "Good Corporate Governance Works: More Evidence from CalPERS," *Journal of Asset Management*, Vol. 5, 3 (February 2004), 149-156. Also see "The Shareholder Wealth Effects of CalPERS' Focus List" by the same authors, published in the *Journal of Applied Corporate Finance*, (Winter 2003), 8-17. The authors found that between 1992 and 2002, publication of the CalPERS' "Focus List" and efforts to improve the corporate governance of companies on that list generated one-year average cumulative excess returns of 59.4%. Cumulative excess return is the cumulative "return earned over and above the risk-adjusted return required for each public corporation."

[4] Gompers, Paul A., Joy L. Ishii, and Andrew Metrick, "Corporate Governance and Equity Prices," *Quarterly Journal of Economics*, 118(1) (February 2003), 107-155. The authors compared the investment performance of some 1,500 U.S.-listed companies against a corporate governance index the authors constructed from 24 distinct governance rules. Also see Lucian Bebchuk, Alma Cohen, and Allen Ferrell, "What Matters in Corporate Governance," (2004), The John M. Olin Center for Law, Economics and Business of Harvard University.

[5] Bauer, Rod, and Nadja Guenster, "Good Corporate Governance Pays Off!: Well-governed companies perform better on the stock market," (2003). This study used Deminor Ratings as the basis for determining which companies relative to corporate governance quality. (www.deminor-rating.com).

[6] Wolfgang Drobetz, Andreas Schillhofer, and Heinz Zimmermann, "Ein Corporate Governance Rating für deutsche Publikumsgesellschaften," WWZ/Department of Finance, Working Paper No. 5/03 (2003) (in German.) (www.unibas.ch/wwz/finanz/publications/researchpapers/5).

[7] Gill, Amar, "Corporate Governance in Emerging Markets—Saints and Sinners: Who's Got Religion?", CLSA Emerging Markets, April 2001. Gill points out that CLSA assigned corporate governance ratings to 495 companies in 25 markets.

[8] The five-year returns reported by Gill amounted to 930% for the well-governed large-cap companies in emerging markets, versus the total average return of 388% for large-cap companies in emerging markets during that period.

- The Board and its committees are structured to act independently from management, individuals or entities that have control over management, and other non-Shareowner groups;
- Appropriate controls and procedures are in place covering management's activities in running the day-to-day operations of the Company; and
- The Company's operating and financial activities, as well as its governance activities, are consistently reported to Shareowners in a fair, accurate, timely, reliable, relevant, complete and verifiable manner.

How well a Company achieves these goals depends, in large part, on the adequacy of the Company's corporate governance structure and the strength of the Shareowner's voice in corporate governance matters, through Shareowner voting rights. The success of the Board in safeguarding Shareowner interests depends on these factors.

This manual focuses on these two areas as a means of evaluating the corporate governance practices of Companies.

Independence

A number of new national corporate governance codes and exchange-based rules prescribe factors to consider in determining the Independence of Board and Board committee Members. Generally, to be considered Independent under these codes and rules, a Board Member must not have a material business or other relationship with the following individuals or groups:

- The Company and its subsidiaries or members of its group, including former employees and executives and their family members;
- Individuals, groups or other entities—such as controlling families and governments—that can exert significant influence on the Company's management;
- Executive management, including their family members;
- Company advisers (including external auditors) and their families; or
- Any entity which has a cross-directorship relationship with the Company.

Board Members

The term "Board Member"—in some jurisdictions called "directors"—in this Manual refers to all individuals who sit on the Board (defined below), including Executive Board Members, Independent Board Members, and Non-Executive Board Members.

Executive Board Members

This term refers to the members of executive management. In a Unitary Board, or Committees System, Executive Board Members also serve as part of the Board in a Unitary Board Structure. In a Two-Tier Board, these individuals only would be part of the Management Board. These individuals are not considered Independent.

Independent Board Members

An Independent Board Member refers to an individual who meets the qualifications listed under "Independence."

Non-Executive Board Members

Non-Executive Board Members are neither Executive Board Members nor Independent Board Members. Individuals in this category may represent interests that may conflict with those of other Shareowners. These may include Board Members who are affiliated with individuals or entities that have control over management, who are part of a cross-directorship arrangement with another listed Company, or are representatives of labor organizations.

Board

The term "Board" in this manual refers to both the Supervisory Board—or a Board of Corporate Auditors in Japan—in countries with a Two-Tier Board Structure, and the Board of Directors in countries that use a Unitary Board. In most cases, corporate structures take the form of one or the other of these, but in some countries such as in France and Japan, Companies have the option of choosing which of the two structures they wish to use.

Two-Tier (Dual) Board

Common in some parts of Europe, particularly in Germany, the Netherlands, Austria and Denmark, this structure has two elements, the Management Board and the Supervisory Board, both of which are described further below:

Management Board

The Management Board consists exclusively of executive management and is charged with running the Company on a daily basis and setting the corporate strategy for the Company, in consultation with the Supervisory Board. Its Members do not sit on the Company's Supervisory Board.

Supervisory Board

The Supervisory Board is charged with overseeing and advising the Company's Management Board and includes only Independent and Non-Executive Board Members.

Corporate Auditors System

In Japan, the Two-Tier Board structure is called the Corporate Auditors System and is used by most large Japanese Companies. It includes a Board—including either Independent Board Members or Non-Executive Board Members who are elected by Shareowners and are responsible for business decisions—and a Board of Corporate Auditors—consisting of corporate auditors, including at least one full-time corporate auditor, and at least half the Members must be outside auditors. These corporate auditors are elected separately by Shareowners and are charged with auditing the performance of the Board.

Unitary Board

In a Unitary Board structure, the Board may include Executive, Non-Executive and Independent Board Members. It oversees and advises management and helps set corporate strategy, though in many jurisdictions it does not engage in corporate decision-making, except in matters such as mergers, acquisitions, divestitures and sales. Jurisdictions increasingly require Independent Board Members to comprise at least a majority of the Board.

Committees System

This is the Unitary Board structure in Japan which uses a Board consisting of Executive Board Members, Independent Board Members and Non-Executive Board Members. The system gets its name because the Board must establish three committees—the audit, nominations and compensation committees—all of which must have at least three members, a majority of whom are either Independent Board Members or Non-Executive Board Members.

Company

The Company is the firm in which the Shareowners have an ownership position, and in which Investors are considering an investment.

Investors

This term refers to all individuals or institutions who are considering investment opportunities in shares and other securities of the Company.

Shareowners

The term "Shareowners" is distinguished from the term Investors by referring only to those individuals, institutions or entities that own shares of common or ordinary stock in the Company in question.

THE BOARD

Board Members owe a duty to make decisions based on what ultimately is best for the long-term interests of Shareowners. In order to do this effectively, Board Members need a combination of three things: Independence, experience and resources.

First, a Board should be composed of at least a majority of Independent Board Members with the autonomy to act Independently from management. Board Members should bring with them a commitment to take an unbiased approach in making decisions that will benefit the Company and long-term Shareowners, rather than simply voting with management. **Second**, Board Members who have appropriate experience and expertise relevant to the Company's business are best able to evaluate what is in the best interests of Shareowners. Depending on the nature of the business, this may require specialized expertise by at least some Board Members. **Third**, there need to be internal mechanisms to support the Independent work of the Board, including the authority to hire outside consultants without management's intervention or approval. This mechanism alone provides the Board with the ability to obtain expert help in specialized areas, to circumvent potential areas of conflict with management, and to preserve the integrity of the Board's Independent oversight function.

These three areas, and how Investors can evaluate them, are discussed in more detail below.

Board Independence

Investors should determine whether a Company's Board has, at a minimum, a majority of Independent Board Members.

What is Independence? Independence, as it relates to Board Members, refers to the degree to which they are not biased or otherwise controlled by Company management or other groups who exert control over management. Factors to consider in determining whether a Board Member meets this definition are provided in the "Definitions" section at the front of this Manual.

Implications for Investors. A Board that is not predominantly Independent, or a committee that is not completely Independent, may be more likely to make decisions that unfairly or improperly benefit the interests of management and those who have influence over management. These decisions may also be detrimental to the long-term interests of Shareowners.

Things to Consider. Investors should determine whether:

- Independent Board Members constitute, at a minimum, a majority of the Board. A Board with this makeup and one which is diverse in its composition is more likely to limit undue influence of management and others over the affairs of the Board.
- Independent Board Members regularly meet without the presence of management and report on their activities at least annually to Shareowners. Such meetings permit these Board Members to discuss issues facing the Company without influence from Executive Board Members.
- the Board chair also holds the title of chief executive. Combining the two positions may give too much influence to Executive Board Members and impair the ability and willingness of Independent Board Members to exercise their Independent judgment. A number of national corporate governance codes require the separation of these two positions.
- Independent Board Members have a lead Member if the Board chair is not Independent.
- the Board chair is a former chief executive of the Company. If so, Investors run the risk that this arrangement could impair the Board's ability to act Independently of undue management influence and in the best interests of Shareowners. Such a situation also increases the risk that the chair may hamper efforts to undo the mistakes made by him/her as chief executive.
- individuals who are aligned with a Company supplier or customer, or are aligned with a manager or adviser to the Company's share-option or pension plan, are Members of the Board. In some cases, a Company with a large number of suppliers, customers and advisers may need to nominate individuals to the Board who are aligned with these entities to ensure that it has the expertise it needs to make reasoned decisions. Investors should determine whether such Board Members recuse themselves on issues that may create a conflict.

Where to find information about the Independence of the Board and its committees:

- In most jurisdictions, Companies disclose the names, credentials and Company affiliations of existing Board Members either in their annual reports to Shareowners, or in their annual proxy statements to Shareowners.

- Companies often devote a special section in their annual reports to a discussion of the issues confronted by the Board and Board committees during the past year.
- The websites of many listed Companies provide information about Board Members' Independence.

Board Member Qualifications

Investors should determine whether Board Members have the qualifications the Company needs for the challenges it faces.

Implications for Investors. Investors should assess whether individual Board Members have the knowledge and experience that is required to advise management in light of the particularities of that Company, its businesses, and the competitive environment. Board Members who lack the skills, knowledge and expertise to conduct a meaningful review of the Company's activities are more likely to defer to management when making decisions. Such reliance on management not only threatens the duty to consider Shareowner interests first, but also could threaten the Company's overall performance if Board Members are not capable of in-depth evaluations of the issues affecting the Company's business. (See also the discussion relating to the nominations committee, on page 175.)

Other Things to Consider. Among the factors Investors should consider when analyzing Board Members'[9] qualifications are whether the Board Members:

- are able to make informed decisions about the Company's future.
- are able to act with care and competence as a result of relevant expertise or understanding of:
  - the principal technologies, products or services offered in the Company's business,
  - financial operations,
  - legal matters,
  - accounting,
  - auditing,
  - strategic planning, and
  - the risks the Company assumes as part of its business operations.
- have made public statements that can provide an indication of their ethical perspectives.
- have had legal or regulatory problems as a result of working for, or serving on, the Board of another Company.
- have experience serving on other Boards, particularly with Companies known for having good corporate governance practices.
- serve on a number of Boards for other Companies, constraining the time needed to serve effectively.[10]
- regularly attend Board and committee meetings.

---

[9] The factors to consider are drawn from an upcoming CFA Institute textbook on corporate finance.

[10] Some corporate governance codes, including the code in Pakistan, put a limit on the number of Company Boards on which Board Members may participate. In Pakistan, for example, the limit is 10 Board mandates for a Board Member.

- have committed to the needs of Shareowners, for example by making significant investments in the Company or by avoiding situations or businesses that could create a conflict of interest with his or her position as a Board Member.
- have the background, expertise, and knowledge in specific subjects needed by the Board.
- have served individually on the Board for more than 10 years. Such long-term participation may enhance the individual Board Member's knowledge of the Company, but it also may cause the Board Member to develop a cooperative relationship with management that could impair his/her willingness to act in the best interests of Shareowners.

Investors should also review:

- disclosures made by the Company about the number of Board and committee meetings held during the past year, and individual Board Member attendance records.
- whether the Board and its committees performed a self-assessment and, if available, any information relating to this assessment. This review will help Investors determine whether the Board has the competence and Independence to respond to the competitive and financial challenges facing the Company.
- whether the Board voluntarily or under the requirement of a governance code provides adequate training for Board Members on their roles and responsibilities.

Where to find information about the qualifications of Board Members:

- Many listed Companies post the names and qualifications of Board Members on their websites. Companies also typically provide information about their Board Members in the annual report to Shareowners and, where applicable, in their annual proxy statements.
- In many countries, Companies report on the number of Board and Board committee meetings, as well as attendance by individual Board Members, in their annual reports, on their websites, or, where applicable, in their annual corporate governance reports and proxy statements.
- Some corporate governance codes in jurisdictions such as Australia, Canada, the United Kingdom, and the United States require listed Companies to disclose in their annual reports if they failed to comply with the codes' provisions and why they did not comply.
- The European Union has adopted a European Commission recommendation that the Board of listed Companies annually discuss their internal organizations, their procedures and the extent to which their self-assessments have led to material changes.
- In the United States, Companies typically list the names and qualifications of Board Members, together with the Board's report to Shareowners, in the annual proxy statement, as well as on their websites. The nominations committee also includes its report concerning its members and activities in the annual proxy statement.

Authority to Hire External Consultants

Investors should determine whether the Board and its committees have budgetary authority to hire Independent third-party consultants without having to receive approval from management.

Implications for Investors. It is important to recognize that Independent Board Members typically have limited time to devote to their Board duties. Consequently Board Members need support in gathering and analyzing a large amount of information relevant to managing and overseeing the Company.

The Board and its committees often need specialized and Independent advice as they consider various corporate issues and risks such as compensation, proposed mergers and acquisitions, legal, regulatory, financial matters and reputational concerns. The ability to hire external consultants without first having to seek management's approval provides the Board with an Independent means of receiving advice uninfluenced by management's interests.

It also ensures that the Board receives specialized advice on technical decisions that could affect Shareowner value.

Other Things to Consider. Among other issues, Investors should determine whether:

- at relevant periods in the past the Board hired external financial consultants to help it consider mergers, acquisitions, divestitures, and risk management issues.
- the nominations committee has used external advisers in the past to recruit qualified nominees for management or for the Board.
- the remuneration committee has hired external advisers in the past to help determine appropriate compensation for key executives.

Where to find information about the authority of the Board to hire external consultants: The most likely places to find information relating to the Board's authority to hire external consultants are:

- the corporate governance section of the Company's annual report;
- the annual corporate governance report to Shareowners;
- the corporate governance section of the Company's website; or
- the charter for the Board or its committees.

Other places to find this kind of information:

- the Company's articles of organization or by-laws; or
- national corporate governance codes or stock exchange-mandated corporate governance requirements.

Other Board Issues

Board Member Terms

Shareowners should determine whether Board Members are elected annually, or whether the Company has adopted an election process that staggers the terms of Board Member elections.

Reasons for Reviewing Board Member Terms. Investors need to understand the mechanisms that provide, limit, or eliminate altogether their ability to exercise their rights to vote on individual Board Members.

Implications for Investors. Companies that prevent Shareowners from approving or rejecting Board Members on an annual basis limit Shareowners' ability to change the Board's composition, for example, when Board Members fail to act on their behalf, or to elect individuals with needed expertise in response to a change in Company strategy.

Things to Consider. When reviewing a Company's policy for the election of Board Members, Investors should consider whether:

- Shareowners may elect Board Members every year, or for staggered multiple-year terms (known as a classified Board). An annually elected Board may provide more flexibility to nominate new Board Members to meet changes in the marketplace, if needed, than a classified Board. Staggered Boards also may serve as an anti-takeover device.[11] On the other hand, a classified Board may provide better continuity of Board expertise.

  In Japan, Shareowners of a Company that uses a Corporate Auditors System elect Board Members for two-year terms, and Members of the Corporate Auditors Board for four-year terms. Shareowners of a Company using a Committees System elect Board Members every year.

- the Board has filled a vacancy for the remainder of a Board Member's term without receiving Shareowner approval at the next annual general meeting.
- Shareowners can vote to remove a Board Member under certain circumstances.
- the Board is the appropriate size for the facts and circumstances of the Company. A large Board may have difficulty coordinating its Members' views, be slow to act, and defer more frequently to the chief executive. A small Board may lack depth of experience and counsel, and may not be able to adequately spread the work load among its Members to operate effectively.

Where to find information about the mechanisms related to Board elections and structure:

- In most cases, the best place to find information regarding the election of Board Members is in the notice of the Company's annual general meeting. In the United States and Canada, this information is typically part of the annual proxy statement to Shareowners.
- Investors also should check the Company's by-laws and articles of organization to determine whether management and the Board can fill any vacancies without Shareowner approval.

Related-Party Transactions

Investors should investigate whether the Company engages in outside business relationships with management or Board Members, or individuals associated with them, for goods and services on behalf of the Company.

---

[11] See especially, "The Powerful Antitakeover Force of Staggered Boards: Theory, Evidence, and Policy," by Lucian A. Bebchuk, John C. Coates, IV, and Guhan Subramanian, *Stanford Law Review*, Vol. 54, Issue 5, pg. 887-952. The authors conclude that the ballot box route to a takeover is illusory for a company with an effective staggered Board because, in part, a bidder must foster interest and votes during two elections spread at least 14 months apart.

Reasons for Reviewing the Company's Policies on Related-Party Transactions. As they relate to Board Members, policies that cover related-party transactions attempt to ensure the Independence of Board Members by discouraging them from engaging in the following practices, among others:

- receiving consultancy fees for work performed on behalf of the Company;
- receiving finders' fees for bringing merger, acquisition or sale partners to the Company's attention;

Implications for Investors. Receiving personal benefits from the Company for which Board Members are supposed to make Independent decisions can create an inherent conflict of interest, when these benefits fall outside the role of a Board Member. Limitations on such transactions, either through the Company's ethical code or Board policies, reduce the likelihood that management can use Company resources to sway Board Members' allegiance away from Shareowners.

Other Things to Consider. When reviewing a Company's policies regarding related-party transactions, Investors should determine whether:

- the Company's ethical code or the Board's policies and procedures limit the circumstances in which insiders, including Board Members and their associates, can accept remuneration from the Company for consulting or other services outside of the scope of their positions as Board Members. The intent of such provisions is not only to discourage actions that could compromise Board Members' Independence, but also to discourage the Company from entering into contracts that may not provide the best value to the Company and its Shareowners.
- the Company has disclosed any material related-party transactions or commercial relationships with existing Board Members or Board nominees. (See a discussion of this issue under Board Independence on page 165.)
- Board Members or executive officers have lent, leased or otherwise provided property or equipment to the Company.
- the Company has paid Board Members finders' fees for their roles in acquisitions or other significant Company transactions.

Where to find information about business transactions between the Company and its Board Members, management, or controlling Shareowners:

- The annual reports of Companies in many countries include a discussion of insider transactions and fees paid to Board Members and controlling Shareowners, often under the heading of "Related-Party" transactions.
- In the United States, listed Companies are required to provide information relating to dealings with insiders in the annual proxy statement, often under the heading of "Related-Party Transactions."
- Investors also should review the prospectus of a Company preceding a public offering of securities for any related-party transactions disclosures. This document should inform Investors about transactions that permit insiders to purchase shares at a discount prior to an offering at a higher price.

Board Committees

Audit Committee

Investors should determine whether the Board has established a committee of Independent Board Members, including those with recent and relevant experience of finance and accounting, to oversee the audit of the Company's financial reports.

The Purpose of the Audit Committee. The audit committee's primary objective is to ensure that the financial information reported by the Company to Shareowners is complete, accurate, reliable, relevant and timely.

To this end, the audit committee is responsible for hiring and supervising the Independent external auditors, ensuring that the external auditors' priorities are aligned with the best interests of Shareowners, and ensuring that:

- the information included in the financial reports to Shareowners is complete, accurate, reliable, relevant, verifiable and timely;
- the financial statements are prepared in accordance with generally accepted accounting principles (GAAP) and regulatory disclosure requirements;
- the audit is conducted in accordance with generally accepted auditing standards (GAAS);
- that the external auditor is Independent of management influence;
- that all conflicts of interest between the external auditor and the Company are resolved in favor of the Shareowners; and
- that the Independent auditors have authority over the audit of the entire corporate group, including foreign subsidiaries and affiliated Companies.

Implications for Investors. If the Independence of the audit committee is undermined, it could compromise the integrity of the financial reporting process and raise doubts about the credibility of the Company's financial statements. Misrepresentations of, or other distortions about, the Company's performance and financial condition ultimately could have a detrimental effect on the Company's share valuation.

What to Consider. Investors should determine whether:

- all of the Board Members serving on the audit committee are Independent. Some jurisdictions permit Board Members who are not Independent to serve on the committee. Japan, for example, requires that the committee have three or more members, a majority of whom are either Independent Board Members or Non-Executive Board Members.[12]
- any of the Board Members serving on the audit committee are considered financial experts.[13]

---

[12] Japan's Commercial Code has similar requirements for remuneration/compensation and nominating committees.

[13] Under SEC rules developed in response to Sarbanes-Oxley, a financial expert is a director who: (i) understands GAAP and financial statements; (ii) can assess the application of GAAP for estimates, accruals and reserves; (iii) has prepared, audited, analyzed or evaluated financial statements similar to those of the Company, or has experience supervising those who performed these functions; (iv) understands internal controls and financial reporting procedures; and (v) understands audit committee functions. They may acquire these attributes through: education and experience as or supervising a principal financial officer, principal accounting officer, controller, public accountant or auditor; overseeing or assessing companies or public accountants in the preparation, auditing or evaluation of financial statements; or from other relevant experience. See: www.sec.gov/rules/final/33-8177.htm, under "Audit Committee Financial Experts."

Implications for Investors. The existence of the committee and its Independence from executive management bias help to ensure that the rewards and incentives offered to management are consistent with the best long-term interests of Shareowners. Committees that lack Independence could be overly pressured by management to award compensation that is excessive when compared with other comparably situated Companies, or to provide incentives for actions that boost short-term share prices at the expense of long-term profitability and value.

Other Things to Consider. As part of their analyses relating to this committee, Investors should determine whether:

- the composition of the compensation packages offered to senior management are appropriate.
- the Company provided loans or the use of Company property and equipment such as airplanes and real estate to Board Members.
- members of the committee regularly attended meetings during the past year.
- the committee has policies and procedures and, if so, what they are.
- the Company has provided detailed information to Shareowners in public documents relating to the compensation paid during the past year to the Company's five highest-paid executives and its Board Members. Investors also should review any disclosures about the major components and amounts paid to these individuals. Some jurisdictions only require Companies to provide summary information about the compensation of senior management and the Board.
- the terms and conditions of options granted to management and employees and whether the terms are reasonable.
- the Company intends to issue newly registered shares to fulfill its share-based remuneration obligations, or whether it intends to settle these options with shares repurchased in the open market.
- the Company and the Board are required to receive Shareowner approval for any share-based remuneration plans. Such plans affect the number of shares outstanding and, consequently, current Shareowners' ownership interests, as well as the basis on which earnings per share are reported and the market valuations of the Company's securities.
- senior executives from other Companies that have cross-directorship links with the Company are members of the committee. Executive remuneration is often based on compensation of similarly positioned individuals at other Companies, and if the committee has individuals who could benefit directly from reciprocal decisions on remuneration, those decisions may not be in the best interests of the subject Company's Shareowners. (Also see a discussion relating to Board Independence on page 165.)

Where to find information about the remuneration/compensation committee:

Australia—Companies that list on the Australian Stock Exchange are required to disclose in their annual reports if they did not comply with the exchange's recommendations for remuneration committees, together with an explanation of why they did not comply.

Canada—The Toronto Stock Exchange requires Companies listed on its markets to report in their annual reports or their management information and proxy circulars whether they have a compensation committee and, if so, whether it is comprised of Independent or Non-Executive Board Members, and whether a majority are Independent.

European Union—European Commission's non-binding recommendations state that Companies should report their remuneration policies and amounts paid to executive management in the annual report. Also, Companies listed in the United Kingdom are required to report in their annual reports on the frequency of, and attendance by, members at remuneration committee meetings. These Companies also must disclose the responsibilities delegated to the committee.

United States—Listed Companies report on whether there is a standing compensation committee in their annual proxy statements. These reports also include names of committee members, summaries of compensation strategies, and the policies and procedures of the committee.

Nominations Committee

Investors should determine if the Company has a nominations committee of Independent Board Members that is responsible for recruiting Board Members.

The purpose of the nominations committee. The nominations committee is responsible for:

- recruiting new Board Members with appropriate qualities and experience in light of the Company's business needs;
- regularly examining the performance, Independence, skills and expertise of existing Board Members to determine whether they meet the current and future needs of the Company and the Board;
- creating nominations policies and procedures;
- preparing for the succession of executive management and the Board.

Implications for Investors. The slate of candidates proposed by this committee will affect whether the Board works for the benefit of Shareowners. It is important for this committee to remain Independent[16] to ensure that it recruits individuals who can and will work on behalf of Shareowners, and to ensure that the performance assessment of current Board Members is fair and appropriate. (Also see Board Member Qualifications on page 166.)

Other Things to Consider. Investors may have to review Company reports over several years to adequately assess whether this committee has recruited Board Members who act in the interests of Shareowners. They also should review:

- the criteria for new Board Members.
- the composition, background and areas of expertise of existing Board Members, and whether new nominees complement the Board's current portfolio of talents.
- how the committee finds potential new Board Members. Among the considerations is whether the committee engages in a search for candidates, such as by using an executive search firm, or whether its members rely upon the advice of management or other Board Members.
- the attendance records of Board Members at regular and special meetings.
- whether the Company has a succession plan for executive management in the event of unforeseen circumstances, such as the sudden incapacitation of the chief operating and finance officers. Investors should examine the information provided by the Company about the plan and determine who is expected to lead and implement it.

[16] Please see a discussion of the Independence of committees, particularly in Japan, under the discussion above concerning the "Audit Committee."

- the report of the committee, including any discussion of its actions and decisions during the previous year (including the number of meetings held, attendance by committee members, and the committee's policies and procedures).

Where to find information about the nominating committee:

- The annual reports of Companies in many countries include a general discussion of the actions taken by the committee during the previous year.
- The annual reports of Companies listed in some countries, such as Australia and the United Kingdom, are required to disclose and explain when a Company fails to comply with applicable nomination committee rules.
- The corporate governance report often includes an explanation of the Company's nominations process and whether they have a specially designated nominations committee.
- In some regions, such as North America, Investors should look in the annual proxy statement to Shareowners for indications about the work of this committee, including the name of each committee member and the number of meetings held.
- The websites of many listed Companies describe the activities and members of the committee and, in some countries, provide information about the committee's charter.

Other Board Committees

Investors should determine whether the Board has other committees that are responsible for overseeing management's activities in certain areas, such as corporate governance, mergers and acquisitions, legal matters or risk management.

Implications for Investors. Depending on the purpose, committees created by the Board can provide additional insight into the goals, focus and strategies of the Company. For example, a committee dedicated to risk management might consider the identification and quantification of risks faced by the Company, and determine its optimal risk exposure.

Whether these committees consist of only Independent Members is an important factor to weigh in evaluating the degree to which the committee is dedicated to achieving what is best for the Company and Shareowners, or may be improperly influenced by management and other insiders.

Other Things to Consider. Because such committees often are not covered by national corporate governance codes or exchange-mandated guidelines in the manner that audit, remuneration or nominations committees are, they are more likely to have members who are part of executive management. Consequently, the Independence of these committees may not, and possibly need not, achieve the levels of Independence expected of such committees as audit, nominations and remuneration.

Where to find information about other Board committees:
As in the case with the audit, compensation and nominations committees, there are four primary places to look for information about special-purpose committees, namely:

- The annual reports to Shareowners;
- The annual corporate governance report, where applicable; and
- In regions like the United States and Canada, the annual proxy statement to Shareowners.
- The websites of listed Companies.

MANAGEMENT

While the Board helps set the strategic, ethical and financial course for a Company in consultation with management, Investors ultimately must rely on management to implement that course. Management also has the responsibility to communicate to Investors and the public about the Company's performance, financial condition and any changes in strategy or corporate initiatives in an effective and timely manner.

Investors are familiar with the reports that management issues with regard to a Company's financial performance and condition. However, they may not be aware of other sources of information that may provide insight into the corporate culture or governance practices of a Company. In fact, there are various sources of information available to Investors for evaluating management's role in corporate governance practices, aside from the financial reports that Companies issue.

To help Investors better understand management's role and responsibilities in corporate governance matters, the following section provides a general discussion of a Company's code of ethics and corporate culture, followed by specific discussions of common areas of focus on ethical practices such as related-party transactions, executive compensation, contractual arrangements, share repurchase programs and takeover defenses.

Implementation of Code of Ethics

Investors should determine whether the Company has adopted a code of ethics, and whether the Company's actions indicate a commitment to an appropriate ethical framework.

The Purpose of a Code of Ethics. A Company's code of ethics sets standards for ethical conduct based on basic principles of integrity, trust, and honesty. It provides personnel with a framework for behavior while conducting the Company's business, as well as guidance for addressing conflicts of interest. In effect, it represents a part of the Company's risk management policies which are intended to prevent Company representatives from engaging in practices that could harm the Company, its products, or Shareowners.

Implications for Investors. Reported breaches of ethics in a Company often result in regulatory sanctions, fines, management turnover, and unwanted negative media coverage, all of which can adversely affect the Company's performance. Adoption and adherence to an appropriate corporate code of ethics indicates a commitment on the part of management to establish and maintain ethical practices. The existence of such a code may also be a mitigating factor from regulatory actions when breaches do occur.

Things to Consider. As part of their analyses of the Company's ethical climate, Investors should determine whether the Company:

- gives the Board access to relevant corporate information in a timely and comprehensive manner.
- is in compliance with the corporate governance code of the country where it is located, or the governance requirements of the stock exchange that lists its securities. Typically, Companies must disclose whether they have failed to adhere to such codes and, if so, give reasons for the failure. In some cases, non-compliance may result in fines or sanctions by regulators. The Company also may face informal sanctions, such as product boycotting from customers or political groups.
- has an ethical code and whether that code prohibits any practice that would provide advantages to Company insiders that are not also offered to

Shareowners. For example, a code might prohibit the Company from offering shares at discounted prices to management, Board Members and other insiders prior to a public offering of securities to prevent dilution of the value and interests of those who buy at the public offering price.

- has designated someone who is responsible for corporate governance.
- has an ethical code that provides waivers from its prohibitions to certain levels of management, and the reasons why.
- waived any of its code's provisions during recent periods, and why.
- regularly performs an audit of its governance policies and procedures to make improvements.

Where to find information about a Company's Code of Ethics and other ethical matters:

- The annual reports of Companies listed in some countries such as Australia disclose when and why a Company failed to meet applicable governance standards regarding the creation and implementation of a code of conduct.
- Companies with ethical codes typically post them on their public websites, in their annual reports to Shareowners, or, in countries that require them, in their annual corporate governance reports.
- Investors may check on the requirements of a country's national corporate governance code or exchange-mandated governance requirements.

Personal Use of Company Assets

Investors should determine whether the Company permits Board Members, management and their family members to use Company assets for personal reasons.

Reasons for Reviewing the Company's Policies on the Personal Use of Company Assets. As they relate to Board Members, policies that limit or prohibit the use of Company assets by insiders attempt to ensure that resources are used in the most efficient and productive manner for the purpose of generating returns for the Company and all of its Shareowners. Such policies and procedures also seek to preserve the Independence of Board Members by attempting to prevent the conflicts of interest that may result when Board Members or their families use Company assets.

Implications for Investors. When insiders such as Board Members, managers and their families use Company assets for personal reasons, those resources are not available for investment in productive and income-generating activities. Such use also creates conflicts of interest for Board Members.

Other Things to Consider. When reviewing a Company's policies regarding the personal use of Company assets, Investors should determine whether the Company:

- has an ethical code or policies and procedures that place strict limits on the ability of insiders to use Company assets for personal benefit.
- has lent cash or other resources to Board Members, management or their families.
- has purchased property or other assets such as houses or airplanes for the personal use of Board Members, management, or their family members.
- has leased assets such as dwellings or transportation vehicles to Board Members, management or their family members, and whether the terms of such contracts are appropriate given market conditions.

Where to find information about insider transactions involving Board Members, management and controlling Shareowners:

- Investors may find information about loans to Company executives, Board Members or their families in the "Related Party Transactions" sections of a Company's annual report, its annual corporate governance report, annual proxy statement to Shareowners, or its website.
- Investors also should review the prospectus of a Company preceding a public offering of securities for any related-party transactions disclosures. This document should inform Investors about transactions that permit insiders to purchase shares at a discount prior to an offering at a higher price.

Corporate Transparency

Executive Compensation

Investors should analyze both the amounts paid to key executives for managing the Company's affairs and the manner in which compensation is provided to determine whether compensation paid to its executives is commensurate with the executives' level of responsibilities and performance, and provides appropriate incentives.

Reasons for Reviewing Executive Compensation Disclosures. Disclosures of how much, in what manner, and on what basis executive management is paid shed light on the Board's stewardship of Shareowner assets. Furthermore, they allow Investors to evaluate whether the compensation is reasonable in light of the apparent return to the Company in terms of performance.

Implications for Shareowners. The manner in which executive management is compensated can affect Shareowner value in a number of ways. A flawed compensation program may encourage executives to make decisions that generate additional compensation to them through short-term gains, rather than implement an appropriate strategy that focuses on long-term growth. It also could dilute the ownership positions of existing Shareowners. On the other hand, an appropriately designed program can create incentives for Company executives to generate positive results for Shareowners.

Things to Consider. When reviewing a Company's executive compensation disclosures, Investors should examine the reported:

- Remuneration/Compensation strategy. An examination of the terms and conditions of the Company's executive compensation program, together with an analysis of summaries of agreements with executives, will help Investors determine whether the program rewards long-term growth, or short-term increases in share value. This review should include a determination of whether the remuneration/compensation committee uses consultants to set pay for Company executives, or whether it relies on internal sources. Investors also should focus on whether the rewards offered to management are based on the performance of the Company relative to its competitors or other peers, or on some other metric.
- Executive compensation. Analysis of the actual compensation paid to the Company's top executives during recent years and the elements of the compensation packages offered to key employees can help Investors determine whether the Company is receiving adequate returns for the investment it has made in executive management.

- Share-based compensation terms. Examination of the terms of this type of remuneration program, including the total shares offered to key executives and other employees, should alert Investors to how the program can affect shares outstanding, dilution of Shareowner interests, and share values. Investors also should determine whether the Company seeks Shareowner approval for creation or amendments to such plans. (See Shareowner Rights section beginning on page 182 for other issues that may require a vote of Shareowners.)
- Stock-option expensing. Compensation, regardless of whether it is paid in cash, shares or share options, involves payment for services received and should appear as an expense on the income statement. International Financial Reporting Standards (IFRS) and U.S. Generally Accepted Accounting Principles both require Companies to expense stock option grants.[17]
- Performance-based compensation. Investors should determine whether stock options and stock grants, as well as stock-appreciation rights and other performance-based compensation programs, are linked to the long-term profitability and share-price performance of the Company relative to its competitors and peers. The purpose of compensation is to reward management for gains attributable directly to superior performance, and linking pay to performance is one way to achieve this purpose.
- Option repricing. Investors should remain aware of efforts by the Company to reprice downward the **strike prices** of stock options previously granted. Changes in the strike price remove the incentives the original options created for management, and therefore reduce the link between long-term profitability and performance and management remuneration.
- Share ownership of management. Investors should determine whether members of management have share holdings other than those related to stock option grants. Such holdings may align the interests of Company executives with those of Shareowners.

Where to find information about executive compensation:

- In many jurisdictions, Companies report information about executive compensation in their annual reports. In some cases, disclosures about amounts paid to individual executives is voluntary, although accounting standards setters and securities regulators are increasingly making such disclosures compulsory.
- In the United States, executive compensation strategies and reports of actual compensation paid to key executives are included in the Company's annual proxy statement to Shareowners.
- Investors also may find such information posted on Companies' websites.

Share-Repurchase and Price Stabilization Programs

Shareowners should inquire into the size, purpose, means of financing and duration of share-repurchase programs and price stabilization efforts.

Reasons for Reviewing Disclosures of Share-Repurchase and Stabilization Programs. A Company will use a share-repurchase program to buy its own shares that are already trading on a public stock exchange. In a stabilization program, the Company has its investment bankers buy and sell shares following a public offering of shares as a means of reducing the price volatility of the shares.

[17] This requirement is applicable for U.S.-listed companies with fiscal years that end after 15 June 2005.

Implications for Investors. Buying shares on the open market can have a positive effect on share values by reducing the number of shares available and increasing the value for the remaining shares outstanding. Price-stabilization programs may reduce the volatility of a security's price following an offering and permit the market to achieve a balance between buyers and sellers, but may provide insiders with an opportunity to trade at a higher price in anticipation that the share price will decline—or to buy at a lower price in anticipation of future price gains.

Things to Consider. When reviewing share-repurchase and stabilization programs, Investors should determine the:

- Intention of the Program. Investors should determine whether the Board intends to use repurchased shares i) to reduce the number of shares outstanding to increase long-term valuations, ii) to fund the future exercise of management share options, or iii) to prevent a hostile takeover. Depending on the perspective of the Investor, the program may enhance or hurt long-term share value. Fixed-income Investors, for example, may view the use of cash to repurchase shares as detrimental to the ability of the Company to repay its outstanding debts.[18] Equity Investors, on the other hand, may see such actions as beneficial to their valuations.
- Size of and Financing for the Program. This information, together with disclosures about whether the Company plans to use internally generated cash from operations or issue debt to finance the purchases can help equity Investors determine how the program will affect the value of the Company's shares.

In addition, Investors should review:

- regular updates on the program's progress. In particular, Investors should review the prices at which open-market purchases of shares were made, the number of shares purchased, cumulative amounts of shares repurchased to date, and the average price paid to date. This information should help them anticipate completion of the program and how that may affect share value. It also should help them determine whether the program is proceeding as planned or exceeding original intentions for scope and cost.
- disclosures relating to stabilization activities. Following a public securities offering, a Company may contract with its securities underwriters to stabilize the price of the offering through the active purchase and sale of the securities in the open market. Investors should determine prior to investing in a public offering of securities whether the Company intends to use such stabilization services, and subsequently review updates about the number of shares purchased and sold under the program, the average price paid and received, and when the activities concluded. This information will indicate whether the Company and its advisers acted as proposed or whether they engaged in unintended or undisclosed activities.

Where to find information about share repurchase and stabilization programs:

- The annual and interim reports of Companies will, in most cases, provide the information relating to a share-repurchase program.
- The prospectus for an offering should include initial information relating

[18] Bond indentures may require that the Company repay outstanding debt securities or receive a waiver from bondholders prior to launching a share repurchase program.

to stabilization activities. Annual and interim financial reports should provide final information about the activities of stabilization programs.

- Investors should look to the prospectus of an offering to determine whether at the time of the offering the Company intended to use agents to perform price stabilization services following the issuance of the securities.

Post-stabilization disclosure. In the European Union, Companies are required by the Market Abuse Directive to disclose whether stabilization activities were undertaken and, if so, the dates the program began and ended, and the range of prices at which such activities were conducted. The ultimate disclosures will come from either the issuer or the lead underwriter.

The U.S. Securities and Exchange Commission currently does not require post-stabilization disclosures like those of the European Union, though it is considering implementation of one.[19] Currently Nasdaq requires market makers to attach a special symbol to an order for this purpose while other exchanges require underwriters to notify the exchange and provide disclosure to the recipient of the bid that such bids are part of a stabilization program.

Likewise, disclosure in many other jurisdictions is required to be made only to the Company and the exchange.

SHAREOWNER RIGHTS

The value of a financial security is determined not only by its claim on the Company's future earnings but also on the rights associated with those securities. Among the rights associated with shares of common stock is the right to elect Board Members and to vote on matters that may affect the value of their holdings, such as mergers or acquisitions. Other rights may include the right to apply the cumulative votes of one's shares to one or a limited number of Board nominees, the ability to nominate persons to the Board, or to propose changes to Company operations.

Shareowners may not have all these rights in all cases, and even when they do they may have difficulty exercising them. For example, Companies in some regions can restrict voting only to those owners who are present at scheduled meetings of Shareowners, or prevent Shareowners from trading for a designated period prior to the annual general meeting in return for exercising that vote. In other cases, individuals and institutions cannot confidentially cast their votes. In still other cases, founding-family members or government Shareowners may exercise disproportional influence over the Companies' affairs though the ownership of special classes of shares that grant them super-voting rights.

Shareowners may have powers to remedy situations in certain cases, though such remedies are not universal. Local laws and regulations also may provide legal or regulatory redress.

---

[19] "Amendments to Regulation M: Anti-Manipulation Rules Concerning Securities Offerings; Proposed Rule," 17 December 2004, (Federal Register, Vol. 69, No. 242, page 75782), under the third question: "Should the Commission consider, in addition to the proposed disclosure, revising Rule 104 to require a general notification to the market (e.g., through a press release, a website posting, or an administrative message sent over the Tape) that [the] activity has commenced (and another notification when [the activity] has ceased)?"

Such issues are of interest not only to equity Investors, but also to Investors interested in **fixed-income investments**. For example, Companies that grant super-voting rights to a certain class of stock and Shareowners historically use debt financing more than equity financing to fund investments in new business opportunities.[20] Such a strategy may raise the financial risk of a Company and, ultimately, increase the possibility of default.

It is important for Investors to recognize what specific rights are attached to the securities they are considering and factor that information into any investment decisions. Doing so may avoid situations that result in reduced valuations and poor investment performance.

Following is a discussion of issues that Investors should consider in evaluating the Shareowner rights of different Companies.

Shareowner Voting

Proxy Voting

Investors should determine whether the Company permits Shareowners to vote their shares by proxy regardless of whether they are able to attend the meetings in person.

Reasons for Evaluating a Company's Voting Rules. The ability to vote one's shares is a fundamental right of share ownership. In some jurisdictions, Shareowners may find it difficult to vote their shares because the Company accepts only those votes cast at its annual general meeting, and does not allow them the right to vote by proxy or imposes other constraints.

Implications for Investors. By making it difficult for Shareowners to vote their common shares, the Company limits a Shareowner's ability to choose Board Members or otherwise to express their views on other initiatives that could alter the Company's course.

Things to Consider. In examining whether a Company permits proxy voting, Investors should consider whether the Company:

- limits Shareowners' ability to cast votes by conditioning the exercise of their right to vote on their presence at the annual general meeting.
- coordinates the timing of its annual general meeting with other Companies in its region to ensure that all of them hold their meetings on the same day but in different locations. In some regions that require Shareowners to attend such meetings to vote, such actions seek to prevent Shareowners from attending all the meetings, and, therefore, from exercising their voting rights.
- permits proxy voting by means of paper ballot, electronic voting, proxy voting services, or by some other remote mechanism.
- is permitted under its national governance code to use share blocking, whereby it prevents Investors that wish to exercise their voting rights to trade their shares during a period prior to the annual general meeting to permit the Company and various financial institutions certify who owns the shares.

Where to find information about the Company's proxy voting rules:

- Investors also can look to the Company's corporate governance statement for information about whether proxy voting is permitted.

[20] A December 2003 study by Gompers, et. al, found that companies with two classes of common shares that separated the voting rights from the cash flow rights resulted in underinvestment and lower valuations. See Gompers, et. al, "Incentives vs. Control: An Analysis of U.S. Dual-Class Companies," knowledge.wharton.upenn.edu/papers/1278.pdf.

- In the United States, the proxy statement will describe the mechanisms by which Shareowners can cast their votes by proxy.
- Investors can look to the Company's articles of organization and by-laws to determine the mechanisms Shareowners can use to vote their shares.

- Also in the United States, state corporation law regulates issues relating to proxies. Consequently, Investors may have to determine the state in which a Company is incorporated—typically found in the Articles of Incorporation—to review the proxy regulations governing the Company.

Confidential Voting and Vote Tabulation

Investors should determine whether Shareowners are able to cast confidential votes.

Reasons for Determining Whether Shareowners Are Able to Cast Confidential Votes. Shareowners are more likely to vote and to do so conscientiously if they are assured that Board Members and management will not find out how they voted.

Implications for Investors. Confidentiality of voting insures that all votes are counted equally, and that the Board Members and management cannot re-solicit the votes of individuals and institutions who vote against the positions of these insiders until the votes are officially recorded.[21]

Things to Consider. In examining whether Shareowners can vote anonymously, Investors should consider whether:

- the Company uses a third-party entity to tabulate Shareowner votes.
- the Company or its third-party agent retains voting records.
- the vote tabulation performed by the Company or its third-party agent is subject to an audit to ensure accuracy.
- Shareowners are permitted to vote only if they are present at a scheduled Company meeting. (See "Proxy Voting" on page 183 for a discussion of this issue.)

Where to find information concerning confidentiality of voting rights:

- Investors should look to the Company's by-laws or articles of organization to determine the procedures for counting and tabulating Shareowner votes.

Cumulative Voting

Shareowners should determine whether Shareowners can cast the cumulative number of votes allotted to their shares for one or a limited number of Board nominees ("cumulative voting").

Implications for Investors. The ability to use cumulative voting enables Shareowners to vote in a manner that enhances the likelihood that their interests are represented on the Board.

Things to Consider. In evaluating how a Company handles cumulative voting, Investors should consider whether:

[21] In the case of pooled investment funds, CFA Institute has taken the position that the funds should disclose to investors how they voted the shares of each company on behalf of the fund's beneficiaries. Such disclosures are different from disclosing those votes to management and the Board in that the investment fund is disclosing its voting record to the beneficiaries on whose behalf it is acting.

- the Company has a significant minority Shareowner group, such as a founding family, that might be able to use cumulative voting to elect Board Members that represent its specific interests at the expense of the interests of other Shareowners.

Where to find information about whether a Company permits cumulative voting:

- The articles of organization and by-laws frequently provide information regarding how a Company regards Shareowner initiatives and rights.
- The prospectus that a listed Company must file with the local regulator will typically describe the circumstances under which Shareowners can exercise their voting rights.
- In the United States, Investors also may look to the Form 8-A that listed Companies must file with the Securities and Exchange Commission for a description of the rights afforded a Company's common shares.

Voting for Other Corporate Changes

Shareowners should determine whether Shareowners can approve changes to corporate structures and policies that may alter the relationship between Shareowners and the Company.

Reasons for Considering Shareowner Input on Corporate Changes. Changes to certain corporate structures have the ability to affect the value, ownership percentage, and rights associated with the Company's securities. Among the issues Shareowners should review is the ability of Shareowners to effect changes to the Company's:

- articles of organization,
- by-laws,
- governance structures,
- voting rights and mechanisms,
- poison pills, and
- change-in-control provisions.

Implications for Investors. Certain changes to the Company's by-laws or articles of organization can affect the Shareowner's interests in the Company. For example, the introduction or modification of an anti-takeover mechanism might make a takeover too expensive for potential acquirers to consider, thereby denying Shareowners full market value for their shares. Likewise, providing large quantities of stock options to management and employees might dilute the value of shares held by existing Shareowners, while redistributing Company resources to insiders without Shareowner approval.

Things to Consider. In reviewing what issues require Shareowner approval, Investors should determine whether Shareowners:

- must approve such proposals with supermajority votes.
- will have an opportunity to vote on the sale of their Company, or a substantial portion of their Company, to a third-party buyer. Investors also may wish to consider whether Shareowners have an opportunity to vote on significant acquisitions and divestitures that could increase or reduce annual revenues by 10% or more and whether there is a threshold for approval of such transactions.

- The prospectus relating to the initial or follow-on offerings of common shares to the public is likely to include a discussion about different classes of common shares, including whether any entity or group of Investors retains sufficient voting power to overrule certain management or Board decisions.
- The notes to the financial statements, particularly in the annual report, will likely disclose the existence of different classes of common shares.

Shareowner Legal Rights

Investors should determine whether the corporate governance code and other legal statutes of the jurisdiction in which the Company is headquartered permit Shareowners to take legal or seek regulatory action to protect and enforce their ownership rights.

Reasons for Determining the Legal Remedies Available to Shareowners. In situations where the Company has failed to fully recognize their rights, Shareowners may have to turn to the courts or national regulators to enforce their rights of ownership.

Things to Consider: When reviewing the local governance code and legal statutes regarding legal and regulatory actions, Investors should determine whether:

- local legal statutes permit Shareowners to take derivative legal actions—which permit Shareowners to initiate legal actions against management or Board Members on behalf of the Company—and, if so, what conditions must be met.
- the regulator in the local market where the Company is headquartered has taken action in other cases to enforce Shareowner rights or to prevent the denial of Shareowner rights.
- Shareowners, either individually or as a class, are permitted to take legal or regulatory action to enforce fraud charges against management or the Board.
- Shareowners have "dissenters' rights" requiring the company to repurchase their shares at fair market value following such transactions.

Where to find information about legal and regulatory relief for Shareowners:

- The regulator in the local market of the Company's headquarters may provide information about the remedies available to Shareowners in a variety of legal regulatory matters.

Takeover Defenses

Shareowners should carefully evaluate the structure of an existing or proposed takeover defenses and analyze how they could affect the value of shares in a normal market environment and in the event of a takeover bid.

Reasons for Reviewing Disclosures Relating to Takeover Defenses. Such disclosures should provide Shareowners with information about the situations in which takeover defenses—such as so-called golden parachutes, poison pills and greenmail—could be used to counter a hostile bid.

Implications for Investors. By forcing an acquiring entity to deal directly with management and the Board, takeover defenses—often referred to as "Shareowner rights plans"—may reduce the potential for the acquirer to succeed, even in situations that would benefit Shareowners. Defenses against takeovers also may cause Investors to discount the value of the Company's shares in normal trading because of the conditions and barriers they create.

Things to Consider. When reviewing a Company's anti-takeover measures, Investors should:

- inquire whether the Company is required to receive Shareowner approval for such measures prior to implementation. It is likely that each Company will structure its measure differently from others. In some cases, Investors may find that the Board is permitted to implement an anti-takeover measure, subject to approval by Shareowners within a set period of time. Others may not require Shareowner approval at all.
- inquire whether the Company has received any formal acquisition overtures during the past two years.
- consider the possibility that the Board and management will use the Company's cash and available credit lines to pay a hostile bidder to forego a takeover. In general, Shareowners should take steps to discourage the Board from taking such actions. If the Company agrees to such payments, Shareowners should review any publicly available information about the terms of such so-called "greenmail" payments.[24]
- consider whether, in some cases, change of control issues are likely to invoke the interest of a national or local government, which might then pressure the seller to change the terms of a proposed acquisition or merger. In such cases, it is unlikely that the Investor will find specific government directives decreeing such defenses, although Investors may find indications about the likelihood of such actions by examining the government's past actions relating to the Company or relating to other companies in similar situations.
- consider whether change-in-control provisions will trigger large severance packages and other payments to Company executives.

Where to find information about takeover provisions:

- A Company's articles of organization are the most likely places to find information about existing takeover defenses.
- Newly created anti-takeover provisions may or may not require Shareowner approval. In either case, the Company may have to provide information to its Shareowners about any amendments to existing defenses.

[24] Greenmail is a premium paid by the object of a hostile takeover bid to the entity making that bid in return for an agreement that the bidding entity will halt its takeover bid for a certain period.

PORTFOLIO MANAGEMENT

STUDY SESSION

Study Session 12 Portfolio Management

TOPIC LEVEL LEARING OUTCOME

The candidate should be able to demonstrate a working knowledge of the key elements of the portfolio management process, including the investment setting, investment policy, and asset allocation.

STUDY SESSION 12
PORTFOLIO MANAGEMENT

As the first discussion within the CFA curriculum on portfolio management, this study session provides the critical framework and context for subsequent Level I study sessions covering equities, fixed income, derivatives, and alternative investments. Furthermore, this study session provides the underlying theories and tools for portfolio management at Levels II and III.

The first reading discusses the asset allocation decision and the portfolio management process—they are an integrated set of steps undertaken in a consistent manner to create and maintain an appropriate portfolio (combination of assets) to meet clients' stated goals. The last two readings focus on the design of a portfolio and introduces the capital asset pricing model (CAPM), a centerpiece of modern financial economics that relates the risk of an asset to its expected return.

READING ASSIGNMENTS

Reading 49 The Asset Allocation Decision
Reading 50 An Introduction to Portfolio Management
Reading 51 An Introduction to Asset Pricing Models

LEARNING OUTCOMES

Reading 49: The Asset Allocation Decision

The candidate should be able to:

a. describe the steps in the portfolio management process, and explain the reasons for a policy statement;

b. explain why investment objectives should be expressed in terms of risk and return, and list the factors that may affect an investor's risk tolerance;

c. describe the return objectives of capital preservation, capital appreciation, current income, and total return;

d. describe the investment constraints of liquidity, time horizon, tax concerns, legal and regulatory factors, and unique needs and preferences;

e. describe the importance of asset allocation, in terms of the percentage of a portfolio's return that can be explained by the target asset allocation, and explain how political and economic factors result in differing asset allocations by investors in various countries.

Reading 50: An Introduction to Portfolio Management

The candidate should be able to:

a. define risk aversion and discuss evidence that suggests that individuals are generally risk averse;
b. list the assumptions about investor behavior underlying the Markowitz model;
c. compute and interpret the expected return, variance, and standard deviation for an individual investment and the expected return and standard deviation for a portfolio;
d. compute and interpret the covariance of rates of return, and show how it is related to the correlation coefficient;
e. list the components of the portfolio standard deviation formula, and explain the relevant importance of these components when adding an investment to a portfolio;
f. describe the efficient frontier, and explain the implications for incremental returns as an investor assumes more risk;
g. explain the concept of an optimal portfolio, and show how each investor may have a different optimal portfolio.

Reading 51: An Introduction to Asset Pricing Models

The candidate should be able to:

a. explain the capital market theory, including its underlying assumptions, and explain the effect on expected returns, the standard deviation of returns, and possible risk/return combinations when a risk-free asset is combined with a portfolio of risky assets;
b. identify the market portfolio, and describe the role of the market portfolio in the formation of the capital market line (CML);
c. define systematic and unsystematic risk, and explain why an investor should not expect to receive additional return for assuming unsystematic risk;
d. explain the capital asset pricing model, including the security market line (SML) and beta, and describe the effects of relaxing its underlying assumptions;
e. calculate, using the SML, the expected return on a security, and evaluate whether the security is overvalued, undervalued, or properly valued.

THE ASSET ALLOCATION DECISION

by Frank K. Reilly and Keith C. Brown

READING **49**

LEARNING OUTCOMES

The candidate should be able to:

a. describe the steps in the portfolio management process, and explain the reasons for a policy statement;

b. explain why investment objectives should be expressed in terms of risk and return, and list the factors that may affect an investor's risk tolerance;

c. describe the return objectives of capital preservation, capital appreciation, current income, and total return;

d. describe the investment constraints of liquidity, time horizon, tax concerns, legal and regulatory factors, and unique needs and preferences;

e. describe the importance of asset allocation, in terms of the percentage of a portfolio's return that can be explained by the target asset allocation, and explain how political and economic factors result in differing asset allocations by investors in various countries.

Note:
Although this reading addresses the taxation of individual investors from the viewpoint of a U.S. investor, candidates are not expected to know the U.S. tax code.

INTRODUCTION 1

Investors know that *risk drives return.* Therefore, the practice of investing funds and managing portfolios should focus primarily on managing risk rather than on managing returns.

This reading examines some of the practical implications of risk management in the context of asset allocation. **Asset allocation** is the process of deciding how to distribute an investor's wealth among different countries and asset classes for investment purposes. An **asset class** is comprised of securities that have similar

The authors acknowledge the collaboration of Professor Edgar Norton of Illinois State University on this reading.

characteristics, attributes, and risk/return relationships. A broad asset class, such as "bonds," can be divided into smaller asset classes, such as Treasury bonds, corporate bonds, and high-yield bonds. We will see that, in the long run, the highest compounded returns will most likely accrue to those investors with larger exposures to risky assets. We will also see that although there are no shortcuts or guarantees to investment success, maintaining a reasonable and disciplined approach to investing will increase the likelihood of investment success over time.

The asset allocation decision is not an isolated choice; rather, it is a component of a structured four-step portfolio management process that we present in this reading. As we will see, the first step in the process is to develop an investment policy statement, or plan, that will guide all future decisions. Much of an asset allocation strategy depends on the investor's policy statement, which includes the investor's goals or objectives, constraints, and investment guidelines.

What we mean by an "investor" can range from an individual to trustees overseeing a corporation's multibillion-dollar pension fund, a university endowment, or invested premiums for an insurance company. Regardless of who the investor is or how simple or complex the investment needs, he or she should develop a policy statement before making long-term investment decisions. Although most of our examples will be in the context of an individual investor, the concepts we introduce here—investment objectives, constraints, benchmarks, and so on—apply to any investor, individual or institutional. We'll review historical data to show the importance of the asset allocation decision and discuss the need for investor education, an important issue for individuals or companies who offer retirement or savings plans to their employees. The reading concludes by examining asset allocation strategies across national borders to show the effect of market environment and culture on investing patterns; what is appropriate for a U.S.-based investor is not necessarily appropriate for a non-U.S.-based investor.

2 INDIVIDUAL INVESTOR LIFE CYCLE

Financial plans and investment needs are as different as each individual. Investment needs change over a person's life cycle. How individuals structure their financial plan should be related to their age, financial status, future plans, risk aversion characteristics, and needs.

The Preliminaries

Before embarking on an investment program, we need to make sure other needs are satisfied. No serious investment plan should be started until a potential investor has adequate income to cover living expenses and has a safety net should the unexpected occur.

Insurance Life insurance should be a component of any financial plan. Life insurance protects loved ones against financial hardship should death occur before our financial goals are met. The death benefit paid by the insurance company can help pay medical bills and funeral expenses and provide cash that family members can use to maintain their lifestyle, retire debt, or invest for future needs (for example, children's education, spouse retirement). Therefore, one of the first steps in developing a financial plan is to purchase adequate life insurance coverage.

Insurance can also serve more immediate purposes, including being a means to meet long-term goals, such as retirement planning. On reaching retirement age, you can receive the cash or surrender value of your life insurance policy and use the proceeds to supplement your retirement lifestyle or for estate planning purposes.

Insurance coverage also provides protection against other uncertainties. *Health* insurance helps to pay medical bills. *Disability* insurance provides continuing income should you become unable to work. *Automobile and home* (or rental) insurances provide protection against accidents and damage to cars or residences.

Although nobody ever expects to use his or her insurance coverage, a first step in a sound financial plan is to have adequate coverage "just in case." Lack of insurance coverage can ruin the best-planned investment program.

Cash Reserve Emergencies, job layoffs, and unforeseen expenses happen, and good investment opportunities emerge. It is important to have a cash reserve to help meet these occasions. In addition to providing a safety cushion, a cash reserve reduces the likelihood of being forced to sell investments at inopportune times to cover unexpected expenses. Most experts recommend a cash reserve equal to about six months' living expenses. Calling it a "cash" reserve does not mean the funds should be in cash; rather, the funds should be in investments you can easily convert to cash with little chance of a loss in value. Money market or short-term bond mutual funds and bank accounts are appropriate vehicles for the cash reserve.

Similar to the financial plan, an investor's insurance and cash reserve needs will change over his or her life. The need for disability insurance declines when a person retires. In contrast, other insurance, such as supplemental Medicare coverage or long-term care insurance, may become more important.

Life Cycle Net Worth and Investment Strategies

Assuming the basic insurance and cash reserve needs are met, individuals can start a serious investment program with their savings. Because of changes in their net worth and risk tolerance, individuals' investment strategies will change over their lifetime. In the following sections, we review various phases in the investment life cycle. Although each individual's needs and preferences are different, some general traits affect most investors over the life cycle. The four life cycle phases are shown in Exhibit 1 (the third and fourth phases—spending and gifting—are shown as concurrent) and described here.

Accumulation Phase Individuals in the early-to-middle years of their working careers are in the accumulation phase. As the name implies, these individuals are attempting to accumulate assets to satisfy fairly immediate needs (for example, a down payment for a house) or longer-term goals (children's college education, retirement). Typically, their net worth is small, and debt from car loans or their own past college loans may be heavy. As a result of their typically long investment time horizon and their future earning ability, individuals in the accumulation phase are willing to make relatively high-risk investments in the hopes of making above-average nominal returns over time.

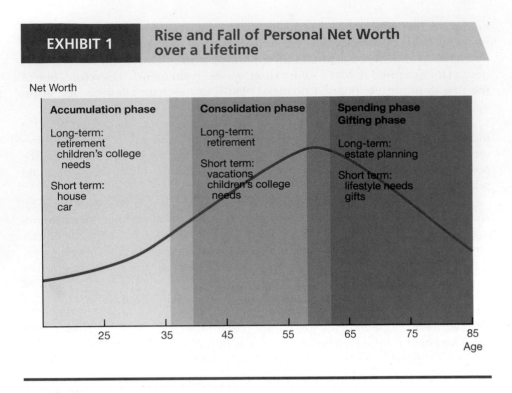

EXHIBIT 1 Rise and Fall of Personal Net Worth over a Lifetime

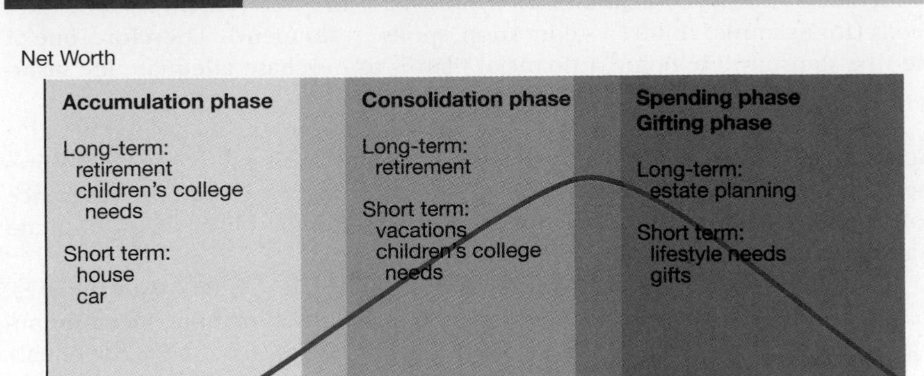

Here we must emphasize the wisdom of investing early and regularly in one's life. Funds invested in early life-cycle phases, with returns compounding over time, will reap financial benefits during later phases. Exhibit 2 shows growth from an initial $10,000 investment over 20, 30, and 40 years at assumed annual returns of 7 and 8 percent. The middle-aged person who invests $10,000 "when he or she can afford it" will only reap the benefits of compounding for 20 years or so before retirement. The younger person who saves will reap the much higher benefits of funds invested for 30 or 40 years. Regularly investing $2,000 a year reaps large

EXHIBIT 2 Benefits of Investing Early

		The Future Value of an Initial \$10,000 Investment	The Future Value of Investing \$2,000 Annually	The Future Value of the Initial Investment Plus the Annual Investment
Interest rate	7.0%			
20 years		\$38,696.84	\$81,990.98	\$120,687.83
30 years		\$76,122.55	\$188,921.57	\$265,044.12
40 years		\$149,744.58	\$399,270.22	\$549,014.80
Interest rate	8.0%			
20 years		\$46,609.57	\$91,523.93	\$138,133.50
30 years		\$100,626.57	\$226,566.42	\$327,192.99
40 years		\$217,245.21	\$518,113.04	\$735,358.25

Source: Calculations by authors.

benefits over time, as well. A person who has invested a total of $90,000—an initial $10,000 investment followed by $2,000 annual investments over 40 years—will have over half a million dollars accumulated from the 7 percent return. If the funds are invested more aggressively and earn the 8 percent return, the accumulation will be nearly three-quarters of a million dollars.

Consolidation Phase Individuals in the consolidation phase are typically past the midpoint of their careers, have paid off much or all of their outstanding debts, and perhaps have paid, or have the assets to pay, their children's college bills. Earnings exceed expenses, so the excess can be invested to provide for future retirement or estate planning needs. The typical investment horizon for this phase is still long (20 to 30 years), so moderately high risk investments are attractive. At the same time, because individuals in this phase are concerned about capital preservation, they do not want to take very large risks that may put their current nest egg in jeopardy.

Spending Phase The **spending phase** typically begins when individuals retire. Living expenses are covered by social security income and income from prior investments, including employer pension plans. Because their earning years have concluded (although some retirees take part-time positions or do consulting work), they seek greater protection of their capital. At the same time, they must balance their desire to preserve the nominal value of their savings with the need to protect themselves against a decline in the *real* value of their savings due to inflation. The average 65-year-old person in the United States has a life expectancy of about 20 years. Thus, although their overall portfolio may be less risky than in the consolidation phase, they still need some risky growth investments, such as common stocks, for inflation (purchasing power) protection.

The transition into the spending phase requires a sometimes difficult change in mindset; throughout our working life we are trying to save; suddenly we can spend. We tend to think that if we spend less, say 4 percent of our accumulated funds annually instead of 5, 6, or 7 percent, our wealth will last far longer. But a bear market early in our retirement can greatly reduce our accumulated funds. Fortunately, there are planning tools that can give a realistic view of what can happen to our retirement funds should markets fall early in our retirement years; this insight can assist in budgeting and planning to minimize the chance of spending (or losing) all the saved retirement funds. Annuities, which transfer risk from the individual to the annuity firm (most likely an insurance company), are another possibility. With an annuity, the recipient receives a guaranteed, lifelong stream of income. Options can allow for the annuity to continue until both a husband and wife die.

Gifting Phase The gifting phase is similar to, and may be concurrent with, the spending phase. In this stage, individuals believe they have sufficient income and assets to cover their current and future expenses while maintaining a reserve for uncertainties. Excess assets can be used to provide financial assistance to relatives or friends, to establish charitable trusts, or to fund trusts as an estate planning tool to minimize estate taxes.

Life Cycle Investment Goals

During the investment life cycle, individuals have a variety of financial goals. **Near-term, high-priority goals** are shorter-term financial objectives that individuals set to fund purchases that are personally important to them, such as accumulating funds to make a house down payment, buy a new car, or take a trip. Parents with teenage children may have a near-term, high-priority goal to accumulate funds to help pay college expenses. Because of the emotional importance of these goals and their short time horizon, high-risk investments are not usually considered suitable for achieving them.

Long-term, high-priority goals typically include some form of financial independence, such as the ability to retire at a certain age. Because of their long-term nature, higher-risk investments can be used to help meet these objectives.

Lower-priority goals are just that—it might be nice to meet these objectives, but it is not critical. Examples include the ability to purchase a new car every few years, redecorate the home with expensive furnishings, or take a long, luxurious vacation. A well-developed policy statement considers these diverse goals over an investor's lifetime. The following sections detail the process for constructing an investment policy, creating a portfolio that is consistent with the policy and the environment, managing the portfolio, and monitoring its performance relative to its goals and objectives over time.

3 THE PORTFOLIO MANAGEMENT PROCESS

The process of managing an investment portfolio never stops. Once the funds are initially invested according to the plan, the real work begins in monitoring and updating the status of the portfolio and the investor's needs.

The first step in the portfolio management process, as seen in Exhibit 3, is for the investor, either alone or with the assistance of an investment advisor, to construct a **policy statement**. The policy statement is a road map; in it, investors specify the types of risks they are willing to take and their investment goals and constraints. All investment decisions are based on the policy statement to ensure they are appropriate for the investor. We examine the process of constructing a policy statement in the following section. Because investor needs change over time, the policy statement must be periodically reviewed and updated.

EXHIBIT 3 The Portfolio Management Process

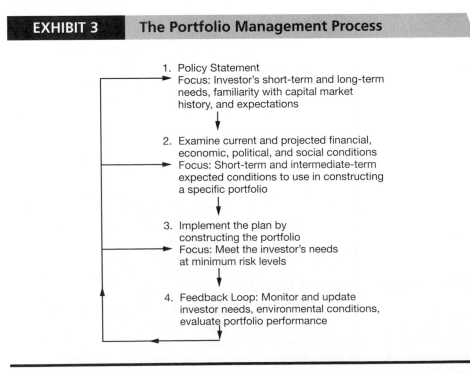

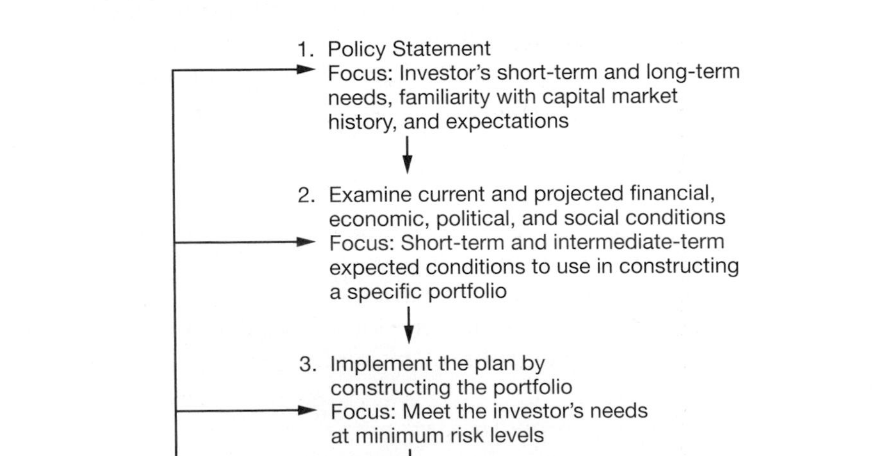

1. Policy Statement
Focus: Investor's short-term and long-term needs, familiarity with capital market history, and expectations
2. Examine current and projected financial, economic, political, and social conditions
Focus: Short-term and intermediate-term expected conditions to use in constructing a specific portfolio
3. Implement the plan by constructing the portfolio
Focus: Meet the investor's needs at minimum risk levels
4. Feedback Loop: Monitor and update investor needs, environmental conditions, evaluate portfolio performance

The process of investing seeks to peer into the future and determine strategies that offer the best possibility of meeting the policy statement guidelines. In the second step of the portfolio management process, the manager should study current financial and economic conditions and forecast future trends. The investor's needs, as reflected in the policy statement, and financial market expectations will jointly determine **investment strategy**. Economies are dynamic; they are affected by numerous industry struggles, politics, and changing demographics and social attitudes. Thus, the portfolio will require constant monitoring and updating to reflect changes in financial market expectations.

The third step of the portfolio management process is to construct the portfolio. With the investor's policy statement and financial market forecasts as input, the advisors implement the investment strategy and determine how to allocate available funds across different countries, asset classes, and securities. This involves constructing a portfolio that will minimize the investor's risks while meeting the needs specified in the policy statement.

The fourth step in the portfolio management process is the continual monitoring of the investor's needs and capital market conditions and, when necessary, updating the policy statement. Based upon all of this, the investment strategy is modified accordingly. A component of the monitoring process is to evaluate a portfolio's performance and compare the relative results to the expectations and the requirements listed in the policy statement. Once you have completed the four steps, it is important to recognize that this is continuous—it is essential to revisit all the steps to ensure that the policy statement is still valid, that the economic outlook has not changed, etc.

THE NEED FOR A POLICY STATEMENT 4

As noted in the previous section, a policy statement is a road map that guides the investment process. Constructing a policy statement is an invaluable planning tool that will help the investor understand his or her needs better as well as assist an advisor or portfolio manager in managing a client's funds. While it does not guarantee investment success, a policy statement will provide discipline for the investment process and reduce the possibility of making hasty, inappropriate decisions. There are two important reasons for constructing a policy statement: First, it helps the investor decide on realistic investment goals after learning about the financial markets and the risks of investing. Second, it creates a standard by which to judge the performance of the portfolio manager.

Understand and Articulate Realistic Investor Goals

When asked about their investment goal, people often say, "to make a lot of money," or some similar response. Such a goal has two drawbacks: First, it may not be appropriate for the investor, and second, it is too open-ended to provide guidance for specific investments and time frames. Such an objective is well suited for someone going to the racetrack or buying lottery tickets, but it is inappropriate for someone investing funds in financial and real assets for the long term.

An important purpose of writing a policy statement is to help investors understand their own needs, objectives, and investment constraints. As part of this, investors need to learn about financial markets and the risks of investing. This background will help prevent them from making inappropriate investment decisions in the future and will increase the possibility that they will satisfy their specific, measurable financial goals.

Thus, the policy statement helps the investor to specify realistic goals and become more informed about the risks and costs of investing. Market values of assets, whether they be stocks, bonds, or real estate, can fluctuate dramatically. For example, during the October 1987 crash, the Dow Jones Industrial Average (DJIA) fell more than 20 percent in one day; in October 1997, the Dow fell "only" 7 percent. A review of market history shows that it is not unusual for asset prices to decline by 10 percent to 20 percent over several months—for example, the months following the market peak in March 2000, and the major decline when the market reopened after September 11, 2001. Investors will typically focus on a single statistic, such as an 11 percent average annual rate of return on stocks, and expect the market to rise 11 percent every year. Such thinking ignores the risk of stock investing. Part of the process of developing a policy statement is for the investor to become familiar with the risks of investing, because we know that a strong positive relationship exists between risk and return.

BOX 1

One expert in the field recommends that investors should think about the following set of questions and explain their answers as part of the process of constructing a policy statement:

1. What are the real risks of an adverse financial outcome, especially in the short run?
2. What probable emotional reactions will I have to an adverse financial outcome?
3. How knowledgeable am I about investments and markets?
4. What other capital or income sources do I have? How important is this particular portfolio to my overall financial position?
5. What, if any, legal restrictions may affect my investment needs?
6. What, if any, unanticipated consequences of interim fluctuations in portfolio value might affect my investment policy?

Adapted from Charles D. Ellis, *Investment Policy: How to Win the Loser's Game* (Homewood, IL: Dow Jones-Irwin, 1985), 25–26. Reproduced with permission of the McGraw-Hill Companies.

In summary, constructing a policy statement is mainly the investor's responsibility. It is a process whereby investors articulate their realistic needs and goals and become familiar with financial markets and investing risks. Without this information, investors cannot adequately communicate their needs to the portfolio manager. Without this input from investors, the portfolio manager cannot construct a portfolio that will satisfy clients' needs; the result of bypassing this step will most likely be future aggravation, dissatisfaction, and disappointment.

Standards for Evaluating Portfolio Performance

The policy statement also assists in judging the performance of the portfolio manager. Performance cannot be judged without an objective standard; the policy statement provides that objective standard. The portfolio's performance should be compared to guidelines specified in the policy statement, not on the portfolio's overall return. For example, if an investor has a low tolerance for risky investments, the portfolio manager should not be fired simply because the portfolio does not perform as well as the risky S&P 500 stock index. Because risk drives returns, the investor's lower-risk investments, as specified in the investor's policy statement, will probably earn lower returns than if all the investor's funds were placed in the stock market.

The policy statement will typically include a **benchmark portfolio**, or comparison standard. The risk of the benchmark, and the assets included in the benchmark, should agree with the client's risk preferences and investment needs. Notably, both the client and the portfolio manager must agree that the benchmark portfolio reflects the risk preferences and appropriate return requirements of the client. In turn, the investment performance of the portfolio manager should be compared to this benchmark portfolio. For example, an investor who specifies low-risk investments in the policy statement should compare the portfolio manager's performance against a low-risk benchmark portfolio. Likewise, an investor seeking high-risk, high-return investments should compare the portfolio's performance against a high-risk benchmark portfolio.

Because it sets an objective performance standard, the policy statement acts as a starting point for periodic portfolio review and client communication with managers. Questions concerning portfolio performance or the manager's faithfulness to the policy can be addressed in the context of the written policy guidelines. Managers should mainly be judged by whether they consistently followed the client's policy guidelines. The portfolio manager who makes unilateral deviations from policy is not working in the best interests of the client. Therefore, even significant deviations that result in higher portfolio returns can and should be grounds for the manager's dismissal.

Thus, we see the importance of the client constructing the policy statement: The client must first understand his or her own needs before communicating them to the portfolio manager. In turn, the portfolio manager must implement the client's desires by following the investment guidelines. As long as policy is followed, shortfalls in performance should not be a major concern. Remember that the policy statement is designed to impose an investment discipline on the client and portfolio manager. The less knowledgeable they are, the more likely clients are to inappropriately judge the performance of the portfolio manager.

Other Benefits

A sound policy statement helps to protect the client against a portfolio manager's inappropriate investments or unethical behavior. Without clear, written guidance, some managers may consider investing in high-risk investments, hoping to earn a quick return. Such actions are probably counter to the investor's specified needs and risk preferences. Though legal recourse is a possibility against such action, writing a clear and unambiguous policy statement should reduce the possibility of such inappropriate manager behavior.

Just because one specific manager currently manages your account does not mean that person will always manage your funds. As with other positions, your portfolio manager may be promoted or dismissed or take a better job. Therefore, after a while, your funds may come under the management of an individual you do not know and who does not know you. To prevent costly delays during this transition, you can ensure that the new manager "hits the ground running" with a clearly written policy statement. A policy statement should prevent delays in monitoring and rebalancing your portfolio and will help create a seamless transition from one money manager to another.

To sum up, a clearly written policy statement helps avoid future potential problems. When the client clearly specifies his or her needs and desires, the portfolio manager can more effectively construct an appropriate portfolio. The policy statement provides an objective measure for evaluating portfolio performance, helps guard against ethical lapses by the portfolio manager, and aids in the transition between money managers. Therefore, the first step before beginning any investment program, whether it is for an individual or a multibillion-dollar pension fund, is to construct a policy statement.

BOX 2

An appropriate policy statement should satisfactorily answer the following questions:

1. Is the policy carefully designed to meet the specific needs and objectives of this particular investor? (Cookie-cutter or one-size-fits-all policy statements are generally inappropriate.)
2. Is the policy written so clearly and explicitly that a competent stranger could use it to manage the portfolio in conformance with the client's needs? In case of a manager transition, could the new manager use this policy statement to handle your portfolio in accordance with your needs?
3. Would the client have been able to remain committed to the policies during the capital market experiences of the past 60 to 70 years? That is, does the client fully understand investment risks and the need for a disciplined approach to the investment process?
4. Would the portfolio manager have been able to maintain the policies specified over the same period? (Discipline is a two-way street; we do not want the portfolio manager to change strategies because of a disappointing market.)
5. Would the policy, if implemented, have achieved the client's objectives? (Bottom line: Would the policy have worked to meet the client's needs?)

Adapted from Charles D. Ellis, *Investment Policy: How to Win the Loser's Game* (Homewood, IL: Dow Jones-Irwin, 1985), 62. Reproduced with permission of the McGraw-Hill Companies.

5 INPUT TO THE POLICY STATEMENT

Before an investor and advisor can construct a policy statement, they need to have an open and frank exchange of information, ideas, fears, and goals. To build a framework for this information-gathering process, the client and advisor need to discuss the client's investment objectives and constraints. To illustrate this framework, we discuss the investment objectives and constraints that may confront "typical" 25-year-old and 65-year-old investors.

Investment Objectives

The investor's **objectives** are his or her investment goals expressed in terms of both risk and returns. The relationship between risk and returns requires that goals not be expressed only in terms of returns. Expressing goals only in terms of returns can lead to inappropriate investment practices by the portfolio manager, such as the use of high-risk investment strategies or account "churning," which involves moving quickly in and out of investments in an attempt to buy low and sell high.

For example, a person may have a stated return goal such as "double my investment in five years." Before such a statement becomes part of the policy statement, the client must become fully informed of investment risks associated with such a goal, including the possibility of loss. *A careful analysis of the client's risk tolerance should precede any discussion of return objectives.* It makes little sense for a person who is risk averse to invest funds in high-risk assets. Investment firms survey clients to gauge their risk tolerance. Sometimes investment magazines or books contain tests that individuals can take to help them evaluate their risk tolerance (see Exhibit 4). Subsequently, an advisor will use the results of this evaluation to categorize a client's risk tolerance and suggest an initial asset allocation such as those contained in Exhibit 5.

Risk tolerance is more than a function of an individual's psychological makeup; it is affected by other factors, including a person's current insurance coverage and cash reserves. Risk tolerance is also affected by an individual's family situation (for example, marital status and the number and ages of children) and by his or her age. We know that older persons generally have shorter investment time frames within which to make up any losses; they also have years of experience, including living through various market gyrations and "corrections" (a euphemism for downtrends or crashes) that younger people have not experienced or whose effect they do not fully appreciate. Risk tolerance is also influenced by one's current net worth and income expectations. All else being equal, individuals with higher incomes have a greater propensity to undertake risk because their incomes can help cover any shortfall. Likewise, individuals with larger net worths can afford to place some assets in risky investments while the remaining assets provide a cushion against losses.

A person's return objective may be stated in terms of an absolute or a relative percentage return, but it may also be stated in terms of a general goal, such as capital preservation, current income, capital appreciation, or total return.

Capital preservation means that investors want to minimize their risk of loss, usually in real terms: They seek to maintain the purchasing power of their investment. In other words, the return needs to be no less than the rate of inflation. Generally, this is a strategy for strongly risk-averse investors or for funds needed in the short-run, such as for next year's tuition payment or a down payment on a house.

Capital appreciation is an appropriate objective when the investors want the portfolio to grow in real terms over time to meet some future need. Under this strategy, growth mainly occurs through capital gains. This is an aggressive strategy for investors willing to take on risk to meet their objective. Generally, longer-term investors seeking to build a retirement or college education fund may have this goal.

When **current income** is the return objective, the investors want the portfolio to concentrate on generating income rather than capital gains. This strategy sometimes suits investors who want to supplement their earnings with income generated by their portfolio to meet their living expenses. Retirees may favor this objective for part of their portfolio to help generate spendable funds.

The objective for the **total return** strategy is similar to that of capital appreciation; namely, the investors want the portfolio to grow over time to meet a future need. Whereas the capital appreciation strategy seeks to do this primarily through capital gains, the total return strategy seeks to increase portfolio value by both capital gains and reinvesting current income. Because the total return strategy has both income and capital gains components, its risk exposure lies between that of the current income and capital appreciation strategies.

Investment Objective: 25-Year-Old What is an appropriate investment objective for our typical 25-year-old investor? Assume he holds a steady job, is a valued employee, has adequate insurance coverage, and has enough money in the bank to provide a cash reserve. Let's also assume that his current long-term, high-priority investment goal is to build a retirement fund. Depending on his risk

EXHIBIT 4 How Much Risk Is Right for You?

You've heard the expression "no pain, no gain"? In the investment world, the comparable phrase would be "no risk, no reward."

How you feel about risking your money will drive many of your investment decisions. The risk-comfort scale extends from very conservative (you don't want to risk losing a penny regardless of how little your money earns) to very aggressive (you're willing to risk much of your money for the possibility that it will grow tremendously). As you might guess, most investors' tolerance for risk falls somewhere in between.

If you're unsure of what your level of risk tolerance is, this quiz should help.

1. You win $300 in an office football pool. You: (a) spend it on groceries, (b) purchase lottery tickets, (c) put it in a money market account, (d) buy some stock.
2. Two weeks after buying 100 shares of a $20 stock, the price jumps to over $30. You decide to: (a) buy more stock; it's obviously a winner, (b) sell it and take your profits, (c) sell half to recoup some costs and hold the rest, (d) sit tight and wait for it to advance even more.
3. On days when the stock market jumps way up, you: (a) wish you had invested more, (b) call your financial advisor and ask for recommendations, (c) feel glad you're not in the market because it fluctuates too much, (d) pay little attention.
4. You're planning a vacation trip and can either lock in a fixed room-and-meals rate of $150 per day or book standby and pay anywhere from $100 to $300 per day. You: (a) take the fixed-rate deal, (b) talk to people who have been there about the availability of last-minute accommodations, (c) book standby and also arrange vacation insurance because you're leery of the tour operator, (d) take your chances with standby.
5. The owner of your apartment building is converting the units to condominiums. You can buy your unit for $75,000 or an option on a unit for $15,000. (Units have recently sold for close to $100,000, and prices seem to be going up.) For financing, you'll have to borrow the down payment and pay mortgage and condo fees higher than your present rent. You: (a) buy your unit, (b) buy your unit and look for another to buy, (c) sell the option and arrange to rent the unit yourself, (d) sell the option and move out because you think the conversion will attract couples with small children.
6. You have been working three years for a rapidly growing company. As an executive, you are offered the option of buying up to 2% of company stock: 2,000 shares at $10 a share. Although the company is privately owned (its stock does not trade on the open market), its majority owner has made handsome profits selling three other businesses and intends to sell this one eventually. You: (a) purchase all the shares you can and tell the owner you would invest more if allowed, (b) purchase all the shares, (c) purchase half the shares, (d) purchase a small amount of shares.
7. You go to a casino for the first time. You choose to play: (a) quarter slot machines, (b) $5 minimum-bet roulette, (c) dollar slot machines, (d) $25 minimum-bet blackjack.
8. You want to take someone out for a special dinner in a city that's new to you. How do you pick a place? (a) read restaurant reviews in the local newspaper, (b) ask coworkers if they know of a suitable place, (c) call the only other person you know in this city, who eats out a lot but only recently moved there, (d) visit the city sometime before your dinner to check out the restaurants yourself.
9. The expression that best describes your lifestyle is: (a) no guts, no glory, (b) just do it!, (c) look before you leap, (d) all good things come to those who wait.
10. Your attitude toward money is best described as: (a) a dollar saved is a dollar earned, (b) you've got to spend money to make money, (c) cash and carry only, (d) whenever possible, use other people's money.

SCORING SYSTEM: Score your answers this way: (1) a-1, b-4, c-2, d-3 (2) a-4, b-1, c-3, d-2 (3) a-3, b-4, c-2, d-1 (4) a-2, b-3, c-1, d-4 (5) a-3, b-4, c-2, d-1 (6) a-4, b-3, c-2, d-1 (7) a-1, b-3, c-2, d-4 (8) a-2, b-3, c-4, d-1 (9) a-4, b-3, c-2, d-1 (10) a-2, b-3, c-1, d-4.

What your total score indicates:

- 10–17: You're not willing to take chances with your money, even though it means you can't make big gains.
- 18–25: You're semi-conservative, willing to take a small chance with enough information.
- 26–32: You're semi-aggressive, willing to take chances if you think the odds of earning more are in your favor.
- 33–40: You're aggressive, looking for every opportunity to make your money grow, even though in some cases the odds may be quite long. You view money as a tool to make more money.

Source: Adapted from *Feathering Your Nest: The Retirement Planner.*

EXHIBIT 5 Initial Risk and Investment Goal Categories and Asset Allocations Suggested by Investment Firms

Fidelity Investments Suggested Asset Allocations

	Cash/ Short-Term	Bonds	Domestic Equities	Foreign Equities
Short-term	100%	0%	0%	0%
Conservative	30	50	20	0
Balanced	10	40	45	5
Growth	5	25	60	10
Aggressive growth	0	15	70	15
Most aggressive	0	0	80	20

Vanguard Investments Suggested Asset Allocations

	Cash/Short-Term	Bonds	Stocks
Income-oriented	0%	100%	0%
	0	80%	20%
	0	70%	30%
Balanced	0%	60%	40%
	0	50%	50%
	0	40%	60%
Growth	0%	30%	70%
	0	20%	80%
	0	0%	100%

T. Rowe Price Matrix

Non-retirement-goals Matrix

Your Time Horizon

Your Risk Tolerance	3–5 years	6–10 years	11+ years
Higher	**Strategy 2** 20% cash 40% bonds 40% stocks	**Strategy 3** 10% cash 30% bonds 60% stocks	**Strategy 5** 100% stocks
Moderate	**Strategy 1** 30% cash 50% bonds 20% stocks	**Strategy 2** 20% cash 40% bonds 40% stocks	**Strategy 4** 20% bonds 80% stocks
Lower	**All Cash** 100% cash	**Strategy 1** 30% cash 50% bonds 20% stocks	**Strategy 3** 10% cash 30% bonds 60% stocks

Source: Based on data sampled from Personal.Fidelity.com, Vanguard.com, and TRowePrice.com.

preferences, he can select a strategy carrying moderate to high amounts of risk because the income stream from his job will probably grow over time. Further, given his young age and income growth potential, a low-risk strategy, such as capital preservation or current income, is inappropriate for his retirement fund goal; a total return or capital appreciation objective would be most appropriate. Here's a possible objective statement:

> Invest funds in a variety of moderate- to higher-risk investments. The average risk of the equity portfolio should exceed that of a broad stock market index, such as the NYSE stock index. Foreign and domestic equity exposure should range from 80 percent to 95 percent of the total portfolio. Remaining funds should be invested in short- and intermediate-term notes and bonds.

Investment Objective: 65-Year-Old Assume our typical 65-year-old investor likewise has adequate insurance coverage and a cash reserve. Let's also assume she is retiring this year. This individual will want less risk exposure than the 25-year-old investor, because her earning power from employment will soon be ending; she will not be able to recover any investment losses by saving more out of her paycheck. Depending on her income from social security and a pension plan, she may need some current income from her retirement portfolio to meet living expenses. Given that she can be expected to live an average of another 20 years, she will need protection against inflation. A risk-averse investor will choose a combination of current income and capital preservation strategy; a more risk-tolerant investor will choose a combination of current income and total return in an attempt to have principal growth outpace inflation. Here's an example of such an objective statement:

> Invest in stock and bond investments to meet income needs (from bond income and stock dividends) and to provide for real growth (from equities). Fixed-income securities should comprise 55–65 percent of the total portfolio; of this, 5–15 percent should be invested in short-term securities for extra liquidity and safety. The remaining 35–45 percent of the portfolio should be invested in high-quality stocks whose risk is similar to the S&P 500 index.

More detailed analyses for our 25-year-old and our 65-year-old would make more specific assumptions about the risk tolerance of each, as well as clearly enumerate their investment goals, return objectives, the funds they have to invest at the present, the funds they expect to invest over time, and the benchmark portfolio that will be used to evaluate performance.

Investment Constraints

In addition to the investment objective that sets limits on risk and return, certain other constraints also affect the investment plan. Investment constraints include liquidity needs, an investment time horizon, tax factors, legal and regulatory constraints, and unique needs and preferences.

Liquidity Needs An asset is **liquid** if it can be quickly converted to cash at a price close to fair market value. Generally, assets are more liquid if many traders are interested in a fairly standardized product. Treasury bills are a highly liquid security; real estate and venture capital are not.

Investors may have liquidity needs that the investment plan must consider. For example, although an investor may have a primary long-term goal, several near-term goals may require available funds. Wealthy individuals with sizable tax obligations need adequate liquidity to pay their taxes without upsetting their investment plan. Some retirement plans may need funds for shorter-term purposes, such as buying a car or a house or making college tuition payments.

Our typical 25-year-old investor probably has little need for liquidity as he focuses on his long-term retirement fund goal. This constraint may change, however, should he face a period of unemployment or should near-term goals, such as honeymoon expenses or a house down payment, enter the picture. Should any changes occur, the investor needs to revise his policy statement and financial plans accordingly.

Our soon-to-be-retired 65-year-old investor has a greater need for liquidity. Although she may receive regular checks from her pension plan and social security, it is not likely that they will equal her working paycheck. She will want some of her portfolio in liquid securities to meet unexpected expenses or bills.

Time Horizon Time horizon as an investment constraint briefly entered our earlier discussion of near-term and long-term high-priority goals. A close (but not perfect) relationship exists between an investor's time horizon, liquidity needs, and ability to handle risk. Investors with long investment horizons generally require less liquidity and can tolerate greater portfolio risk: less liquidity because the funds are not usually needed for many years; greater risk tolerance because any shortfalls or losses can be overcome by returns earned in subsequent years.

Investors with shorter time horizons generally favor more liquid and less risky investments because losses are harder to overcome during a short time frame.

Because of life expectancies, our 25-year-old investor has a longer investment time horizon than our 65-year-old investor. But, as discussed earlier, this does not mean the 65-year-old should place all her money in short-term CDs; she needs the inflation protection that long-term investments such as common stock can provide. Still, because of the time horizon constraint, the 25-year-old will probably have a greater proportion of his portfolio in equities—including stocks in small firms and international firms—than the 65-year-old.

Tax Concerns Investment planning is complicated by the tax code; taxes complicate the situation even more if international investments are part of the portfolio. Taxable income from interest, dividends, or rents is taxable at the investor's marginal tax rate. The marginal tax rate is the proportion of the next one dollar in income paid as taxes. Exhibit 6 shows the marginal tax rates for different levels of taxable income. As of 2004, the top federal marginal tax rate was 35 percent.

Capital gains or losses arise from asset price changes. They are taxed differently than income. Income is taxed when it is received; capital gains or losses are taxed only when an asset is sold and the gain or loss, relative to its initial cost or **basis**, is realized. **Unrealized capital gains** (or *losses*) reflect the price change in currently held assets that have *not* been sold; the tax liability on unrealized capital gains can be deferred indefinitely. If appreciated assets are passed on to an heir upon the investor's death, the basis of the assets is considered to be their value on the date of the holder's death. The heirs can then sell the assets and pay lower capital gains taxes if they wish. **Realized capital gains** occur when an appreciated asset has been sold; taxes are due on the realized capital gains only. As of 2004, the maximum tax rate on stock dividends and long-term capital gains is 15 percent.

Some find the difference between average and marginal income tax rates confusing. The **marginal tax rate** is the part of each additional dollar in income that is paid as tax. Thus, a married person, filing jointly, with an income of $50,000 will have a marginal tax rate of 15 percent. The 15 percent marginal tax rate should be used to determine after-tax returns on investments.

EXHIBIT 6 **Individual Marginal Tax Rates, 2004**

	If Taxable Income		The Tax Is		
			Then		
	Is Over	But Not Over	This Amount	Plus This %	Of the Excess Over
Single	$0	$7,150	$0	10%	$0
	$7,150	$29,050	$715	15%	$7,150
	$29,050	$70,350	$4,000	25%	$29,050
	$70,350	$146,750	$14,325	28%	$70,350
	$146,750	$319,100	$35,717	33%	$146,750
	$319,100	—	$92,592	35%	$319,100
Married Filing Jointly	$0	$14,300	$0	10%	$0
	$14,300	$58,100	$1,430	15%	$14,300
	$58,100	$117,250	$8,000	25%	$58,600
	$117,250	$178,650	$22,787	28%	$117,250
	$178,650	$319,100	$39,979	33%	$178,650
	$319,100	—	$86,328	35%	$319,100

Note: For updates, go to the IRS website, www.irs.gov.

The **average tax rate** is simply a person's total tax payment divided by their total income. It represents the average tax paid on each dollar the person earned. From Exhibit 6, a married person, filing jointly, will pay $6,785 in tax on a $50,000 income [$1,430 + 0.15($50,000 − $14,300)]. This average tax rate is $6,785/$50,000 or 13.6 percent. Note that the average tax rate is a weighted average of the person's marginal tax rates paid on each dollar of income. The first $14,000 of income has a 10 percent marginal tax rate; the next $36,000 has a 15 percent marginal tax rate:

$$\frac{\$14{,}000}{\$50{,}000} \times 0.10 + \frac{\$36{,}000}{\$50{,}000} \times 0.15 = 0.136, \text{ or the average tax rate of 13.6 percent}$$

Another tax factor is that some sources of investment income are exempt from federal and state taxes. For example, interest on federal securities, such as Treasury bills, notes, and bonds, is exempt from state taxes. Interest on municipal bonds (bonds issued by a state or other local governing body) is exempt from federal taxes. Further, if investors purchase municipal bonds issued by a local governing body of the state in which they live, the interest is exempt from both state and federal income tax. Thus, high-income individuals have an incentive to purchase municipal bonds to reduce their tax liabilities.

The after-tax return on taxable investment income is

$$\text{After-Tax Income Return} = \text{Pre-Tax Income Return} \times (1 - \text{Marginal Tax Rate}) \qquad \text{(49-1)}$$

Thus, the after-tax return on a taxable bond investment should be compared to that of municipals before deciding which a tax-paying investor should purchase.[1] Alternatively, we could compute a municipal's equivalent taxable yield, which is what a taxable bond investment would have to offer to produce the same after-tax return as the municipal. It is given by

$$\text{Equivalent Taxable Yield} = \frac{\text{Municipal Yield}}{(1 - \text{Marginal Tax Rate})} \quad \textbf{(49-2)}$$

To illustrate, if an investor is in the 28 percent marginal tax bracket, a taxable investment yield of 8 percent has an after-tax yield of 8 percent × (1 − 0.28) or 5.76 percent; an equivalent-risk municipal security offering a yield greater than 5.76 percent offers the investor greater after-tax returns. On the other hand, a municipal bond yielding 6 percent has an equivalent taxable yield of 6 percent/(1 − 0.28) = 8.33 percent; to earn more money after taxes, an equivalent-risk taxable investment has to offer a return greater than 8.33 percent.

There are other means of reducing investment tax liabilities. Contributions to an IRA (individual retirement account) may qualify as a tax deduction if certain income limits are met. Even without that deduction, taxes on any investment returns of an IRA, including any income, are deferred until the funds are withdrawn from the account. Any funds withdrawn from an IRA are taxable as current income, regardless of whether growth in the IRA occurs as a result of capital gains, income, or both. For this reason, to minimize taxes advisors recommend investing in stocks in taxable accounts and bonds in tax-deferred accounts such as IRAs. When funds are withdrawn from a tax-deferred account such as a regular IRA, assets are taxed (at most) at a 35 percent income tax rate (Exhibit 6)—even if the source of the stock return is primarily capital gains. In a taxable account, capital gains are taxed at the maximum 15 percent capital gains rate.

The benefits of deferring taxes can dramatically compound over time. For example, $1,000 invested in an IRA at a tax-deferred rate of 8 percent grows to $10,062.66 over thirty years; in a taxable account (assuming a 28 percent marginal (federal + state) tax rate), the funds would grow to only $5,365.91. After thirty years, the value of the tax-deferred investment has grown to be nearly twice as large as the taxable investment.

With various stipulations, as of 2005, tax-deductible contributions of up to $4,000 (to be raised to $5,000 by 2008) can be made to a traditional IRA. A Roth IRA contribution is *not* tax-deductible, and contribution limits mirror those of the traditional IRA. The returns in a Roth IRA will grow on a tax-deferred basis and can be withdrawn, tax-free, if the funds are invested for at least five years and are withdrawn after the investor reaches age $59\frac{1}{2}$.[2]

For money you intend to invest in some type of IRA, the advantage of the Roth IRA's tax-free withdrawals will outweigh the tax-deduction benefit from the regular IRA—unless you expect your tax rate when the funds are withdrawn to be substantially less than when you initially invest the funds. Let's illustrate this with a hypothetical example.

Suppose you are considering investing $2,000 in either a regular or Roth IRA. Let's assume for simplicity that your combined federal and state marginal tax rate is 28 percent and that, over your 20-year time horizon, your $2,000

[1] Realized capital gains on municipal securities are taxed, as are all other capital gains; similarly for capital losses. Only the income from municipals is exempt from federal income tax.

[2] Earlier tax-free withdrawals are possible if the funds are to be used for educational purposes or first-time home purchases.

investment will grow to $20,000, tax-deferred in either account; this represents an average annual return of 12.2 percent.

In a Roth IRA, no tax is deducted when the $2,000 is invested; in a regular IRA, the $2,000 investment is tax-deductible and will lower your tax bill by $560 (0.28 × $2,000).

Thus, in a Roth IRA, only $2,000 is assumed to be invested; for a regular IRA, both the $2,000 and the $560 tax savings are assumed to be invested. We will assume the $560 is invested at an after-tax rate of 12.2% × (1 − 0.28) = 8.8 percent. After 20 years, this amount will grow to $3,025. The calculations in Exhibit 7 show that at the end of the 20-year time horizon the Roth IRA will give you more after-tax dollars unless you believe your tax bracket will be lower then *and you invest the regular IRA tax savings.*

Another tax-deferred investment is the cash value of life insurance contracts; these accumulate tax-free until the funds are withdrawn. Also, employers may offer 401(k) or 403(b) plans, which allow the employee to reduce taxable income by making tax-deferred investments. Many times employee contributions are matched by employer donations (up to a specified limit), thus allowing the employees to double their investment with little risk.

At times investors face a trade-off between taxes and diversification needs. If entrepreneurs concentrate much of their wealth in equity holdings of their firm, or if employees purchase substantial amounts of their employer's stock through payroll deduction plans during their working life, their portfolios may contain a large amount of unrealized capital gains. In addition, the risk position of such a portfolio may be quite high because it is concentrated in a single company. The decision to sell some of the company stock in order to diversify the portfolio's risk by reinvesting the proceeds in other assets must be balanced against the resulting tax liability.

EXHIBIT 7 Comparing the Regular versus Roth IRA Returns

	Regular IRA	Roth IRA
Invested funds	$2,000 + $560 tax savings on the tax-deductible IRA investment	$2,000 (no tax deduction)
Time horizon	20 years	20 years
Rate of return assumption	12.2 percent tax-deferred on the IRA investment; 8.8 percent on invested tax savings (represents the after-tax return on 12.2 percent)	12.2 percent tax-deferred on the IRA investment
Funds available after 20 years (taxes ignored)	$20,000 (pre-tax) from IRA investment; $3,025 (after-tax) from invested tax savings	$20,000 from IRA investment
Funds available after 20 years, 15 percent marginal tax rate at retirement	$20,000 less tax (0.15 × $20,000) plus $3,025 from invested tax savings equals $20,025	$20,000
Funds available after 20 years, 28 percent marginal tax rate at retirement	$20,000 less tax (0.28 × $20,000) plus $3,025 from invested tax savings equals $17,425	$20,000
Funds available after 20 years, 40 percent marginal tax rate at retirement	$20,000 less tax (0.40 × $20,000) plus $3,025 from invested tax savings equals $15,025	$20,000

Our typical 25-year-old investor probably is in a fairly low tax bracket, so detailed tax planning and tax-exempt income, such as that available from municipals, will not be major concerns. Nonetheless, he should still invest as much as possible into such tax-deferred plans as IRAs or 401(k)s for the retirement portion of his portfolio. If other funds are available for investment, they should be allocated based on his shorter- and longer-term investment goals.

Our 65-year-old investor may face a different situation. If she had been in a high tax bracket prior to retiring—and therefore had sought tax-exempt income and tax-deferred investments—her situation may change shortly after retirement. After her retirement, without large regular paychecks, the need for tax-deferred investments or tax-exempt income becomes less. Taxable income may then offer higher after-tax yields than tax-exempt municipals if her tax bracket is lower. If her employer's stock is a large component of her retirement account, she must make careful decisions regarding the need to diversify versus the cost of realizing large capital gains (in her lower tax bracket).

Legal and Regulatory Factors Both the investment process and the financial markets are highly regulated and subject to numerous laws. At times, these legal and regulatory factors constrain the investment strategies of individuals and institutions.

For example, funds removed from a regular IRA, Roth IRA, or 401(k) plan before age $59\frac{1}{2}$ are taxable and subject to an additional 10 percent withdrawal penalty. You may also be familiar with the tag line in many bank CD advertisements—"substantial interest penalty upon early withdrawal." Regulations and rules such as these may make such investments unattractive for investors with substantial liquidity needs in their portfolios.

Regulations can also constrain the investment choices available to someone in a fiduciary role. A *fiduciary,* or trustee, supervises an investment portfolio of a third party, such as a trust account or discretionary account.[3] The fiduciary must make investment decisions in accordance with the owner's wishes; a properly written policy statement assists this process. In addition, trustees of a trust account must meet the prudent-man standard, which means that they must invest and manage the funds as a prudent person would manage his or her own affairs. Notably, the prudent-man standard is based on the composition of the entire portfolio, not each individual asset.[4]

All investors must respect certain laws, such as insider trading prohibitions against the purchase and sale of securities on the basis of important information that is not publicly known. Typically, the people possessing such private, or insider, information are the firm's managers, who have a fiduciary duty to their shareholders. Security transactions based on access to insider information violates the fiduciary trust the shareholders have placed with management because the managers seek personal financial gain from their privileged position as agents for the shareholders.

For our typical 25-year-old investor, legal and regulatory matters will be of little concern, with the possible exception of insider trading laws and the penalties associated with early withdrawal of funds from tax-deferred retirement accounts. Should he seek a financial advisor to assist him in constructing a financial plan, that advisor would have to obey the regulations pertinent to a client-advisor relationship. Similar concerns confront our 65-year-old investor. In addition, as a

[3] A discretionary account is one in which the fiduciary, many times a financial planner or stockbroker, has the authority to purchase and sell assets in the owner's portfolio without first receiving the owner's approval.

[4] As we will discuss in Reading 50, it is sometimes wise to hold assets that are individually risky in the context of a well-diversified portfolio, even if the investor is strongly risk averse.

retiree, if she wants to do estate planning and set up trust accounts, she should seek legal and tax advice to ensure her plans are properly implemented.

Unique Needs and Preferences This category covers the individual and sometimes idiosyncratic concerns of each investor. Some investors may want to exclude certain investments from their portfolio solely on the basis of personal preference or for social consciousness reasons. For example, they may request that no firms that manufacture or sell tobacco, alcohol, pornography, or environmentally harmful products be included in their portfolio. Some mutual funds screen according to this type of social responsibility criterion.

Another example of a personal constraint is the time and expertise a person has for managing his or her portfolio. Busy executives may prefer to relax during nonworking hours and let a trusted advisor manage their investments. Retirees, on the other hand, may have the time but believe they lack the expertise to choose and monitor investments, so they also may seek professional advice.

In addition, a business owner with a large portion of her wealth—and emotion—tied up in her firm's stock may be reluctant to sell even when it may be financially prudent to do so and then reinvest the proceeds for diversification purposes. Further, if the stock holdings are in a private company, it may be difficult to find a buyer unless shares are sold at a discount from their fair market value. Because each investor is unique, the implications of this final constraint differ for each person; there is no "typical" 25-year-old or 65-year-old investor. Each individual will have to decide—and then communicate specific goals in a well-constructed policy statement.

6 CONSTRUCTING THE POLICY STATEMENT

As we have seen, the policy statement allows the investor to communicate his or her objectives (risk and return) and constraints (liquidity, time horizon, tax, legal and regulatory, and unique needs and preferences). This communication gives the advisor a better chance of implementing an investment strategy that will satisfy the investor. Even if an advisor is not used, each investor needs to take this first important step of the investment process and develop a financial plan to guide the investment strategy. To do without a plan or to plan poorly is to place the success of the financial plan in jeopardy.

General Guidelines

Constructing a policy statement is the investor's responsibility, but investment advisors often assist in the process. The following lists of recommendations for both the investor and the advisor provide guidelines for good policy statement construction.

BOX 3

In the process of constructing a policy statement, investors should think about the following set of questions and be able to explain their answers:

1. What are the real risks of an adverse financial outcome, especially in the short run?
2. What probable emotional reactions will I have to an adverse financial outcome?
3. How knowledgeable am I about investments and markets?

4. What other capital or income sources do I have? How important is this particular portfolio to my overall financial position?
5. What, if any, legal restrictions may affect my investment needs?
6. What, if any, unanticipated consequences of interim fluctuations in portfolio value might affect my investment policy?

Adapted from Charles D. Ellis, *Investment Policy: How to Win the Loser's Game.* Homewood IL: Dow Jones-Irwin, 1985, pp. 25–26.

BOX 4

In assisting an investor in the policy statement process, an advisor should ensure that the policy statement satisfactorily answers the following questions:

1. Is the policy carefully designed to meet the specific needs and objectives of this particular investor? (Cookie-cutter or one-size-fits-all policy statements are generally inappropriate.)
2. Is the policy written so clearly and explicitly that a competent stranger could manage the portfolio in conformance with the client's needs? In case of a manager transition, could the new manager use this policy to handle the portfolio in accordance with the client's needs?
3. Would the client have been able to remain committed to the policies during the capital market experiences of the past 60 to 70 years? That is, does the client fully understand investment risks and the need for a disciplined approach to the investment process?
4. Would the portfolio manager have been able to maintain fidelity to the policy over the same period? (Discipline is a two-way street; we do not want the portfolio manager to change strategies because of a disappointing market.)
5. Would the policy, if implemented, achieve the client's objectives? (Bottom line: would the policy have worked to meet the client's needs?)

Adapted from Charles D. Ellis, *Investment Policy: How to Win the Loser's Game.* Homewood IL: Dow Jones-Irwin, 1985, p. 62.

Some Common Mistakes

When constructing their policy statements, participants in employer-sponsored retirement plans need to realize that through such plans 30–40 percent of their retirement funds may be invested in their employer's stock. Having so much money invested in one asset violates diversification principles and could be costly. To put this in context, most mutual funds are limited by law to having no more than 5 percent of their assets in any one company's stock; a firm's pension plan can invest no more than 10 percent of their funds in its own stock. As noted by Schulz (1996), individuals are unfortunately doing what government regulations prevent many institutional investors from doing. In addition, some studies point out that the average stock allocation in retirement plans is lower than it should be to allow for growth of principal over time.

Another consideration is the issue of stock trading. A number of studies by Barber and Odean (1999, 2000, 2001) and Odean (1998, 1999) have shown that many individual investors trade stocks too often (driving up commissions), sell stocks with gains too early (prior to further price increases), and hold onto losers too long (as the price continues to fall). These results are especially true for men and online traders.

Investors, in general, seem to neglect that important first step to achieve financial success: they do not plan for the future. Studies of retirement plans discussed by Ruffenach (2001) and Clements (1997a, b, c) show that Americans are not saving enough to finance their retirement years and they are not planning sufficiently for what will happen to their savings after they retire. Around 25 percent of workers have saved less than $50,000 for their retirement and 60 percent of workers surveyed confessed they were "behind schedule" in planning and saving for retirement.

7 THE IMPORTANCE OF ASSET ALLOCATION

A major reason why investors develop policy statements is to determine an overall investment strategy. Though a policy statement does not indicate which specific securities to purchase and when they should be sold, it should provide guidelines as to the asset classes to include and the relative proportions of the investor's funds to invest in each class. How the investor divides funds into different asset classes is the process of asset allocation. Rather than present strict percentages, asset allocation is usually expressed in ranges. This allows the investment manager some freedom, based on his or her reading of capital market trends, to invest toward the upper or lower end of the ranges. For example, suppose a policy statement requires that common stocks be 60 percent to 80 percent of the value of the portfolio and that bonds should be 20 percent to 40 percent of the portfolio's value. If a manager is particularly bullish about stocks, she will increase the allocation of stocks toward the 80 percent upper end of the equity range and decrease bonds toward the 20 percent lower end of the bond range. Should she be more optimistic about bonds, that manager may shift the allocation closer to 40 percent of the funds invested in bonds with the remainder in equities.

A review of historical data and empirical studies provides strong support for the contention that the asset allocation decision is a critical component of the portfolio management process. In general, there are four decisions involved in constructing an investment strategy:

- What asset classes should be considered for investment?
- What policy weights should be assigned to each eligible asset class?
- What are the allowable allocation ranges based on policy weights?
- What specific securities or funds should be purchased for the portfolio?

The asset allocation decision comprises the first two points. How important is the asset allocation decision to an investor? In a word, *very*. Several studies by Ibbotson and Kaplan (2000); Brinson, Hood, and Beebower (1986); and Brinson, Singer, and Beebower (1991) have examined the effect of the normal policy weights on investment performance, using data from both pension funds and mutual funds, from periods of time extending from the early 1970s to the late 1990s. The studies all found similar results: About 90 percent of a fund's returns over time can be explained by its target asset allocation policy. Exhibit 8 shows the

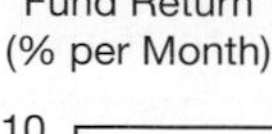

EXHIBIT 8 **Time-Series Regression of Monthly Fund Return versus Fund Policy Return: One Mutual Fund, April 1988–March 1998**

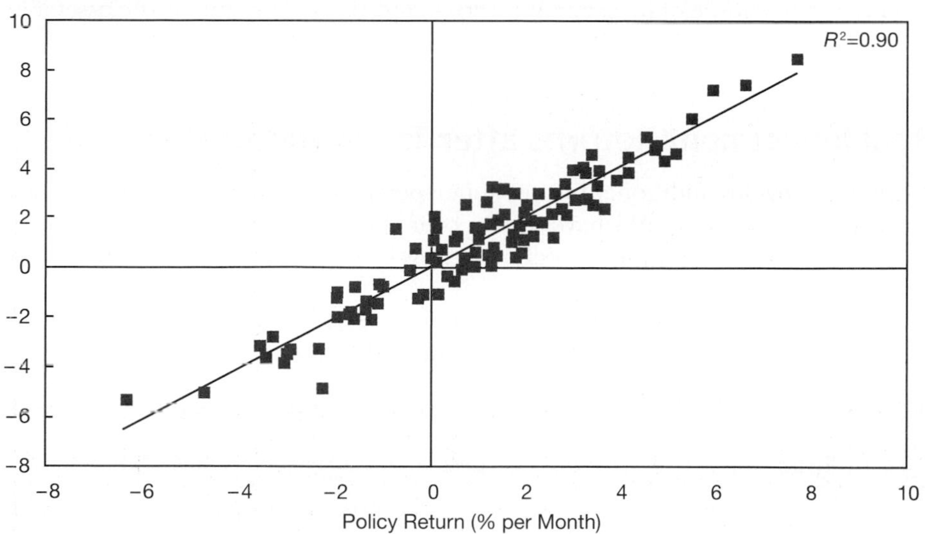

Note: The sample fund's policy allocations among the general asset classes were 52.4 percent U.S. large-cap stocks, 9.8 percent U.S. small-cap stocks, 3.2 percent non-U.S. stocks, 20.9 percent U.S. bonds, and 13.7 percent cash.

Source: Copyright 2000, Association for Investment Management and Research. Reproduced and republished from "Does Asset Allocation Policy Explain 40, 90 or 100 Percent of Performance?" in the *Financial Analysts Journal,* January/February 2000, with permission from the CFA Institute. All Rights Reserved.

relationship between returns on the target or policy portfolio allocation and actual returns on a sample mutual fund.

Rather than looking at just one fund and how the target asset allocation determines its returns, some studies have looked at how much the asset allocation policy affects returns on a variety of funds with different target weights. For example, Ibbotson and Kaplan (2000) found that, across a sample of funds, about 40 percent of the difference in fund returns is explained by differences in asset allocation policy. And what does asset allocation tell us about the *level* of a particular fund's returns? The studies by Brinson and colleagues (1986, 1991) and Ibbotson and Kaplan (2000) answered that question as well. They divided the policy return (what the fund return would have been had it been invested in indexes at the policy weights) by the actual fund return (which includes the effects of varying from the policy weights and security selection). Thus, a fund that was passively invested at the target weights would have a ratio value of 1.0, or 100 percent. A fund managed by someone with skill in market timing (for moving in and out of asset classes) and security selection would have a ratio less than 1.0 (or less than 100 percent); the manager's skill would result in a policy return less than the actual fund return. The studies showed the opposite: The policy return/actual return ratio averaged over 1.0, showing that asset allocation explains slightly more than 100 percent of the level of a fund's returns. Because of market efficiency, fund managers practicing market timing and security selection, on average, have difficulty surpassing passively invested index returns, after taking into account the expenses and fees of investing.

Thus, asset allocation is a very important decision. Across all funds, the asset allocation decision explains an average of 40 percent of the variation in fund returns. For a single fund, asset allocation explains 90 percent of the fund's variation in returns over time and slightly more than 100 percent of the average fund's level of return.

Good investment managers may add some value to portfolio performance, but the major source of investment return—and risk—over time is the asset allocation decision (Brown, 2000).

Real Investment Returns after Taxes and Costs

Exhibit 9 provides additional historical perspectives on returns. It indicates how an investment of $1 would have grown over the 1981–2004 period and, using fairly conservative assumptions, examines how investment returns are affected by taxes and inflation.

Focusing first on stocks, funds invested in 1981 in the Dow Jones Wilshire 5000 stocks would have averaged a 12.36 percent annual return by the end of

EXHIBIT 9 The Effect of Taxes and Inflation on Investment Returns: 1981–2004

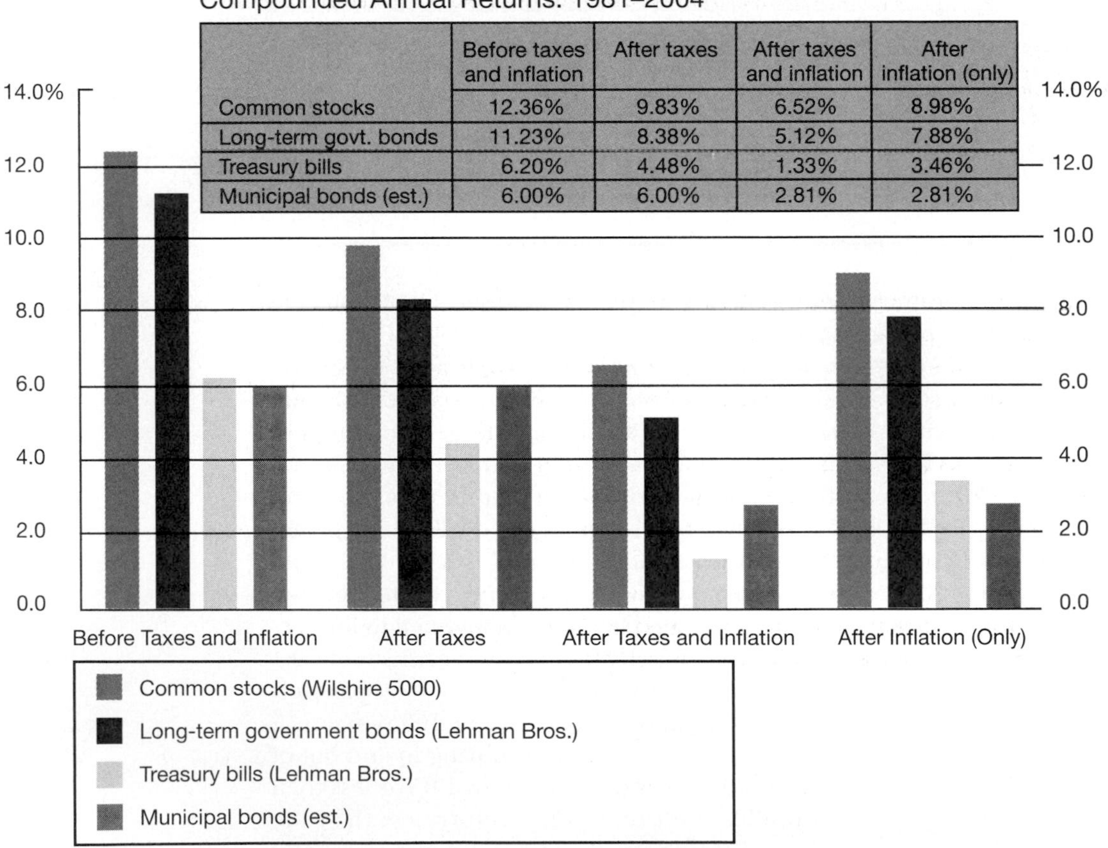

	Before taxes and inflation	After taxes	After taxes and inflation	After inflation (only)
Common stocks	12.36%	9.83%	6.52%	8.98%
Long-term govt. bonds	11.23%	8.38%	5.12%	7.88%
Treasury bills	6.20%	4.48%	1.33%	3.46%
Municipal bonds (est.)	6.00%	6.00%	2.81%	2.81%

Assumptions: 28 percent tax rate on income; 20 percent on price change. Compound inflation rate was 3.1 percent for full period.
Source: Computations by authors, using data indicated.

2004. Unfortunately, this return is unrealistic because if the funds were invested over time, taxes would have to be paid and inflation would erode the real purchasing power of the invested funds.

Except for tax-exempt investors and tax-deferred accounts, annual tax payments reduce investment returns. Incorporating taxes into the analysis lowers the after-tax average annual return of a stock investment to 9.83 percent.

But the major reduction in the value of our investment is caused by inflation. The real after-tax average annual return on a stock over this time frame was only 6.52 percent, which is quite a bit less than our initial unadjusted 12.36 percent return!

This example shows the long-run impact of taxes and inflation on the real value of a stock portfolio. For bonds and bills, however, the results in Exhibit 9 show something even more surprising. After adjusting for taxes, long-term bonds maintained their purchasing power; T-bills barely provided value in real terms. One dollar invested in long-term government bonds in 1981 gave the investor an annual average after-tax real return of 5.12 percent. An investment in Treasury bills earned an average rate of only 1.33 percent after taxes and inflation. Municipal bonds, because of the protection they offer from taxes, earned an average annual real return of almost 3.00 percent during this time.

This historical analysis demonstrates that, for taxable investments, a reasonable way to maintain purchasing power over time when investing in financial assets is to invest in common stocks. Put another way, an asset allocation decision for a taxable portfolio that does not include a substantial commitment to common stocks makes it difficult for the portfolio to maintain real value over time.[5]

Notably, the fourth column, labeled "After inflation (only)," is more encouraging since it refers to results for a tax-free retirement account that is only impacted by inflation. These results should encourage investors to take advantage of such opportunities.

Returns and Risks of Different Asset Classes

By focusing on returns, we have ignored its partner—risk. Assets with higher long-term returns have these returns to compensate for their risk. Exhibit 10 illustrates returns (unadjusted for costs and taxes) for several asset classes over time. As expected, the higher returns available from equities (both large cap and small cap) come at the cost of higher risk. This is precisely why investors need a policy statement and why the investor and manager must understand the capital markets and have a disciplined approach to investing. Safe Treasury bills will sometimes outperform equities, and, because of their higher risk, common stocks sometimes lose significant value. These are times when undisciplined and uneducated investors become frustrated, sell their stocks at a loss, and vow never to invest in equities again. In contrast, these are times when disciplined investors stick to their investment plan and position their portfolios for the next bull market.[6] By holding

[5] Of course other equity-oriented investments, such as venture capital or real estate, may also provide inflation protection after adjusting for portfolio costs and taxes. Future studies of the performance of Treasury inflation-protected securities (TIPs) will likely show their usefulness in protecting investors from inflation as well.

[6] Newton's law of gravity seems to work two ways in financial markets. What goes up must come down; it also appears over time that what goes down may came back up. Contrarian investors and some "value" investors use this concept of reversion to the mean to try to outperform the indexes over time.

EXHIBIT 10 Summary Statistics of Annual Returns, 1984–2003, U.S. Securities

	Geometric Mean (%)	Arithmetic Mean (%)	Standard Deviation (%)
Large company stocks (S&P 500)	13.33	14.74	17.92
Small company stocks (S&P SmallCap 600)	10.82	12.86	21.21
Government bonds (Lehman Brothers)	9.07	9.20	5.33
Corporate bonds (Lehman Brothers)	10.07	10.24	5.99
Intermediate-term corporate bonds (Lehman Brothers)	9.25	9.34	4.37
Intermediate-term government bonds (Lehman Brothers)	8.43	8.50	3.84
30-day Treasury bill	5.23	5.23	0.64
U.S. inflation	3.01	3.01	0.81

Source: Calculations by authors, using data noted.

on to their stocks and perhaps purchasing more at depressed prices, the equity portion of the portfolio will experience a substantial increase in the future.

The asset allocation decision determines to a great extent both the returns and the volatility of the portfolio. Exhibit 10 indicates that stocks are riskier than bonds or T-bills. Exhibit 11 shows that stocks have sometimes earned returns lower than those of T-bills for extended periods of time. Sticking with an investment policy and riding out the difficult times can earn attractive long-term rates of return.[7]

EXHIBIT 11 Higher Returns Offered by Equities over Long Time Periods Time Frame: 1934–2003

Length of Holding Period (calendar years)	Percentage of Periods That Stock Returns Trailed T-Bill Returns[a]
1	35.7%
5	18.2
10	11.5
20	0.0
30	0.0

[a] Price change plus reinvested income.

Source: Author calculations.

[7] The added benefits of diversification—combining different asset classes in the portfolio—may reduce overall portfolio risk without harming potential return. The topic of diversification is discussed in Reading 50.

One popular way to measure risk is to examine the variability of returns over time by computing a standard deviation or variance of annual rates of return for an asset class. This measure, which is contained in Exhibit 10, indicates that stocks are risky and T-bills are relatively safe. Another intriguing measure of risk is the probability of *not* meeting your investment return objective. From this perspective, the results in Exhibit 11 show that if the investor has a long time horizon (i.e., approaching 20 years), the risk of equities is small and that of T-bills is large because of their differences in long-term expected returns.

Asset Allocation Summary

A carefully constructed policy statement determines the types of assets that should be included in a portfolio. The asset allocation decision, not the selection of specific stocks and bonds, determines most of the portfolio's returns over time. Although seemingly risky, investors seeking capital appreciation, income, or even capital preservation over long time periods will do well to include a sizable allocation to the equity portion in their portfolio. As noted in this section, a strategy's risk may depend on the investor's goals and time horizon. As demonstrated, investing in T-bills may be a riskier strategy than investing in common stocks due to reinvestment risks and the risk of not meeting long-term investment return goals after considering inflation and taxes.

Asset Allocation and Cultural Differences Thus far, our analysis has focused on U.S. investors. Non-U.S. investors make their asset allocation decisions in much the same manner; but because they face different social, economic, political, and tax environments, their allocation decisions differ from those of U.S. investors. Exhibit 12 shows the equity allocations of pension funds in several countries. As shown, the equity allocations vary dramatically from 79 percent in Hong Kong to 37 percent in Japan and only 8 percent in Germany.

National differences can explain much of the divergent portfolio strategies. Of these six nations, the average age of the population is highest in Germany and Japan and lowest in the United States and the United Kingdom, which helps explain the greater use of equities in the latter countries. Government privatization programs during the 1980s in the United Kingdom encouraged equity ownership among individual and institutional investors. In Germany, regulations

EXHIBIT 12 Equity Allocations in Pension Fund Portfolios

Country	Percentage in Equities
Hong Kong	79
United Kingdom	78
Ireland	68
United States	58
Japan	37
Germany	8

Source: Copyright 1998, Association for Investment Management and Research. Reproduced and republished from "Client Expectations and the Demand to Minimize Downside Risk" from the seminar proceedings *Asset Allocation in a Changing World*, 1998, with permission from the CFA Institute. All Rights Reserved.

prevent insurance firms from having more than 20 percent of their assets in equities. Both Germany and Japan have banking sectors that invest privately in firms and whose officers sit on corporate boards. Since 1980, the cost of living in the United Kingdom has increased at a rate about two times that of Germany; this inflationary bias in the U.K. economy favors equities in U.K. asset allocations. Exhibit 13 shows the positive relationship between the level of inflation in a country and its pension fund allocation to equity. These results indicate that the general economic environment, as well as demographics, has an effect on the asset allocation in a country.

The need to invest in equities for portfolio growth is less in Germany, where workers receive generous state pensions. Germans tend to show a cultural aversion to the stock market: Many Germans are risk averse and consider stock investing a form of gambling. Although this attitude is changing, the German stock market is rather illiquid, and Gumbel (1995) noted that only a handful of stocks account for 50 percent of total stock trading volume. New legislation that encourages 401(k)-like plans in Germany may encourage citizens to invest more in equities.

Other Organization for Economic Cooperation and Development (OECD) countries place regulatory restrictions on institutional investors. As noted by Witschi (1998) and Chernoff (1996), pension funds in Austria must have at least 50 percent of their assets in bank deposits or schilling-denominated bonds. Belgium limits pension funds to a minimum 15 percent investment in government bonds. Finland places a 5 percent limit on investments outside its borders by pension funds, and French pension funds must invest a minimum of 34 percent in public debt instruments.

Asset allocation policy and strategy are determined in the context of an investor's objectives and constraints. Among the factors that explain differences in investor behavior across countries, however, are their political and economic environments.

EXHIBIT 13 Asset Allocation and Inflation for Different Countries' Equity Allocation as of December 1997; Average Inflation Measured over 1980–1997

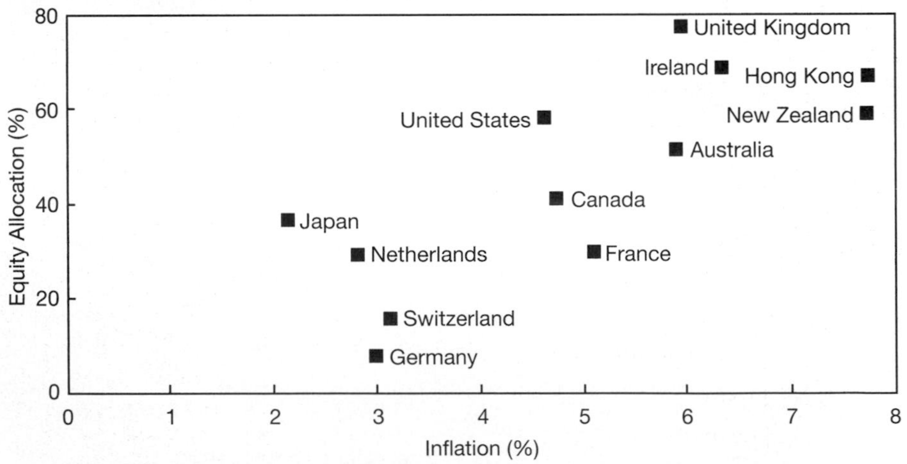

Source: Copyright 1998, Association for Investment Management and Research. Reproduced and republished from "Are U.K. Investors Turning More Conservative?" from the seminar proceedings *Asset Allocation in a Changing World,* 1998, with permission from the CFA Institute. All Rights Reserved.

THE INTERNET

Investments Online

Many inputs go into an investment policy statement as an investor maps out his or her objectives and constraints. Some inputs and helpful information are available in the following websites. Many of the sites mentioned contain important information and insights about asset allocation decisions, as well.

www.ssa.gov Information on a person's expected retirement funds from Social Security can be obtained by using the Social Security Administration's website.

www.ibbotson.com Ibbotson is the source of much data and analysis that is helpful to the investor education and asset allocation process. Many professional financial planners make use of Ibbotson's data and education resources.

www.mfea.com/InvestmentStrategies/Calculators/default.asp contains links to calculators on websites of mutual fund families.

Sites with information and sample Monte Carlo simulations for spending plans in retirement include: *www.financialengines.com*, *www.troweprice.com* (after getting to the individual investor page, click on investment planning and tools, then tools, and calculators, investment planning tools, then investment strategy planner); *www3.troweprice.com/ric/RIC/* (for a retirement income calculator), and *www.decisioneering.com*.

Many professional organizations have websites for use by their members, those interested in seeking professional finance designations, and those interested in seeking advice from a professional financial advisor. These sites include:

www.cfainstitute.org CFA Institute awards the CFA (Chartered Financial Analyst) designation. This site provides information about the CFA designation, CFA Institute publications, investor education, and various Internet resources.

www.theamericancollege.edu This is the website for The American College, which is the training arm of the insurance industry. The American College offers the CLU and ChFC designations, which are typically earned by insurance professionals.

www.cfp.net The Certified Financial Planner Board of Standards home page. Contains links to find a CFP™ mark holder and other information about the financial planning profession.

www.napfa.org This is the home page for the National Association of Personal Financial Advisors. This is the trade group for fee-only financial planners. Fee-only planners do not sell products on commission, or, should they recommend a commission-generating product, they pass the commission on to the investor. This site features press releases, finding a fee-only planner in your area, a list of financial resources on the Web, and position openings in the financial planning field.

www.fpanet.org The Financial Planning Association's website. The site offers features and topics of interest to financial planners including information on earning the CFP designation and receiving the *Journal of Financial Planning.*

www.aset.org The home page of the American Saving Education Council.

SUMMARY

- In this reading, we saw that investors need to prudently manage risk within the context of their investment goals and preferences. Income, spending, and investing behavior will change over a person's lifetime.
- We reviewed the importance of developing an investment policy statement before implementing a serious investment plan. By forcing investors to examine their needs, risk tolerance, and familiarity with the capital markets, policy statements help investors correctly identify appropriate objectives and constraints. In addition, the policy statement becomes a standard by which to judge the performance of the portfolio manager.
- We also reviewed the importance of the asset allocation decision in determining long-run portfolio investment returns and risks. Because the asset allocation decision follows setting the objectives and constraints, it is clear that the success of the investment program depends on the first step, the construction of the policy statement.

AN INTRODUCTION TO PORTFOLIO MANAGEMENT

by Frank K. Reilly and Keith C. Brown

READING

50

LEARNING OUTCOMES

The candidate should be able to:

a. define risk aversion and discuss evidence that suggests that individuals are generally risk averse;

b. list the assumptions about investor behavior underlying the Markowitz model;

c. compute and interpret the expected return, variance, and standard deviation for an individual investment and the expected return and standard deviation for a portfolio;

d. compute and interpret the covariance of rates of return, and show how it is related to the correlation coefficient;

e. list the components of the portfolio standard deviation formula, and explain the relevant importance of these components when adding an investment to a portfolio;

f. describe the efficient frontier, and explain the implications for incremental returns as an investor assumes more risk;

g. explain the concept of an optimal portfolio, and show how each investor may have a different optimal portfolio.

INTRODUCTION 1

One of the major advances in the investment field during the past few decades has been the recognition that the creation of an optimum investment portfolio is not simply a matter of combining numerous unique individual securities that have desirable risk-return characteristics. Specifically, it has been shown that an investor must consider the relationship *among* the investments to build an optimum portfolio that will meet investment objectives. The recognition of what is important in creating a portfolio was demonstrated in the derivation of portfolio theory.

In this reading we explain portfolio theory step by step. We introduce the basic portfolio risk formula for combining different assets. Once you understand this formula and its implications, you will understand not only *why* you should diversify your portfolio but also *how* you should diversify.

2 SOME BACKGROUND ASSUMPTIONS

Before presenting portfolio theory, we need to clarify some general assumptions of the theory. This includes not only what we mean by an *optimum portfolio* but also what we mean by the terms *risk aversion* and *risk*.

One basic assumption of portfolio theory is that as an investor you want to maximize the returns from your total set of investments for a given level of risk. To adequately deal with such an assumption, certain ground rules must be laid. First, your portfolio should *include all of your assets and liabilities*, not only your stocks or even your marketable securities but also such items as your car, house, and less marketable investments such as coins, stamps, art, antiques, and furniture. The full spectrum of investments must be considered because the returns from all these investments interact, and *this relationship among the returns for assets in the portfolio is important*. Hence, a good portfolio is not simply a collection of individually good investments.

Risk Aversion

Portfolio theory also assumes that investors are basically **risk averse**, meaning that, given a choice between two assets with equal rates of return, they will select the asset with the lower level of risk. Evidence that most investors are risk averse is that they purchase various types of insurance, including life insurance, car insurance, and health insurance. Buying insurance basically involves an outlay of a given known amount to guard against an uncertain, possibly larger, outlay in the future. Further evidence of risk aversion is the difference in promised yield (the required rate of return) for different grades of bonds that supposedly have different degrees of credit risk. Specifically, the promised yield on corporate bonds increases from AAA (the lowest risk class) to AA to A, and so on, indicating that investors require a higher rate of return to accept higher risk.

This does not imply that everybody is risk averse, or that investors are completely risk averse regarding all financial commitments. The fact is, not everybody buys insurance for everything. Some people have no insurance against anything, either by choice or because they cannot afford it. In addition, some individuals buy insurance related to some risks such as auto accidents or illness, but they also buy lottery tickets and gamble at race tracks or in casinos, where it is known that the expected returns are negative (which means that participants are willing to pay for the excitement of the risk involved). This combination of risk preference and risk aversion can be explained by an attitude toward risk that depends on the amount of money involved. Researchers such as Friedman and Savage (1948) speculate that this is the case for people who like to gamble for small amounts (in lotteries or slot machines) but buy insurance to protect themselves against large losses such as fire or accidents.

While recognizing such attitudes, our basic assumption is that most investors committing large sums of money to developing an investment portfolio are risk averse. Therefore, we expect a positive relationship between expected return and expected risk. Notably, this is also what we generally find in terms of historical results—that is, most studies find a positive relationship between the rates of return on various assets and their measures of risk.

Definition of Risk

Although there is a difference in the specific definitions of *risk* and *uncertainty*, for our purposes and in most financial literature the two terms are used interchangeably. For most investors, *risk* means *the uncertainty of future outcomes.* An alternative definition might be *the probability of an adverse outcome.* In our subsequent discussion of portfolio theory, we will consider several measures of risk that are used when developing and applying the theory.

MARKOWITZ PORTFOLIO THEORY 3

In the early 1960s, the investment community talked about risk, but there was no specific measure for the term. To build a portfolio model, however, investors had to quantify their risk variable. The basic portfolio model was developed by Harry Markowitz (1952, 1959), who derived the **expected rate of return** for a portfolio of assets and an expected risk measure. Markowitz showed that the variance of the rate of return was a meaningful measure of portfolio risk under a reasonable set of assumptions, and he derived the formula for computing the variance of a portfolio. This portfolio variance formula not only indicated the importance of diversifying investments to reduce the total risk of a portfolio but also showed *how* to effectively diversify. The Markowitz model is based on several assumptions regarding investor behavior.

1. Investors consider each investment alternative as being represented by a probability distribution of expected returns over some holding period.
2. Investors maximize one-period **expected utility**, and their utility curves demonstrate **diminishing marginal** utility of wealth.
3. Investors estimate the risk of the portfolio on the basis of the variability of expected returns.
4. Investors base decisions solely on expected return and risk, so their utility curves are a function of expected return and the expected variance (or standard deviation) of returns only.
5. For a given risk level, investors prefer higher returns to lower returns. Similarly, for a given level of expected return, investors prefer less risk to more risk.

Under these assumptions, *a single asset or portfolio of assets is considered to be efficient if no other asset or portfolio of assets offers higher expected return with the same (or lower) risk or lower risk with the same (or higher) expected return.*

Alternative Measures of Risk

One of the best-known measures of risk is the *variance,* or *standard deviation of expected returns.*[1] It is a statistical measure of the dispersion of returns around the

[1] We consider the variance and standard deviation as one measure of risk because the standard deviation is the square root of the variance.

expected value whereby a larger variance or standard deviation indicates greater dispersion. The idea is that the more disperse the expected returns, the greater the uncertainty of future returns.

Another measure of risk is the *range of returns*. It is assumed that a larger range of expected returns, from the lowest to the highest expected return, means greater uncertainty and risk regarding future expected returns.

Instead of using measures that analyze all deviations from expectations, some observers believe that investors should be concerned only with returns below expectations, which means only deviations below the mean value. A measure that only considers deviations below the mean is the *semivariance.* An extension of the semivariance measure only computes expected returns *below zero* (that is, negative returns), or returns below the returns of some specific asset such as T-bills, the rate of inflation, or a benchmark. These measures of risk implicitly assume that investors want to *minimize the damage* (regret) from returns less than some target rate. Assuming that investors would welcome returns above some target rate, the returns above such a target rate are not considered when measuring risk.

Although there are numerous potential measures of risk, we will use the variance or standard deviation of returns because (1) this measure is somewhat intuitive, (2) it is a correct and widely recognized risk measure, and (3) it has been used in most of the theoretical asset pricing models.

Expected Rates of Return

We compute the **expected rate of return** for an *individual investment* as shown in Exhibit 1. The expected return for an individual risky asset with the set of potential returns and an assumption of the different probabilities used in the example would be 10.3 percent.

The expected rate of return for a *portfolio* of investments is simply the weighted average of the expected rates of return for the individual investments in the portfolio. The weights are the proportion of total value for the individual investment.

The expected rate of return for a hypothetical portfolio with four risky assets is shown in Exhibit 2. The expected return for this portfolio of investments would be 11.5 percent. The effect of adding or dropping any investment from the portfolio would be easy to determine; we would use the new weights

EXHIBIT 1 Computation of the Expected Return for an Individual Asset

Probability	Possible Rate of Return (percent)	Expected Return (percent)
0.35	0.08	0.0280
0.30	0.10	0.0300
0.20	0.12	0.0240
0.15	0.14	0.0210
		E(R) = 0.1030

EXHIBIT 2 **Computation of the Expected Return for a Portfolio of Risky Assets**

Weight (w_i) (percent of portfolio)	Expected Security Return (R_i)	Expected Portfolio Return ($w_i \times R_i$)
0.20	0.10	0.0200
0.30	0.11	0.0330
0.30	0.12	0.0360
0.20	0.13	0.0260
		$E(R_{port}) = 0.1150$

based on value and the expected returns for each of the investments. We can generalize this computation of the expected return for the portfolio $E(R_{port})$ as follows:

$$E(R_{port}) = \sum_{i=1}^{n} w_i R_i \tag{50-1}$$

where

w_i = the weight of an individual asset in the portfolio, or the percent of the portfolio in Asset i

R_i = the expected rate of return for Asset i

Variance (Standard Deviation) of Returns for an Individual Investment

As noted, we will be using the variance or the standard deviation of returns as the measure of risk. Therefore, at this point we demonstrate how to compute the standard deviation of returns for an individual investment. Subsequently, after discussing some other statistical concepts, we will consider the determination of the standard deviation for a *portfolio* of investments.

The variance, or standard deviation, is a measure of the variation of possible rates of return R_i from the expected rate of return $E(R_i)$ as follows:

$$\text{Variance} = \sigma^2 = \sum_{i=1}^{n} [R_i - E(R_i)]^2 P_i \tag{50-2}$$

where

P_i = probability of the possible rate of return R_i

$$\text{Standard Deviation} = \sigma = \sqrt{\sum_{i=1}^{n} [R_i - E(R_i)]^2 P_i} \tag{50-3}$$

The computation of the variance and standard deviation of returns for the individual risky asset in Exhibit 1 is set forth in Exhibit 3.

EXHIBIT 3 Computation of the Variance for an Individual Risky Asset

Possible Rate of Return (R_i)	Expected Return $E(R_i)$	$R_i - E(R_i)$	$[R_i - E(R_i)]^2$	P_i	$[R_i - E(R_i)]^2 P_i$
0.08	0.103	−0.023	0.0005	0.35	0.000185
0.10	0.103	−0.003	0.0000	0.30	0.000003
0.12	0.103	0.017	0.0003	0.20	0.000058
0.14	0.103	0.037	0.0014	0.15	0.000205
					0.000451

Variance = σ^2 = 0.000451.

Standard Deviation = σ = 0.021237.

Variance (Standard Deviation) of Returns for a Portfolio

Two basic concepts in statistics, covariance and correlation, must be understood before we discuss the formula for the variance of the rate of return for a portfolio.

Covariance of Returns In this subsection we discuss what the covariance of returns is intended to measure, give the formula for computing it, and present an example of its computation. **Covariance** is a measure of the degree to which two variables move together relative to their individual mean values over time. In portfolio analysis, we usually are concerned with the covariance of *rates of return* rather than prices or some other variable.[2] A positive covariance means that the rates of return for two investments tend to move in the same direction relative to their individual means during the same time period. In contrast, a negative covariance indicates that the rates of return for two investments tend to move in different directions relative to their means during specified time intervals over time. The *magnitude* of the covariance depends on the variances of the individual return series, as well as on the relationship between the series.

Exhibit 4 contains the monthly closing index values for U.S. stocks (measured by the Wilshire 5000 index) and bonds (measured by the Lehman Brothers Treasury Bond Index). Both indexes are total return indexes—that is, the stock index includes dividends paid and the bond index includes **accrued interest**, as discussed in Reading 53 of Volume 5. We can use these data to compute monthly rates of return for these two assets during 2004. Exhibits 5 and 6 contain a time-series plot of the monthly rates of return for the two assets during 2004. Although the rates of return for the two assets moved together during some months, in other months they moved in opposite directions. The covariance statistic provides an *absolute* measure of how they moved together over time.

[2] Returns, of course, can be measured in a variety of ways, depending on the type of asset. We defined returns (R_i) as:

$$R_i = \frac{EV - BV + CF}{BV}$$

where EV is ending value, BV is beginning value, and CF is the cash flow during the period.

EXHIBIT 4 Computation of Monthly Rates of Return for U.S. Stocks and Bonds

	Wilshire 5000 Index	Lehman Brothers Treasury Bonds
Date	Monthly Rate of Return (%)	Monthly Rate of Return (%)
Jan-04	2.23	1.77
Feb-04	1.46	2.00
Mar-04	−1.07	1.50
Apr-04	−2.13	−5.59
May-04	1.38	−0.54
Jun-04	2.08	0.95
Jul-04	−3.82	1.73
Aug-04	0.33	3.74
Sep-04	1.78	0.84
Oct-04	1.71	1.51
Nov-04	4.68	−2.19
Dec-04	3.63	2.31
	Mean = 1.02	Mean = 0.67

Sources: Wilshire Associates and Lehman Brothers.

EXHIBIT 5 Time-Series Plot of Monthly Returns for Wilshire 5000 Index, 2004

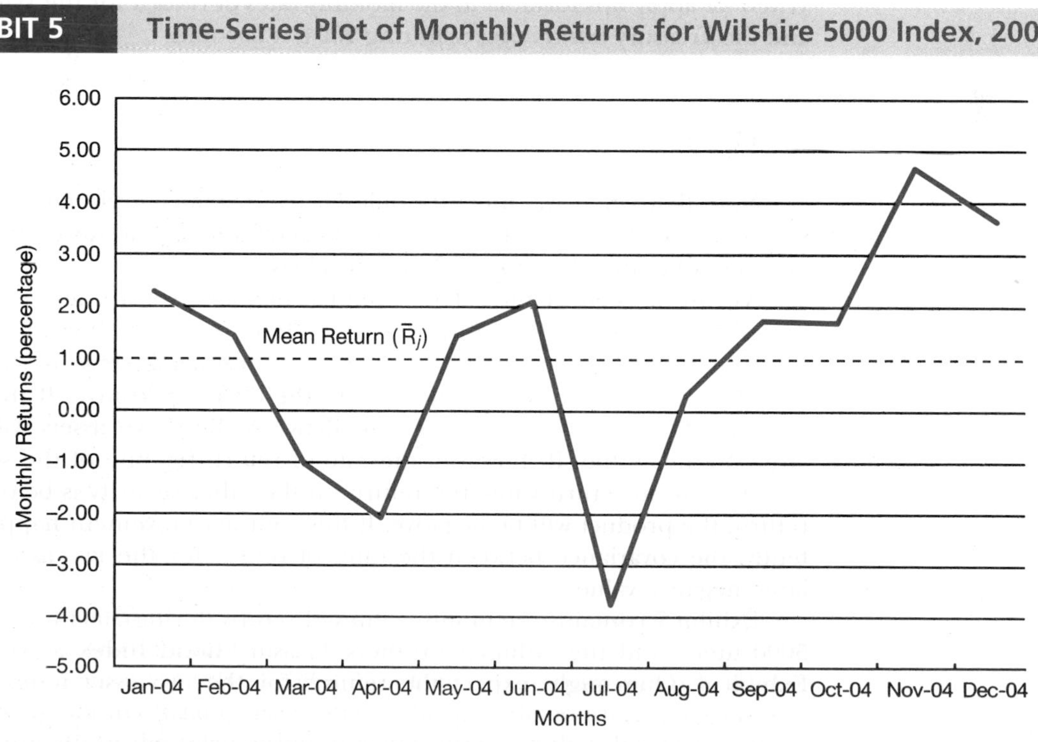

EXHIBIT 8 Scatterplot of Monthly Returns for Wilshire 5000 and Lehman Brothers Treasury Bond Index, 2004

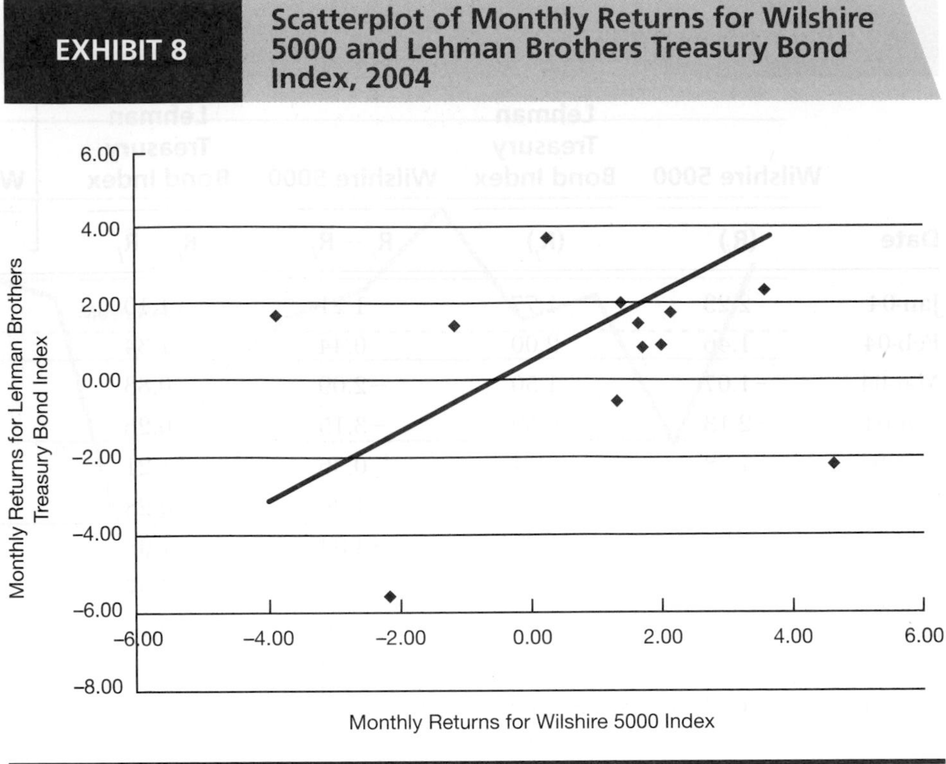

during 2004 was not very strong, since during five months the two assets moved counter to each other. As a result, the overall covariance was a small positive value.

Covariance and Correlation Covariance is affected by the variability of the two individual return indexes. Therefore, a number such as the 0.637 in our example might indicate a weak positive relationship if the two individual indexes were volatile, but would reflect a strong positive relationship if the two indexes were stable. Obviously, we want to standardize this covariance measure. We do so by taking into consideration the variability of the two individual return indexes, as follows:

$$r_{ij} = \frac{\text{Cov}_{ij}}{\sigma_i \sigma_j} \quad \textbf{(50-5)}$$

where:

r_{ij} = the correlation coefficient of returns
σ_i = the standard deviation of R_{it}
σ_j = the standard deviation of R_{jt}

Standardizing the covariance by the product of the individual standard deviations yields the **correlation coefficient** r_{ij}, which can vary only in the range −1 to +1. A value of +1 indicates a perfect positive linear relationship between R_i and R_j, meaning the returns for the two-assets move together in a completely linear manner. A value of −1 indicates a perfect negative relationship between the two return indexes, so that when one asset's rate of return is above its mean, the other asset's rate of return will be below its mean by a comparable amount.

To calculate this standardized measure of the relationship, we need to compute the standard deviation for the two individual return indexes. We already have the values for $(R_{it} - \overline{R}_i)$ and $(R_{jt} - \overline{R}_j)$ in Exhibit 7. We can square each of

EXHIBIT 9 Computation of Standard Deviation of Returns for the Wilshire 5000 Index and Lehman Brothers Treasury Bond Index, 2004

	Wilshire 5000 Index		Lehman Brothers Treasury Bonds	
Date	$R_i - \bar{R}_i$	$(R_i - \bar{R}_i)^2$	$R_j - \bar{R}_j$	$(R_j - \bar{R}_j)^2$
Jan-04	1.21	1.46	1.10	1.21
Feb-04	0.44	0.19	1.34	1.79
Mar-04	−2.09	4.38	0.83	0.69
Apr-04	−3.15	9.93	−6.26	39.17
May-04	0.36	0.13	−1.21	1.47
Jun-04	1.06	1.12	0.28	0.08
Jul-04	−4.84	23.44	1.06	1.13
Aug-04	−0.69	0.48	3.07	9.42
Sep-04	0.76	0.58	0.17	0.03
Oct-04	0.69	0.47	0.84	0.70
Nov-04	3.66	13.38	−2.86	8.18
Dec-04	2.61	6.80	1.64	2.69
		Sum = 62.36		Sum = 66.56

$\text{Variance}_i = 62.36/11 = 5.67.$
$\text{Standard Deviation}_i = (5.67)^{1/2} = 2.38.$

$\text{Variance}_j = 66.56/11 = 6.05.$
$\text{Standard Deviation}_j = (6.05)^{1/2} = 2.46.$

these values and sum them as shown in Exhibit 9 to calculate the variance of each return series; again, we divide by $(n - 1)$ to avoid statistical bias.

$$\sigma_i^2 = \frac{1}{11}62.36 = 5.67$$

and

$$\sigma_j^2 = \frac{1}{11}66.56 = 6.05$$

The standard deviation for each index is the square root of the variance for each, as follows:

$$\sigma_i = \sqrt{5.67} = 2.38$$
$$\sigma_j = \sqrt{6.05} = 2.46$$

Thus, based on the covariance between the two indexes and the individual standard deviations, we can calculate the correlation coefficient between returns for common stocks and Treasury bonds during 2004:

$$\text{r}_{ij} = \frac{\text{Cov}_{ij}}{\sigma_i\sigma_j} = \frac{0.637}{(2.38)(2.46)} = \frac{0.637}{5.8548} = 0.109$$

Obviously, this formula also implies that

$$\text{Cov}_{ij} = \text{r}_{ij}\sigma_i\sigma_j = (0.109)(2.38)(2.46) = 0.638$$

Standard Deviation of a Portfolio

As noted, a correlation of +1.0 indicates perfect positive correlation, and a value of −1.0 means that the returns moved in completely opposite directions. A value of zero means that the returns had no linear relationship, that is, they were uncorrelated statistically. That does *not* mean that they are independent. The value of $r_{ij} = 0.109$ is not significantly different from zero. This insignificant positive correlation is not unusual for stocks versus bonds during short time intervals such as one year.

Portfolio Standard Deviation Formula Now that we have discussed the concepts of covariance and correlation, we can consider the formula for computing the standard deviation of returns for a *portfolio* of assets, our measure of risk for a portfolio. In Exhibit 2, we showed that the expected rate of return of the portfolio was the weighted average of the expected returns for the individual assets in the portfolio; the weights were the percentage of value of the portfolio. One might assume it is possible to derive the standard deviation of the portfolio in the same manner, that is, by computing the weighted average of the standard deviations for the individual assets. This would be a mistake. Markowitz (1959) derived the general formula for the standard deviation of a portfolio as follows:

$$\sigma_{\text{port}} = \sqrt{\sum_{i=1}^{n} w_i^2 \sigma_i^2 + \sum_{\substack{i=1 \\ i \neq j}}^{n} \sum_{j=1}^{n} w_i w_j \text{Cov}_{ij}} \tag{50-6}$$

where

σ_{port} = the standard deviation of the portfolio
w_i = the weights of an individual asset in the portfolio, where weights are determined by the proportion of value in the portfolio
σ_i^2 = the variance of rates of return for asset *i*
Cov_{ij} = the covariance between the rates of return for assets *i* and *j*, where $\text{Cov}_{ij} = r_{ij}\sigma_i\sigma_j$

This formula indicates that the standard deviation for a portfolio of assets is a function of the weighted average of the individual variances (where the weights are squared), *plus* the weighted covariances between all the assets in the portfolio. The very important point is that the standard deviation for a portfolio of assets encompasses not only the variances of the individual assets but *also* includes the covariances between all the pairs of individual assets in the portfolio. Further, it can be shown that, in a portfolio with a large number of securities, this formula reduces to the sum of the weighted covariances.

Impact of a new security in a portfolio. Although in most of the following discussion we will consider portfolios with only two assets (because it is possible to show the effect in two dimensions), we will also demonstrate the computations for a three-asset portfolio. Still, it is important at this point to consider what happens in a large portfolio with many assets. Specifically, what happens to the portfolio's standard deviation when we add a new security to such a portfolio? As shown by the formula, we see two effects. The first is the asset's own variance of returns, and the second is the covariance between the returns of this new asset and the returns of *every other asset that is already in the portfolio.* The relative weight of these numerous covariances is substantially greater than the asset's unique variance; the more assets in the portfolio, the more this is true. This means that the important factor to consider when adding an investment to a portfolio that contains a number of other investments is *not* the new security's own variance but *its average covariance with all the other investments in the portfolio.*

Portfolio Standard Deviation Calculation Because of the assumptions used in developing the Markowitz portfolio model, any asset or portfolio of assets can be described by two characteristics: the expected rate of return and the expected standard deviation of returns. Therefore, the following demonstrations can be applied to two *individual* assets, two *portfolios* of assets, or two *asset classes* with the indicated return—standard deviation characteristics and correlation coefficients.

Equal risk and return—changing correlations. Consider first the case in which both assets have the same expected return and expected standard deviation of return. As an example, let's assume

$$E(R_1) = 0.20, \qquad E(\sigma_1) = 0.10$$
$$E(R_2) = 0.20, \qquad E(\sigma_2) = 0.10$$

To show the effect of different covariances, we assume different levels of correlation between the two assets. We also assume that the two assets have equal weights in the portfolio ($w_1 = 0.50$; $w_2 = 0.50$). Therefore, the only value that changes in each example is the correlation between the returns for the two assets.

Now consider the following five correlation coefficients and the covariances they yield. Since $Cov_{ij} = r_{ij}\sigma_i\sigma_j$, the covariance will be equal to $r_{1,2}$ (0.10)(0.10) because the standard deviation of both assets is 0.10.

a. For $r_{1,2} = 1.00$, $\quad Cov_{1,2} = (1.00)(0.10)(0.10) = 0.01$
b. For $r_{1,2} = 0.50$, $\quad Cov_{1,2} = (0.50)(0.10)(0.10) = 0.005$
c. For $r_{1,2} = 0.00$, $\quad Cov_{1,2} = (0.00)(0.10)(0.10) = 0.000$
d. For $r_{1,2} = -0.50$, $\quad Cov_{1,2} = (-0.50)(0.10)(0.10) = -0.005$
e. For $r_{1,2} = -1.00$, $\quad Cov_{1,2} = (-1.00)(0.10)(0.10) = -0.01$

Now let's see what happens to the standard deviation of the portfolio under these five conditions.

When we apply the general portfolio formula from Equation 6 to a two-asset portfolio, it is

$$\sigma_{port} = \sqrt{w_1^2\sigma_1^2 + w_2^2\sigma_2^2 + 2w_1w_2r_{1,2}\sigma_1\sigma_2} \qquad \textbf{(50-7)}$$

or

$$\sigma_{port} = \sqrt{w_1^2\sigma_1^2 + w_2^2\sigma_2^2 + 2w_1w_2Cov_{1,2}}$$

Thus, in Case a:

$$\begin{aligned}\sigma_{port(a)} &= \sqrt{(0.5)^2(0.10)^2 + (0.5)^2(0.10)^2 + 2(0.5)(0.5)(0.01)}\\ &= \sqrt{(0.25)(0.01) + (0.25)(0.01) + 2(0.25)(0.01)}\\ &= \sqrt{0.01}\\ &= 0.10\end{aligned}$$

In this case, where the returns for the two assets are perfectly positively correlated, the standard deviation for the portfolio is, in fact, the weighted average of the individual standard deviations. The important point is that we get no real benefit from combining two assets that are perfectly correlated; they are like one asset already because their returns move together.

We will use the previous set of correlation coefficients, but we must recalculate the covariances because this time the standard deviations of the assets are different. The results are shown in the following table.

Case	Correlation Coefficient ($r_{1,2}$)	Covariance ($r_{1,2}\sigma_1\sigma_2$)
a	+1.00	0.0070
b	+0.50	0.0035
c	0.00	0.0000
d	−0.50	−0.0035
e	−1.00	−0.0070

Because we are assuming the same weights in all cases (0.50 − 0.50), the expected return in every instance will be

$$\begin{aligned} E(R_{port}) &= 0.50(0.10) + 0.50(0.20) \\ &= 0.15 \end{aligned}$$

The portfolio standard deviation for Case a will be

$$\begin{aligned} \sigma_{port(a)} &= \sqrt{(0.5)^2(0.07)^2 + (0.5)^2(0.10)^2 + 2(0.5)(0.5)(0.0070)} \\ &= \sqrt{0.007225} \\ &= 0.085 \end{aligned}$$

Again, with perfect positive correlation, the portfolio standard deviation is the weighted average of the standard deviations of the individual assets:

$$(0.5)(0.07) + (0.5)(0.10) = 0.085$$

As you might envision, changing the weights with perfect positive correlation causes the portfolio standard deviation to change in a linear fashion. This will be an important point to remember when we discuss the capital asset pricing model (CAPM).

For Cases b, c, d, and e, the portfolio standard deviations are as follows:[4]

$$\begin{aligned} \sigma_{port(b)} &= \sqrt{(0.001225) + (0.0025) + (0.5)(0.0035)} \\ &= \sqrt{0.005475} \\ &= 0.07399 \end{aligned}$$

$$\begin{aligned} \sigma_{port(c)} &= \sqrt{(0.001225) + (0.0025) + (0.5)(0.00)} \\ &= 0.0610 \end{aligned}$$

$$\begin{aligned} \sigma_{port(d)} &= \sqrt{(0.001225) + (0.0025) + (0.5)(-0.0035)} \\ &= 0.0444 \end{aligned}$$

$$\begin{aligned} \sigma_{port(e)} &= \sqrt{(0.003725) + (0.5)(-0.0070)} \\ &= 0.015 \end{aligned}$$

[4] In all the following examples, we will skip some steps because you are now aware that only the last term changes. You are encouraged to work out the individual steps to ensure that you understand the computational procedure.

Portfolio Standard Deviation Calculation Because of the assumptions used in developing the Markowitz portfolio model, any asset or portfolio of assets can be described by two characteristics: the expected rate of return and the expected standard deviation of returns. Therefore, the following demonstrations can be applied to two *individual* assets, two *portfolios* of assets, or two *asset classes* with the indicated return—standard deviation characteristics and correlation coefficients.

Equal risk and return—changing correlations. Consider first the case in which both assets have the same expected return and expected standard deviation of return. As an example, let's assume

$$E(R_1) = 0.20, \qquad E(\sigma_1) = 0.10$$
$$E(R_2) = 0.20, \qquad E(\sigma_2) = 0.10$$

To show the effect of different covariances, we assume different levels of correlation between the two assets. We also assume that the two assets have equal weights in the portfolio ($w_1 = 0.50$; $w_2 = 0.50$). Therefore, the only value that changes in each example is the correlation between the returns for the two assets.

Now consider the following five correlation coefficients and the covariances they yield. Since $Cov_{ij} = r_{ij}\sigma_i\sigma_j$, the covariance will be equal to $r_{1,2}$ (0.10)(0.10) because the standard deviation of both assets is 0.10.

a. For $r_{1,2} = 1.00$, $\quad Cov_{1,2} = (1.00)(0.10)(0.10) = 0.01$
b. For $r_{1,2} = 0.50$, $\quad Cov_{1,2} = (0.50)(0.10)(0.10) = 0.005$
c. For $r_{1,2} = 0.00$, $\quad Cov_{1,2} = (0.00)(0.10)(0.10) = 0.000$
d. For $r_{1,2} = -0.50$, $\quad Cov_{1,2} = (-0.50)(0.10)(0.10) = -0.005$
e. For $r_{1,2} = -1.00$, $\quad Cov_{1,2} = (-1.00)(0.10)(0.10) = -0.01$

Now let's see what happens to the standard deviation of the portfolio under these five conditions.

When we apply the general portfolio formula from Equation 6 to a two-asset portfolio, it is

$$\sigma_{port} = \sqrt{w_1^2\sigma_1^2 + w_2^2\sigma_2^2 + 2w_1w_2r_{1,2}\sigma_1\sigma_2} \qquad \textbf{(50-7)}$$

or

$$\sigma_{port} = \sqrt{w_1^2\sigma_1^2 + w_2^2\sigma_2^2 + 2w_1w_2Cov_{1,2}}$$

Thus, in Case a:

$$\begin{aligned}\sigma_{port(a)} &= \sqrt{(0.5)^2(0.10)^2 + (0.5)^2(0.10)^2 + 2(0.5)(0.5)(0.01)}\\ &= \sqrt{(0.25)(0.01) + (0.25)(0.01) + 2(0.25)(0.01)}\\ &= \sqrt{0.01}\\ &= 0.10\end{aligned}$$

In this case, where the returns for the two assets are perfectly positively correlated, the standard deviation for the portfolio is, in fact, the weighted average of the individual standard deviations. The important point is that we get no real benefit from combining two assets that are perfectly correlated; they are like one asset already because their returns move together.

Now consider Case b, where $r_{1,2}$ equals 0.50.

$$\begin{aligned}\sigma_{port(b)} &= \sqrt{(0.5)^2(0.10)^2 + (0.5)^2(0.10)^2 + 2(0.5)(0.5)(0.005)} \\ &= \sqrt{(0.0025) + (0.0025) + 2(0.25)(0.005)} \\ &= \sqrt{0.0075} \\ &= 0.0866\end{aligned}$$

The only term that changed from Case a is the last term, $Cov_{1,2}$, which changed from 0.01 to 0.005. As a result, the standard deviation of the portfolio declined by about 13 percent, from 0.10 to 0.0866. Note that *the expected return of the portfolio did not change* because it is simply the weighted average of the individual expected returns; it is equal to 0.20 in both cases.

You should be able to confirm through your own calculations that the standard deviations for Portfolios c and d are as follows:

c. 0.0707
d. 0.05

The final case, where the correlation between the two assets is −1.00, indicates the ultimate benefits of diversification.

$$\begin{aligned}\sigma_{port(e)} &= \sqrt{(0.5)^2(0.10)^2 + (0.5)^2(0.10)^2 + 2(0.5)(0.5)(-0.01)} \\ &= \sqrt{(0.0050) + (-0.0050)} \\ &= \sqrt{0} \\ &= 0\end{aligned}$$

Here, the negative covariance term exactly offsets the individual variance terms, leaving an overall standard deviation of the portfolio of zero. *This would be a risk-free portfolio.*

Exhibit 10 illustrates a graph of such a pattern. Perfect negative correlation gives a mean combined return for the two securities over time equal to the mean for each of them, so the returns for the portfolio show no variability. Any returns above and below the mean for each of the assets are *completely offset* by the return

EXHIBIT 10 Time Patterns of Returns for Two Assets with Perfect Negative Correlation

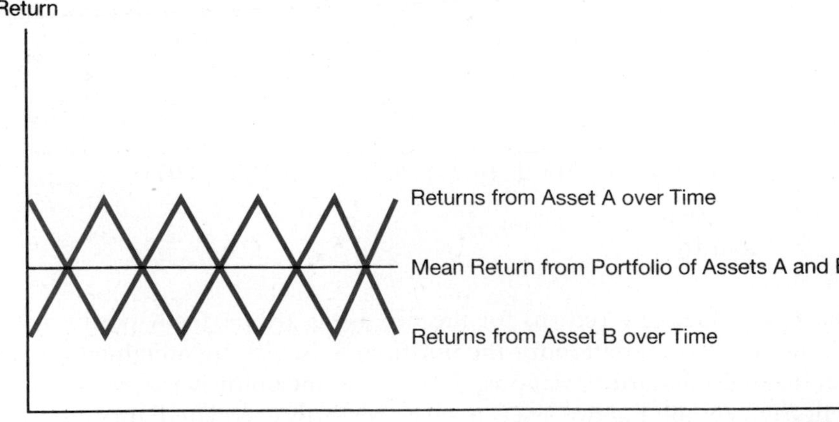

EXHIBIT 11 **Risk-Return Plot for Portfolios with Equal Returns and Standard Deviations but Different Correlations**

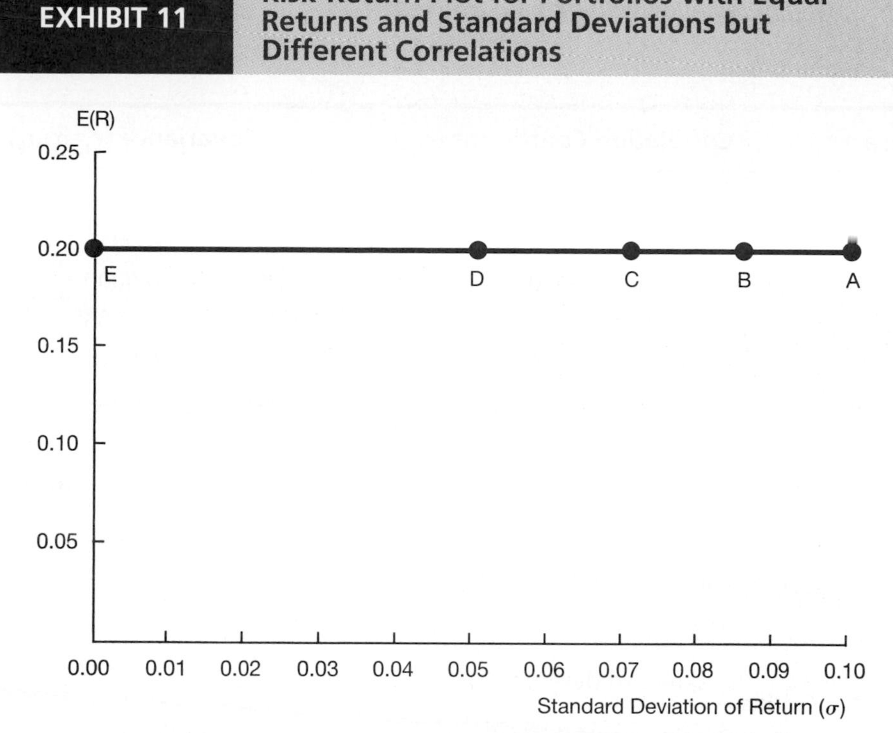

for the other asset, so there is *no variability* in total returns—that is, *no risk*—for the portfolio. Thus, a pair of completely negatively correlated assets provides the maximum benefits of diversification by completely eliminating risk.

The graph in Exhibit 11 shows the difference in the risk-return posture for our five cases. As noted, the only effect of the change in correlation is the change in the standard deviation of this two-asset portfolio. Combining assets that are not perfectly correlated does *not* affect the expected return of the portfolio, but it *does* reduce the risk of the portfolio (as measured by its standard deviation). When we eventually reach the ultimate combination of perfect negative correlation, risk is eliminated.

Combining stocks with different returns and risk. We have seen what happens when only the correlation coefficient (covariance) differs between the assets. We now consider two assets (or portfolios) with different expected rates of return and individual standard deviations.[3] We will show what happens when we vary the correlations between them. We will assume two assets with the following characteristics.

Asset	E(R)	w	σ^2	σ_1
1	0.10	0.50	0.0049	0.07
2	0.20	0.50	0.0100	0.10

[3] As noted, these could be two asset classes. For example, Asset 1 could be low risk-low return bonds and Asset 2 could be higher return-higher risk stocks.

We will use the previous set of correlation coefficients, but we must recalculate the covariances because this time the standard deviations of the assets are different. The results are shown in the following table.

Case	Correlation Coefficient ($r_{1,2}$)	Covariance ($r_{1,2}\sigma_1\sigma_2$)
a	+1.00	0.0070
b	+0.50	0.0035
c	0.00	0.0000
d	−0.50	−0.0035
e	−1.00	−0.0070

Because we are assuming the same weights in all cases (0.50 − 0.50), the expected return in every instance will be

$$\begin{aligned} E(R_{port}) &= 0.50(0.10) + 0.50(0.20) \\ &= 0.15 \end{aligned}$$

The portfolio standard deviation for Case a will be

$$\begin{aligned} \sigma_{port(a)} &= \sqrt{(0.5)^2(0.07)^2 + (0.5)^2(0.10)^2 + 2(0.5)(0.5)(0.0070)} \\ &= \sqrt{0.007225} \\ &= 0.085 \end{aligned}$$

Again, with perfect positive correlation, the portfolio standard deviation is the weighted average of the standard deviations of the individual assets:

$$(0.5)(0.07) + (0.5)(0.10) = 0.085$$

As you might envision, changing the weights with perfect positive correlation causes the portfolio standard deviation to change in a linear fashion. This will be an important point to remember when we discuss the capital asset pricing model (CAPM).

For Cases b, c, d, and e, the portfolio standard deviations are as follows:[4]

$$\begin{aligned} \sigma_{port(b)} &= \sqrt{(0.001225) + (0.0025) + (0.5)(0.0035)} \\ &= \sqrt{0.005475} \\ &= 0.07399 \end{aligned}$$

$$\begin{aligned} \sigma_{port(c)} &= \sqrt{(0.001225) + (0.0025) + (0.5)(0.00)} \\ &= 0.0610 \end{aligned}$$

$$\begin{aligned} \sigma_{port(d)} &= \sqrt{(0.001225) + (0.0025) + (0.5)(-0.0035)} \\ &= 0.0444 \end{aligned}$$

$$\begin{aligned} \sigma_{port(e)} &= \sqrt{(0.003725) + (0.5)(-0.0070)} \\ &= 0.015 \end{aligned}$$

[4] In all the following examples, we will skip some steps because you are now aware that only the last term changes. You are encouraged to work out the individual steps to ensure that you understand the computational procedure.

EXHIBIT 12 Risk-Return Plot for Portfolios with Different Returns, Standard Deviations, and Correlations

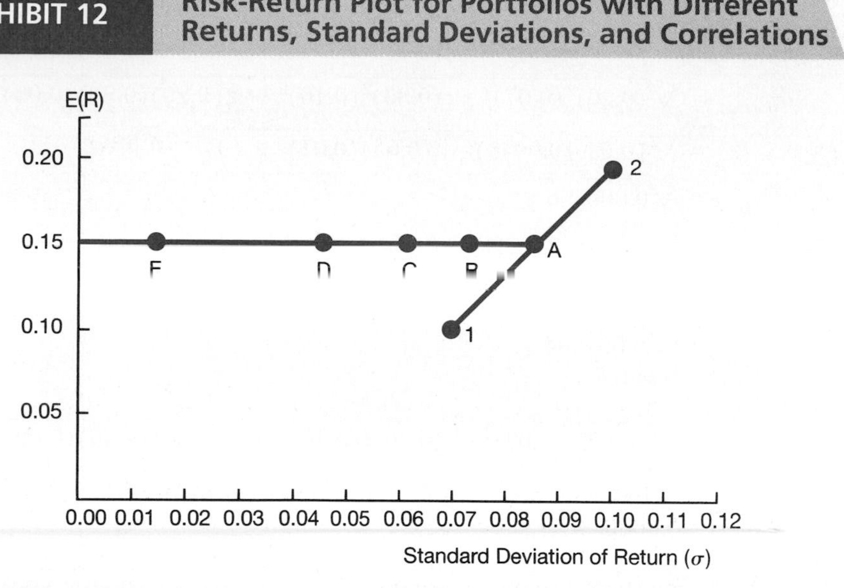

Note that, in this example, with perfect negative correlation the portfolio standard deviation is not zero. This is because the different examples have equal weights, but the asset standard deviations are not equal.

Exhibit 12 shows the results for the two individual assets and the portfolio of the two assets assuming the correlation coefficients vary as set forth in Cases a through e. As before, the expected return does not change because the proportions are always set at 0.50–0.50, so all the portfolios lie along the horizontal line at the return, R = 0.15.

Constant correlation with changing weights. If we changed the weights of the two assets while holding the correlation coefficient constant, we would derive a set of combinations that trace an ellipse starting at Asset 2, going through the 0.50–0.50 point, and ending at Asset 1. We can demonstrate this with Case c, in which the correlation coefficient of zero eases the computations. We begin with 100 percent in Asset 2 (Case f) and change the weights as follows, ending with 100 percent in Asset 1 (Case l):

Case	w_1	w_2	$E(R_i)$
f	0.00	1.00	0.20
g	0.20	0.80	0.18
h	0.40	0.60	0.16
i	0.50	0.50	0.15
j	0.60	0.40	0.14
k	0.80	0.20	0.12
l	1.00	0.00	0.10

We already know the standard deviation (σ) for portfolio (i). In Cases f, g, h, j, k, and l, the standard deviations are[5]

$$\begin{aligned}\sigma_{port(g)} &= \sqrt{(0.20)^2(0.07)^2 + (0.80)^2(0.10)^2 + 2(0.20)(0.80)(0.00)}\\ &= \sqrt{(0.04)(0.0049) + (0.64)(0.01) + (0)}\\ &= \sqrt{0.006596}\\ &= 0.0812\end{aligned}$$

$$\begin{aligned}\sigma_{port(h)} &= \sqrt{(0.40)^2(0.07)^2 + (0.60)^2(0.10)^2 + 2(0.40)(0.60)(0.00)}\\ &= \sqrt{0.004384}\\ &= 0.0662\end{aligned}$$

$$\begin{aligned}\sigma_{port(j)} &= \sqrt{(0.60)^2(0.07)^2 + (0.40)^2(0.10)^2 + 2(0.60)(0.40)(0.00)}\\ &= \sqrt{0.003364}\\ &= 0.0580\end{aligned}$$

$$\begin{aligned}\sigma_{port(k)} &= \sqrt{(0.80)^2(0.07)^2 + (0.20)^2(0.10)^2 + 2(0.80)(0.20)(0.00)}\\ &= \sqrt{0.003536}\\ &= 0.0595\end{aligned}$$

The various weights with a constant correlation yield the following risk-return combinations.

Case	w_1	w_2	$E(R_i)$	$E(\sigma_{port})$
f	0.00	1.00	0.20	0.1000
g	0.20	0.80	0.18	0.0812
h	0.40	0.60	0.16	0.0662
i	0.50	0.50	0.15	0.0610
j	0.60	0.40	0.14	0.0580
k	0.80	0.20	0.12	0.0595
l	1.00	0.00	0.10	0.0700

A graph of these combinations appears in Exhibit 13. We could derive a complete curve by simply varying the weighting by smaller increments.

A notable result is that with low, zero, or negative correlations, it is possible to derive portfolios that have *lower risk than either single asset.* In our set of examples where $r_{ij} = 0.00$, this occurs in Cases h, i, j, and k. This ability to reduce risk is the essence of diversification.

As shown in Exhibit 13, assuming the normal risk-return relationship where assets with higher risk (larger standard deviation of returns) provide high rates of return, it is possible for a conservative investor to experience *both* lower risk *and* higher return by diversifying into a higher risk-higher return asset, assuming that the correlation between the two assets is fairly low. Exhibit 13 shows that, in

[5] Again, you are encouraged to fill in the steps we skipped in the computations.

EXHIBIT 13 Portfolio Risk-Return Plots for Different Weights When $r_{i,j}$ = +1.00, +0.50, 0.00, −0.50, −1.00

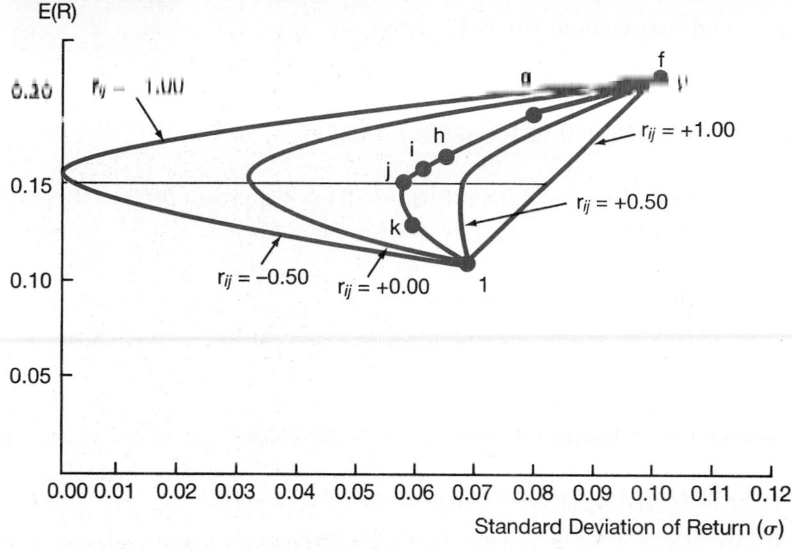

the case where we used the correlation of zero (0.00), the low-risk investor at Point 1—who would receive a return of 10 percent and risk of 7 percent—could *increase* the return to 14 percent *and* experience a *decline* in risk to 5.8 percent by investing (diversifying) 40 percent of the portfolio in riskier Asset 2. As noted, the benefits of diversification are critically dependent on the correlation between assets. The exhibit shows that there is even some benefit when the correlation is 0.50 rather than zero.

Exhibit 13 also shows that the curvature in the graph depends on the correlation between the two assets or portfolios. With r_{ij} = +1.00, the combinations lie along a straight line between the two assets. When r_{ij} = 0.50, the curve is to the right of the r_{ij} = 0.00 curve; when r_{ij} = −0.50, it is to the left. Finally, when r_{ij} = −1.00, the graph would be two straight lines that would touch at the vertical line (zero risk) with some combination. It is possible to solve for the specified set of weights that would give a portfolio with zero risk. In this case, it is w_1 = 0.412 and w_2 = 0.588.

A Three-Asset Portfolio

A demonstration of what occurs with a three-asset portfolio is useful because it shows the dynamics of the portfolio process when assets are added. It also shows the rapid growth in the computations required, which is why we will stop at three! We will assume the following characteristics for the next example:

Asset Classes	E(R)	E(σ)	w
Stocks (S)	0.12	0.20	0.60
Bonds (B)	0.08	0.10	0.30
Cash equivalent (C)	0.04	0.03	0.10

In this example, we will combine three asset classes we have been discussing: stocks, bonds, and cash equivalents.[6] The correlations are

$$r_{S,B} = 0.25;\ r_{S,C} = -0.08;\ r_{B,C} = 0.15$$

Given the weights specified, the $E(R_{port})$ is

$$\begin{aligned} E(R_{port}) &= (0.60)(0.12) + (0.30)(0.08) + (0.10)(0.04) \\ &= (0.072 + 0.024 + 0.004) = 0.100 = 10.00\% \end{aligned}$$

When we apply the generalized formula from Equation 50-6 to the expected standard deviation of a three-asset portfolio, it is

$$\begin{aligned} \sigma^2_{port} = {} & (w_S^2\sigma_S^2 + w_B^2\sigma_B^2 + w_C^2\sigma_C^2) \\ & + (2w_Sw_B\sigma_S\sigma_B r_{S,B} + 2w_Sw_C\sigma_S\sigma_C r_{S,C} + 2w_Bw_C\sigma_B\sigma_C r_{B,C}) \end{aligned} \quad \textbf{(50-8)}$$

From the characteristics specified, the standard deviation of this three-asset-class portfolio (σ_{port}) would be

$$\begin{aligned} \sigma^2_{port} &= [(0.6)^2(0.20)^2 + (0.3)^2(0.10)^2 + (0.1)^2(0.03)^2] \\ &\quad + \{[2(0.6)(0.3)(0.20)(0.10)(0.25)] + [2(0.6)(0.1)(0.20)(0.03)(-0.08)] \\ &\quad + [2(0.3)(0.1)(0.10)(0.03)(0.15)]\} \\ &= [0.015309 + (0.0018) + (-0.0000576) + (0.000027)] \\ &= 0.0170784 \end{aligned}$$

$$\sigma_{port} = (0.0170784)^{1/2} = 0.1306 = 13.06\%$$

Estimation Issues

It is important to keep in mind that the results of this portfolio asset allocation depend on the accuracy of the statistical inputs. In the current instance, this means that for every asset (or asset class) being considered for inclusion in the portfolio, we must estimate its expected returns and standard deviation. We must also estimate the correlation coefficient among the entire set of assets. The number of correlation estimates can be significant—for example, for a portfolio of 100 securities, the number is 4,950 (that is, 99 + 98 + 97 +. . .). The potential source of error that arises from these approximations is referred to as *estimation risk.*

We can reduce the number of correlation coefficients that must be estimated by assuming that stock returns can be described by the relationship of each stock to a market index—that is, a single index market model, as follows:

$$R_i = a_i + b_iR_m + \varepsilon_i \quad \textbf{(50-9)}$$

where

b_i = the slope coefficient that relates the returns for Security i to the returns for the aggregate stock market

R_m = the returns for the aggregate stock market

[6] The asset allocation articles regularly contained in the *Wall Street Journal* generally refer to these three asset classes.

If all the securities are similarly related to the market and a slope coefficient b_i is derived for each one, it can be shown that the correlation coefficient between two Securities i and j is

$$r_{ij} = b_i b_j \frac{\sigma_m^2}{\sigma_i \sigma_j} \quad \textbf{(50-10)}$$

where

σ_m^2 = the variance of returns for the aggregate stock market

This reduces the number of estimates from 4,950 to 100—that is, once we have derived a slope estimate b_i for each security, we can compute the correlation estimates. Keep in mind that this assumes that the single index market model provides a good estimate of security returns.

The Efficient Frontier

If we examined different two-asset combinations and derived the curves assuming all the possible weights, we would have a graph like that in Exhibit 14. The envelope curve that contains the best of all these possible combinations is referred to as the **efficient frontier**. Specifically, the efficient frontier represents that set of portfolios that has the maximum rate of return for every given level of risk or the minimum risk for every level of return. An example of such a frontier is shown in Exhibit 15. Every portfolio that lies on the efficient frontier has either a higher rate of return for equal risk or lower risk for an equal rate of return than some portfolio beneath the frontier. Thus, we would say that Portfolio A in Exhibit 15 *dominates* Portfolio C because it has an equal rate of return but substantially less risk. Similarly, Portfolio B dominates Portfolio C because it has equal risk but a higher expected rate of return. Because of the benefits of diversification among imperfectly correlated assets, we would expect the efficient frontier to be made

EXHIBIT 14 Numerous Portfolio Combinations of Available Assets

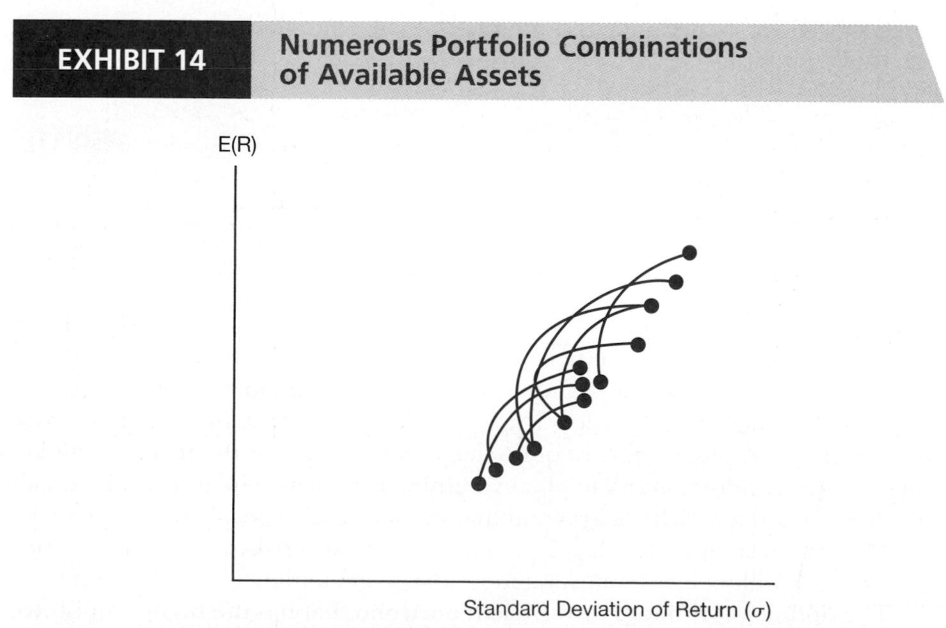

EXHIBIT 15 Efficient Frontier for Alternative Portfolios

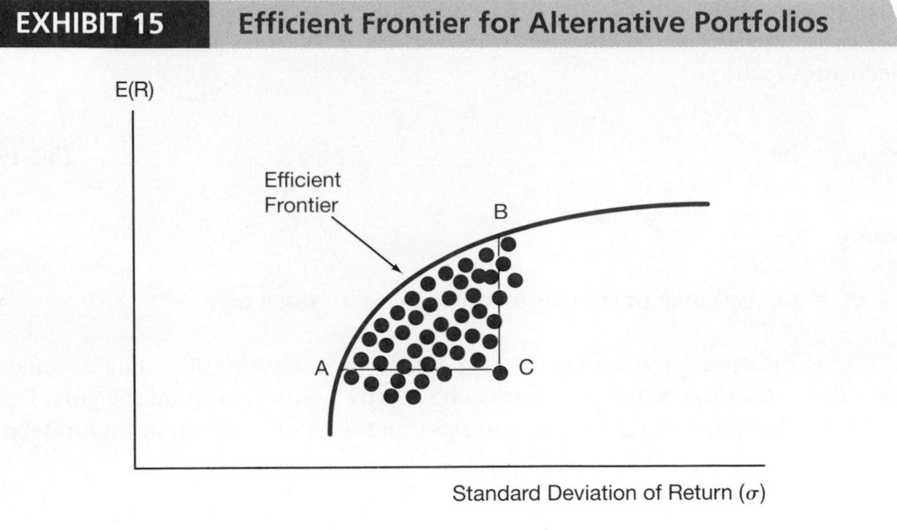

up of *portfolios* of investments rather than individual securities. Two possible exceptions arise at the end points, which represent the asset with the highest return and the asset with the lowest risk.

As an investor, you will target a point along the efficient frontier based on your *utility function,* which reflects your attitude toward risk. No portfolio on the efficient frontier can dominate any other portfolio on the efficient frontier. All of these portfolios have different return and risk measures, with expected rates of return that increase with higher risk.

The Efficient Frontier and Investor Utility

The curve in Exhibit 15 shows that the slope of the efficient frontier curve decreases steadily as we move upward. This implies that adding equal increments of risk as we move up the efficient frontier gives diminishing increments of expected return. To evaluate this situation, we calculate the slope of the efficient frontier as follows:

$$\frac{\Delta E(R_{port})}{\Delta E(\sigma_{port})} \tag{50-11}$$

An individual investor's utility curves specify the trade-offs he or she is willing to make between expected return and risk. In conjunction with the efficient frontier, these utility curves determine which *particular* portfolio on the efficient frontier best suits an individual investor. Two investors will choose the same portfolio from the efficient set only if their utility curves are identical.

Exhibit 16 shows two sets of utility curves along with an efficient frontier of investments. The curves labeled U_1, U_2, and U_3 are for a strongly risk-averse investor. These utility curves are quite steep, indicating that the investor will not tolerate much additional risk to obtain additional returns. The investor is equally disposed toward any $E(R)$, $E(\sigma)$ combinations along the specific utility curve U_1.

The curves labeled ($U_{3'}$, $U_{2'}$, $U_{1'}$) characterize a less risk-averse investor. Such an investor is willing to tolerate a bit more risk to get a higher expected return.

The optimal portfolio is the **efficient portfolio** that has the highest utility for a given investor. It lies at the point of tangency between the efficient frontier and the U_1 curve with the highest possible utility. A conservative investor's highest

EXHIBIT 16 Selecting an Optimal Risky Portfolio

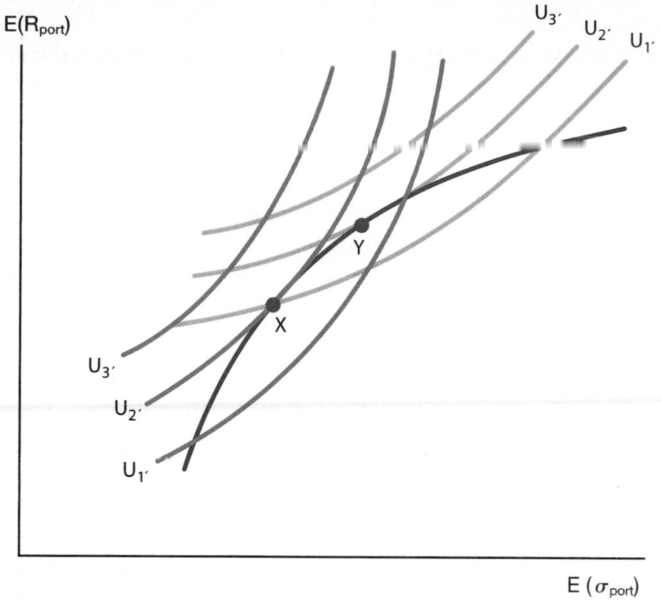

utility is at Point X in Exhibit 16, where the U_2 curve just touches the efficient frontier. A less risk-averse investor's highest utility occurs at Point Y, which represents a portfolio on the efficient frontier with higher expected returns and higher risk than the portfolio at X.

THE INTERNET

Investments Online

By seeking to operate on the efficient frontier, portfolio managers try to minimize risk for a certain level of return, or maximize return for a given level of risk. Software programs, called optimizers, are used by portfolio managers to determine the shape of the efficient frontier as well as to determine some of the portfolios which lie on it. Financial planners use information on past returns and manager performance, in addition to **optimizers**, to make recommendations to their clients. Some interesting websites for money managers include:

www.pionline.com This is the home page for *Pensions and Investments,* a newspaper for money managers. Items on the home page include links to news of interest to managers, and ePIPER performance data on a number of equity, fixed income, real estate, and global portfolios from money manager and pension funds. It contains many links to organizations such as central banks, consultants, and sellers of investment-related products.

www.investmentnews.com Investment News is a sister publication to *Pensions and Investments,* with a focus toward the financial advisor. This site includes information on financial planning, the mutual fund industry, regulation, equity performance, and industry trends.

Software for creating efficient frontiers is available from firms such as Ibbotson Associates (*www.ibbotson.com*), Zephyr Associates (*www.styleadvisor.com*), Wagner Associates (*www.wagner.com*), and Efficient Solutions, Inc. (*www.effisols.com*).

William J. Bernstein's website, *www.efficientfrontier.com*, offers articles from his web-zine, *Efficient Frontier,* an online journal of practical asset allocation.

SUMMARY

- The basic Markowitz portfolio model derives the expected rate of return for a portfolio of assets and a measure of expected risk, which is the standard deviation of expected rate of return. Markowitz showed that the expected rate of return of a portfolio is the weighted average of the expected return for the individual investments in the portfolio. The standard deviation of a portfolio is a function not only of the standard deviations for the individual investments but *also* of the covariance between the rates of return for all the pairs of assets in the portfolio. In a large portfolio, these covariances are the important factors.
- Different weights or amounts of a portfolio held in various assets yield a curve of potential combinations. Correlation coefficients among assets are the critical factor to consider when selecting investments. Investors can maintain their rate of return while reducing the risk level of their portfolio by combining assets or portfolios that have low-positive or negative correlation.
- Assuming numerous assets and a multitude of combination curves, the efficient frontier is the envelope curve that encompasses all of the best combinations. It defines the set of portfolios that has the highest expected return for each given level of risk or the minimum risk for each given level of return. From this set of dominant portfolios, investors select the one that lies at the point of tangency between the efficient frontier and their highest utility curve. Because risk-return utility functions differ, the point of tangency and, therefore, the portfolio choice will differ among investors.

At this point, you understand that an optimum portfolio is a combination of investments, each having desirable individual risk-return characteristics that also fit together based on their correlations. Because many foreign stock and bond investments provide superior rates of return compared with U.S. securities *and* have low correlations with portfolios of U.S. stocks and bonds, including these foreign securities in your portfolio will help you to reduce the overall risk of your portfolio while possibly increasing your rate of return.

AN INTRODUCTION TO ASSET PRICING MODELS

by Frank K. Reilly and Keith C. Brown

READING 51

LEARNING OUTCOMES

The candidate should be able to:

a. explain the capital market theory, including its underlying assumptions, and explain the effect on expected returns, the standard deviation of returns, and possible risk/return combinations when a risk-free asset is combined with a portfolio of risky assets;

b. identify the market portfolio, and describe the role of the market portfolio in the formation of the capital market line (CML);

c. define systematic and unsystematic risk, and explain why an investor should not expect to receive additional return for assuming unsystematic risk;

d. explain the capital asset pricing model, including the security market line (SML) and beta, and describe the effects of relaxing its underlying assumptions;

e. calculate, using the SML, the expected return on a security, and evaluate whether the security is overvalued, undervalued, or properly valued.

INTRODUCTION 1

Following the development of portfolio theory by Markowitz, two major theories have been put forth that derive a model for the valuation of risky assets. In this reading, we introduce one of these two models—that is, the capital asset pricing model (CAPM). The background on the CAPM is important at this point in the book because the risk measure implied by this model is a necessary input for our subsequent discussion on the valuation of risky assets. The presentation concerns capital market theory and the capital asset pricing model that was developed almost concurrently by three individuals. Subsequently, an alternative

PRACTICE PROBLEMS FOR READING 50

1. The following are the monthly rates of return for Madison Corp. and for Sophie Electric during a six-month period.

Month	Madison Corp.	Sophie Electric
1	−0.04	0.07
2	0.06	−0.02
3	−0.07	−0.10
4	0.12	0.15
5	−0.02	−0.06
6	0.05	0.02

Compute the following:

A. Average monthly rate of return $\bar{R}_i$ for each stock

B. Standard deviation of returns for each stock

C. Covariance between the rates of return

D. The correlation coefficient between the rates of return

What level of correlation did you expect? How did your expectations compare with the computed correlation? Would these two stocks offer a good chance for diversification? Why or why not?

2. You are considering two assets with the following characteristics:

$E(R_1) = 0.15 \quad E(\sigma_1) = 0.10 \quad w_1 = 0.5$

$E(R_2) = 0.20 \quad E(\sigma_2) = 0.20 \quad w_2 = 0.5$

Compute the mean and standard deviation of two portfolios if $r_{1,2} =$ 0.40 and −0.60, respectively. Plot the two portfolios on a risk-return graph and briefly explain the results.

3. Given: $E(R_1) = 0.10$

$E(R_2) = 0.15$

$E(\sigma_1) = 0.03$

$E(\sigma_2) = 0.05$

Calculate the expected returns and expected standard deviations of a two-stock portfolio in which Stock 1 has a weight of 60 percent under the following conditions:

A. $r_{1,2} = 1.00$

B. $r_{1,2} = 0.75$

C. $r_{1,2} = 0.25$

D. $r_{1,2} = 0.00$

E. $r_{1,2} = -0.25$

F. $r_{1,2} = -0.75$

G. $r_{1,2} = -1.00$

CFA
2005 exam

4. An investor has an equal amount invested in each of the following four securities:

Security	Expected Annual Rate of Return
W	0.10
X	0.12
Y	0.16
Z	0.22

The investor plans to sell Security Y and use the proceeds to purchase a new security that has the same expected return as the current portfolio. The expected return for the investor's new portfolio, compared to the current portfolio, will be

A. lower regardless of changes in the correlation of returns among securities.

B. the same regardless of changes in the correlation of returns among securities.

C. lower only if the correlation of the new security with Securities W, X, and Z is lower than the correlation of Security Y.

D. the same only if the correlation of the new security with Securities W, X, and Z is lower than the correlation of Security Y.

CFA
2005 exam

5. Markowitz Portfolio Theory is *most* accurately described as including an assumption that

A. risk is measured by the range of expected returns.

B. investors have the ability to borrow or lend at the risk-free rate of return.

C. investor utility curves demonstrate diminishing marginal utility of wealth.

D. investment decision-making is based on both rational and irrational factors.

Risk-Free Asset

As noted, the assumption of a risk-free asset in the economy is critical to asset pric ing theory. Therefore, this section explains the meaning of a risk-free asset anc shows the effect on the risk and return measures when this risk-free asset is com bined with a portfolio on the Markowitz efficient frontier.

We have defined a **risky asset** as one from which future returns are uncertain and we have measured this uncertainty by the variance, or standard deviation, o expected returns. Because the expected return on a risk-free asset is entirely cer tain, the standard deviation of its expected return is zero ($\sigma_{RF} = 0$). The rate o return earned on such an asset should be the risk-free rate of return *(RFR),* whicl should equal the expected long-run growth rate of the economy with an adjust ment for short-run liquidity. The next subsections show what happens when we introduce this risk-free asset into the risky world of the Markowitz portfolic model.

Covariance with a Risk-Free Asset Recall that the covariance between two sets o returns is

$$\text{Cov}_{ij} = \sum_{t=1}^{n} [R_{it} - E(R_{it})][R_{jt} - E(R_{jt})]/(n-1) \quad \textbf{(51-1)}$$

Because the returns for the risk-free asset are certain, $\sigma_{RF} = 0$, which mean that $R_i = E(R_i)$ during all periods. Thus, $R_i - E(R_i)$ will equal zero, and the prod uct of this expression with any other expression will equal zero. Consequently, the covariance of the risk-free asset with any risky asset or portfolio of assets will al ways equal zero. Similarly, the correlation between any risky asset *i,* and the risk free asset, RF, would be zero because it is equal to

$$r_{RF,i} = \text{Cov}_{RF,i}/\sigma_{RF}\sigma_j$$

Combining a Risk-Free Asset with a Risky Portfolio What happens to the aver age rate of return and the standard deviation of returns when you combine a risk free asset with a portfolio of risky assets such as those that exist on the Markowitz efficient frontier?

Expected return. Like the expected return for a portfolio of two risky assets, the expected rate of return for a portfolio that includes a risk-free asset is the weighted average of the two returns:

$$E(R_{port}) = w_{RF}(RFR) + (1 - w_{RF})E(R_i)$$

where

w_{RF} = the proportion of the portfolio invested in the risk-free asset
$E(R_i)$ = the expected rate of return on risky Portfolio i

Standard deviation. Recall from Reading 50 (Equation 50-7) that the expectec variance for a two-asset portfolio is

$$\sigma^2_{port} = w_1^2\sigma_1^2 + w_2^2\sigma_2^2 + 2w_1w_2r_{1,2}\sigma_1\sigma_2$$

Substituting the risk-free asset for Security 1, and the risky asset portfolio foı Security 2, this formula would become

$$\sigma^2_{port} = w_{RF}^2\sigma_{RF}^2 + (1 - w_{RF})^2\sigma_i^2 + 2w_{RF}(1 - w_{RF})r_{RF,i}\sigma_{RF}\sigma_i$$

EXHIBIT 2 Derivation of Capital Market Line Assuming Lending or Borrowing at the Risk-Free Rate

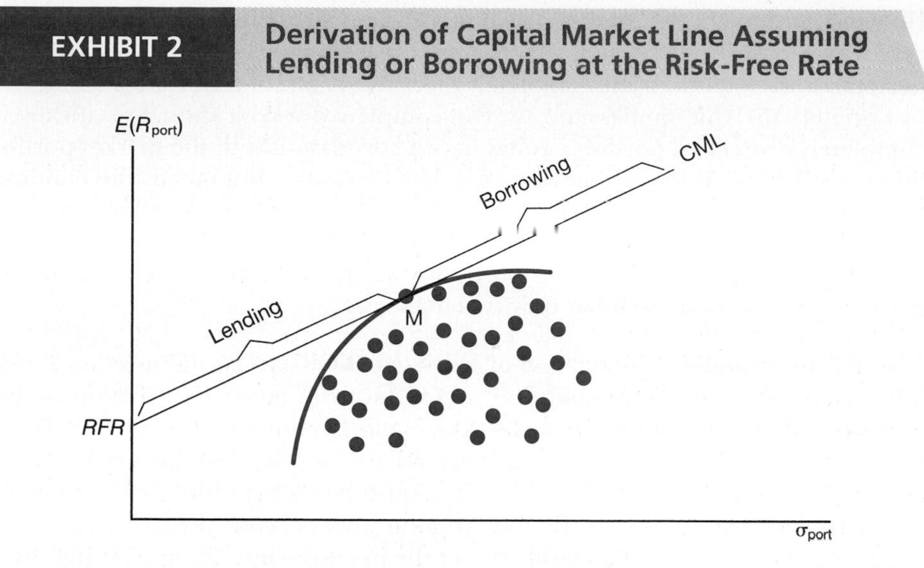

the alternative portfolios on the CML is the magnitude of the variability, which is caused by the proportion of the risky asset portfolio in the total portfolio.

The Market Portfolio

Because Portfolio M lies at the point of tangency, it has the highest portfolio possibility line, and everybody will want to invest in Portfolio M and borrow or lend to be somewhere on the CML. This portfolio must, therefore, include *all risky assets.* If a risky asset were not in this portfolio in which everyone wants to invest, there would be no demand for it and therefore it would have no value.

Because the market is in equilibrium, it is also necessary that all assets are included in this portfolio *in proportion to their market value.* If, for example, an asset accounts for a higher proportion of the M portfolio than its market value justifies, excess demand for this asset will increase its price until its relative market value becomes consistent with its proportion in the M portfolio.

This portfolio that includes all risky assets is referred to as the **market portfolio.** It includes not only U.S. common stocks but *all* risky assets, such as non-U.S. stocks, U.S. and non-U.S. bonds, options, real estate, coins, stamps, art, or antiques. Because the market portfolio contains all risky assets, it is a **completely diversified portfolio**, which means that all the risk unique to individual assets in the portfolio is diversified away. Specifically, the unique risk of any single asset is offset by the unique variability of all the other assets in the portfolio.

This unique (diversifiable) risk is also referred to as **unsystematic risk**. This implies that only **systematic risk**, which is defined as the variability in all risky assets caused by macro-economic variables, remains in the market portfolio. This systematic risk, measured by the standard deviation of returns of the market portfolio, can change over time if and when there are changes in the macroeconomic variables that affect the valuation of all risky assets.[1] Examples of such macroeconomic variables would be variability of growth in the money supply, interest rate volatility, and variability in such factors as industrial production, corporate earnings, and corporate cash flow.

[1] For an analysis of changes in the standard deviation (volatility) of returns for stocks and bonds in the United States, see Schwert (1989); Spiro (1990); Officer (1973); and Reilly, Wright, and Chan (2000).

How to Measure Diversification As noted earlier, all portfolios on the CML are perfectly positively correlated, which means that all portfolios on the CML are perfectly correlated with the completely diversified market Portfolio M. As noted by Lorie (1975), this implies a measure of complete diversification. Specifically, a completely diversified portfolio would have a correlation with the market portfolio of +1.00. This is logical because complete diversification means the elimination of all the unsystematic or unique risk. Once you have eliminated all unsystematic risk, only systematic risk is left, which cannot be diversified away. Therefore, completely diversified portfolios would correlate perfectly with the market portfolio because it has only systematic risk.

Diversification and the Elimination of Unsystematic Risk As discussed in Reading 50, the purpose of diversification is to reduce the standard deviation of the total portfolio. This assumes imperfect correlations among securities.[2] Ideally, as you add securities, the average covariance for the portfolio declines. An important question is, about how many securities must be included to arrive at a completely diversified portfolio? To discover the answer, you must observe what happens as you increase the sample size of the portfolio by adding securities that have some positive correlation. The typical correlation between U.S. securities is about 0.5 to 0.6.

One set of studies examined the average standard deviation for numerous portfolios of randomly selected stocks of different sample sizes. Specifically, Evans and Archer (1968) and Tole (1982) computed the standard deviation for portfolios of increasing numbers up to 20 stocks. The results indicated a large initial impact wherein the major benefits of diversification were achieved rather quickly. Specifically, about 90 percent of the maximum benefit of diversification was derived from portfolios of 12 to 18 stocks. Exhibit 3 shows a graph of the effect.

A subsequent study by Statman (1987) compared the benefits of lower risk from diversification to the added transaction costs with more securities. It

EXHIBIT 3 **Number of Stocks in a Portfolio and the Standard Deviation of Portfolio Return**

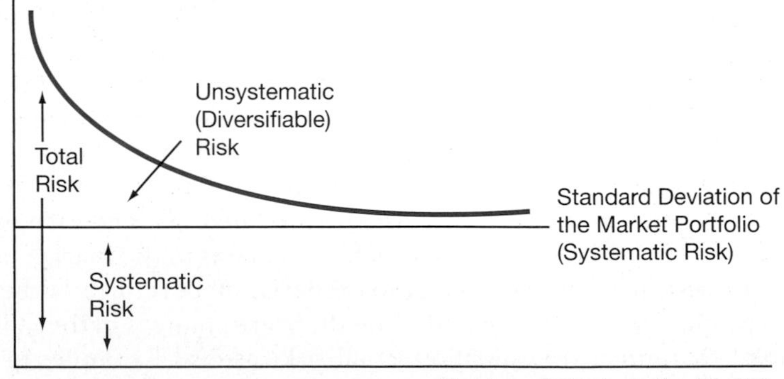

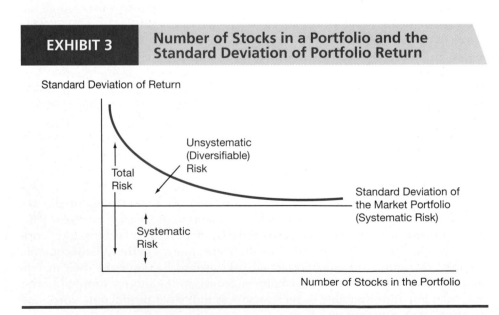

[2] The discussion in Reading 50 leads one to conclude that securities with negative correlation would be ideal. Although this is true in theory, it is difficult to find such assets in the real world.

concluded that a well-diversified stock portfolio must include at least 30 stocks for a borrowing investor and 40 stocks for a lending investor.

An important point to remember is that, by adding stocks to the portfolio that are not perfectly correlated with stocks in the portfolio, you can reduce the overall standard deviation of the portfolio but you *cannot eliminate variability.* The standard deviation of your portfolio will eventually reach the level of the market portfolio, where you will have diversified away all unsystematic risk, but you still have market or systematic risk. You cannot eliminate the variability and uncertainty of macroeconomic factors that affect all risky assets. At the same time, you can attain a lower level of systematic risk by diversifying globally versus only diversifying within the United States because some of the systematic risk factors in the U.S. market (such as U.S. monetary policy) are not correlated with systematic risk variables in other countries such as Germany and Japan. As a result, if you diversify globally, you eventually get down to a world systematic risk level.

The CML and the Separation Theorem The CML leads all investors to invest in the same risky asset portfolio, the M portfolio. Individual investors should only differ regarding their position on the CML, which depends on their risk preferences.

In turn, how they get to a point on the CML is based on their *financing decisions.* If you are relatively risk averse, you will lend some part of your portfolio at the *RFR* by buying some risk-free securities and investing the remainder in the market portfolio of risky assets. For example, you might invest in the portfolio combination at Point A in Exhibit 4. In contrast, if you prefer more risk, you might borrow funds at the *RFR* and invest everything (all of your capital plus what you borrowed) in the market portfolio, building the portfolio at Point B. This financing decision provides more risk but greater returns than the market portfolio. As discussed earlier, because portfolios on the CML dominate other portfolio possibilities, the CML becomes the efficient frontier of portfolios, and investors decide where they want to be along this efficient frontier. Tobin (1958)

EXHIBIT 4 Choice of Optimal Portfolio Combinations on the CML

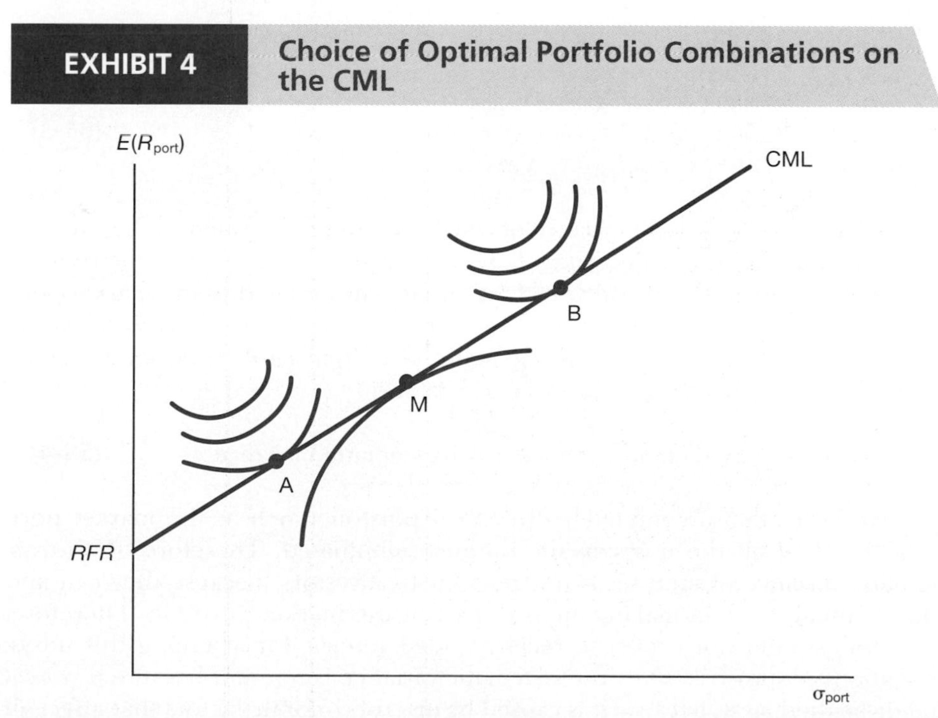

called this division of the investment decision from the financing decision the **separation theorem**. Specifically, to be somewhere on the CML efficient frontier, you initially decide to invest in the market Portfolio M, which means that you will be on the CML. This is your *investment* decision. Subsequently, based on your risk preferences, you make a separate *financing* decision either to borrow or to lend to attain your preferred risk position on the CML.

A Risk Measure for the CML In this section, we show that the relevant risk measure for risky assets is *their covariance with the M portfolio,* which is referred to as their systematic risk. The importance of this covariance is apparent from two points of view.

First, in discussing the Markowitz portfolio model, we noted that the relevant risk to consider when adding a security to a portfolio is *its average covariance with all other assets in the portfolio.* In this reading, we have shown that *the only relevant portfolio is the M portfolio.* Together, these two findings mean that the only important consideration for any individual risky asset is its average covariance with all the risky assets in the M portfolio or, simply, *the asset's covariance with the market portfolio.* This covariance, then, is the relevant risk measure for an individual risky asset.

Second, because all individual risky assets are a part of the M portfolio, one can describe their rates of return in relation to the returns for the M portfolio using the following linear model:

$$R_{it} = a_i + b_i R_{Mt} + \varepsilon \tag{51-2}$$

where

$R_{i,t}$ = return for asset i during period t
a_i = constant term for asset i
b_i = slope coefficient for asset i
R_{Mt} = return for the M portfolio during period t
ε = random error term

The variance of returns for a risky asset could be described as

$$\begin{aligned} \mathrm{Var}(R_{it}) &= \mathrm{Var}(a_i + b_i R_{Mt} + \varepsilon) \\ &= \mathrm{Var}(a_i) + \mathrm{Var}(b_i R_{Mt}) + \mathrm{Var}(\varepsilon) \\ &= 0 + \mathrm{Var}(b_i R_{Mt}) + \mathrm{Var}(\varepsilon) \end{aligned} \tag{51-3}$$

Note that $\mathrm{Var}(b_i R_{Mt})$ is the variance of return for an asset related to the variance of the market return, or the *systematic variance or risk.* Also, $\mathrm{Var}(\varepsilon)$ is the residual variance of return for the individual asset that is not related to the market portfolio. This residual variance is the variability that we have referred to as the unsystematic or *unique risk* or unsystematic or unique *variance* because it arises from the unique features of the asset. Therefore:

$$\mathrm{Var}(R_{i,t}) = \text{Systematic Variance} + \text{Unsystematic Variance} \tag{51-4}$$

We know that a completely diversified portfolio such as the market portfolio has had all the unsystematic variance eliminated. Therefore, the unsystematic variance of an asset is not relevant to investors, because they can and do eliminate it when making an asset part of the market portfolio. Therefore, investors should not expect to receive added returns for assuming this unsystematic (unique) risk. Only the systematic variance is relevant because it *cannot* be diversified away, because it is caused by macroeconomic factors that affect all risky assets.

THE CAPITAL ASSET PRICING MODEL: EXPECTED RETURN AND RISK

3

Up to this point, we have considered how investors make their portfolio decisions, including the significant effects of a risk-free asset. The existence of this risk-free asset resulted in the derivation of a capital market line (CML) that became the relevant efficient frontier. Because all investors want to be on the CML, an asset's covariance with the market portfolio of risky assets emerged as the relevant risk measure.

Now that we understand this relevant measure of risk, we can proceed to use it to determine an appropriate expected rate of return on a risky asset. This step takes us into the **capital asset pricing model (CAPM)**, which is a model that indicates what should be the expected or required rates of return on risky assets. This transition is important because it helps you to value an asset by providing an appropriate discount rate to use in any valuation model. Alternatively, if you have already estimated the rate of return that you think you will earn on an investment, you can compare this ***estimated* rate of return** to the *required* rate of return implied by the CAPM and determine whether the asset is undervalued, overvalued, or properly valued.

To accomplish the foregoing, we demonstrate the creation of a security market line (SML) that visually represents the relationship between risk and the expected or the required rate of return on an asset. The equation of this SML, together with estimates for the return on a risk-free asset and on the market portfolio, can generate expected or required rates of return for any asset based on its systematic risk. You compare this required rate of return to the rate of return that you estimate that you will earn on the investment to determine if the investment is undervalued or overvalued. After demonstrating this procedure, we finish the section with a demonstration of how to calculate the systematic risk variable for a risky asset.

The Security Market Line (SML)

We know that the relevant risk measure for an individual risky asset is its covariance with the market portfolio ($Cov_{i,M}$). Therefore, we can draw the risk-return relationship as shown in Exhibit 5 with the systematic covariance variable ($Cov_{i,M}$) as the risk measure.

The return for the market portfolio (R_M) should be consistent with its own risk, which is the covariance of the market with itself. If you recall the formula for covariance, you will see that the covariance of any asset with itself is its variance, $Cov_{i,i} = \sigma_i^2$. In turn, the covariance of the market with itself is the variance of the market rate of return $Cov_{M,M} = \sigma_M^2$. Therefore, the equation for the risk-return line in Exhibit 5 is:

$$\begin{aligned} E(R_i) &= RFR + \frac{R_M - RFR}{\sigma_M^2}(Cov_{i,M}) \\ &= RFR + \frac{Cov_{i,M}}{\sigma_M^2}(R_M - RFR) \end{aligned} \quad \textbf{(51-5)}$$

Defining $Cov_{i,M}/\sigma_M^2$ as beta, (β_i), this equation can be stated:

$$E(R_i) = RFR + \beta_i(R_M - RFR) \quad \textbf{(51-6)}$$

Beta can be viewed as a *standardized* measure of systematic risk. Specifically, we already know that the covariance of any asset i with the market portfolio (Cov_{iM})

EXHIBIT 5 Graph of Security Market Line

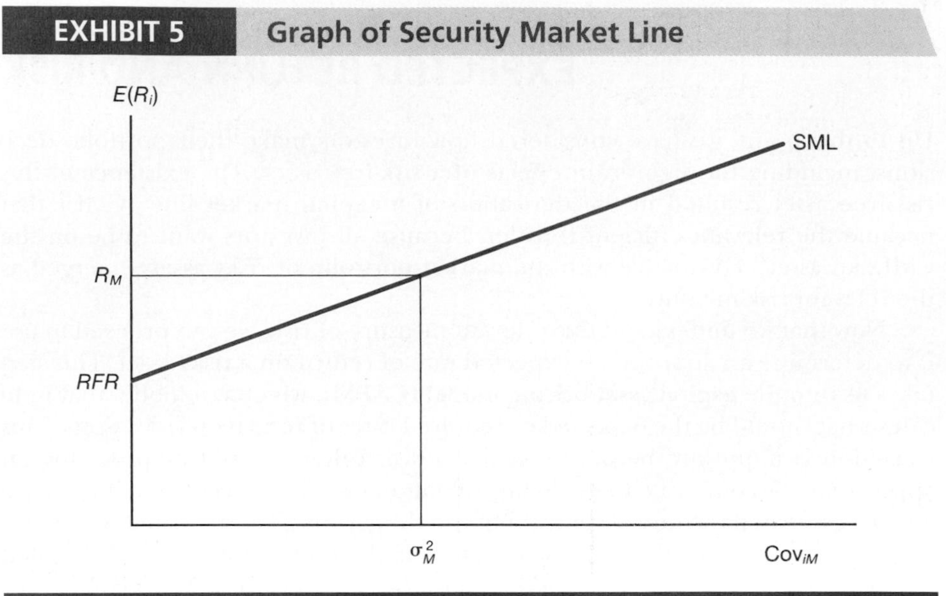

is the relevant risk measure. Beta is a standardized measure of risk because it relates this covariance to the variance of the market portfolio. As a result, the market portfolio has a beta of 1. Therefore, if the β_i for an asset is above 1.0, the asset has higher normalized systematic risk than the market, which means that it is more volatile than the overall market portfolio.

Given this standardized measure of systematic risk, the SML graph can be expressed as shown in Exhibit 6. This is the same graph as in Exhibit 5, except there is a different measure of risk. Specifically, the graph in Exhibit 6 replaces the covariance of an asset's returns with the market portfolio as the risk measure with the standardized measure of systematic risk (beta), which is the covariance of an asset with the market portfolio divided by the variance of the market portfolio.

Determining the Expected Rate of Return for a Risky Asset Equation 51-6 and the graph in Exhibit 6 tell us that the expected (required) rate of return for a

EXHIBIT 6 Graph of SML with Normalized Systematic Risk

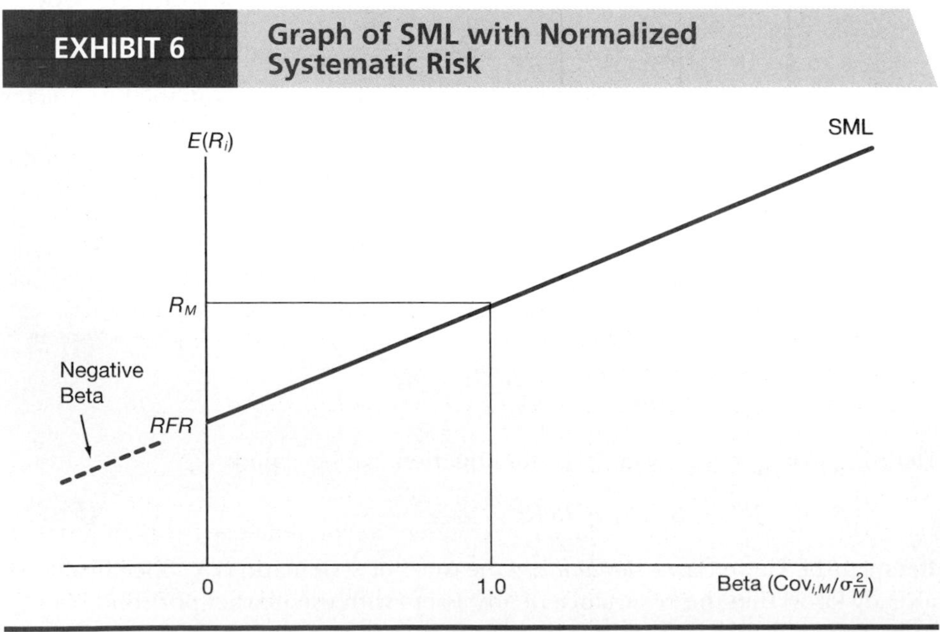

risky asset is determined by the *RFR* plus a risk premium for the individual asset. In turn, the risk premium is determined by the systematic risk of the asset (β_i), and the prevailing **market risk premium** ($R_M - RFR$). To demonstrate how you would compute the expected or required rates of return, consider the following example stocks assuming you have already computed betas:

Stock	Beta
A	0.70
B	1.00
C	1.15
D	1.40
E	−0.30

Assume that we expect the economy's *RFR* to be 5 percent (0.05) and the return on the market portfolio (R_M) to be 9 percent (0.09). This implies a market risk premium of 4 percent (0.04). With these inputs, the SML equation would yield the following expected (required) rates of return for these five stocks:

$$\begin{aligned}
E(R_i) &= RFR + \beta_i(R_M - RFR)\\
E(R_A) &= 0.05 + 0.70\ (0.09 - 0.05)\\
&= 0.078 = 7.80\%\\
E(R_B) &= 0.05 + 1.00(0.09 - 0.05)\\
&= 0.09 = 9.00\%\\
E(R_C) &= 0.05 + 1.15(0.09 - 0.05)\\
&= 0.096 = 9.60\%\\
E(R_D) &= 0.05 + 1.40(0.09 - 0.05)\\
&= 0.106 = 10.60\%\\
E(R_E) &= 0.05 + (-0.30)\ (0.09 - 0.05)\\
&= 0.05 - 0.012\\
&= 0.038 = 3.8\%
\end{aligned}$$

As stated, these are the expected (required) rates of return that these stocks should provide based on their systematic risks and the prevailing SML.

Stock A has lower risk than the aggregate market, so you should not expect (require) its return to be as high as the return on the market portfolio of risky assets. You should expect (require) Stock A to return 7.80 percent. Stock B has systematic risk equal to the market's (beta = 1.00), so its required rate of return should likewise be equal to the expected market return (9 percent). Stocks C and D have systematic risk greater than the market's, so they should provide returns consistent with their risk. Finally, Stock E has a *negative* beta (which is quite rare in practice), so its required rate of return, if such a stock could be found, would be below the *RFR* of 5 percent.

In equilibrium, *all* assets and *all* portfolios of assets should plot on the SML. That is, all assets should be priced so that their **estimated rates of return**, which are the actual holding period rates of return that you anticipate, are consistent with their levels of systematic risk. Any security with an estimated rate of return that plots above the SML would be considered underpriced because it implies that you *estimated* you would receive a rate of return on the security that is above its *required* rate of return based on its systematic risk. In contrast, assets with estimated rates of return that plot below the SML would be considered overpriced. This

EXHIBIT 7 Price, Dividend, and Rate of Return Estimates

Stock	Current Price (P_t)	Expected Price (P_{t+1})	Expected Dividend (D_{t+1})	Estimated Future Rate of Return (percent)
A	25	26	1.00	8.00%
B	40	42	0.50	6.20
C	33	37	1.00	15.15
D	64	66	1.10	5.16
E	50	53	—	6.00

position relative to the SML implies that your estimated rate of return is below what you should require based on the asset's systematic risk.

In a completely efficient market in equilibrium, you would not expect any assets to plot off the SML because, in equilibrium, all stocks should provide holding period returns that are equal to their required rates of return. Alternatively, a market that is fairly efficient but not completely efficient may misprice certain assets because not everyone will be aware of all the relevant information for an asset.

A superior investor has the ability to derive value estimates for assets that are consistently superior to the consensus market evaluation. As a result, such an investor will earn better rates of return than the average investor on a risk-adjusted basis.

Identifying Undervalued and Overvalued Assets Now that we understand how to compute the rate of return one should expect or require for a specific risky asset using the SML, we can compare this *required* rate of return to the asset's *estimated* rate of return over a specific investment horizon to determine whether it would be an appropriate investment. To make this comparison, you need an independent estimate of the return outlook for the security based on either fundamental or technical analysis techniques, which will be discussed in subsequent readings. Let us continue the example for the five assets discussed in the previous subsection.

Assume that analysts in a major trust department have been following these five stocks. Based on extensive fundamental analysis, the analysts provide the expected price and dividend estimates contained in Exhibit 7. Given these projections, you can compute the estimated rates of return the analysts would anticipate during this holding period.

EXHIBIT 8 Comparison of Required Rate of Return to Estimated Rate of Return

Stock	Beta	Required Return $E(R_i)$	Estimated Return	Estimated Return Minus $E(R_i)$	Evaluation
A	0.70	7.80	8.00	0.20	Properly valued
B	1.00	9.00	6.20	−2.80	Overvalued
C	1.15	9.60	15.15	5.55	Undervalued
D	1.40	10.60	5.16	−5.44	Overvalued
E	−0.30	3.80	6.00	2.20	Undervalued

EXHIBIT 9 **Plot of Estimated Returns on SML Graph**

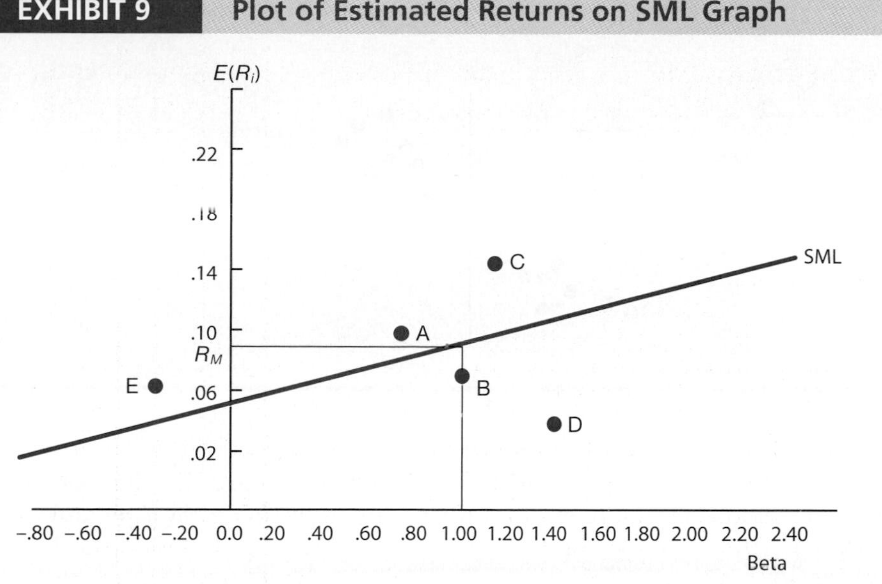

Exhibit 8 summarizes the relationship between the required rate of return for each stock based on its systematic risk as computed earlier, and its estimated rate of return (from Exhibit 7) based on the current and future prices, and its dividend outlook. This difference between estimated return and expected (required) return is sometimes referred to as a stock's ***alpha*** or its excess return. This alpha can be positive (the stock is undervalued) or negative (the stock is overvalued). If the alpha is zero, the stock is on the SML and is properly valued in line with its systematic risk.

Plotting these estimated rates of return and stock betas on the SML we specified earlier gives the graph shown in Exhibit 9. Stock A is almost exactly on the line, so it is considered properly valued because its estimated rate of return is almost equal to its required rate of return. Stocks B and D are considered overvalued because their estimated rates of return during the coming period are less than what an investor should expect (require) for the risk involved. As a result, they plot below the SML. In contrast, Stocks C and E are expected to provide rates of return greater than we would require based on their systematic risk. Therefore, both stocks plot above the SML, indicating that they are undervalued stocks.

Assuming that you trusted your analyst to forecast estimated returns, you would take no action regarding Stock A, but you would buy Stocks C and E and sell Stocks B and D. You might even sell Stocks B and D short if you favored such aggressive tactics.

Calculating Systematic Risk: The Characteristic Line The systematic risk input for an individual asset is derived from a regression model, referred to as the asset's **characteristic line** with the market portfolio:

$$R_{i,t} = \alpha_i + \beta_i R_{M,t} + \varepsilon \qquad \textbf{(51-7)}$$

where:

$R_{i,t}$ = the rate of return for Asset i during Period t

$R_{M,t}$ = the rate of return for the market portfolio M during Period t

α_i = the constant term, or intercept, of the regression, which equals $\overline{R}_i - \beta_i \overline{R}_M$

β_i = the systematic risk (beta) of Asset i equal to $\text{Cov}_{i,M}/\sigma_M^2$

ε = the random error term

EXHIBIT 10 Scatterplot of Rates of Return

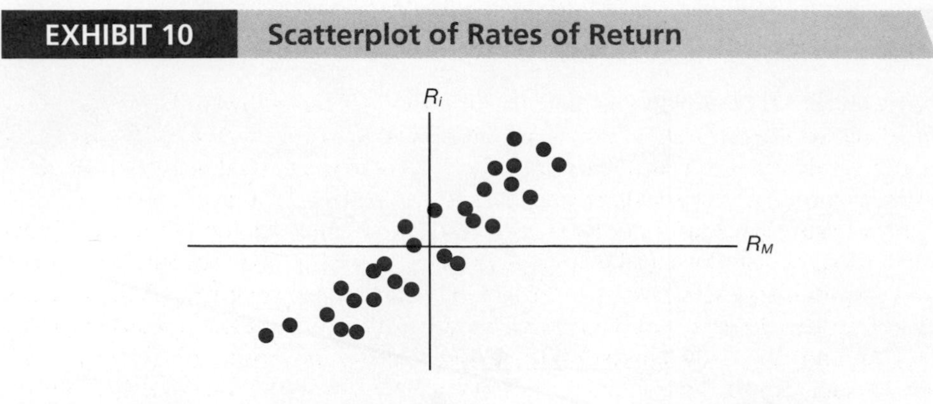

The characteristic line (Equation 51-7) is the regression line of best fit through a scatterplot of rates of return for the individual risky asset and for the market portfolio of risky assets over some designated past period, as shown in Exhibit 10.

The impact of the time interval. In practice, the number of observations and the time interval used in the regression vary. Value Line Investment Services derives characteristic lines for common stocks using weekly rates of return for the most recent five years (260 weekly observations). Merrill Lynch, Pierce, Fenner & Smith uses monthly rates of return for the most recent five years (60 monthly observations). Because there is no theoretically correct time interval for analysis, we must make a trade-off between enough observations to eliminate the impact of random rates of return and an excessive length of time, such as 15 or 20 years, over which the subject company may have changed dramatically. Remember that what you really want is the *expected* systematic risk for the potential investment. In this analysis, you are analyzing historical data to help you derive a reasonable estimate of the asset's expected systematic risk.

A couple of studies have considered the effect of the time interval used to compute betas (weekly versus monthly). Statman (1981) examined the relationship between Value Line (VL) betas and Merrill Lynch (ML) betas and found a relatively weak relationship. Reilly and Wright (1988) analyzed the differential effects of return computation, market index, and the time interval and showed that the major cause of the differences in beta was the use of monthly versus weekly return intervals. Also, the interval effect depended on the sizes of the firms. The shorter weekly interval caused a larger beta for large firms and a smaller beta for small firms. For example, the average beta for the smallest decile of firms using monthly data was 1.682, but the average beta for these small firms using weekly data was only 1.080. The authors concluded that the return time interval makes a difference, and its impact increases as the firm size declines.

The effect of the market proxy. Another significant decision when computing an asset's characteristic line is which indicator series to use as a proxy for the market portfolio of all risky assets. Most investigators use the Standard & Poor's 500 Composite Index as a proxy for the market portfolio, because the stocks in this index encompass a large proportion of the total market value of U.S. stocks and it is a value-weighted series, which is consistent with the theoretical market series. Still, this series contains only large-cap U.S. stocks, most of them listed on the NYSE. Previously, it was noted that the market portfolio of all risky assets should include U.S. stocks and bonds, non-U.S. stocks and bonds, real estate, coins, stamps, art, antiques, and any other marketable risky asset from around the world.[3]

Example Computations of a Characteristic Line The following examples show how you would compute characteristic lines for General Electric (GE) based on the monthly rates of return during 2004.[4] Twelve monthly rates are not enough observations for statistical purposes, but they provide a good example. We demonstrate the computations using two different proxies for the market portfolio. First, we use the standard S&P 500 as the market proxy. Second, we use the Morgan Stanley (M-S) World Equity Index as the market proxy. This analysis demonstrates the effect of using a global portfolio of stocks as the market proxy.

The monthly price changes are computed using the closing prices for the last day of each month. These data for GE, the S&P 500, and the M-S World Index are contained in Exhibit 11. Exhibit 12 contains the scatterplot of the percentage price changes for GE and the S&P 500. During this 12-month period, there were only 2 months when GE had returns that were not consistent with the S&P 500. As a result, the covariance between GE and the S&P 500 series was a reasonable positive value (3.57). The covariance divided by the variance of the S&P 500 market portfolio (4.38) indicates that GE's beta relative to the S&P 500 was equal to 0.82. This analysis indicates that, during this limited time period, GE was less risky than the aggregate market proxied by the S&P 500. When we draw the computed characteristic line on Exhibit 12, the scatterplots are reasonably close to the characteristic line except for two observations, which is consistent with the correlation coefficient of 0.43.

The computation of the characteristic line for GE using the M-S World Index as the proxy for the market is contained in Exhibit 11, and the scatterplots are in Exhibit 13. At this point, it is important to consider what one might expect to be the relationship between the beta relative to the S&P 500 versus the betas with the M-S World Index. This requires a consideration of the two components that go into the computation of beta: (1) the covariance between the stock and the benchmark and (2) the variance of returns for the benchmark series. Notably, there is no obvious answer regarding what will happen to the beta for either series because one would expect both components to change. Specifically, the covariance of GE with the S&P 500 will probably be higher than the covariance with the global series because you are matching a U.S. stock with a U.S. market index rather than a world index. Thus, one would expect the covariance with the global index to be smaller. At the same time, the variance of returns for the world stock index should also be smaller than the variance for the S&P 500 because the world index is a more diversified stock portfolio.

Therefore, the direction of change for the beta will depend on the relative change in the two components. Empirically, as demonstrated by Reilly and Akhtar (1995), the beta is typically smaller with the world stock index because the covariance is definitely lower, but the variance is only slightly smaller. The results of this example were consistent with these expectations. The beta of GE with the world stock index was definitely smaller (0.59 vs. 0.82) because the covariance of GE with the global index was smaller as expected (3.30 vs. 3.57), but the variance of the global market proxy was not smaller as hypothesized (it was 5.59 vs. 4.38). The fact that the betas with the alternative market proxies differed is significant

[3] Substantial discussion surrounds the market index used and its impact on the empirical results and usefulness of the CAPM. This concern is discussed further and demonstrated in the next subsection on computing an asset's characteristic line.

[4] These betas are computed using only monthly price changes for GE, the S&P 500, and the M-S World Index (dividends are not included). This is done for simplicity but it is also based on a study by Sharpe and Cooper (1972a) that indicated that betas derived with and without dividends have a correlation coefficient of 0.99.

EXHIBIT 11 Computation of Beta for General Electric with Selected Indexes

Date	Index			Return			S&P 500 R(S&P) − R̄(S&P)	MSCI World R(MSCI) − R̄(MSCI)	GE R̄(GE) − R(GE)		
	S&P 500	MSCI World	GE	S&P 500	MSCI World	GE	(1)	(2)	(3)	(4)[a]	(5)[b]
Dec-03	1111.92	1,036.32	30.98	–	–	–					
Jan-04	1131.13	1,052.29	33.63	1.73	1.54	8.55	0.99	0.50	7.11	7.02	3.58
Feb-04	1144.94	1,068.65	32.52	1.22	1.55	(3.30)	0.48	0.52	(4.75)	(2.28)	(2.46)
Mar-04	1126.21	1,059.16	30.52	(1.64)	(0.89)	(6.15)	(2.38)	(1.93)	(7.60)	18.05	14.63
Apr-04	1107.3	1,035.66	29.95	(1.68)	(2.22)	(1.87)	(2.42)	(3.26)	(3.32)	8.02	10.79
May-04	1120.68	1,042.63	31.12	1.21	0.67	3.91	0.47	(0.36)	2.46	1.15	(0.90)
Jun-04	1140.84	1,062.51	32.40	1.80	1.91	4.11	1.06	0.87	2.67	2.82	2.32
Jul-04	1101.72	1,026.99	33.25	(3.43)	(3.34)	2.62	(4.17)	(4.38)	1.18	(4.90)	(5.15)
Aug-04	1104.24	1,029.63	32.79	0.23	0.26	(1.38)	(0.51)	(0.78)	(2.83)	1.45	2.21
Sep-04	1114.58	1,047.86	33.58	0.94	1.77	2.41	0.20	0.73	0.96	0.19	0.71
Oct-04	1130.2	1,072.70	34.12	1.40	2.37	1.61	0.66	1.33	0.16	0.11	0.21
Nov-04	1173.82	1,127.34	35.36	3.86	5.09	3.63	3.12	4.06	2.19	6.82	8.87
Dec-04	1211.92	1,169.34	36.50	3.25	3.73	3.22	2.51	2.69	1.78	4.45	4.78
Average (R)			0.74	1.04	1.45				Total =	42.89	39.59
Standard Deviation			2.09	2.36	3.97						

$\text{Cov}_{(GE,\ S\&P)} = 42.89/12 = 3.57$

$\text{Cov}_{(GE,\ MSCI)} = 39.59/12 = 3.30$

$\text{Correlation Coef.}_{(GE,\ S\&P)} = 3.57/(2.09 \times 3.97) = 0.430$

$\text{Var}_{(S\&P)} = \text{St. Dev.}_{(S\&P)}{}^2 = 2.09^2 = 4.38$

$\text{Var}_{(MSCI)} = \text{St. Dev.}_{(MSCI)}{}^2 = 2.36^2 = 5.59$

$\text{Beta}_{(GE,\ S\&P)} = 3.57/4.38 = 0.82$

$\text{Beta}_{(GE,\ MSCI)} = 3.30/5.59 = 0.59$

$\text{Alpha}_{(GE,\ S\&P)} = 1.45 - (0.82 \times 0.74) = 0.843$

$\text{Alpha}_{(GE,\ MSCI)} = 1.45 - (0.59 \times 1.04) = 0.836$

$\text{Correlation Coef.}_{(GE,\ MSCI)} = 3.30/(2.36 \times 3.97) = 0.352$

[a] Column 4 is equal to Column 1 multiplied by Column 3.

[b] Column 5 is equal to Column 2 multiplied by Column 3.

EXHIBIT 12 Scatterplot of General Electric (GE) and the S&P 500 with Characteristic Line for GE, 2004

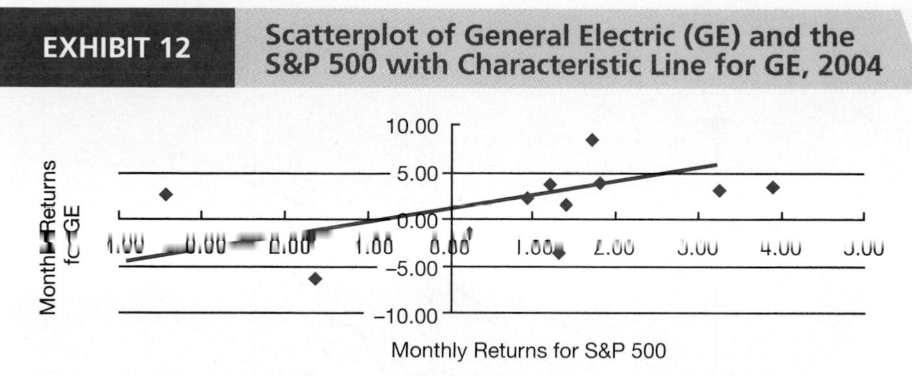

and reflects the potential problem in a global investment environment. Specifically, it means that selecting the appropriate proxy for the market portfolio is an important decision when measuring risk.

RELAXING THE ASSUMPTIONS 4

Earlier in the reading, several assumptions were set forth related to the CAPM. In this section, we discuss the impact on the capital market line (CML) and the security market line (SML) when we relax several of these assumptions.

Differential Borrowing and Lending Rates

One of the first assumptions of the CAPM was that investors could borrow and lend any amount of money at the risk-free rate. It is reasonable to assume that investors can *lend* unlimited amounts at the risk-free rate by buying government securities (e.g., T-bills). In contrast, one may question the ability of investors to borrow unlimited amounts at the T-bill rate because most investors must pay a premium relative to the prime rate when borrowing money. For example, when T-bills are yielding 4 percent, the prime rate will probably be about 6 percent, and most individuals would have to pay about 7 percent to borrow at the bank.

EXHIBIT 13 Scatterplot of General Electric (GE) and the MSCI World Index with Characteristic Line for GE, 2004

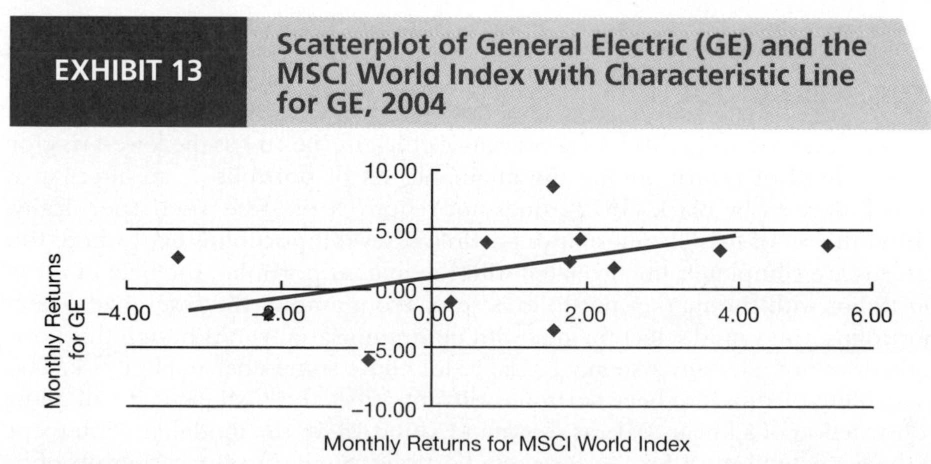

EXHIBIT 14 **Investment Alternatives When the Cost of Borrowing Is Higher than the Cost of Lending**

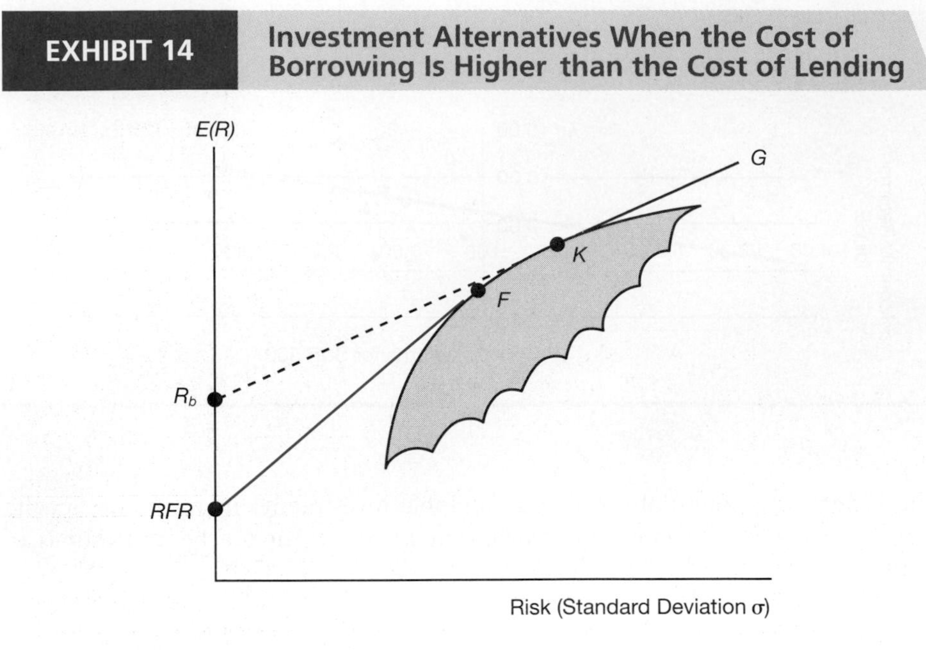

Because of this differential, there will be two different lines going to the Markowitz efficient frontier, as shown in Exhibit 14. The segment *RFR-F* indicates the investment opportunities available when an investor combines risk-free assets (i.e., lending at the *RFR*) and Portfolio F on the Markowitz efficient frontier. It is not possible to extend this line any farther if it is assumed that you cannot borrow at this risk-free rate to acquire further units of Portfolio F. If it is assumed that you can borrow at R_b, the point of tangency from this rate would be on the curve at Point K. This indicates that you could borrow at R_b and use the proceeds to invest in Portfolio K to extend the CML along the line segment *K-G*. Therefore, the CML is made up of *RFR-F-K-G;* that is, a line segment (*RFR-F*), a curve segment (*F-K*), and another line segment (*K-G*). As noted by Brennan (1969), this implies that you can either lend or borrow, but the borrowing portfolios are not as profitable as when it was assumed that you could borrow at the *RFR*. In this instance, because you must pay a borrowing rate that is higher than the *RFR*, your net return is less—that is, the slope of the borrowing line (*K-G*) is below that for *RFR-F*.

Zero-Beta Model

If the market portfolio (M) is mean-variance efficient (i.e., it has the lowest risk for a given level of return among the attainable set of portfolios), an alternative model, derived by Black (1972), does not require a risk-free asset. Specifically, within the set of feasible alternative portfolios, several portfolios exist where the returns are completely uncorrelated with the market portfolio; the beta of these portfolios with the market portfolio is zero. From among the several zero-beta portfolios, you would select the one with minimum variance. Although this portfolio does not have any systematic risk, it does have some unsystematic risk. The availability of this zero-beta portfolio will not affect the CML, but it will allow construction of a linear SML, as shown in Exhibit 15. In the model, the intercept is the expected return for the zero-beta portfolio. Similar to the earlier proof in this reading, the combinations of this zero-beta portfolio and the market portfolio

EXHIBIT 15 **Security Market Line with a Zero-Beta Portfolio**

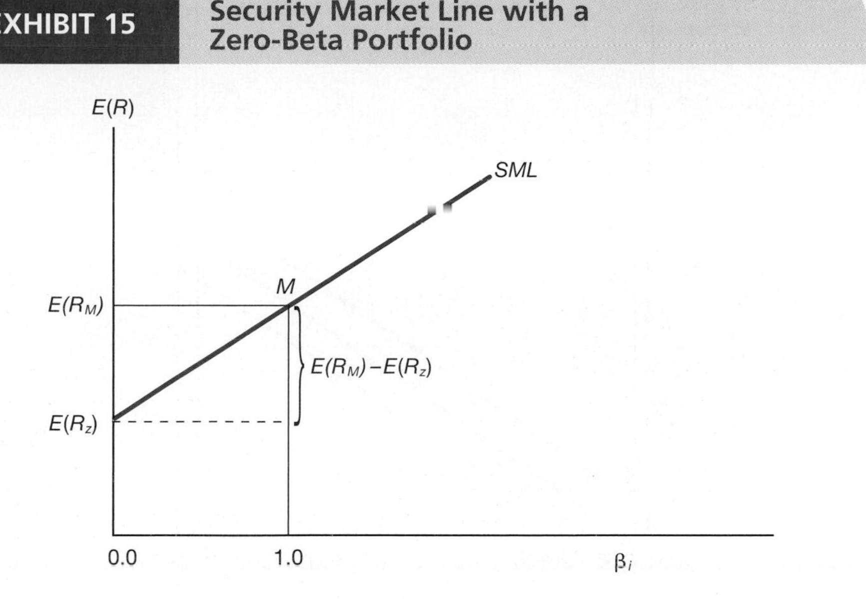

will be a linear relationship in return and risk because the covariance between the zero-beta portfolio (R_z) and the market portfolio is similar to what it was with the risk-free asset. Assuming the return for the zero-beta portfolio is greater than that for a risk-free asset, the slope of the line through the market portfolio would not be as steep; that is, the market risk premium would be smaller. The equation for this zero-beta CAPM line would be:

$$E(R_i) = E(R_z) + B_i[E(R_M) - E(R_z)] \quad \textbf{(51-8)}$$

Obviously, the risk premiums for individual assets would be a function of the beta for the individual security and the market risk premium:

$$[E(R_M) - E(R_z)]$$

Some of the empirical results discussed in the next section support this model with its higher intercept and flatter slope. Alternatively, several studies have specifically tested this model and had conflicting results. Specifically, studies by Gibbons (1982) and Shanken (1985b) rejected the model, while a study by Stambaugh (1982) supported the zero-beta CAPM.

Transaction Costs

The basic assumption is that there are no transaction costs, so investors will buy or sell mispriced securities until they again plot on the SML. For example, if a stock plots above the SML, it is underpriced so investors should buy it and bid up its price until its estimated return is in line with its risk—that is, until it plots on the SML. Assuming there are transaction costs, investors will not correct all mispricing because in some instances the cost of buying and selling the mispriced security will offset any potential excess return. Therefore, securities will plot very close to the SML—but not exactly on it. Thus, the SML will be a band of securities, as shown in Exhibit 16, rather than a single line. Obviously, the width of the

EXHIBIT 16 Security Market Line with Transaction Costs

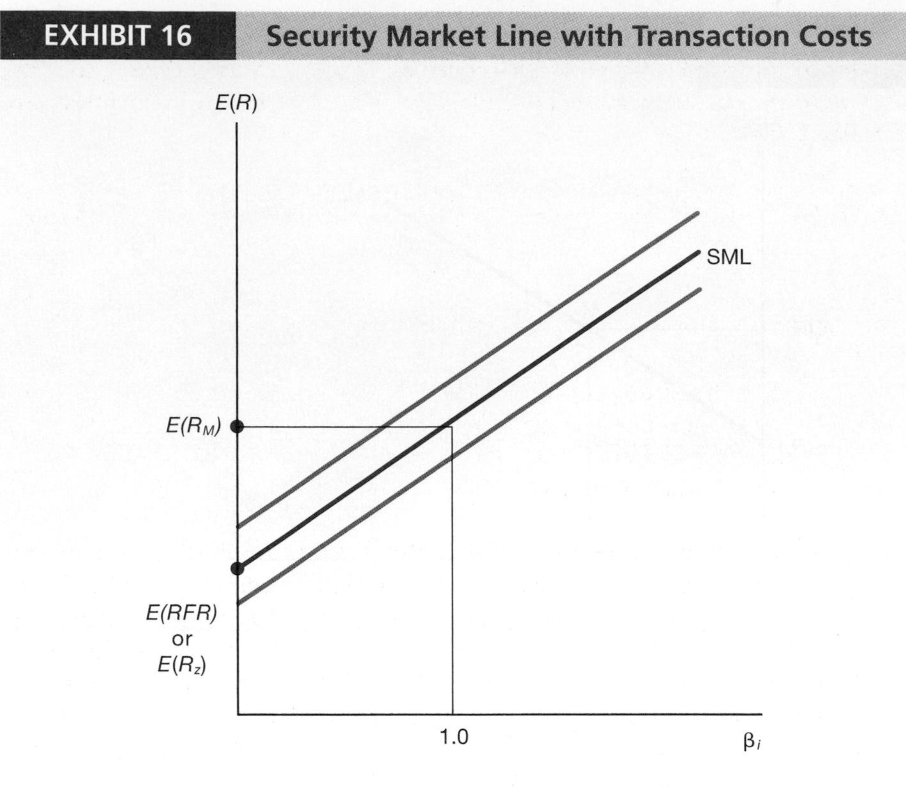

band is a function of the amount of the transaction costs. In a world with a large proportion of trading by institutions at pennies per share and with discount brokers available for individual investors, the band should be quite narrow.

Dimson (1979) considered the existence of transaction costs and how they affect the extent of diversification by investors. Earlier in the reading, we discussed the relationship between the number of stocks in a portfolio and the variance of the portfolio (see Exhibit 3). Initially, the variance declined rapidly, approaching about 90 percent of complete diversification with about 15 to 18 securities. An important question is, How many securities must be added to derive the last 10 percent? Because of transaction costs, Brennan and Subramanyam (1996) show that at some point the additional cost of diversification would exceed its benefit, especially when considering the costs of monitoring and analyzing the added securities.

Heterogeneous Expectations and Planning Periods

If all investors had different expectations about risk and return, each would have a unique CML and/or SML, and the composite graph would be a set (band) of lines with a breadth determined by the divergence of expectations. If all investors had similar information and background, the band would be reasonably narrow.

The impact of *planning periods* is similar. Recall that the CAPM is a one-period model, corresponding to the planning period for the individual investor. Thus, if you are using a one-year planning period, your CML and SML could differ from mine, if I assume a one-month planning period.

Taxes

The rates of return that we normally record and that were used throughout the model were pretax returns. In fact, the actual returns for most investors are affected as follows:

$$E(R_i)(AT) = \frac{(P_e - P_b) \times (1 - T_{cg}) + (Div) \times (1 - T_i)}{P_b} \quad \textbf{(51-9)}$$

where

$R_i(AT)$ = after-tax rate of return
P_e = ending price
P_b = beginning price
T_{cg} = tax on capital gain or loss
Div = dividend paid during period
T_i = tax on ordinary income

Clearly, tax rates differ between individuals and institutions. For institutions that do not pay taxes, the original pretax model is correctly specified—that is, T_{cg} and T_i take on values of zero. As noted by Black and Scholes (1979) and Litzenberger and Ramaswamy (1979), because investors have heavy tax burdens, this could cause major differences in the CML and SML among investors. Studies by Elton, Gruber, and Rentzler (1983); Miller and Scholes (1982); and Christie (1990) have examined the effect of the differential taxes on dividends versus capital gains but the evidence is not unanimous.

EMPIRICAL TESTS OF THE CAPM 5

When we discussed the assumptions of capital market theory, we pointed out that a theory should not be judged on the basis of its assumptions, but on *how well it explains the relationships that exist in the real world.* When testing the CAPM, there are two major questions. First, *How stable is the measure of systematic risk (beta)?* Because beta is our principal risk measure, it is important to know whether past betas can be used as estimates of future betas. Also, how do the alternative published estimates of beta compare? Second, *Is there a positive linear relationship as hypothesized between beta and the rate of return on risky assets?* More specifically, how well do returns conform to the following SML equation, discussed earlier as Equation 51-6.

$$E(R_i) = RFR + \beta_i(R_M - RFR)$$

Some specific questions might include:

- Does the intercept approximate the prevailing *RFR*?
- Was the slope of the line positive and was it consistent with the slope implied by the prevailing risk premium ($R_M - RFR$)?

We consider these two major questions in the following section.

Stability of Beta

Numerous studies have examined the stability of beta and generally concluded that the risk measure was *not* stable for individual stocks, but the stability of the

beta for *portfolios* of stocks increased dramatically. Further, the larger the portfolio of stocks (e.g., over 50 stocks) and the longer the period (over 26 weeks), the more stable the beta of the portfolio. Also, the betas tended to regress toward the mean. Specifically, high-beta portfolios tended to decline over time toward unity (1.00), whereas low-beta portfolios tended to increase over time toward unity.

Carpenter and Upton (1981) considered the influence of the trading volume on beta stability and contended that the predictions of betas were slightly better using the volume-adjusted betas. A **small-firm effect** wherein the beta for low-volume securities was biased downward was documented by Ibbotson, Kaplan, and Peterson (1997).

Comparability of Published Estimates of Beta

In contrast to deriving your own estimate of beta for a stock, you may want to use a published source for speed or convenience, such as Merrill Lynch's *Security Risk Evaluation Report* (published monthly) and the weekly *Value Line Investment Survey*. Both services use the following market model equation:

$$(R_{i,t}) = RFR + \beta_i R_{M,t} + E_t$$

Notably, they differ in the data used. Specifically, Merrill Lynch uses *60 monthly observations* and the S&P 500 as the market proxy, whereas the *Value Line* estimates beta using *260 weekly observations* and the NYSE composite series as the market proxy. They both use an adjustment process because of the regression tendencies.

As noted earlier, Statman (1981) documented a difference between the betas for the two services. Subsequently, Reilly and Wright (1988) showed that the reason for the difference was due to the return interval used (weekly vs. monthly) by the two services and demonstrated that market value also made a difference. Handa, Kothari, and Wasley (1989) concurred with the differences in betas and showed that the specific reason the return interval was the cause was that an asset's covariance with the market and the market's variance did not change proportionally with the returns interval. They also confirmed that size impacted the effect.

6 RELATIONSHIP BETWEEN SYSTEMATIC RISK AND RETURN

The ultimate question regarding the CAPM is whether it is useful in explaining the return on risky assets. Specifically, is there a positive linear relationship between the systematic risk and the rates of return on these risky assets? Sharpe and Cooper (1972b) found a positive relationship between return and risk, although it was not completely linear.

Because of the statistical problems with individual stocks, Black, Jensen, and Scholes (1972) examined the risk and return for portfolios of stocks and found a positive linear relationship between monthly excess return and portfolio beta, although the intercept was higher than the zero value expected. Exhibit 17 contains charts from this study, which show that (1) most of the measured SMLs had a positive slope, (2) the slopes change between periods, (3) the intercepts are not zero, and (4) the intercepts likewise change between periods.

EXHIBIT 17 Average Excess Monthly Rates of Return Compared to Systematic Risk during Alternative Time Periods

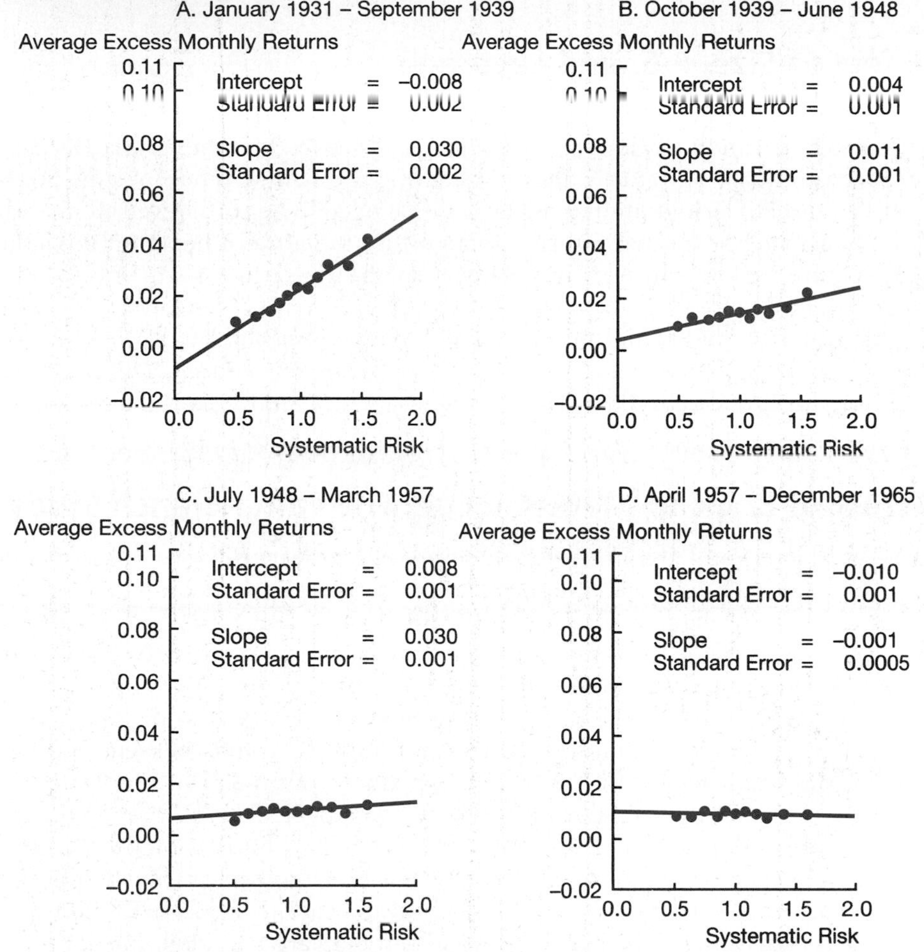

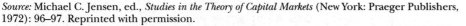

Source: Michael C. Jensen, ed., *Studies in the Theory of Capital Markets* (New York: Praeger Publishers, 1972): 96–97. Reprinted with permission.

Effect of Skewness on the Relationship

Beyond the analysis of return and beta, several authors also have considered the impact of skewness on expected returns. You will recall from your statistics course that skewness reflects the presence of too many large positive or negative observations in a distribution. A normal distribution is symmetric, which means that balance exists between positive and negative observations. In contrast, positive skewness indicates an abnormal number of large positive price changes.

Investigators contended that skewness helped explain the prior results wherein the model appeared to underprice low-beta stocks (so investors received returns above expectations) and overprice high-beta stocks (so investors received returns lower than expected). Some early results confirmed these expectations, but also found that high-beta stocks had high-positive skewness, which implied that investors prefer stocks with high-positive skewness that provide an opportunity for very large returns.

Kraus and Litzenberger (1976) tested a CAPM with a skewness term and confirmed that investors are willing to pay for positive skewness. The importance of skewness was supported in studies by Sears and Wei (1988) and subsequently by Lim (1989).

Effect of Size, P/E, and Leverage

In the efficient markets hypothesis (EMH) reading, we discussed the size effect (the small-firm anomaly) and the P/E effect and showed that these variables have an inverse impact on returns after considering the CAPM. These results imply that size and P/E are additional risk factors that need to be considered along with beta. Specifically, expected returns are a positive function of beta, but investors also require higher returns from relatively small firms and for stocks with relatively low P/E ratios.

Bhandari (1988) found that financial leverage also helps explain the cross section of average returns after both beta and size are considered. This implies a multivariate CAPM with three risk variables: beta, size, and financial leverage.

Effect of Book-to-Market Value: The Fama-French Study

A study by Fama and French (1992) attempted to evaluate the joint roles of market beta, size, E/P, financial leverage, and the book-to-market equity ratio in the cross section of average returns on the NYSE, AMEX, and Nasdaq stocks. While some earlier studies found a significant positive relationship between returns and beta, this study finds that the relationship between beta and the average rate of return disappears during the recent period 1963 to 1990, even when beta is used alone to explain average returns. In contrast, univariate tests between average returns and size, leverage, E/P, and book-to-market equity (BE/ME) indicate that all of these variables are significant and have the expected sign.

In the multivariate tests, the results contained in Exhibit 18 show that the negative relationship between size [In (ME)] and average returns is robust to the inclusion of other variables. Further, the positive relation between BE/ME and average returns also persists when the other variables are included. Interestingly, when both of these variables are included, the book-to-market value ratio (BE/ME) has the consistently stronger role in explaining average returns. The joint effect of size and BE/ME is shown in Exhibit 18. The seventh regression that includes both of these variables indicates that both coefficients are significant. Further, they are still significant when the two P/E ratio variables are included in the tenth regression.

Fama and French conclude that between 1963 and 1990, size and book-to-market equity capture the cross-sectional variation in average stock returns associated with size, E/P, book-to-market equity, and leverage. Moreover, of the two variables, the book-to-market equity ratio appears to subsume E/P and leverage. Following these results, Fama and French (1993) suggested the use of a three-factor CAPM model. This model was used by Fama and French (1996) to explain a number of the anomalies from prior studies.

Summary of CAPM Risk-Return Empirical Results

Most of the early evidence regarding the relationship between rates of return and systematic risk of portfolios supported the CAPM; there was evidence that the intercepts were generally higher than implied by the *RFR* that prevailed, which is either consistent with a zero-beta model or the existence of higher borrowing

EXHIBIT 18 Average Slopes (t-Statistics) from Month-by-Month Regressions of Stock Returns on β, Size, Book-to-Market Equity, Leverage, and E/P: July 1963 to December 1990

Stocks are assigned the post-ranking β of the size-β portfolio they are in at the end of June of year *t*. BE is the book value of common equity plus balance-sheet deferred taxes, A is total book assets, and E is earnings (income before extraordinary items, plus income-statement deferred taxes, minus preferred dividends). BE, A, and E are for each firm's latest fiscal year ending in calendar year $t - 1$. The accounting ratios are measured using market equity ME in December of year $t - 1$. Firm size ln(ME) is measured in June of year *t*. In the regressions, these values of the explanatory variables for individual stocks are matched with returns for the CRSP tapes from the University of Chicago for the months from July of year *t* to June of year $t + 1$. The gap between the accounting data and the returns ensures that the accounting data are available prior to the returns. If earnings are positive, E(+)/P is the ratio of total earnings to market equity and E/P dummy is 0. If earnings are negative, E(+)/P is 0 and E/P dummy is 1.

The average slope is the time-series average of the monthly regression slopes for July 1963 to December 1990, and the *t*-statistic is the average slope divided by its time-series standard error.

On average, there are 2,267 stocks in the monthly regressions. To avoid giving extreme observations heavy weight in the regressions, the smallest and largest 0.5% of the observations of E(+)/P, BE/ME, A/ME, and A/BE are set equal to the next largest or smallest values of the ratios (the 0.005 and 0.995 fractiles). This has no effect on inferences.

β	ln(ME)	ln(BE/ME)	ln(A/ME)	ln(A/BE)	E/P Dummy	E(−)/P
0.15						
(0.46)						
	−0.15					
	(−2.58)					
−0.37	−0.17					
(−1.21)	(−3.41)					
		0.50				
		(5.71)				
			0.50	−0.57		
			(5.69)	(−5.34)		
					0.57	4.72
					(2.28)	(4.57)
	−0.11	0.35				
	(−1.99)	(4.44)				
	−0.11		0.35	−0.50		
	(−2.06)		(4.32)	(−4.56)		
	−0.16				0.06	2.99
	(−3.06)				(0.38)	(3.04)
	−0.13	0.33			−0.14	0.87
	(−2.47)	(4.46)			(−0.90)	(1.23)
	−0.13		0.32	−0.46	−0.08	1.15
	(−2.47)		(4.28)	(−4.45)	(−0.56)	(1.57)

Source: Eugene F. Fama and Kenneth French, "The Cross Section of Expected Stock Returns," *Journal of Finance* 47, no. 2 (June 1992): 439. Reprinted with permission of Blackwell Publishing.

rates. In a search for other variables that could explain these unusual returns, additional variables were considered including the third moment of the distribution (skewness). The results indicated that positive skewness and high betas were correlated.

The efficient markets literature provided extensive evidence that size, the P/E ratio, financial leverage, and the book-to-market value ratio have explanatory power regarding returns beyond beta.

The Fama-French study considered most of the variables suggested and concluded that the two dominant variables were size and the book value to market value ratio.

In contrast to Fama and French, who measure beta with monthly returns, Kothari, Shanken, and Sloan (1995) measured beta with annual returns to avoid trading problems and found substantial compensation for beta risk. They suggested that the results obtained by Fama and French may have been periodic to this time frame and might not be significant over a longer period. Pettengill, Dundaram, and Matthur (1995) noted that empirical studies typically use realized returns to test the CAPM model when theory specifies expected returns. When they adjusted for negative market excess returns, they found a consistent and significant relationship between beta and rates of return. When Jagannathan and Wang (1996) employed a conditional CAPM that allows for changes in betas and in the market risk premium, this model performed well in explaining the cross section of returns. Grundy and Malkiel (1996) also contend that beta is a very useful measure of risk during declining markets, which is when it is important. Finally, when Reilly and Wright (2004) examined the risk-adjusted performance for 31 different asset classes utilizing betas computed using a very broad proxy for the market portfolio, the risk-return relationship was significant and as expected in theory.

7 THE MARKET PORTFOLIO: THEORY VERSUS PRACTICE

Throughout our presentation of the CAPM, we noted that the market portfolio included *all* the risky assets in the economy. Further, in equilibrium, the various assets would be included in the portfolio in proportion to their market value. Therefore, this market portfolio should contain not only U.S. stocks and bonds but also real estate, options, art, stamps, coins, foreign stocks and bonds, and so on, with weights equal to their relative market value.

Although this concept of a market portfolio of all risky assets is reasonable in theory, it is difficult to implement when testing or using the CAPM. The easy part is getting a stock series for U.S. and foreign stocks. As noted in Reading 53 of Volume 5, there also are some well-regarded U.S. and global bond series available. Because of the difficulty in deriving series that are available monthly in a timely fashion for numerous other assets, most studies have been limited to using a stock or bond series alone. In fact, the vast majority of studies have chosen the S&P 500 series or some other broad stock series that is obviously limited to only U.S. stocks, which constitutes *less than 20 percent* of a truly global risky asset portfolio. At best, it was assumed that the particular series used as a proxy for the market portfolio was highly correlated with the true market portfolio.

Most academicians recognize this potential problem but assume that the deficiency is not serious. Several articles by Roll (1977a, 1978, 1980, 1981), however, concluded that, on the contrary, the use of these indexes as a proxy for the market portfolio had very serious implications for tests of the model and especially for using the model when evaluating portfolio performance. Roll referred to this problem as a **benchmark error** because the practice is to compare the per-

formance of a portfolio manager to the return of an unmanaged portfolio of equal risk—that is, the market portfolio adjusted for risk would be the benchmark. Roll's point is that, if the benchmark is mistakenly specified, you cannot measure the performance of a portfolio manager properly. A mistakenly specified market portfolio can have two effects. First, the beta computed for alternative portfolios would be wrong because the market portfolio used to compute the portfolio's systematic risk is inappropriate. Second, the SML derived would be wrong because it goes from the *RFR* through the improperly specified M portfolio. Exhibit 19 shows an example where the true portfolio risk (β_T) is underestimated (β_e), possibly because of the proxy market portfolio used in computing the estimated beta. As shown, the portfolio being evaluated may appear to be above the SML using β_e, which would imply superior management. If, in fact, the true risk (β_T) is greater, the portfolio being evaluated will shift to the right and be below the SML, which would indicate inferior performance.

Exhibit 20 indicates that the intercept and slope will differ if (1) there is an error in selecting a proper risk-free asset and (2) if the market portfolio selected is not the correct mean-variance efficient portfolio. Obviously, it is very possible that under these conditions, a portfolio judged to be superior relative to the first SML (i.e., the portfolio plotted above the measured SML) could be inferior relative to the true SML (i.e., the portfolio would plot below the true SML).

Roll contends that a test of the CAPM requires an analysis of whether the proxy used to represent the market portfolio is mean-variance efficient (on the Markowitz efficient frontier) and whether it is the true optimum market portfolio. Roll showed that if the proxy market portfolio (e.g., the S&P 500 index) is mean-variance efficient, it is mathematically possible to show a linear relationship between returns and betas derived with this portfolio. Unfortunately, this is not a true test of the CAPM because you are not working with the true SML (see Exhibit 21).

A demonstration of the impact of the benchmark problem is provided in a study by Reilly and Akhtar (1995). Exhibit 22 shows the substantial difference in average beta for the 30 stocks in the DJIA during three alternative periods using two

EXHIBIT 19 Differential Performance Based on an Error in Estimating Systematic Risk

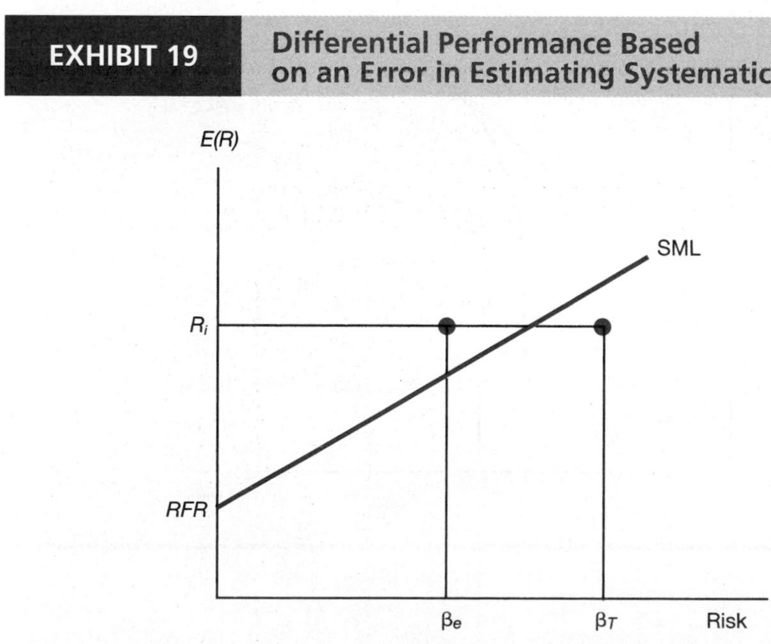

EXHIBIT 20 Differential SML Based on Measured Risk-Free Asset and Proxy Market Portfolio

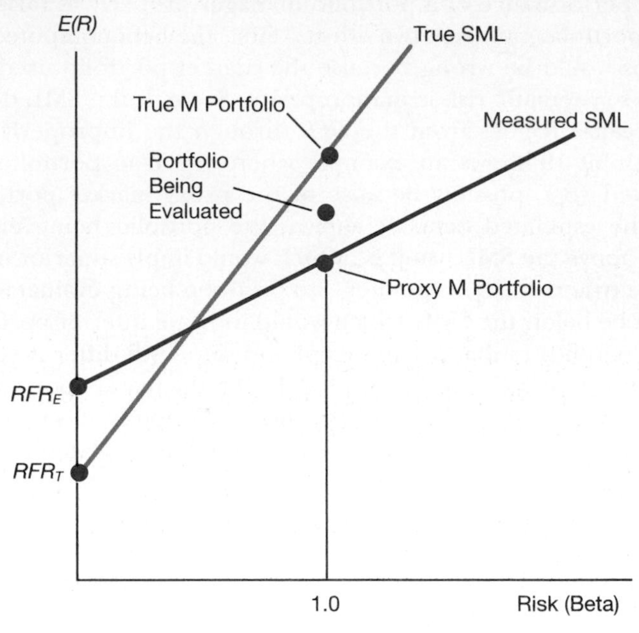

EXHIBIT 21 Differential SML Using Market Proxy That Is Mean-Variance Efficient

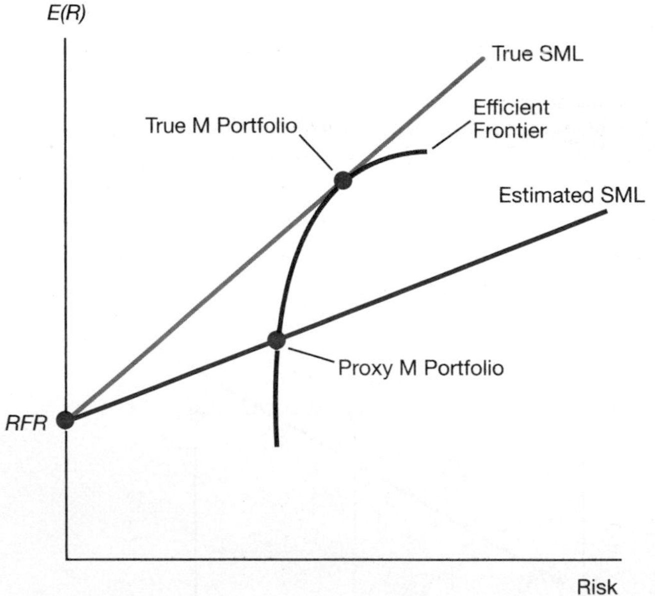

different proxies for the market portfolio: (1) the S&P 500 Index, and (2) the Brinson Partners Global Security Market Index (GSMI). The GSMI includes not only U.S. and international stocks but also U.S. and international bonds. The results in Exhibit 22 are as one would expect because, as we know from earlier discussions in this reading (Equations 51-5 and 51-6), beta is equal to:

$$\text{Beta} = \frac{\text{Cov}_{i,M}}{\sigma^2_M}$$

where

$\text{Cov}_{i,M}$ = the covariance between asset *i* and the M portfolio

σ^2_M = the variance of the M portfolio

As we change from an all-U.S. stock index to a world stock and bond index (GSMI), we would expect the covariance with U.S. stocks to decline. The other component of beta is the variance for the market portfolio. As shown in Exhibit 22, although the covariance between the U.S. stocks and the GSMI is lower, the variance of the GSMI market portfolio, which is highly diversified with stocks *and* bonds from around the world, is substantially lower (about 25 to 33 percent). As a result, the beta is substantially larger (about 27 to 48 percent larger) when the Brinson GSMI is used rather than the S&P 500 Index. Notably, the Brinson GSMI has a composition of assets that is substantially closer to the true M portfolio than the S&P 500 proxy that contains only U.S. stocks. Notably, the results for the recent period were completely consistent with the original results from 1983-1994.

EXHIBIT 22 The Average Beta for the 30 Stocks in the Dow Jones Industrial Average during Alternative Time Periods Using Different Proxies for the Market Portfolio

	Alternative Market Proxies	
Time Period	**S&P 500**	**Brinson GSMI**
2000–2004		
Average beta	0.961	1.305
Mean index return	−0.006	0.001
Standard deviation of index returns	0.048	0.031
1989–1994		
Average beta	0.991	1.264
Mean index return	0.010	0.008
Standard deviation of index returns	0.036	0.026
1983–1988		
Average beta	0.820	1.215
Mean index return	0.014	0.014
Standard deviation of index returns	0.049	0.031

Source: Adapted from Frank K. Reilly and Rashid A. Akhtar, "The Benchmark Error Problem with Global Capital Markets," *Journal of Portfolio Management* 22, no. 1 (Fall 1995): 33–52. The updated results were provided by Frank K. Reilly. This copyrighted material is reprinted with permission from *Journal of Portfolio Management,* a publication of Institutional Investor, Inc.

EXHIBIT 23 Components of Security Market Lines Using Alternative Market Proxies

	2000–2004			1989–1994			1983–1988		
	R_M	RFR	$(R_M - RFR)$	R_M	RFR	$(R_M - RFR)$	R_M	RFR	$(R_M - RFR)$
S&P 500	−2.01	3.05	−5.06	13.07	5.71	7.36	18.20	8.31	9.90
Brinson GSMI	3.02	3.05	−0.03	10.18	5.71	4.48	18.53	8.31	10.22

Source: Adapted from Frank K. Reilly and Rashid A. Akhtar, "The Benchmark Error Problem with Global Capital Markets," *Journal of Portfolio Management* 22, no. 1 (Fall 1995): 33–52. The updated results were provided by Frank K. Reilly. This copyrighted material is reprinted with permission from *Journal of Portfolio Management,* a publication of Institutional Investor, Inc.

There also was a difference in the SMLs implied by each of the market proxies. Exhibit 23 contains the average *RFR,* the market returns, and the slope of the SML during three time periods for the two indexes. Clearly, the slopes differ dramatically among the alternative indexes and over time. Needless to say, the benchmark used does make a difference.

In summary, an incorrect market proxy will affect both the beta risk measures and the position and slope of the SML that is used to evaluate portfolio performance. In general, the errors will tend to overestimate the performance of portfolio managers because the proxy used for the market portfolio is probably not as efficient as the true market portfolio, so the slope of the SML will be underestimated. Also, the beta measure generally will be underestimated because the true market portfolio will have a lower variance than the typical market proxy because the true market portfolio is more diversified.

Roll's benchmark problems, however, do not invalidate the value of the CAPM as *a normative model of asset pricing;* they only indicate a problem in *measurement* when attempting to test the theory and when using this model for evaluating portfolio performance. Therefore, it is necessary to develop a better market portfolio proxy similar to the Brinson GSMI.

8 WHAT IS NEXT?

At this point, we have discussed the basic theory of the CAPM, the impact of changing some of its major assumptions, the empirical evidence that does and does not support the theory, and its dependence on a market portfolio of all risky assets. In addition, the model assumes that investors have quadratic utility functions and that the distribution of security prices is normal (symmetrically distributed), with a variance term that can be estimated.

The tests of the CAPM indicated that the beta coefficients for individual securities were not stable, but the portfolio betas generally were stable assuming long enough sample periods and adequate trading volume. There was mixed support for a positive linear relationship between rates of return and systematic risk for portfolios of stock, with some recent evidence indicating the need to consider additional risk variables. In addition, several papers have criticized the tests of the model and the usefulness of the model in portfolio evaluation because of its dependence on a market portfolio of risky assets that is not currently available.

Consequently, the academic community has considered alternative asset pricing models.

THE INTERNET

Investments Online

Asset pricing models show how risk measures or underlying return-generating factors will affect asset returns. Estimates from such models are usually proprietary and are available from providers only by buying their research. Of course, users can always purchase their raw data elsewhere (see some of our earlier Internet discussions) and develop their own estimates of beta and factor sensitivities.

www.valueline.com The Value Line Investment Survey has been a long-time favorite of investors and many local and college/university libraries subscribe to it. It is a popular source of finding a stock's beta. Value Line Publishing, Inc.'s website contains useful information for the on-line researcher and student of investments. Its site features investment-related articles, sample pages from the Value Line Investment Survey, and a product directory, which lists the venerable investment survey as well as Value Line's mutual fund, options, and convertibles survey, and others.

www.wsharpe.com William F. Sharpe, the 1990 winner of the Nobel prize in Economics because of his development of the Capital Asset Pricing Model, has a home page on the Internet. Among other items, Web surfers can read drafts of a sophisticated textbook in progress, some of his published papers, and case studies he has written. Sharpe's site offers monthly returns data on a number of mutual funds, stock indices, and bond indices, and links to other finance sites.

http://gsb.uchicago.edu/fac/eugene.fama/ The home page of Eugena Fama, whose empirical work first found support … and then lack of support...for beta as a risk measure.

www.moneychimp.com This is an informative education site on investments and includes CAPM calculators for estimating a stock's return and a "market simulator" to show the effect of randomness on a portfolio's return over time.

SUMMARY

- The assumptions of capital market theory expand on those of the Markowitz portfolio model and include consideration of the risk-free rate of return. The correlation and covariance of any asset with a risk-free asset are zero, so that any combination of an asset or portfolio with the risk-free asset generates a linear return and risk function. Therefore, when you combine the risk-free asset with any risky asset on the Markowitz efficient frontier, you derive a set of straight-line portfolio possibilities.
- The dominant line is the one that is tangent to the efficient frontier. This dominant line is referred to as the *capital market line (CML),* and all investors should target points along this line depending on their risk preferences.
- Because all investors want to invest in the risky portfolio at the point of tangency, this portfolio—referred to as the market portfolio—must contain all risky assets in proportion to their relative market values. Moreover, the investment decision and the financing decision can be separated because, although everyone will want to invest in the market portfolio, investors will make different financing decisions about whether to lend or borrow based on their individual risk preferences.
- Given the CML and the dominance of the market portfolio, the relevant risk measure for an individual risky asset is its covariance with the market portfolio, that is, its *systematic risk.* When this covariance is standardized by the covariance for the market portfolio, we derive the well-known beta measure of systematic risk and a security market line (SML) that relates the expected or required rate of return for an asset to its beta. Because all individual securities and portfolios should plot on this SML, you can determine the expected (required) return on a security based on its systematic risk (its beta).
- Alternatively, assuming security markets are not always completely efficient, you can identify undervalued and overvalued securities by comparing your estimate of the rate of return to be earned on an investment to its expected (required) rate of return. The systematic risk variable (beta) for an individual risky asset is computed using a regression model that generates an equation referred to as the asset's *characteristic line.*
- When we relax several of the major assumptions of the CAPM, the required modifications are reasonably minor and do not change the overall concept of the model. Empirical studies have indicated stable portfolio betas, especially when enough observations were used to derive the betas and there was adequate volume. Although the early tests confirmed the expected relationship between returns and systematic risk (with allowance for the zero-beta model), several subsequent studies indicated that the univariate beta model needed to be supplemented with additional variables that considered skewness, size, P/E, leverage, and the book value/market value ratio. A study by Fama and French contended that during the period 1963 to 1990, beta was not relevant. In their study, the most significant variables were book-to-market value (BE/ME) and size. Subsequent studies both supported their findings and differed with them because some more recent authors have found a significant relationship between beta and rates of return on stocks.
- Another problem has been raised by Roll, who contends that it is not possible to empirically derive a true market portfolio, so it is not possible to test the CAPM model properly or to use the model to evaluate portfolio performance. A study by Reilly and Akhtar provided empirical support for this contention by demonstrating significant differences in betas, SMLs, and expected returns with alternative benchmarks.

PRACTICE PROBLEMS FOR READING 51

1. You expect an *RFR* of 10 percent and the market return (R_M) of 14 percent. Compute the expected (required) return for the following stocks, and plot them on an SML graph.

Stock	Beta	*E(R)*
U	0.85	
N	1.25	
D	−0.20	

2. **[Adapted from the 1998 CFA Level II Examination]**
An analyst expects a risk-free return of 4.5 percent, a market return of 14.5 percent, and the returns for Stocks A and B that are shown in the following table.

Stock Information		
Stock	**Beta**	**Analyst's Estimated Return**
A	1.2	16%
B	0.8	14%

   A. Show on the graph provided in the answer book:
      i. Where Stocks A and B would plot on the security market line (SML) if they were fairly valued using the capital asset pricing model (CAPM).
      ii. Where Stocks A and B actually plot on the same graph according to the returns estimated by the analyst and shown in the table. [6 minutes]

   B. State whether Stocks A and B are undervalued or overvalued if the analyst uses the SML for strategic investment decisions. [4 minutes]

3. An investor with a portfolio located on the capital market line to the left of the market portfolio has
   A. lower unsystematic risk than the market portfolio.
   B. higher unsystematic risk than the market portfolio.
   C. less than 100 percent of his wealth invested in the market portfolio.
   D. more than 100 percent of his wealth invested in the market portfolio.

4. All else equal, as the correlations of returns among a set of securities increase, will a portfolio composed of those securities *most likely* experience an increase in expected:

	return?	risk?
A.	No	No
B.	No	Yes
C.	Yes	No
D.	Yes	Yes

5. With respect to the security market line, beta is *most* accurately defined as a(n)
   A. absolute measure of systematic risk.
   B. absolute measure of unsystematic risk.
   C. standardized measure of systematic risk.
   D. standardized measure of unsystematic risk.

6. With respect to the security market line, if two risky assets have the same covariance with the market portfolio, will the two assets *most likely* have the same:

	beta?	expected (required) rate of return?
A.	No	No
B.	No	Yes
C.	Yes	No
D.	Yes	Yes

7. An analyst gathered the following information about McGettrick Enterprises and the market:

Beta for McGettrick common stock	1.1
Estimated annual rate of return for McGettrick common stock	12.8%
Market risk premium	8.0%
Risk-free rate of return	4.0%

Another stock that the analyst is following, Jimma Industries, has the same estimated rate of return as McGettrick stock but a higher covariance of returns with the market portfolio. Based on the security market line, are the stocks of McGettrick and Jimma, respectively, *most* appropriately described as undervalued, properly valued, or overvalued?

	McGettrick Stock	Jimma Stock
A.	Undervalued	Overvalued
B.	Undervalued	Undervalued
C.	Properly valued	Overvalued
D.	Properly valued	Undervalued

8. An analyst gathered the following information about four common stocks:

Common Stock	Beta
A	0.9
B	1.0
C	1.1
D	1.2

The expected risk-free rate of return is 4 percent and the market risk premium is 8 percent. With respect to the security market line, if all four stocks have the same estimated annual return of 12.4 percent, what is the number of stocks that are overvalued and undervalued, respectively?

	Number of Overvalued Stocks	Number of Undervalued Stocks
A.	1	1
B.	1	2
C.	2	1
D.	2	2

9. When using a regression model to evaluate the return on an individual asset, the asset's systematic risk is estimated using the

A. efficient frontier.

B. characteristic line.

C. capital market line.

D. security market line.

APPENDIX

SOLUTIONS FOR READING 44

1. C is correct.

$$NPV = -50{,}000 + \frac{15{,}000}{1.08} + \frac{15{,}000}{1.08^2} + \frac{20{,}000}{1.08^3} + \frac{10{,}000}{1.08^4} + \frac{5{,}000}{1.08^5}$$

$$NPV = -50{,}000 + 13{,}888.89 + 12{,}860.08 + 15{,}876.64 + 7{,}350.30 + 3{,}402.92$$

$$NPV = -50{,}000 + 53{,}378.83 = 3{,}378.83$$

The IRR, found with a financial calculator, is 10.88 percent.

2. C is correct.

Year	0	1	2	3	4	5
Cash flow	−50,000	15,000	15,000	20,000	10,000	5,000
Cumulative cash flow	−50,000	−35,000	−20,000	0	10,000	15,000
Discounted cash flow	−50,000	13,888.89	12,860.08	15,876.64	7,350.30	3,402.92
Cumulative DCF	−50,000	−36,111.11	−23,251.03	−7,374.38	−24.09	3,378.83

As the table shows, the cumulative cash flow offsets the initial investment in exactly three years. The payback period is 3.00 years. The discounted payback period is between four and five years. The discounted payback period is 4 years plus 24.09/3,402.92 = 0.007 of the fifth year cash flow, or 4.007 = 4.01 years. The discounted payback period is 4.01 − 3.00 = 1.01 years longer than the payback period.

3. B is correct.

$$NPV = \sum_{t=0}^{3} \frac{CF_t}{(1+r)^t} = -100 + \frac{40}{1.20} + \frac{80}{1.20^2} + \frac{120}{1.20^3} = \$58.33$$

4. D is correct. The IRR can be found using a financial calculator or with trial and error. Using trial and error, the total PV is equal to zero if the discount rate is 28.79 percent.

		Present Value			
Year	Cash Flow	28.19%	28.39%	28.59%	28.79%
0	−150,000	−150,000	−150,000	−150,000	−150,000
1	100,000	78,009	77,888	77,767	77,646
2	120,000	73,025	72,798	72,572	72,346
Total		1,034	686	338	−8

A more precise IRR of 28.7854 percent has a total PV closer to zero.

5. A is correct.

$$\text{The NPV} = -750 + \sum_{t=1}^{7} \frac{175}{1.10^t} = -750 + 851.97 = 101.97 \text{ million won.}$$

The IRR, found with a financial calculator, is 14.02 percent. (The PV is −750, N = 7, and PMT = 175.)

6. B is correct.

Year	0	1	2	3	4	5	6	7
Cash flow	−750	175	175	175	175	175	175	175
Cumulative cash flow	−750	−575	−400	−225	−50	125	300	475

The payback period is between four and five years. The payback period is four years plus 50/175 = 0.29 of the fifth year cash flow, or 4.29 years.

Year	0	1	2	3	4	5	6	7
Cash flow	−750	175	175	175	175	175	175	175
Discounted cash flow	−750	159.09	144.63	131.48	119.53	108.66	98.78	89.80
Cumulative DCF	−750	−590.91	−446.28	−314.80	−195.27	−86.61	12.17	101.97

The discounted payback period is between five and six years. The discounted payback period is five years plus 86.61/98.78 = 0.88 of the sixth year cash flow, or 5.88 years.

7. D is correct.

The present value of future cash flows is $PV = \dfrac{2{,}000}{0.08} = 25{,}000$

The profitability index is $PI = \dfrac{PV}{\text{Investment}} = \dfrac{25{,}000}{20{,}000} = 1.25$

8. C is correct.

$$PV = \sum_{t=1}^{7} \frac{115}{1.10^t} + \frac{50}{1.10^7} = 585.53 \text{ million euros}$$

$$PI = \frac{585.53}{375} = 1.56$$

9. C is correct. The IRR would stay the same because both the initial outlay and the after-tax cash flows double, so that the return on each dollar invested remains the same. All of the cash flows and their present values double. The difference between total present value of the future cash flows and the initial outlay (the NPV) also doubles.

10. A is correct. If the cumulative cash flow in one year equals the outlay and additional cash flows are not very large, this scenario is possible. For example, assume the outlay is 100, the cash flow in year 1 is 100, and the cash flow in year 2 is 5. The required return is 10 percent. This project would have a payback of 1.0 years, an NPV of −4.96, and an IRR of 4.77 percent.

11. A is correct. The vertical intercept changes from 60 to 65, and the horizontal intercept changes from 21.86 percent to 20.68 percent.

12. B is correct. When valuing mutually exclusive projects, the decision should be made with the NPV method because this method uses the most realistic discount rate, namely the opportunity cost of funds. In this example, the reinvestment rate for the NPV method (here 10 percent) is more realistic than the reinvestment rate for the IRR method (here 21.86 percent or 18.92 percent).

13. B is correct. For these projects, a discount rate of 13.16 percent would yield the same NPV for both (an NPV of 6.73).

14. C is correct. Discount rates of 0 percent and approximately 61.8 percent both give a zero NPV.

Rate	0%	20%	40%	60%	61.8%	80%	100%
NPV	0.00	4.40	3.21	0.29	0.00	−3.02	−6.25

15. A is correct. The crossover rate is the discount rate at which the NPV profiles for two projects cross; it is the only point where the NPVs of the projects are the same.

16. B is correct. The vertical axis represents a discount rate of zero. The point where the profile crosses the vertical axis is simply the sum of the cash flow from the project or the maximum possible NPV.

17. D is correct. The horizontal axis represents a NPV of zero. By definition, the project's IRR equals an NPV of zero.

18. B is correct. Costs to finance the project are taken into account when the cash flows are discounted at the appropriate cost of capital; including interest costs in the cash flows would result in double-counting the cost of debt.

SOLUTIONS FOR READING 45

1. B is correct. The cost of equity is defined as the rate of return required by stockholders.
2. B is correct.

   Wrong answers:

   A. The appropriate rate of tax to use is the marginal tax rate, not the average tax rate.

   C. The investment opportunity schedule is downward sloping.

   D. The target capital structure is that capital structure for which the company has as an objective, which may or may not be represented by its current capital structure.
3. D is correct. First calculate the growth rate using the sustainable growth calculation, and then calculate the cost of equity using the rearranged dividend discount model:

   g = (1 − dividend payout ratio)(return on equity) = (1 − 0.30)(15%) = 10.5%

   $r_e = (D_1 / P_0) + g = (\$2.30 / \$45) + 10.50\% = 15.61\%$
4. C is correct. FV = \$1,000; PMT = \$40; N = 10; PV = \$900.

   Solve for i. The six-month yield, i, is 5.3149%.

   YTM = 5.3149% × 2 = 10.62985%

   $r_d(1 - t) = 10.62985\%(1 - 0.38) = 6.5905\%$
5. C is correct. The bond rating approach depends on knowledge of the company's rating and can be compared with yields on bonds in the public market.
6. B is correct. The company can issue preferred stock at 6.5%.

   $P_p = \$1.75/0.065 = \$26.92$

   Note: Dividends are not tax-deductible so there is no adjustment for taxes.
7. B is correct.

   Cost of equity $= D_1/P_0 + g = \$1.50 / \$30 + 7\% = 5\% + 7\% = 12\%$

   WACC = [(0.445) (0.08)(1 − 0.4)] + [(0.555)(0.12)] = 8.8%
8. B is correct. The weighted average cost of capital, using weights derived from the current capital structure, is the best estimate of the cost of capital for the average-risk project of a company.
9. C is correct.

   $w_d = \$63/(\$220 + 63) = 0.223$

   $w_e = \$220/(\$220 + 63) = 0.777$
10. A is correct. Asset risk does not change with a higher debt-to-equity ratio. Equity risk rises with higher debt.
11. B is correct. The debt-to-equity ratio of the new product should be used when making the adjustment from the asset beta, derived from the comparables, to the equity beta of the new product.

12. B is correct. Capital structure:

Market value of debt: FV = \$10,000,000, PMT = \$400,000, N = 10, I/YR = 13.65% solving for PV gives the answer \$7,999,688

Market value of equity: 1.2 million shares outstanding @ \$10 = \$12,000,000

Market value of debt	\$ 7,999,688	40%
Market value of equity	12,000,000	60%
Total capital	\$19,999,688	100%

To raise \$7.5 million of new capital while maintaining the same capital structure, the company would issue \$7.5 million × 40% = \$3.0 million in bonds, which results in a before-tax rate of 16 percent.

$r_d(1 - t) = 0.16(1 - 0.3) = 0.112$ or 11.2%

$r_e = 0.03 + 2.2\ (0.10 - 0.03) = 0.184$ or 18.4%

WACC = [0.40(0.112)] + [0.6(0.184)] = 0.0448 + 0.1104 = 0.1552 or 15.52%

13. B is correct.

$r_e = 0.0425 + (1.3)(0.0482) = 0.1052$ or 10.52%

14. B is correct.

WACC = [(€900/€3300) .0925 (1 − 0.375)] + [(€2400/€3300) (0.1052)] = 0.0923 or 9.23%

15. A is correct.

Asset beta = Unlevered beta = 1.3/(1 + [(1 − 0.375) (€900/€2400)] = 1.053

16. D is correct.

Project beta = 1.053 {1 + [(1 − 0.375) (€80/€20)] } = 1.053 {3.5} = 3.686

17. D is correct.

$r_e = 0.0425 + 3.686(0.0482 + 0.0188) = 0.2895$ or 28.95%

18. C is correct.

Cost of equity without the country risk premium:

$r_e = 0.0425 + 3.686\ (0.0482) = 0.2202$ or 22.02%

Cost of equity with the country risk premium:

$r_e = 0.0425 + 3.686\ (0.0482 + 0.0188) = 0.2895$ or 28.95%

Weighted average cost of capital without the country risk premium:

$$\text{WACC} = [0.80\ (0.0925)\ (1 - 0.375)\ ] + [0.20\ (0.2202)]$$
$$= 0.04625 + 0.04404 = 0.09038 \text{ or } 9.03 \text{ percent}$$

Weighted average cost of capital with the country risk premium:

$$\text{WACC} = [0.80\ (0.0925)\ (1 - 0.375)\ ] + [0.20\ (0.2895)]$$
$$= 0.04625 + 0.0579 = 0.1042 \text{ or } 10.42 \text{ percent}$$

NPV without the country risk premium:

$$\text{NPV} = \frac{€48 \text{ million}}{(1 + 0.0903)^1} + \frac{€52 \text{ million}}{(1 + 0.0903)^2} + \frac{€54.4 \text{ million}}{(1 + 0.0903)^3} - €100 \text{ million}$$
$$= €44.03 \text{ million} + 43.74 \text{ million} + 41.97 \text{ million} - €100 \text{ million}$$
$$= €29.74 \text{ million}$$

NPV with the country risk premium:

$$\text{NPV} = \frac{€48 \text{ million}}{(1 + 0.1042)^1} + \frac{€52 \text{ million}}{(1 + 0.1042)^2} + \frac{€54.4 \text{ million}}{(1 + 0.1042)^3} - €100 \text{ million}$$

$$= €43.47 \text{ million} + 42.65 \text{ million} + 40.41 \text{ million} - €100 \text{ million}$$

$$= €26.53 \text{ million}$$

19. B is correct.

Asset betas: $\beta_{equity}/[1+(1-t)(D/E)]$
Relevant = 1.702/[1+ (0.77)(0)] = 1.702
ABJ = 2.8/[1 + (0.77)(0.003)]= 2.7918
Opus = 3.4/1 + [(0.77)(0.013)]= 3.3663

20. D is correct. Weights are determined based on relative market values:

Pure-Play	Market value of equity in billions	Proportion of total
Relevant	\$3.800	0.5490
ABJ	2.150	0.3106
Opus	0.972	0.1404
Total	\$6.922	1.0000

Weighted average beta (0.5490)(1.702) + (0.3106)(2.7918) + (0.1404)(3.3572) = 2.27

21. B is correct.

Asset beta = 2.27
Levered beta = 2.27 {1 + [(1 − 0.23)(0.01)]} = 2.2875
Cost of equity capital = 0.0525 + (2.2875)(0.07) = 0.2126 or 21.26%

22. D is correct.

For debt: FV = 2,400,000; PV = 2,156,000; n = 10; PMT = 150,000
Solve for i. i = 0.07748. YTM = 15.5%

Before-tax cost of debt = 15.5%

Market value of equity = 1 million shares outstanding plus 1 million newly issued shares = 2 million shares at \$8 = \$16 million

Total market capitalization = \$2.156 million + \$16 million = \$18.156 million

Levered beta = 2.27 {1 + [(1 − 0.23)(2.156/16)]} = 2.27 (1.1038) = 2.5055

Cost of equity = 0.0525 + 2.5055 (0.07) = 0.2279 or 22.79%

Debt weight = \$2.156/\$18.156 = 0.1187

Equity weight = \$16/\$18.156 = 0.8813

TagOn's MCC = [(0.1187)(0.155)(1 − 0.23)] + [(0.8813)(0.2279)]
= 0.01417 + 0.20083
= 0.2150 or 21.50%

23. B is correct. The relevant cost is the marginal cost of debt. The before-tax marginal cost of debt can be estimated by the yield to maturity on a comparable outstanding. After adjusting for tax, the after-tax cost is 7(1 − 0.4) = 7(0.6) = 4.2%.

24. D is correct. The expected return is the sum of the expected dividend yield plus expected growth. The expected growth is $(1 - 0.4)15\% = 9\%$. The expected dividend yield is $\$2.18/\$28 = 7.8\%$. The sum is 16.8%.

25. B is correct. Using the CAPM approach, $4\% + 1.3(9\%) = 15.7\%$.

26. C is correct. Inferring the asset beta for the public company: unlevered beta $= 1.75/[1 + (1 - 0.35)(0.90)] = 1.104$. Relevering to reflect the target debt ratio of the private firm: levered beta $= 1.104 \times [1 + (1 - 0.30)(1.00)] = 1.877$.

27. D is correct. The country equity premium can be estimated as the sovereign yield spread times the volatility of the country's stock market relative to its bond market. Paragon's equity premium is $(10.5\% - 4.5\%) \times (35\%/25\%) = 6\% \times 1.4 = 8.40\%$.

SOLUTIONS FOR READING 46

1. B is correct.

Current ratio = Current assets/€100 million = 2.5

Therefore, current assets = €250 million

Quick ratio = (€250 million − Inventory)/€100 million = 1.5

Therefore, Inventory = €100 million

2. D is correct.

Number of days of inventory = \$2,300/(\$20,000/365) = 41.975 days
Number of days of receivables = \$2,500/(\$25,000/365) = 36.5 days
Operating cycle = 41.975 + 36.5 days = 78.475 days

Note: The net operating cycle is 47.9 days.

3. A is correct.

Number of days of inventory = \$2,000/(\$30,000/365) = 24.333 days
Number of days of receivables = \$3,000/(\$40,000/365) = 27.375 days
Operating cycle = 24.333 + 27.375 days = 51.708 days
Purchases = \$30,000 + \$2,000 − \$1,500 = \$30,500
Number of days of payables = \$4,000/(\$30,500/365) = 47.869 days
The net operating cycle is 51.708 − 47.869 = 3.839 days

4. C is correct.

Bond equivalent yield = [(\$10,000 − 9,725)/ \$9,725] × (365/182)
= 5.671 percent

Note that the discount yield is 5.44 percent.

5. B is correct.

6. D is correct.

$$\text{Cost} = \left(1 + \frac{0.02}{0.98}\right)^{365/40} - 1 = 20.24 \text{ percent}$$

7. B is correct.

$$\text{Line cost} = \frac{\text{Interest + commitment fee}}{\text{Net Proceeds}} \times 12$$

$$= \frac{(0.072 \times \$1{,}000{,}000 \times 1/12) + (0.005 \times \$1{,}000{,}000 \times 1/12)}{\$1{,}000{,}000} \times 12$$

$$= \frac{\$6{,}000 + 416.67}{\$1{,}000{,}000} \times 12 = 0.077 \text{ or } 7.7 \text{ percent}$$

$$\text{Banker's acceptance cost} = \frac{\text{Interest}}{\text{Net proceeds}} \times 12$$

$$= \frac{0.071 \times \$1{,}000{,}000 \times 1/12}{\$1{,}000{,}000 - (0.071 \times \$1{,}000{,}000 \times 1/12)} \times 12$$

$$= \frac{\$5{,}916.67}{\$994{,}083.33} \times 12 = 0.0714 \text{ or } 7.14 \text{ percent}$$

$$\text{Commercial paper cost} = \frac{\text{Interest + Dealer's commission + Back-up costs}}{\text{Net proceeds}} \times 12$$

$$= \frac{(0.069 \times \$1{,}000{,}000 \times 1/12) + (0.0025 \times \$1{,}000{,}000 \times 1/12) + (0.003333 \times \$1{,}000{,}000 \times 1/12)}{\$1{,}000{,}000 - (0.069 \times \$1{,}000{,}000 \times 1/12)} \times 1/12$$

$$= \frac{\$5{,}750 + 208.33 + 277.78}{\$1{,}000{,}000 - 5{,}750} \times 12 = 0.0753 \text{ or } 7.53 \text{ percent}$$

8. B is correct.

Company A: \$1.0 million/(\$5.0 million/365) = 73.0 days
Company B: \$1.2 million/(\$3.0 million/365) = 146.0 days
Company C: \$0.8 million/(\$2.5 million/365) = 116.8 days
Company D: \$0.1 million/(\$0.5 million/365) = 73.0 days

9. B is correct.

Company A: \$6.0 million/\$1.2 million = 5.00
Company B: \$4.0 million/\$1.5 million = 2.67
Company C: \$3.0 million/\$1.0 million = 3.00
Company D: \$0.6 million/\$0.2 million = 3.00

10. B is correct.

20X1: 73 days
20X2: 70.393

Note: If the number of days decreased from 20X1 to 20X2, the receivable turnover increased.

11. B is correct. Company B increased its accounts receivable (A/R) turnover and reduced its number of days of receivables between 20X1 and 20X2.

	20X1		20X2	
Company	A/R Turnover	Number of Days of Receivables	A/R Turnover	Number of Days of Receivables
A	5.000	73.000	5.000	73.000
B	2.500	146.000	2.667	136.875
C	3.125	116.800	3.000	121.667
D	5.000	73.000	3.000	121.667

12. B is correct.

Company A number of days of inventory = 100 − 73 = 27 days
Company D number of days of inventory = 145 − 121.67 = 23.33 days
Company A's turnover = 365/27 = 13.5 times
Company D's inventory turnover = 365/23.3 = 15.6 times

SOLUTIONS FOR READING 47

1. D is correct. This is the DuPont "triangle," in which profit margins and turnovers are used to explain returns.
2. A is correct.

$$\text{Return on equity} = \left(\frac{\text{Net income}}{\text{Revenues}} \times \frac{\text{Revenues}}{\text{Total assets}}\right) \times \frac{\text{Total assets}}{\text{Shareholders' equity}}$$

$$\text{Return on equity} = \text{Return on assets} \times \frac{\text{Total assets}}{\text{Shareholders' equity}}$$

3. A is correct.

$$\text{Return on equity} = \frac{\text{Net income}}{\text{Average total equity}} = \frac{\text{Net income}}{\text{Revenues}} = \frac{\text{Revenues}}{\text{Average total assets}} = \frac{\text{Average total assets}}{\text{Average total equity}}$$

$$\text{Return on equity} = -5\% \times 1.5 \times 1.2 = -9.0\%$$

4. B is correct.

LaPearla Company
Income Statement for Year 0
(in millions)

	2005	Percent of Sales	Pro Forma	Explanation
Revenues	€10,000	100.0	€11,000	110 percent of 2005 sales
Cost of goods sold	5,500	55.0	6,050	55 percent of projected sales
Gross profit	€ 4,500	45.0	€ 4,950	
Selling, general, and admin. expenses	800	8.0	880	8 percent of projected sales
Operating income	€ 3,700	37.0	€ 4,070	37 percent of projected sales
Interest expense	500	5.0	550	5 percent of projected sales
Earnings before taxes	€ 3,200		€ 3,520	
Taxes	960		1,056	30 percent of earnings before taxes
Net income	€ 2,240		€ 2,464	

5. D is correct.

LaPearla Company
Income Statement for Year 0
(in millions)

	2005	Percent of Sales	Pro Forma	Explanation
Revenues	€10,000	100.0	€11,000	110 percent of 2005 sales
Cost of goods sold	5,500	55.0	6,050	55 percent of projected sales
Gross profit	€ 4,500	45.0	€ 4,950	
Selling, general, and admin. expenses	800	8.0	880	8 percent of projected sales
Operating income	€ 3,700	37.0	€ 4,070	37 percent of projected sales
Interest expense	500	5.0	500	Fixed because long-term debt is fixed
Earnings before taxes	€ 3,200		€ 3,570	
Taxes	960		1,071	30 percent of earnings before taxes
Net income	€ 2,240		€ 2,499	

LaPearla Company
Balance Sheet, End of Year 0
(in millions)

	2005	Percent of Sales	Pro Forma	Explanation
Current assets	€ 2,000	20.0	€ 2,200	20 percent of projected sales
Net plant and equipment	18,000	180.0	19,800	180 percent of projected sales
Total assets	€20,000	200.0	€22,000	200 percent of projected sales
Current liabilities	€ 1,000	10.0	€ 1,100	10 percent of projected sales
Long-term debt	5,000		5,000	Fixed at €5,000
Common stock and paid-in capital	500		500	Fixed at €500
Retained earnings	13,500			
Total liabilities and equity	€20,000	200.0	€22,000	200 percent of projected sales

No dividends: Financing surplus

Without paying dividends,

Retained earnings = €13,500 + €2,499 = €15,999

With no dividends:

Total liabilities and equity	€22,000
Less:	
Current liabilities	1,100
Long-term debt	5,000
Common stock and paid in capital	500
Retained earnings without dividends	15,999
Financing deficiency or (surplus)	(€599)

Paying 50 percent of net income in dividends: Financing deficiency

Paying 50 percent of net income as dividends,

Retained earnings = €13,500 + €2,499 − €1,249.5 = €14,749.5

Total liabilities and equity	€22,000.0
Less:	
Current liabilities	1,100.0
Long-term debt	5,000.0
Common stock and paid in capital	500.0
Retained earnings with dividends	14,749.5
Financing deficiency or (surplus)	€ 650.5

Paying 100 percent of net income as dividends: Financing deficiency

Retained earnings = €13,500 + €2,499 − €2,499 = €13,500

Total liabilities and equity	€22,000
Less:	
Current liabilities	1,100
Long-term debt	5,000
Common stock and paid in capital	500
Retained earnings with dividends	13,500
Financing deficiency or (surplus)	€ 1,900

SOLUTIONS FOR READING 50

1.

Month	Madison (R_i)	General Electric (R_j)	$R_i - E(R_i)$	$R_j - E(R_j)$	$[R_i - E(R_i)] \times [R_j - E(R_j)]$
1	−.04	.07	−.057	.06	−.0034
2	.06	−.02	.043	−.03	−.0013
3	−.07	−.10	−.087	−.11	.0096
4	.12	.15	.103	.14	.0144
5	−.02	−.06	−.037	−.07	.0026
6	.05	.02	.033	.01	.0003
Sum	.10	.06			.0222

A.

$$E(R_{Madison}) = .10/6 = .0167 \qquad E(R_{GE}) = .06/6 = .01$$

B.

$$\sigma_{Madison} = \sqrt{.0257/6} = \sqrt{.0043} = .06549$$

$$\sigma_{GE} = \sqrt{.04120/6} = \sqrt{.006867} = .08287$$

C.

$$COV_{ij} = 1/6(.0222) = .0037$$

D.

$$r_{ij} = \frac{.0037}{(.06549)(.08287)} = \frac{.0037}{.005427} = .682$$

One should have expected a positive correlation between the two stocks, since they tend to move in the same direction(s). Risk can be reduced by combining assets that have low positive or negative correlations, which is not the case for Madison and General Electric.

2.

$$E(R_1) = .15 \quad E(\sigma_1) = .10 \quad w_1 = .5$$
$$E(R_2) = .20 \quad E(\sigma_2) = .20 \quad w_2 = .5$$
$$E(R_{port}) = .5(.15) + .5(.20) = .175$$
If $r_{1,2} = .40$

$$\sigma_p = \sqrt{(.5)^2(.10)^2 + (.5)^2(.20)^2 + 2(.5)(.5)(.10)(.20)(.40)}$$
$$= \sqrt{.0025 + .01 + .004}$$
$$= \sqrt{.0165}$$
$$= 0.12845$$

If $r_{1,2} = -.60$

$$\sigma_p = \sqrt{(.5)^2(.10)^2 + (.5)^2(.20)^2 + 2(.5)(.5)(.10)(.20)(-.60)}$$
$$= \sqrt{.0025 + .01 + (-.006)}$$
$$= \sqrt{.0065}$$
$$= .08062$$

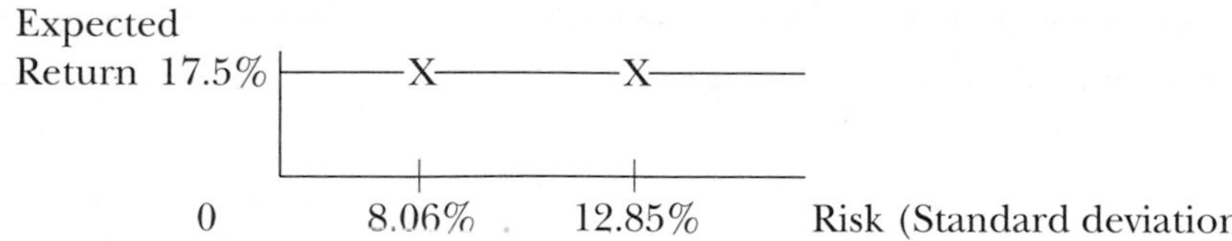

The negative correlation coefficient reduces risk without sacrificing return.

3. For all values of $r_{1,2}$:

$$E(R_{port}) = (.6 \times .10) + (.4 \times .15) = .12$$
$$\sigma_{port} = \sqrt{(.6)^2(.03)^2 + (.4)^2(.05)^2 + 2(.6)(.4)(.03)(.05)(r_{1,2})}$$
$$= \sqrt{.000324 + .0004 + .00072(r_{1,2})}$$
$$= \sqrt{.000724 + .00072(r_{1,2})}$$

A. $\sqrt{.000724 + .00072(1.0)} = \sqrt{.001444} = .0380$

B. $\sqrt{.000724 + .00072(.75)} = \sqrt{.001264} = .0356$

C. $\sqrt{.000724 + .00072(.25)} = \sqrt{.000904} = .0301$

D. $\sqrt{.000724 + .00072(.00)} = \sqrt{.000724} = .0269$

E. $\sqrt{.000724 + .00072(-.25)} = \sqrt{.000544} = .0233$

F. $\sqrt{.000724 + .00072(-.75)} = \sqrt{.000184} = .0136$

G. $\sqrt{.000724 + .00072(-1.0)} = \sqrt{.000004} = .0020$

4. A is correct. The current portfolio has an equal amount invested in each of the four securities. The return on the current portfolio is a simple average of the individual securities. (0.10 + 0.12 + 0.16 + 0.22)/4 = 0.15 or 15 percent. Replacing a security with a 16 percent return with a security having only a 15 percent return will lower the expected return of the portfolio. Correlations have no effect on the return calculation.

5. C is correct. MPT assumes investors maximize one-period expected utility, and their utility curves demonstrate diminishing marginal utility of wealth.

SOLUTIONS FOR READING 51

1. $E(R_i) = RFR + \beta_i(R_M - RFR)$
$= .10 + \beta_i(.14 - .10)$
$= .10 + .04\beta_i$

Stock	Beta	(Required Return) $E(R_i) = .10 + .04\beta_i$
U	85	$.10 + .04(.85) = .10 + .034 = .134$
N	1.25	$.10 + .04(1.25) = .10 + .05 = .150$
D	−.20	$.10 + .04(-.20) = .10 + .008 = .092$

2. CFA Examination II (1998)

A. Security Market Line

i. *Fair-value plot.* The following template shows, using the CAPM, the expected return, ER, of Stock A and Stock B on the SML. The points are consistent with the following equations:

ER on stock = Risk-free rate + Beta × (Market return − Risk-free rate)

ER for A = 4.5% + 1.2(14.5% − 4.5%)
= 16.5%

ER for B = 4.5% + 0.8(14.5% − 4.5%)
= 12.5%

ii. *Analyst estimate plot.* Using the analyst's estimates, Stock A plots below the SML and Stock B, above the SML.

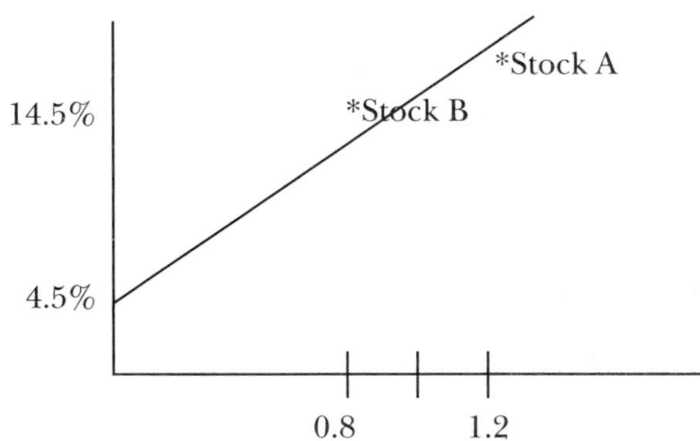

B. Over versus Undervalue

Stock A is overvalued because it should provide a 16.5% return according to the CAPM whereas the analyst has estimated only a 16.0% return.

Stock B is undervalued because it should provide a 12.5% return according to the CAPM whereas the analyst has estimated a 14% return.

3. C is correct. An investor with a portfolio that is on the CML and to the left of the market portfolio has a lending portfolio; some portion of the investor's wealth is invested in the risk-free asset.
4. B is correct. The standard deviation (risk) of the portfolio will increase as correlations increase; the expected return remains the same.
5. C is correct. Beta measures systematic risk and is a standardized measure because it relates an asset's covariance with the market portfolio to the variance of the market portfolio.
6. D is correct. The variance of the market portfolio is the same for all assets, so if the covariance with the market portfolio is the same, the assets must have the same beta. The two assets should plot at the same place on the SML and have the same required rate of return.
7. C is correct. The required rate of return for McGettrick is 12.8 percent, the same as the estimated rate of return based on the current stock price. Using the CAPM: 4% + 1.1(8%) = 12.8%. If Jimma has a higher covariance with the market portfolio than McGettrick, it has a higher beta and a higher required rate of return. Since the estimated rate of return is below the required rate of return for Jimma, the stock is overvalued.
8. D is correct. The required rates of return with a risk-free rate of 4% and a market risk premium of 8% are

    A = 11.2%.

    B = 12.0%.

    C = 12.8%.

    D = 13.6%.

    Stocks A and B are undervalued; stocks C and D are overvalued.
9. B is correct. An asset's characteristic line is a regression model used to derive the asset's beta (systematic risk input). It is the regression line of best fit that relates the rate of return for an individual risky asset to returns from the market portfolio.

GLOSSARY

A priori probability A probability based on logical analysis rather than on observation or personal judgment.

Abandonment option The ability to terminate a project at some future time if the financial results are disappointing.

Abnormal rate of return The amount by which a security's actual return differs from its expected rate of return which is based on the market's rate of return and the security's relationship with the market.

Above full-employment equilibrium A macroeconomic equilibrium in which real GDP exceeds potential GDP.

Absolute dispersion The amount of variability present without comparison to any reference point or benchmark.

Absolute frequency The number of observations in a given interval (for grouped data).

Accelerated method A method of depreciation that allocates relatively large amounts of the depreciable cost of an asset to earlier years and reduced amounts to later years.

Accelerated methods of depreciation Depreciation methods that allocate a relatively large proportion of the cost of an asset to the early years of the asset's useful life.

Account With the accounting systems, a formal record of increases and decreases in a specific asset, liability, component of owners' equity, revenue, or expense.

Account format A method of presentation of accounting transactions in which effects on assets appear at the left and effects on liabilities and equity appear at the right of a central dividing line; also known as T-account format.

Accounting risk The risk associated with accounting standards that vary from country to country or with any uncertainty about how certain transactions should be recorded.

Accounts payable Amounts that a business owes to its vendors for goods and services that were purchased from them but which have not yet been paid.

Accounts receivable turnover Ratio of sales on credit to the average balance in accounts receivable.

Accrual accounting The system of recording financial transactions as they come into existence as a legally enforceable claim, rather than when they settle.

Accrued expenses (accrued liabilities) Liabilities related to expenses that have been incurred but not yet paid as of the end of an accounting period—an example of an accrued expense is rent that has been incurred but not yet paid, resulting in a liability "rent payable."

Accrued interest Interest earned but not yet paid.

Accumulated depreciation An offset to property, plant, and equipment (PPE) reflecting the amount of the cost of PPE that has been allocated to current and previous accounting periods.

Active factor risk The contribution to active risk squared resulting from the portfolio's different-than-benchmark exposures relative to factors specified in the risk model.

Active return The return on a portfolio minus the return on the portfolio's benchmark.

Active risk The standard deviation of active returns.

Active risk squared The variance of active returns; active risk raised to the second power.

Active specific risk or asset selection risk The contribution to active risk squared resulting from the portfolio's active weights on individual assets as those weights interact with assets' residual risk.

Active strategy In reference to short-term cash management, an investment strategy characterized by monitoring and attempting to capitalize on market conditions to optimize the risk and return relationship of short-term investments.

Activity ratios (asset utilization or operating efficiency ratios) Ratios that measure how efficiently a company performs day-to-day tasks, such as the collection of receivables and management of inventory.

Addition rule for probabilities A principle stating that the probability that *A* or *B* occurs (both occur) equals the probability that *A* occurs, plus the probability that *B* occurs, minus the probability that both *A* and *B* occur.

Additional information Information that is required or recommended under the GIPS standards and is not considered as "supplemental information" for the purposes of compliance.

Additions Enlargements to the physical layout of a plant asset.

Add-on interest A procedure for determining the interest on a bond or loan in which the interest is added onto the face value of a contract.

Adjusted beta Historical beta adjusted to reflect the tendency of beta to be mean reverting.

Adjusted R^2 A measure of goodness-of-fit of a regression that is adjusted for degrees of freedom and hence does not automatically increase when another independent variable is added to a regression.

Administrative fees All fees other than the trading expenses and the investment management fee. Administrative fees include custody fees, accounting fees, consulting fees, legal fees, performance measurement fees, or other related fees. These administrative fees are typically outside the control of the investment management firm and are not included in either the gross-of-fees return or the net-of-fees return. However, there are some markets and investment vehicles where administrative fees are controlled by the firm. (See the term "bundled fee.")

Aggregate demand The relationship between the quantity of real GDP demanded and the price level.

Aggregate hours The total number of hours worked by all the people employed, both full time and part time, during a year.

Aggregate production function The relationship between the quantity of real GDP supplied and the quantities of labor and capital and the state of technology.

Aging schedule In the context of accounts receivable, it is an analysis of accounts receivable categorized by days outstanding.

Allocative efficiency A situation in which we cannot produce more of any good without giving up some of another good that we value more highly.

Allowance for bad debts An offset to accounts receivable for the amount of accounts receivable that are estimated to be uncollectible.

Alpha A term commonly used to describe a manager's abnormal rate of return, which is the difference between the return the portfolio actually produced and the expected return given its risk level.

Alternative hypothesis The hypothesis accepted when the null hypothesis is rejected.

American Depository Receipts (ADRs) Certificates of ownership issued by a U.S. bank that represent indirect ownership of a certain number of shares of a specific foreign firm. Shares are held on deposit in a bank in the firm's home country.

American option An option contract that can be exercised at any time until its expiration date

American terms With reference to U.S. dollar exchange rate quotations, the U.S. dollar price of a unit of another currency.

Amortization The process of allocating the cost of intangible long-term assets having a finite useful life to accounting periods; the allocation of the amount of a bond premium or discount to the periods remaining until bond maturity.

Amortizing and accreting swaps A swap in which the notional principal changes according to a formula related to changes in the underlying.

Analysis of variance (ANOVA) The analysis of the total variability of a dataset (such as observations on the dependent variable in a regression) into components representing different sources of variation; with reference to regression, ANOVA provides the inputs for an *F*-test of the significance of the regression as a whole.

Annual percentage rate The cost of borrowing expressed as a yearly rate.

Annuity A finite set of level sequential cash flows.

Annuity due An annuity having a first cash flow that is paid immediately.

Anomalies Security price relationships that appear to contradict a well-regarded hypothesis; in this case, the efficient market hypothesis.

Anticipation stock Excess inventory that is held in anticipation of increased demand, often because of seasonal patterns of demand.

Antidilutive With reference to a transaction or a security, one that would increase earnings per share (EPS) or result in EPS higher than the company's basic EPS—antidilutive securities are not included in the calculation of diluted EPS.

Arbitrage (1) The simultaneous purchase of an undervalued asset or portfolio and sale of an overvalued but equivalent asset or portfolio, in order to obtain a riskless profit on the price differential. Taking advantage of a market inefficiency in a risk-free manner. (2) A trading strategy designed to generate a guaranteed profit from a transaction that requires no capital commitment or risk bearing on the part of the trader. A simple example of an arbitrage trade would be the simultaneous purchase and sale of the same security in different markets at different prices. (3) The condition in a financial market in which equivalent assets or combinations of assets sell for two different prices, creating an opportunity to profit at no risk with no commitment of money. In a well-functioning financial market, few arbitrage opportunities are possible. (4) A risk-free operation that earns an expected positive net profit but requires no net investment of money.

Arbitrage opportunity An opportunity to conduct an arbitrage; an opportunity to earn an expected positive net profit without risk and with no net investment of money.

Arbitrage portfolio The portfolio that exploits an arbitrage opportunity.

Arbitrage pricing theory (APT) A theory that posits that the expected return to a financial asset can be described by its relationship with several common risk factors. The multifactor APT can be contrasted with the single-factor CAPM.

Arithmetic mean The sum of the observations divided by the number of observations.

Arrears swap A type of interest rate swap in which the floating payment is set at the end of the period and the interest is paid at that same time.

Asian call option A European-style option with a value at maturity equal to the difference between the stock price at maturity and the average stock price during the life of the option, or $0, whichever is greater.

Asset allocation The process of deciding how to distribute an investor's wealth among different asset classes for investment purposes.

Asset beta The unlevered beta; reflects the business risk of the assets.

Asset class Securities that have similar characteristics, attributes, and risk/return relationships.

Asset impairment Loss of revenue-generating potential of a long-lived asset before the end of its useful life; the difference between an asset's carrying value and its fair value, as measured by the present value of the expected cash flows.

Asset-based loans A loan that is secured with company assets.

Assets under management (AUM) The total market value of the assets managed by an investment firm.

Assets Resources controlled by an enterprise as a result of past events and from which future economic benefits to the enterprise are expected to flow.

Assignment of accounts receivable The use of accounts receivable as collateral for a loan

At the money An option in which the underlying value equals the exercise price.

At-the-money option An option for which the strike (or exercise) price is close to (at) the current market price of the underlying asset.

Autocorrelation The correlation of a time series with its own past values.

Automated Clearing House An electronic payment network available to businesses, individuals, and financial institutions in the United States, U.S. Territories, and Canada.

Automatic fiscal policy A change in fiscal policy that is triggered by the state of the economy.

Automatic stabilizers Mechanisms that stabilize real GDP without explicit action by the government.

Autonomous expenditure The sum of those components of aggregate planned expenditure that are not influenced by real GDP. Autonomous expenditure equals investment, government purchases, exports, and the autonomous parts of consumption expenditure and imports.

Autoregressive (AR) model A time series regressed on its own past values, in which the independent variable is a lagged value of the dependent variable.

Available-for-sale securities Securities that a company does not intend to actively trade or (in the case of debt securities) hold to maturity.

Average cost pricing rule A rule that sets price to cover cost including normal profit, which means setting the price equal to average total cost.

Average fixed cost Total fixed cost per unit of output—total fixed cost divided by output.

Average product The average product of a resource. It equals total product divided by the quantity of the resource employed.

Average tax rate A person's total tax payment divided by his or her total income.

Average total cost Total cost per unit of output.

Average variable cost Total variable cost per unit of output.

Backtesting With reference to portfolio strategies, the application of a strategy's portfolio selection rules to historical data to assess what would have been the strategy's historical performance.

Backwardation A condition in the futures markets in which the benefits of holding an asset exceed the costs, leaving the futures price less than the spot price.

Balance of payments (1) A summary of all economic transactions between a country and all other countries for a specific time period, usually a year. The balance-of-payments account reflects all payments and liabilities to foreigners (debits) and all payments and obligations received from foreigners (credits). (2) A record of all financial flows crossing the borders of a country during a given time period (a quarter or a year).

Balance of payments accounts A country's record of international trading, borrowing, and lending.

Balance of trade *See* Trade balance.

Balance sheet A financial statement that shows what assets the firm controls at a fixed point in time and how it has financed these assets.

Balance sheet ratios Financial ratios involving balance sheet items only.

Balance sheet (statement of financial position or statement of financial condition) The financial statement that presents an entity's current financial position by disclosing resources the entity controls (its assets) and the claims on those resources (its liabilities and equity claims), as of a particular point in time (the date of the balance sheet).

Balanced budget A government budget in which tax revenues and expenditures are equal.

Balanced budget multiplier The magnification on aggregate demand of a *simultaneous* change in government purchases and taxes that leaves the budget balance unchanged.

Balanced fund A mutual fund with, generally, a three-part investment objective: (1) to conserve the investor's principal, (2) to pay current income, and (3) to increase both principal and income. The fund aims to achieve this by owning a mixture of bonds, preferred stocks, and common stocks.

Bank discount basis A quoting convention that annualizes, on a 360-day year, the discount as a percentage of face value.

Barriers to entry Legal or natural constraints that protect a firm from potential competitors.

Barter The direct exchange of one good or service for other goods and services.

Basic earnings per share Net earnings available to common shareholders (i.e., net income minus preferred dividends) divided by the weighted average number of common shares outstanding during the period.

Basis The difference between the spot price of the underlying asset and the futures contract price at any point in time (e.g., the *initial* basis at the time of contract origination, the *cover* basis at the time of contract termination).

Basis point value (BPV) Also called *present value of a basis point* or *price value of a basis point* (PVBP), the change in the bond price for a 1 basis point change in yield.

Basis swap (1) An interest rate swap involving two floating rates. (2) A swap in which both parties pay a floating rate.

Bayes' formula A method for updating probabilities based on new information.

Bear spread An option strategy that involves selling a put with a lower exercise price and buying a put with a higher exercise price. It can also be executed with calls.

Behavioral finance Involves the analysis of various psychological traits of individuals and how these traits affect how they act as investors, analysts, and portfolio managers.

Below full-employment equilibrium A macroeconomic equilibrium in which potential GDP exceeds real GDP.

Benchmark A comparison portfolio; a point of reference or comparison.

Benchmark bond A bond representative of current market conditions and used for performance comparison.

Benchmark error Situation where an inappropriate or incorrect benchmark is used to compare and assess portfolio returns and management.

Benchmark portfolio A comparison standard of risk and assets included in the policy statement and similar to the investor's risk preference and investment needs, which can be used to evaluate the investment performance of the portfolio manager.

Bernoulli random variable A random variable having the outcomes 0 and 1.

Bernoulli trial An experiment that can produce one of two outcomes.

Beta A standardized measure of systematic risk based upon an asset's covariance with the market portfolio.

Betterments Improvements that do not add to the physical layout of a plant asset.

Bid-ask spread The difference between the quoted ask and the bid prices.

Big tradeoff A tradeoff between equity and efficiency.

Bill-and-hold basis Sales on a bill-and-hold basis involve selling products but not delivering those products until a later date.

Binomial model A model for pricing options in which the underlying price can move to only one of two possible new prices.

Binomial option pricing model A valuation equation that assumes the price of the underlying asset changes through a series of discrete upward or downward movements.

Binomial random variable The number of successes in n Bernoulli trials for which the probability of success is constant for all trials and the trials are independent.

Binomial tree The graphical representation of a model of asset price dynamics in which, at each period, the asset moves up with probability p or down with probability $(1 - p)$.

Black market An illegal trading arrangement in which the price exceeds the legally imposed price ceiling.

Black-Scholes option pricing model A valuation equation that assumes the price of the underlying asset changes continuously through the option's expiration date by a statistical process known as *geometric Brownian motion.*

Block Orders to buy or sell that are too large for the liquidity ordinarily available in dealer networks or stock exchanges.

Bond A long-term debt security with contractual obligations regarding interest payments and redemption.

Bond-equivalent basis A basis for stating an annual yield that annualizes a semiannual yield by doubling it.

Bond-equivalent yield The yield to maturity on a basis that ignores compounding.

Bond equivalent yield A calculation of yield that is annualized using the ratio of 365 to the number of days to maturity. Bond equivalent yield allows for the restatement and comparison of securities with different compounding periods.

Bond option An option in which the underlying is a bond; primarily traded in over-the-counter markets.

Bond price volatility The percentage changes in bond prices over time.

Bond yield plus risk premium approach An estimate of the cost of common equity that is produced by summing the before-tax cost of debt and a risk premium that captures the additional yield on a company's stock relative to its bonds. The additional yield is often estimated using historical spreads between bond yields and stock yields.

Book value equity per share The amount of the book value (also called carrying value) of common equity per share of common stock, calculated by dividing the book value of shareholders' equity by the number of shares of common stock outstanding.

Book value of equity (or book value) (1) Shareholders' equity (total assets minus total liabilities) minus the value of preferred stock; common shareholders' equity. (2) The accounting value of a firm.

Book value per share Book value of equity divided by the number of common shares outstanding.

Bottom-up analysis With reference to investment selection processes, an approach that involves selection from all securities within a specified investment universe, i.e., without prior narrowing of the universe on the basis of macroeconomic or overall market considerations.

Box spread An option strategy that combines a bull spread and a bear spread having two different exercise prices, which produces a risk-free payoff of the difference in the exercise prices.

Brady bonds Bonds issued by emerging countries under a debt-reduction plan named after Mr. Brady, former U.S. Secretary of the Treasury.

Brand name A registered name that can be used only by its owner to identify a product or service.

Break point In the context of the weighted average cost of capital (WACC), a break point is the amount of capital at which the cost of one or more of the sources of capital changes, leading to a change in the WACC.

Breusch-Pagan test A test for conditional heteroskedasticity in the error term of a regression.

Broker (1) An agent who executes orders to buy or sell securities on behalf of a client in exchange for a commission. (2) *See* Futures commission merchants.

Budget deficit A government's budget balance that is negative—expenditures exceed tax revenues.

Budget surplus A government's budget balance that is positive—tax revenues exceed expenditures.

Bull spread An option strategy that involves buying a call with a lower exercise price and selling a call with a higher exercise price. It can also be executed with puts.

Bundled fee A fee that combines multiple fees into one "bundled" fee. Bundled fees can include any combination of management, transaction, custody, and other administrative fees. Two specific examples of bundled fees are the wrap fee and the all-in fee.

All-in fee Due to the universal banking system in some countries, asset management, brokerage, and custody are often part of the same company. This allows banks to offer a variety of choices to customers regarding how the fee will be charged. Customers are offered numerous fee models in which fees may be bundled together or charged separately. All-in fees can include any combination of investment management, trading expenses, custody, and other administrative fees.

Wrap fee Wrap fees are specific to a particular investment product. The U.S. Securities and Exchange Commission (SEC) defines a wrap fee account (now more commonly known as a separately managed account or SMA) as "any advisory program under which a specified fee or fees not based upon transactions in a client's account is charged for investment advisory services (which may include portfolio management or advice concerning the selection of other investment advisers) and execution of client transactions." A typical separately managed account has a contract or contracts (and fee) involving a sponsor (usually a broker or independent provider) acting as the investment advisor, an investment management firm typically as the subadvisor, other services (custody, consulting, reporting, performance, manager selection, monitoring, and execution of trades), distributor, and the client (brokerage customer). Wrap fees can be all-inclusive, asset-based fees (which may include any combination of management, transaction, custody, and other administrative fees).

Conditional expected value (1) Expected value of a variable conditional on some available information set. The expected value changes over time with changes in the information set. (2) The expected value of a stated event given that another event has occurred.

Conditional heteroskedasticity Heteroskedasticity in the error variance that is correlated with the values of the independent variable(s) in the regression.

Conditional probability The probability of an event given (conditioned on) another event.

Conditional variance (1) Variance of a variable conditional on some available information set. (2) The variance of one variable, given the outcome of another.

Conditional variances The variance of one variable, given the outcome of another.

Confidence interval A range that has a given probability that it will contain the population parameter it is intended to estimate.

Consistency A desirable property of estimators; a consistent estimator is one for which the probability of estimates close to the value of the population parameter increases as sample size increases.

Consistent With reference to estimators, describes an estimator for which the probability of estimates close to the value of the population parameter increases as sample size increases.

Consolidated Quotation System (CQS) An electronic quotation service for issues listed on the NYSE, the AMEX, or regional exchanges and traded on the Nasdaq InterMarket.

Constant maturity swap or CMT swap A swap in which the floating rate is the rate on a security known as a constant maturity treasury or CMT security.

Constant maturity treasury or CMT A hypothetical U.S. Treasury note with a constant maturity. A CMT exists for various years in the range of 2 to 10.

Constant returns to scale Features of a firm's technology that leads to constant long-run average cost as output increases. When constant returns to scale are present, the *LRAC* curve is horizontal.

Consumer Price Index (CPI) An index that measures the average of the prices paid by urban consumers for a fixed "basket" of the consumer goods and services.

Consumer surplus The value of a good minus the price paid for it, summed over the quantity bought.

Consumption expenditure The total payment for consumer goods and services.

Contango A situation in a futures market where the current futures price is greater than the current spot price for the underlying asset.

Contestable market A market in which firms can enter and leave so easily that firms in the market face competition from potential entrants.

Contingent claims Derivatives in which the payoffs occur if a specific event occurs; generally referred to as options.

Continuous market A market where stocks are priced and traded continuously by an auction process or by dealers when the market is open.

Continuous random variable A random variable for which the range of possible outcomes is the real line (all real numbers between $-\infty$ and ∞) or some subset of the real line.

Continuous time Time thought of as advancing in extremely small increments.

Continuously compounded return The natural logarithm of 1 plus the holding period return, or equivalently, the natural logarithm of the ending price over the beginning price.

Contra account An account that offsets another account.

Contract price The transaction price specified in a forward or futures contract.

Convenience yield The nonmonetary return offered by an asset when the asset is in short supply, often associated with assets with seasonal production processes.

Conventional cash flow A conventional cash flow pattern is one with an initial outflow followed by a series of inflows.

Conversion factor An adjustment used to facilitate delivery on bond futures contracts in which any of a number of bonds with different characteristics are eligible for delivery.

Conversion value The value of the convertible security if converted into common stock at the stock's current market price.

Convertible bonds A bond with the added feature that the bondholder has the option to turn the bond back to the firm in exchange for a specified number of common shares of the firm.

Convexity (1) A measure of the change in duration with respect to changes in interest rates. (2) A measure of the degree to which a bond's price-yield curve departs from a straight line. This characteristic affects estimates of a bond's price volatility for a given change in yields.

Cooperative equilibrium The outcome of a game in which the players make and share the monopoly profit.

Copyright A government-sanctioned exclusive right granted to the inventor of a good, service, or productive process to produce, use, and sell the invention for a given number of years.

Correlation A number between −1 and 1 that measures the co-movement (linear association) between two random variables.

Correlation analysis The analysis of the strength of the linear relationship between two data series.

Correlation coefficient A standardized measure of the relationship between two variables that ranges from 2 1.00 to 1 1.00.

Cost averaging The periodic investment of a fixed amount of money.

Cost of capital The rate of return that the suppliers of capital-bondholders and owners-require as compensation for their contribution of capital.

Cost of carry The cost associated with holding some asset, including financing, storage, and insurance costs. Any yield received on the asset is treated as a negative carrying cost.

Cost of carry model A model for pricing futures contracts in which the futures price is determined by adding the cost of carry to the spot price.

Cost of debt The cost of debt financing to a company, such as when it issues a bond or takes out a bank loan.

Cost of goods sold For a given period, equal to beginning inventory minus ending inventory plus the cost of goods acquired or produced during the period.

Cost of preferred stock The cost to a company of issuing preferred stock; the dividend yield that a company must commit to pay preferred stock holders.

Cost recovery method A method of revenue recognition in which is the seller does not report any profit until the cash amounts paid by the buyer—including principal and interest on any financing from the seller—are greater than all the seller's costs for the merchandise sold.

Cost-push inflation An inflation that results from an initial increase in costs.

Council of Economic Advisers In the executive branch of the U.S. government, a council whose main work is to monitor the economy and keep the President and the public well informed about the current state of the economy and the best available forecasts of where it is heading.

Counterparty A participant to a derivative transaction.

Country risk Uncertainty due to the possibility of major political or economic change in the country where an investment is located. Also called *political risk.*

Coupon Indicates the interest payment on a debt security. It is the coupon rate times the par value that indicates the interest payments on a debt security.

Covariance A measure of the co-movement (linear association) between two random variables.

Covariance matrix A matrix or square array whose entries are covariances; also known as a variance-covariance matrix.

Covariance stationary Describes a time series when its expected value and variance are constant and finite in all periods and when its covariance with itself for a fixed number of periods in the past or future is constant and finite in all periods.

Covered call An option strategy involving the holding of an asset and sale of a call on the asset.

Covered interest arbitrage A transaction executed in the foreign exchange market in which a currency is purchased (sold) and a forward contract is sold (purchased) to lock in the exchange rate for future delivery of the currency. This transaction should earn the risk-free rate of the investor's home country.

Credit With respect to double-entry accounting, a credit records increases in liability, owners' equity, and revenue accounts or decreases in asset accounts; with respect to borrowing, the willingness and ability of the borrower to make promised payments on the borrowing.

Credit analysis The evaluation of credit risk; the evaluation of the creditworthiness of a borrower or counterparty.

Credit derivatives A contract in which one party has the right to claim a payment from another party in the event that a specific credit event occurs over the life of the contract.

Credit-linked notes Fixed-income securities in which the holder of the security has the right to withhold payment of the full amount due at maturity if a credit event occurs.

Credit risk (or default risk) The risk of loss caused by a counterparty's or debtor's failure to make a promised payment.

Credit scoring model A statistical model used to classify the creditworthiness of borrowers.

Credit spread option An option on the yield spread on a bond.

Credit swap A type of swap transaction used as a credit derivative in which one party makes periodic payments to the other and receives the promise of a payoff if a third party defaults.

Credit union A depository institution owned by a social or economic group such as firm's employees that accepts savings deposits and makes mostly consumer loans.

Credit VAR, Default VAR, or Credit at risk A variation of VAR that reflects credit risk.

Creditor nation A country that during its entire history has invested more in the rest of the world than other countries have invested in it.

Creditworthiness The perceived ability of the borrower to pay what is owed on the borrowing in a timely manner; it represents the ability of a company to withstand adverse impacts on its cash flows.

Cross elasticity of demand The responsiveness of the demand for a good to the price of a substitute or complement, other things remaining the same. It is calculated as the percentage change in the quantity demanded of the good divided by the percentage change in the price of the substitute or complement.

Cross-product netting Netting the market values of all contracts, not just derivatives, between parties.

Cross-sectional analysis Analysis that involves comparisons across individuals in a group over a given time period or at a given point in time.

Cross-sectional data Observations over individual units at a point in time, as opposed to time-series data.

Crowding-out effect The tendency for a government budget deficit to decrease in investment.

Cumulative distribution function A function giving the probability that a random variable is less than or equal to a specified value.

Cumulative relative frequency For data grouped into intervals, the fraction of total observations that are less than the value of the upper limit of a stated interval.

Currency The bills and coins that we use today. A record of the payments for imports of goods and services, receipts from exports of goods and services, interest income, and net transfers.

Currency appreciation The rise in the value of one currency in terms of another currency.

Currency depreciation The fall in the value of one currency in terms of another currency.

Currency drain An increase in currency held outside the banks.

Currency forward A forward contract in which the underlying is a foreign currency.

Currency option An option that allows the holder to buy (if a call) or sell (if a put) an underlying currency at a fixed exercise rate, expressed as an exchange rate.

Currency swap A swap in which each party makes interest payments to the other in different currencies.

Current assets Assets that are expected to be consumed or converted into cash in the near future, typically one year or less.

Current cost With reference to assets, the amount of cash or cash equivalents that would have to be paid to buy the same or an equivalent asset today; with reference to liabilities, the undiscounted amount of cash or cash equivalents that would be required to settle the obligation today.

Current credit risk The risk associated with the possibility that a payment currently due will not be made.

Current income A return objective in which the investor seeks to generate income rather than capital gains; generally a goal of an investor who wants to supplement earnings with income to meet living expenses.

Current liabilities Those liabilities that are expected to be settled in the near future, typically one year or less (e.g. accounts payable, wages payable).

Current P/E *See* Trailing P/E.

Current ratio The ratio of current assets to current liabilities; a measure of a company's ability to satisfy its current liabilities with its current assets.

Current taxes payable Tax expenses that have been recognized and recorded on a company's income statement but which have not yet been paid.

Current yield A bond's yield as measured by its current income (coupon) as a percentage of its market price.

Customer list A list of customers or subscribers.

Cyclical businesses Businesses with high sensitivity to business- or industry-cycle influences.

Cyclical company A firm whose earnings rise and fall with general economic activity.

Cyclical stock A stock with a high beta; its gains typically exceed those of a rising market and its losses typically exceed those of a falling market.

Cyclical surplus or deficit The actual surplus or deficit minus the structural surplus or deficit.

Cyclical unemployment The fluctuations in unemployment over the business cycle.

Daily settlement See *marking to market.*

Data mining The practice of determining a model by extensive searching through a dataset for statistically significant patterns.

Day trader A trader holding a position open somewhat longer than a scalper but closing all positions at the end of the day.

Days of inventory on hand (DOH) An activity ratio equal to the number of days in the period divided by inventory turnover over the period.

Days of sales outstanding (DSO) An activity ratio equal to the number of days in period divided by receivables turnover.

Deadweight loss A measure of inefficiency. It is equal to the decrease in consumer surplus and producer surplus that results from an inefficient level of production.

Dealing securities Securities held by banks or other financial intermediaries for trading purposes.

Debentures Bonds that promise payments of interest and principal but pledge no specific assets. Holders have first claim on the issuer's income and unpledged assets. Also known as *unsecured bonds*.

Debit With respect to double-entry accounting, a debit records increases of asset and expense accounts or decreases in liability and owners' equity accounts.

Debt incurrence test A financial covenant made in conjunction with existing debt that restricts a company's ability to incur additional debt at the same seniority based on one or more financial tests or conditions.

Debtor nation A country that during its entire history has borrowed more from the rest of the world than it has lent to it.

Debt-rating approach A method for estimating a company's before-tax cost of debt based upon the yield on comparably rated bonds for maturities that closely match that of the company's existing debt.

Debt-to-assets ratio A solvency ratio calculated as total debt divided by total assets; a measure of the proportion of assets that is financed with debt (both short-term and long-term debt).

Debt-to-capital ratio A solvency ratio calculated as total debt divided by total debt plus total shareholders' equity.

Debt-to-equity ratio A solvency ratio calculated as total debt divided by total shareholders' equity; compares the proportions of a company's assets that are financed through the use of debt relative to equity, evaluated using book values of the capital sources.

Decentralized risk management A system that allows individual units within an organization to manage risk. Decentralization results in duplication of effort but has the advantage of having people closer to the risk be more directly involved in its management.

Deciles Quantiles that divide a distribution into 10 equal parts.

Decision rule With respect to hypothesis testing, the rule according to which the null hypothesis will be rejected or not rejected; involves the comparison of the test statistic to rejection point(s).

Declining-balance method An accelerated method of depreciation in which depreciation is computed by applying a fixed rate to the carrying value (the declining balance) of a tangible long-lived asset.

Declining trend channel The range defined by security prices as they move progressively lower.

Deep in the money Options that are far in-the-money.

Deep out of the money Options that are far out-of-the-money.

Default risk The risk that an issuer will be unable to make interest and principal payments on time.

Default risk premium An extra return that compensates investors for the possibility that the borrower will fail to make a promised payment at the contracted time and in the contracted amount.

Defensive competitive strategy Positioning the firm so that its capabilities provide the best means to deflect the effect of the competitive forces in the industry.

Defensive interval ratio A liquidity ratio that estimates the number of days that an entity could meet cash needs from liquid assets; calculated as (cash + short-term marketable investments + receivables) divided by daily cash expenditures.

Defensive stock A stock whose return is not expected to decline as much as that of the overall market during a bear market (a beta less than one).

Deflation A process in which the price level falls—a negative inflation.

Degree of confidence The probability that a confidence interval includes the unknown population parameter.

Degrees of freedom (df) The number of independent observations used.

Delivery A process used in a deliverable forward contract in which the long pays the agreed-upon price to the short, which in turn delivers the underlying asset to the long.

Delivery option The feature of a futures contract giving the short the right to make decisions about what, when, and where to deliver.

Delta The relationship between the option price and the underlying price, which reflects the sensitivity of the price of the option to changes in the price of the underlying.

Delta hedge An option strategy in which a position in an asset is converted to a risk-free position with a position in a specific number of options. The number of options per unit of the underlying changes through time, and the position must be revised to maintain the hedge.

Delta-normal method A measure of VAR equivalent to the analytical method but that refers to the use of delta to estimate the option's price sensitivity.

Demand The relationship between the quantity of a good that consumers plan to buy and the price of the good when all other influences on buyers' plans remain the same. It is described by a demand schedule and illustrated by a demand curve.

Demand curve A curve that shows the relationship between the quantity demanded of a good and its price when all other influences on consumers' planned purchases remain the same.

Demand for labor The relationship between the quantity of labor demanded and the real wage rate when all other influences on firm's hiring plans remain the same.

Demand-pull inflation An inflation that results from an initial increase in aggregate demand.

Dependent With reference to events, the property that the probability of one event occurring depends on (is related to) the occurrence of another event.

Dependent variable The variable whose variation about its mean is to be explained by the regression; the left-hand-side variable in a regression equation.

Depletion The exhaustion of a natural resource through mining, cutting, pumping, or other extraction, and the way in which the cost is allocated.

Depository institution A firm that takes deposits from households and firms and makes loans to other households and firms.

Depreciable cost The cost of an asset less its residual value.

Depreciation The process of systematically allocating the cost of long-lived (tangible) assets to the periods during which the assets are expected to provide economic benefits.

Derivative A financial instrument that offers a return based on the return of some other underlying asset or factor (e.g., a stock price, an interest rate, or exchange rate).

Derivative security An instrument whose market value ultimately depends upon, or derives from, the value of a more fundamental investment vehicle called the underlying asset or security.

Derivatives (1) Securities bearing a contractual relation to some underlying asset or rate. Options, futures, forward, and swap contracts, as well as many forms of bonds, are derivative securities. (2) A financial instrument that offers a return based on the return of some other underlying asset.

Derivatives dealers Commercial and investment banks that make markets in derivatives. .

Derived demand The demand for a productive resource, which is derived from the demand for the goods and services produced by the resource.

Descriptive statistics The study of how data can be summarized effectively.

Diff swaps A swap in which the payments are based on the difference between interest rates in two countries but payments are made in only a single currency.

Diffuse prior The assumption of equal prior probabilities.

Diluted earnings per share Net income, minus preferred dividends, divided by the number of common shares outstanding considering all dilutive securities (e.g., convertible debt and options); the EPS that would result if all dilutive securities were converted into common shares.

Diluted shares The number of shares that would be outstanding if all potentially dilutive claims on common shares (e.g., convertible debt, convertible preferred stock, and employee stock options) were exercised.

Diminishing balance method An accelerated depreciation method, i.e., one that allocates a relatively large proportion of the cost of an asset to the early years of the asset's useful life.

Diminishing marginal returns The tendency for the marginal product of an additional unit of a factor of production to be less than the marginal product of the previous unit of the factor.

Diminishing marginal utility The decrease in marginal utility as the quantity consumed increases.

Direct debit program An arrangement whereby a customer authorizes a debit to a demand account; typically used by companies to collect routine payments for services.

Direct format (direct method) With reference to the cash flow statement, a format for the presentation of the statement in which cash flow from operating activities is shown as operating cash receipts less operating cash disbursements.

Direct method The procedure for converting the income statement from an accrual basis to a cash basis by adjusting each item on the income statement.

Direct write-off method An approach to recognizing credit losses on customer receivables in which the company waits until such time as a customer has defaulted and only then recognizes the loss.

Disbursement float The amount of time between check issuance and a check's clearing back against the company's account.

Discount To reduce the value of a future payment in allowance for how far away it is in time; to calculate the present value of some future amount. Also, the amount by which an instrument is priced below its face value.

Discount interest A procedure for determining the interest on a loan or bond in which the interest is deducted from the face value in advance.

Discounting The conversion of a future amount of money to its present value.

Discouraged workers People who are available and willing to work but have not made specific efforts to find a job within the previous four weeks.

Discrete random variable A random variable that can take on at most a countable number of possible values.

Discrete time Time thought of as advancing in distinct finite increments.

Discretionary fiscal policy A policy action that is initiated by an act of Congress.

Discretionary policy A policy that responds to the state of the economy in a possibly unique way that uses all the information available, including perceived lessons from past "mistakes."

Discriminant analysis A multivariate classification technique used to discriminate between groups, such as companies that either will or will not become bankrupt during some time frame.

Diseconomies of scale Features of a firm's technology that leads to rising long-run average cost as output increases.

Dispersion The variability around the central tendency.

Disposable income Aggregate income minus taxes plus transfer payments.

Distinct business entity A unit, division, department, or office that is organizationally and functionally segregated from other units, divisions, departments, or offices and retains discretion over the assets it manages and autonomy over the investment decision-making process. Possible criteria that can be used to determine this include: (a) being a legal entity; (b) having a distinct market or client type (e.g., institutional, retail, private client, etc.); (c) using a separate and distinct investment process.

Dividend discount model (DDM) A technique for estimating the value of a stock issue as the present value of all future dividends.

Dividend discount model based approach or implied risk premium approach An approach for estimating a country's equity risk premium. The market rate of return is estimated as the sum of the dividend yield and the growth rate in dividends for a market index. Subtracting the risk-free rate of return from the estimated market return produces an estimate for the equity risk premium.

Dividend payout ratio The ratio of dividends paid to earnings for a period; more specifically, the ratio of dividends paid to common shareholders to net income attributable to common shares.

Dividends per share The dollar amount of cash dividends paid during a period per share of common stock.

Dominant strategy equilibrium A Nash equilibrium in which the best strategy of each player is to cheat (deny) regardless of the strategy of the other player.

Double declining balance depreciation An accelerated depreciation method that involves depreciating the asset at double the straight-line rate.

Double-declining-balance method An accelerated method of depreciation in which a fixed rate equal to twice the straight-line percentage is applied to the carrying value (the declining balance) of a tangible long-lived asset.

Double-entry accounting The accounting system of recording transactions in which every recorded transaction affects at least two accounts so as to keep the basic accounting equation (assets = liabilities + owners' equity) in balance.

Down transition probability The probability that an asset's value moves down in a model of asset price dynamics.

Drag on liquidity When receipts lag, creating pressure from the decreased available funds.

Dummy variable A type of qualitative variable that takes on a value of 1 if a particular condition is true and 0 if that condition is false.

Dumping The sale by a foreign firm of exports at a lower price that the cost of production.

Duopoly A market structure in which two producers of a good or service compete.

DuPont analysis An approach to decomposing return on investment, e.g., return on equity, as the product of other financial ratios.

DuPont system A method of examining ROE by breaking it down into three component parts: (1) profit margin, (2) total asset turnover, and (3) financial leverage.

Duration A measure of an option-free bond's average maturity. Specifically, the weighted average maturity of all future cash flows paid by a security, in which the weights are the present value of these cash flows as a fraction of the bond's price. A measure of a bond's price sensitivity to interest rate movements.

Dutch Book Theorem A result in probability theory stating that inconsistent probabilities create profit opportunities.

Dynamic comparative advantage A comparative advantage that a person or country possesses as a result of having specialized in a particular activity and then, as a result of learning-by-doing, having become the producer with the lowest opportunity cost.

Dynamic hedging A strategy in which a position is hedged by making frequent adjustments to the quantity of the instrument used for hedging in relation to the instrument being hedged.

Earnings at risk (EAR) A variation of VAR that reflects the risk of a company's earnings instead of its market value.

Earnings momentum A strategy in which portfolios are constructed of stocks of firms with rising earnings.

Earnings multiplier model A technique for estimating the value of a stock issue as a multiple of its earnings per share.

Earnings per share (EPS) The amount of income earned during a period per share of common stock; (net income − preferred dividends) divided by the weighted average number of common shares outstanding.

Earnings surprise A company announcement of earnings that differ from analysts' prevailing expectations.

Earnings yield Earnings per share divided by price; the reciprocal of the P/E ratio.

EBITDA Earnings before interest, taxes, depreciation, and amortization.

Economic depreciation The change in the market value of capital over a given period.

Economic efficiency A situation that occurs when the firm produces a given output at the least cost.

Economic exposure The risk associated with changes in the relative attractiveness of products and services offered for sale, arising out of the competitive effects of changes in exchange rates.

Economic growth The expansion of production possibilities that results from capital accumulation and technological change.

Economic information Data on prices, quantities, and qualities of goods and services and factors of production.

Economic model A description of some aspect of the economic world that includes only those features of the world that are needed for the purpose at hand.

Economic order quantity-reorder point An approach to managing inventory based on expected demand and the predictability of demand; the ordering point for new inventory is determined based on the costs of ordering and carrying inventory, such that the total cost associated with inventory is minimized.

Economic profit A firm's total revenue minus its opportunity cost.

Economic rent The income received by the owner of a factor of production over and above the amount required to induce that owner to offer the factor for use.

Economic theory A generalization that summarizes what we think we understand about the economic choices that people make and the performance of industries and entire economies.

Economic value added (EVA) Internal management performance measure that compares net operating profit to total cost of capital. Indicates how profitable company projects are as a sign of management performance.

Economics The social science that studies the *choices* that individuals, businesses, governments, and entire societies make and how they cope with *scarcity* and the *incentives* that influence and reconcile those choices.

Economies of scale Features of a firm's technology that leads to a falling long-run average cost as output increases.

Economies of scope Decreases in average total cost that occur when a firm uses specialized resources to produce a range of goods and services.

Effective annual rate The amount by which a unit of currency will grow in a year with interest on interest included.

Effective annual yield (EAY) An annualized return that accounts for the effect of interest on interest; EAY is computed by compounding 1 plus the holding period yield forward to one year, then subtracting 1.

Effective duration Direct measure of the interest rate sensitivity of a bond (or any financial instrument) based upon price changes derived from a pricing model.

Efficiency In statistics, a desirable property of estimators; an efficient estimator is the unbiased estimator with the smallest variance among unbiased estimators of the same parameter.

Efficient capital market A market in which security prices rapidly reflect all information about securities.

Efficient frontier The portion of the minimum-variance frontier beginning with the global minimum-variance portfolio and continuing above it; the graph of the set of portfolios offering the maximum expected return for their level of variance of return.

Efficient market A market in which the actual price embodies all currently available relevant information. Resources are sent to their highest valued use.

Efficient portfolio A portfolio offering the highest expected return for a given level of risk as measured by variance or standard deviation of return.

Elastic demand Demand with a price elasticity greater than 1; other things remaining the same, the percentage change in the quantity demanded exceeds the percentage change in price.

Elasticity of demand The responsiveness of the quantity demanded of a good to a change in its price, other things remaining the same.

Elasticity of supply The responsiveness of the quantity supplied of a good to a change in its price, other things remaining the same.

Electronic funds transfer The use of computer networks to conduct financial transactions electronically.

Empirical probability The probability of an event estimated as a relative frequency of occurrence.

Employment Act of 1946 A landmark Congressional act that recognized a role for government actions to keep unemployment, keep the economy expanding, and keep inflation in check.

Employment-to-population ratio The percentage of people of working age who have jobs.

Ending market value (private equity) The remaining equity that a limited partner has in a fund. Also referred to as net asset value or residual value.

Enhanced derivatives products companies (EDPC or special purpose vehicles SPVs) A type of subsidiary engaged in derivatives transactions that is separated from the parent company in order to have a higher credit rating than the parent company.

Enterprise risk management A form of *centralized risk management* that typically encompasses the management of a broad variety of risks, including insurance risk.

Entrepreneurship The human resource that organizes labor, land, and capital. Entrepreneurs come up with new ideas about what and how to produce, make business decisions, and bear the risks that arise from their decisions.

Equation of exchange An equation that states that the quantity of money multiplied by the velocity of circulation equals GDP.

Equilibrium price The price at which the quantity demanded equals the quantity supplied.

Equilibrium quantity The quantity bought and sold at the equilibrium price.

Equitizing cash A strategy used to replicate an index. It is also used to take a given amount of cash and turn it into an equity position while maintaining the liquidity provided by the cash.

Equity Assets less liabilities; the residual interest in the assets after subtracting the liabilities.

Equity forward A contract calling for the purchase of an individual stock, a stock portfolio, or a stock index at a later date at an agreed-upon price.

Equity options Options on individual stocks; also known as stock options.

Equity risk premium The expected return on equities minus the risk-free rate; the premium that investors demand for investing in equities.

Equity swap A swap transaction in which at least one cash flow is tied to the return to an equity portfolio position, often an equity index.

Error autocorrelation The autocorrelation of the error term.

Error term The portion of the dependent variable that is not explained by the independent variable(s) in the regression.

Estimate The particular value calculated from sample observations using an estimator.

Estimated (or fitted) parameters With reference to regression analysis, the estimated values of the population intercept and population slope coefficient(s) in a regression.

Estimated rate of return The rate of return an investor anticipates earning from a specific investment over a particular future holding period.

Estimated useful life The total number of service units expected from a long-term asset.

Estimation With reference to statistical inference, the subdivision dealing with estimating the value of a population parameter.

Estimator An estimation formula; the formula used to compute the sample mean and other sample statistics are examples of estimators.

Eurobonds Bonds denominated in a currency not native to the country in which they are issued.

Eurodollar A dollar deposited outside the United States.

European option An option contract that can only be exercised on its expiration date.

European terms With reference to U.S. dollar exchange rate quotations, the price of a U.S. dollar in terms of another currency.

European-style option or European option An option exercisable only at maturity.

European Union (EU) A formal association of European countries founded by the Treaty of Rome in 1957. Formerly known as the EEC.

Event Any outcome or specified set of outcomes of a random variable.

Event study Research that examines the reaction of a security's price to a specific company, world event, or news announcement.

Ex-ante Before the fact.

Excess kurtosis Degree of peakedness (fatness of tails) in excess of the peakedness of the normal distribution.

Excess reserves A bank's actual reserves minus its required reserves.

Exchange for physicals (EFP) A permissible delivery procedure used by futures market participants, in which the long and short arrange a delivery procedure other than the normal procedures stipulated by the futures exchange.

Exchange rate risk Uncertainty due to the denomination of an investment in a currency other than that of the investor's own country.

Exchange-traded fund (ETF) A tradable depository receipt that gives investors a pro rata claim to the returns associated with a portfolio of securities (often designed to mimic an index, such as the Standard & Poor's 500) held in trust by a financial institution.

Exercise (or exercising the option) The process of using an option to buy or sell the underlying.

Exercise price (or strike price or striking price, or strike) The fixed price at which an option holder can buy or sell the underlying.

Exercise rate or strike rate The fixed rate at which the holder of an interest rate option can buy or sell the underlying.

Exhaustive Covering or containing all possible outcomes.

Expansion A business cycle phase between a trough and a peak-phase in which real GDP increases.

Expected rate of return The return that analysts' calculations suggest a security should provide, based on the market's rate of return during the period and the security's relationship to the market.

Expected return The rate of return that an investor expects to get on an investment.

Expected utility The average utility arising from all possible outcomes.

Expected value The probability-weighted average of the possible outcomes of a random variable.

Expenditure A payment or obligation to make future payment for an asset or a service.

Expensed Taken as a deduction in arriving at net income.

Expenses Outflows of economic resources or increases in liabilities that result in decreases in equity (other than decreases because of distributions to owners).

Expiration date The date on which a derivative contract expires.

Expiry The expiration date of a derivative security.

Exports The goods and services that we sell to people in other countries.

Extended DuPont System A method of examining *ROE* by breaking it down into five component parts.

External benefits Benefits that accrue to people other than the buyer of the good.

External cash flow Cash, securities, or assets that enter or exit a portfolio.

External costs Costs that are not borne by the producer of the good but borne by someone else.

External diseconomies Factors outside the control of a firm that raise the firm's costs as the industry produces a larger output.

External economies Factors beyond the control of a firm that lower the firm's costs as the industry produces a larger output.

External valuation (real estate) An external valuation is an assessment of market value performed by a third party who is a qualified, professionally designated, certified, or licensed commercial property valuer/appraiser. External valuations must be completed following the valuation standards of the local governing appraisal body.

Externality A cost or a benefit that arises from production that falls on someone other than the producer or a cost or a benefit that arises from consumption that falls on someone other than the consumer.

Extraordinary repairs Repairs that affect the estimated residual value or estimated useful life of an asset thereby increasing its carrying value.

Face value The promised payment at maturity separate from any coupon payment.

Factor A common or underlying element with which several variables are correlated.

Factor risk premium (or factor price) The expected return in excess of the risk-free rate for a portfolio with a sensitivity of 1 to one factor and a sensitivity of 0 to all other factors.

Factor sensitivity (also factor betas or factor loadings) A measure of the response of return to each unit of increase in a factor, holding all other factors constant.

Factors of production The productive resources that businesses use to produce goods and services.

Fair market value The market price of an asset or liability that trades regularly.

Fair value The amount at which an asset could be exchanged or a liability settled, between knowledgeable, willing parties in an arm's-length transaction.

Federal budget The annual statement of the expenditures and tax revenues of the government of the United States together with the laws and regulations that approve and support those expenditures and taxes.

Federal funds rate The interest rate that banks charge each other on overnight loans of reserves.

Federal Open Market Committee The main policy-making organ of the Federal Reserve System.

Federal Reserve System The central bank of the United States.

Fee Schedule The firm's current investment management fees or bundled fees for a particular presentation. This schedule is typically listed by asset level ranges and should be appropriate to the particular prospective client.

Feedback-rule policy A rule that specifies how policy actions respond to changes in the state of the economy.

Fiduciary A person who supervises or oversees the investment portfolio of a third party, such as in a trust account, and makes investment decisions in accordance with the owner's wishes.

Fiduciary call A combination of a European call and a risk-free bond that matures on the option expiration day and has a face value equal to the exercise price of the call.

FIFO method The first in, first out, method of accounting for inventory, which matches sales against the costs of items of inventory in the order in which they were placed in inventory.

Financial account A component of the balance of payments covering investments by residents abroad and investments by nonresidents in the home country. Examples include direct investment made by companies, portfolio investments in equity and bonds, and other investments and liabilities.

Financial analysis The process of selecting, evaluating, and interpreting financial data, along with other pertinent information, in order to formulate an assessment of the company's present and future financial condition and performance.

Financial flexibility The ability to react and adapt to financial adversities and opportunities.

Financial futures Futures contracts in which the underlying is a stock, bond, or currency.

Financial innovation The development of new financial products—new ways of borrowing and lending.

Financial leverage The extent to which a company can effect, through the use of debt, a proportional change in the return on common equity that is greater than a given proportional change in operating income; also, short for the financial leverage ratio.

Financial leverage ratio (or equity multiplier) A measure of financial leverage calculated as average total assets divided by average total equity, indicates the extent to which assets are financed with debt relative to equity.

Financial risk Uncertainty of net income and net cash flows attributed to the use of financing that has a fixed cost, such as debt and leases.

Financing activities Activities related to obtaining or repaying capital to be used in the business (e.g., equity and long-term debt).

Firm (1) For purposes of the GIPS standards, the term "firm" refers to the entity defined for compliance with the GIPS standards. See the term "distinct business entity." (2) An economic unit that hires factors of production and organizes those factors to produce and sell goods and services.

First-differencing A transformation that subtracts the value of the time series in period $t - 1$ from its value in period t.

First-order serial correlation Correlation between adjacent observations in a time series.

Fiscal imbalance The present value of the government's commitments to pay benefits minus the present value of its tax revenues.

Fiscal policy The government's attempt to achieve macroeconomic objectives such as full employment, sustained economic growth, and price level stability by setting and changing taxes, making transfer payments, and purchasing goods and services.

Fixed asset turnover An activity ratio calculated as total revenue divided by average net fixed assets.

Fixed charge coverage A solvency ratio measuring the number of times interest and lease payments are covered by operating income, calculated as (EBIT + lease payments) divided by (interest payments + lease payments).

Fixed costs Costs that stay the same within some range of activity.

Fixed exchange rate An exchange rate that is set at a determined amount by government policy.

Fixed exchange rate regime A system in which the exchange rate between two currencies remains fixed at a preset level, known as official parity.

Fixed rate perpetual preferred stock Nonconvertible, noncallable preferred stock that has a fixed dividend rate and no maturity date.

Fixed-income forward A forward contract in which the underlying is a bond.

Fixed-income investments Loans with contractually mandated payment schedules from firms or governments to investors.

Fixed-rule policy A rule that specifies an action to be pursued independently of the state of the economy.

Flat trend channel The range defined by security prices as they maintain a relatively steady level.

Flexible exchange rate system A system in which exchange rates are determined by supply and demand.

Flexible exchange rates Exchange rates that are determined by the market forces of supply and demand. They are sometimes called floating exchange rates.

Float In the context of customer receipts, the amount of money that is in transit between payments made by customers and the funds that are usable by the company.

Float factor An estimate of the average number of days it takes deposited checks to clear; average daily float divided by average daily deposit.

Floating-rate loan A loan in which the interest rate is reset at least once after the starting date.

Floor A combination of interest rate put options designed to hedge a lender against lower rates on a floating-rate loan.

Floor brokers Independent members of an exchange who act as brokers for other members.

Floor traders or locals Market makers that buy and sell by quoting a bid and an ask price. They are the primary providers of liquidity to the market.

Floored swap A swap in which the floating payments have a lower limit.

Floorlet Each component put option in a floor.

Flotation cost Fees charged to companies by investment bankers and other costs associated with raising new capital.

Flow A quantity per unit of time.

Foreign bond A bond issued by a foreign company on the local market and in the local currency (e.g., Yankee bonds in the United States, Bulldog bonds in the United Kingdom, or Samurai bonds in Japan).

Foreign exchange expectation A relation that states that the forward exchange rate, quoted at time 0 for delivery at time 1, is equal to the expected value of the spot exchange rate at time 1. When stated relative to the current spot exchange rate, the relation states that the forward discount (premium) is equal to the expected exchange rate movement.

Foreign exchange market The market in which the currency of one country is exchanged for the currency of another.

Foreign exchange rate The price at which one currency exchanges for another.

Forward contract An agreement between two parties in which one party, the buyer, agrees to buy from the other party, the seller, an underlying asset at a later date for a price established at the start of the contract.

Forward discount A situation where, from the perspective of the domestic country, the spot exchange rate is smaller than the forward exchange rate with a foreign country.

Forward P/E *See* Leading P/E.

Forward premium A situation where, from the perspective of the domestic country, the spot exchange rate is larger than the forward exchange rate with a foreign country.

Forward price or forward rate The fixed price or rate at which the transaction scheduled to occur at the expiration of a forward contract will take place. This price is agreed on at the initiation date of the contract.

Forward rate A short-term yield for a future holding period implied by the spot rates of two securities with different maturities.

Forward rate agreement (FRA) A forward contract calling for one party to make a fixed interest payment and the other to make an interest payment at a rate to be determined at the contract expiration.

Forward swap A forward contract to enter into a swap.

Four-firm concentration ratio A measure of market power that is calculated as the percentage of the value of sales accounted for by the four largest firms in an industry.

Franchise The right or license to an exclusive territory or market.

Franchise factor A firm's unique competitive advantage that makes it possible for a firm to earn excess returns (rates of return above a firm's cost of capital) on its capital projects. In turn, these excess returns and the franchise factor cause the firm's stock price to have a *P/E* ratio above its base *P/E* ratio that is equal to $1/k$.

Free cash flow The excess of operating cash flow over capital expenditures.

Free cash flow to equity The cash flow available to holders of the company's common equity after all operating expenses, interest, and principal payments have been paid and necessary investments in working capital and fixed capital have been made.

Free cash flow to the firm The cash flow available to the company's suppliers of capital after all operating expenses (including taxes) have been paid and necessary investments in working capital (e.g., inventory) and fixed capital (e.g., plant and equipment) have been made.

Free-rider problem The absence of an incentive for people to pay for what they consume.

Frequency distribution A tabular display of data summarized into a relatively small number of intervals.

Frequency polygon A graph of a frequency distribution obtained by drawing straight lines joining successive points representing the class frequencies.

Frictional unemployment The unemployment that arises from normal labor turnover-from people entering and leaving the labor force and from the ongoing creation and destruction of jobs.

Full employment A situation in which the quantity of labor demanded equal the quantity supplied. At full employment, there is no cyclical unemployment—all unemployment is frictional and structural.

Full price The price of a security including accrued interest.

Full-costing A method of accounting for the costs of exploring and developing oil and gas resources in which all costs are recorded as assets and depleted over the estimated life of the producing resources.

Full-costing method A method of accounting for the costs of exploring and developing oil and gas resources in which all costs are recorded as assets and depleted over the estimated life of the producing resources.

Fundamental beta A beta that is based at least in part on fundamental data for a company.

Fundamental factor models A multifactor model in which the factors are attributes of stocks or companies that are important in explaining cross-sectional differences in stock prices.

Future value (FV) The amount to which a payment or series of payments will grow by a stated future date.

Futures commission merchants (FCMs) Individuals or companies that execute futures transactions for other parties off the exchange.

Futures contract A variation of a forward contract that has essentially the same basic definition but with some additional features, such as a clearinghouse guarantee against credit losses, a daily settlement of gains and losses, and an organized electronic or floor trading facility.

Futures exchange A legal corporate entity whose shareholders are its members. The members of the exchange have the privilege of executing transactions directly on the exchange.

Gains Asset inflows not directly related to the ordinary activities of the business.

Game theory A tool that economists use to analyze strategic behavior—behavior that takes into account the expected behavior of others and the mutual recognition of independence.

Gamma A numerical measure of how sensitive an option's delta is to a change in the underlying.

GDP deflator One measure of the price level, which is the average of current-year prices as a percentage of base-year prices.

General Agreement on Tariffs and Trade An international agreement signed in 1947 to reduce tariffs on international trade.

Generalized least squares A regression estimation technique that addresses heteroskedasticity of the error term.

Generally accepted accounting principles (GAAP) Accounting principles formulated by the Financial Accounting Standards Board and used to construct financial statements.

Generational accounting An accounting system that measures the lifetime tax burden and benefits of each generation.

Generational imbalance The division of the fiscal imbalance between the current and future generations, assuming that the current generation will enjoy the existing levels of taxes and benefits

Generic *See* Plain-vanilla.

Geometric mean A measure of central tendency computed by taking the nth root of the product of n non-negative values.

Giro system An electronic payment system used widely in Europe and Japan.

Goods and services The objects that people value and produce to satisfy their wants.

Goodwill An intangible asset that represents the excess of the purchase price of an acquired company over the fair value of the net assets acquired.

Government budget deficit The deficit that arises when federal government spends more than it collects in taxes.

Government budget surplus The surplus that arises when the federal government collects more in taxes than it spends.

Government debt The total amount of borrowing that the government has borrowed. It equals the sum of past budget deficits minus budget surpluses.

Government purchases Goods and services bought by the government.

Government purchases multiplier The magnification effect of a change in government purchases of goods and services on aggregate demand.

Government sector surplus or deficit An amount equal to net taxes minus government purchases of goods and services.

Great Depression A decade (1929-1939) of high unemployment and stagnant production throughout the world economy.

Gross domestic product (GDP) The market value of all the final goods and services produced within a country during a given time period—usually a year.

Gross investment The total amount spent on purchases of new capital and on replacing depreciated capital.

Gross-Of-Fees Return The return on assets reduced by any trading expenses incurred during the period.

Gross profit (gross margin) Sales minus the cost of sales (i.e., the cost of goods sold for a manufacturing company).

Gross profit margin A profitability ratio calculated as gross profit divided by revenue; indicates how much of every dollar of revenues is left after the cost of goods sold.

Group depreciation The grouping of similar items to calculate depreciation.

Grouping by function With reference to the presentation of expenses in an income statement, the grouping together of expenses serving the same function, e.g. all items that are costs of good sold.

Grouping by nature With reference to the presentation of expenses in an income statement, the grouping together of expenses by similar nature, e.g., all depreciation expenses.

Growth company A company that consistently has the opportunities and ability to invest in projects that provide rates of return that exceed the firm's cost of capital. Because of these investment opportunities, it retains a high proportion of earnings, and its earnings grow faster than those of average firms.

Growth investors With reference to equity investors, investors who seek to invest in high-earnings-growth companies.

Growth option or expansion option The ability to make additional investments in a project at some future time if the financial results are strong.

Growth stock A stock issue that generates a higher rate of return than other stocks in the market with similar risk characteristics.

Harmonic mean A type of weighted mean computed by averaging the reciprocals of the observations, then taking the reciprocal of that average.

Hedge A trading strategy in which derivative securities are used to reduce or completely offset a counter-party's risk exposure to an underlying asset.

Hedge fund An investment vehicle designed to manage a private, unregistered portfolio of assets according to any of several strategies. The investment strategy often employs arbitrage trading and significant financial leverage (e.g., short selling, borrowing, derivatives) while the compensation arrangement for the manager typically specifies considerable profit participation.

Hedge ratio The relationship of the quantity of an asset being hedged to the quantity of the derivative used for hedging.

Hedging A general strategy usually thought of as reducing, if not eliminating, risk.

Held-for-trading securities (trading securities) Securities that a company intends to trade.

Held-to-maturity securities (Fixed-income) Securities that a company intends to hold to maturity; these are presented at their original cost, updated for any amortization of discounts or premiums.

Herfindahl-Hirschman Index A measure of market power that is calculated as the square of the market share of each firm (as a percentage) summed over the largest 50 firms (or over all firms if there are fewer than 50) in a market.

Heteroskedastic With reference to the error term of a regression, having a variance that differs across observations.

Heteroskedasticity The property of having a nonconstant variance; refers to an error term with the property that its variance differs across observations.

Heteroskedasticity-consistent standard errors Standard errors of the estimated parameters of a regression that correct for the presence of heteroskedasticity in the regression's error term.

High-yield bond A bond rated below investment grade. Also referred to as *speculative-grade bonds* or *junk bonds.*

Histogram A bar chart of data that have been grouped into a frequency distribution.

Historical cost In reference to assets, the amount paid to purchase an asset, including any costs of acquisition and/or preparation; with reference to liabilities, the amount of proceeds received in exchange in issuing the liability.

Historical equity risk premium approach An estimate of a country's equity risk premium that is based upon the historical averages of the risk-free rate and the rate of return on the market portfolio.

Historical method A method of estimating VAR that uses data from the returns of the portfolio over a recent past period and compiles this data in the form of a histogram.

Historical simulation (or back simulation) method Another term for the historical method of estimating VAR. This method involves not a *simulation* of the past but rather what *actually happened* in the past, sometimes adjusted to reflect the fact that a different portfolio may have existed in the past than is planned for the future.

Holding period return (HPR) The return that an investor earns during a specified holding period; a synonym for total return.

Holding period yield (HPY) The return that an investor earns during a specified holding period; holding period return with reference to a fixed-income instrument.

Homogenization Creating a contract with standard and generally accepted terms, which makes it more acceptable to a broader group of participants.

Homoskedasticity The property of having a constant variance; refers to an error term that is constant across observations.

Horizontal analysis Common-size analysis that involves comparing a specific financial statement with that statement in prior or future time periods; also, cross-sectional analysis of one company with another.

Horizontal common-size analysis An analysis in which financial statement accounts are compared to a benchmark in a different reporting period. Accounts in subsequent periods are restated as a percentage of the base period's value for the same account.

Human capital The value of skills and knowledge possessed by the workforce.

Hurdle rate The rate of return that must be met for a project to be accepted.

Hypothesis With reference to statistical inference, a statement about one or more populations.

Hypothesis testing With reference to statistical inference, the subdivision dealing with the testing of hypotheses about one or more populations.

Identifiable intangible An intangible that can be acquired singly and is typically linked to specific rights or privileges having finite benefit periods (e.g., a patent or trademark).

If-converted method A method for accounting for the effect of convertible securities on earnings per share (EPS) that specifies what EPS would have been if the convertible securities had been converted at the beginning of the period, taking account of the effects of conversion on net income and the weighted average number of shares outstanding.

Impairment Diminishment in value.

Implicit rental rate The firm's opportunity cost of using its own capital.

Implied repo rate The rate of return from a cash-and-carry transaction implied by the futures price relative to the spot price.

Implied volatility The volatility that option traders use to price an option, implied by the price of the option and a particular option-pricing model.

Implied yield A measure of the yield on the underlying bond of a futures contract implied by pricing it as though the underlying will be delivered at the futures expiration.

Imports The goods and services that we buy from people in other countries.

In the money An option that has positive intrinsic value.

Incentive A reward that encourages or a penalty that discourages an action.

Incentive system A method of organizing production that uses a market-like mechanism inside the firm.

Income Increases in economic benefits in the form of inflows or enhancements of assets, or decreases of liabilities that result in an increase in equity (other than increases resulting from contributions by owners).

Income effect The effect of a change in income on consumption, other things remaining the same.

Income elasticity of demand The responsiveness of demand to a change in income, other things remaining the same. It is calculated as the percentage change in the quantity demanded divided by the percentage change in income.

Income statement (statement of operations or profit and loss statement) A financial statement that provides information about a company's profitability over a stated period of time.

Income statement A financial statement that shows the flow of the firm's sales, expenses, and earnings over a period of time.

Incremental cash flows The changes or increments to cash flows resulting from a decision or action;

the cash flow with a decision minus the cash flow without that decision.

Indenture The legal agreement that lists the obligations of the issuer of a bond to the bondholder, including payment schedules, call provisions, and sinking funds.

Independent With reference to events, the property that the occurrence of one event does not affect the probability of another event occurring.

Independent and identically distributed (IID) With respect to random variables, the property of random variables that are independent of each other but follow the identical probability distribution.

Independent projects Independent projects are projects whose cash flows are independent of each other.

Independent variable A variable used to explain the dependent variable in a regression; a right-hand-side variable in a regression equation.

Index amortizing swap An interest rate swap in which the notional principal is indexed to the level of interest rates and declines with the level of interest rates according to a predefined scheduled. This type of swap is frequently used to hedge securities that are prepaid as interest rates decline, such as mortgage-backed securities.

Index option An option in which the underlying is a stock index.

Indexing An investment strategy in which an investor constructs a portfolio to mirror the performance of a specified index.

Indirect format (indirect method) With reference to cash flow statements, a format for the presentation of the statement which, in the operating cash flow section, begins with net income then shows additions and subtractions to arrive at operating cash flow.

Indirect method The procedure for converting the income statement from an accrual basis to a cash basis by adjusting net income for items that do not affect cash flows, including depreciation, amortization, depletion, gains, losses, and changes in current assets and current liabilities.

Individual transferable quota (ITQ) A production limit that is assigned to an individual who is free to transfer the quota to someone else.

Induced taxes Taxes that vary with real GDP.

Industry life cycle analysis An analysis that focuses on the industry's stage of development.

Inelastic demand A demand with a price elasticity between 0 and 1; the percentage change in the quantity demanded is less than the percentage change in price.

Infant-industry argument The argument that it is necessary to protect a new industry to enable it to grow into a mature industry that can compete in world markets.

Inferior good A good for which demand decreases as income increases.

Inflation A process in which the price level is rising and money is losing value.

Inflation premium An extra return that compensates investors for expected inflation.

Inflation rate The percentage change in the price level from one year to the next.

Inflationary gap The amount by which real GDP exceeds potential GDP.

Information An attribute of a good market that includes providing buyers and sellers with timely, accurate information on the volume and prices of past transactions and on all currently outstanding bids and offers.

Information ratio (IR) Mean active return divided by active risk.

Information ratio Statistic used to measure a portfolio's average return in excess of a comparison, benchmark portfolio divided by the standard deviation of this excess return.

Informationally efficient market A more technical term for an efficient capital market that emphasizes the role of information in setting the market price.

Initial margin requirement The margin requirement on the first day of a transaction as well as on any day in which additional margin funds must be deposited.

Initial public offering (IPO) A new issue by a firm that has no existing public market.

In-sample forecast errors The residuals from a fitted time-series model within the sample period used to fit the model.

Instability in the minimum-variance frontier The characteristic of minimum-variance frontiers that they are sensitive to small changes in inputs.

Installment Said of a sale in which proceeds are to be paid in installments over an extended period of time.

Installment method (installment-sales method) With respect to revenue recognition, a method that specifies that the portion of the total profit of the sale that is recognized in each period is determined by the percentage of the total sales price for which the seller has received cash.

Intangible asset An asset without physical substance.

Intellectual property rights Property rights for discoveries owned by the creators of knowledge.

Interest coverage A solvency ratio calculated as EBIT divided by interest payments.

Interest coverage ratio (or times-interest-earned ratio) Ratio of EBIT to interest payments; a comparison of the earnings available to meet interest obligations with existing interest obligations.

Interest rate A rate of return that reflects the relationship between differently dated cash flows; a discount rate.

Interest rate call An option in which the holder has the right to make a known interest payment and receive an unknown interest payment.

Interest rate cap or cap A series of call options on an interest rate, with each option expiring at the date on which the floating loan rate will be reset, and with each option having the same exercise rate. A cap in general can have an underlying other than an interest rate.

Interest rate collar A combination of a long cap and a short floor, or a short cap and a long floor. A collar in general can have an underlying other than an interest rate.

Interest rate floor or floor A series of put options on an interest rate, with each option expiring at the date on which the floating loan rate will be reset, and with each option having the same exercise rate. A floor in general can have an underlying other than the interest rate.

Interest rate forward (See *forward rate agreement*)

Interest rate option An option in which the underlying is an interest rate.

Interest rate parity A formula that expresses the equivalence or parity of spot and forward rates, after adjusting for differences in the interest rates.

Interest rate put An option in which the holder has the right to make an unknown interest payment and receive a known interest payment.

Interest rate risk The uncertainty of returns on an investment due to possible changes in interest rates over time.

Interest rate swap A swap in which the underlying is an interest rate. Can be viewed as a currency swap in which both currencies are the same and can be created as a combination of currency swaps.

Interest The income that capital earns.

Interest-on-interest Bond income from reinvestment of coupon payments.

Intergenerational data mining A form of data mining that applies information developed by previous researchers using a dataset to guide current research using the same or a related dataset.

Intermarket Trading System (ITS) A computerized system that connects competing exchanges and dealers who trade stocks listed on a U.S. exchange. Its purpose is to help customers find the best market for these stocks at a point in time.

Internal liquidity (solvency) ratios Financial ratios that measure the ability of the firm to meet future short-term financial obligations.

Internal rate of return (IRR) The discount rate that makes net present value equal 0; the discount rate that makes the present value of an investment's costs (outflows) equal to the present value of the investment's benefits (inflows).

Internal Rate of Return (Private Equity) (IRR) IRR is the annualized implied discount rate (effective compounded rate) that equates the present value of all the appropriate cash inflows (paid-in capital, such as drawdowns for net investments) associated with an investment with the sum of the present value of all the appropriate cash outflows (such as distributions) accruing from it and the present value of the unrealized residual portfolio (unliquidated holdings). For an interim cumulative return measurement, any IRR depends on the valuation of the residual assets.

Internal Valuation (Real Estate) An internal valuation is an advisor's or underlying third-party manager's best estimate of market value based on the most current and accurate information available under the circumstances. An internal valuation could include industry practice techniques, such as discounted cash flow, sales comparison, replacement cost, or a review of all significant events (both general market and asset specific) that could have a material impact on the investment. Prudent assumptions and estimates must be used, and the process must be applied consistently from period to period, except where a change would result in better estimates of market value.

International Fisher relation The assertion that the interest rate differential between two countries should equal the expected inflation rate differential over the term of the interest rates.

Interquartile range The difference between the third and first quartiles of a dataset.

Interval With reference to grouped data, a set of values within which an observation falls.

Interval scale A measurement scale that not only ranks data but also gives assurance that the differences between scale values are equal.

In-the-money option An option that, if exercised, would result in the value received being worth more than the payment required to exercise (apart from transaction costs).

Intrinsic value The portion of a call option's total value equal to the greater of either zero or the difference between the current value of the underlying asset and the exercise price; for a put option, intrinsic value is the greater of either zero or the exercise price less the underlying asset price. For a stock, it is the value derived from fundamental analysis of the stock's expected returns or cash flows.

Intrinsic value or exercise value The value obtained if an option is exercised based on current conditions.

Inventory The unsold units of product on hand.

Inventory blanket lien The use of inventory as collateral for a loan. Though the lender has claim to some or all of the company's inventory, the company may still sell or use the inventory in the ordinary course of business.

Inventory turnover An activity ratio calculated as cost of goods sold divided by average inventory; an indication of the resources tied up in inventory relative to the speed at which inventory is sold during the period.

Inverse floater A floating-rate note or bond in which the coupon is adjusted to move opposite to a benchmark interest rate.

Inverse relationship A relationship between variables that move in opposite directions.

Invested Capital (Private Equity) The amount of paid-in capital that has been invested in portfolio companies.

Investing activities Activities which are associated with the acquisition and disposal of property, plant, and equipment; intangible assets; other long-term assets; and both long-term and short-term investments in the equity and debt (bonds and loans) issued by other companies.

Investment The purchase of new plant, equipment, and buildings and additions to inventories.

Investment Advisor (Private Equity) Any individual or institution that supplies investment advice to clients on a per fee basis. The investment advisor inherently has no role in the management of the underlying portfolio companies of a partnership/fund.

Investment company A firm that sells shares of the company and uses the proceeds to buy portfolios of stock, bonds, or other financial instruments.

Investment decision process Estimation of intrinsic value for comparison with market price to determine whether or not to invest.

Investment demand The relationship between investment and real interest rate, other things remaining the same.

Investment horizon The time period used for planning and forecasting purposes or the future time at which the investor requires the invested funds.

Investment management company A company separate from the investment company that manages the portfolio and performs administrative functions.

Investment Management Fee The fee payable to the investment management firm for the on-going management of a portfolio. Investment management fees are typically asset based (percentage of assets), performance based (based on performance relative to a benchmark), or a combination of the two but may take different forms as well.

Investment Multiple (TVPI Multiple) (Private Equity) The ratio of total value to paid-in-capital. It represents the total return of the investment to the original investment not taking into consideration the time invested. Total value can be found by adding the residual value and distributed capital together.

Investment opportunity schedule A graphical depiction of a company's investment opportunities ordered from highest to lowest expected return. A company's optimal capital budget is found where the investment opportunity schedule intersects with the company's marginal cost of capital.

Investment strategy A decision by a portfolio manager regarding how he or she will manage the portfolio to meet the goals and objectives of the client. This will include either active or passive management and, if active, what style in terms of top-down or buttom-up or fundamental versus technical.

IRR The discount rate which forces the PV of a project's inflows to equal the PV of its costs.

IRR rule An investment decision rule that accepts projects or investments for which the IRR is greater than the opportunity cost of capital.

January effect A frequent empirical anomaly where risk-adjusted stock returns in the month of January are significantly larger than those occurring in any other month of the year.

Job search The activity of looking for acceptable vacant jobs.

Joint probability The probability of the joint occurrence of stated events.

Joint probability function A function giving the probability of joint occurrences of values of stated random variables.

Just-in-time method (JIT) Method of managing inventory that minimizes in-process inventory stocks.

Keynesian An economist who believes that left alone, the economy would rarely operate at full employment and that to achieve full employment, active help from fiscal policy and monetary policy is required.

***k*th Order autocorrelation** The correlation between observations in a time series separated by *k* periods.

Kurtosis The statistical measure that indicates the peakedness of a distribution.

Labor The work time and work effort that people devote to producing goods and services.

Labor force The sum of the people who are employed and who are unemployed.

Labor force participation rate The percentage of the working-age population who are members of the labor force.

Labor productivity Real GDP per hour of work.

Labor union An organized group of workers whose purpose is to increase wages and to influence other job conditions.

Laddering strategy A form of active strategy which entails scheduling maturities on a systematic basis within the investment portfolio such that investments are spread out equally over the term of the ladder.

Laffer curve The relationship between the tax rate and the amount of tax revenue collected.

Land The gifts of nature that we use to produce goods and services.

Law of demand Other things remaining the same, the higher the price of a good, the smaller is the quantity demanded of it.

Law of diminishing returns As a firm uses more of a variable input, with a given quantity of other inputs (fixed inputs), the marginal product of the variable input eventually diminishes.

Law of one price The condition in a financial market in which two financial instruments or combinations of financial instruments can sell for only one price. Equivalent to the principle that no arbitrage opportunities are possible.

Law of supply Other things remaining the same, the higher the price of a good, the greater is the quantity supplied of it.

Leading indicators A set of economic variables whose values reach peaks and troughs in advance of the aggregate economy.

Leading P/E (or forward P/E or prospective P/E) A stock's current price divided by the next year's expected earnings.

Learning-by-doing People become more productive in an activity (learn) just by repeatedly producing a particular good or service (doing).

Leasehold A right to occupy land or buildings under a long-term rental contract.

Leasehold improvements Improvements to leased property that become the property of the lessor at the end of the lease.

Legal monopoly A market structure in which there is one firm and entry is restricted by the granting of a public franchise, government license, patent, or copyright.

Legal risk The risk that the legal system will not enforce a contract in case of dispute or fraud.

Leptokurtic Describes a distribution that is more peaked than a normal distribution.

Level of significance The probability of a Type I error in testing a hypothesis.

Leveraged floating-rate note or leveraged floater A floating-rate note or bond in which the coupon is adjusted at a multiple of a benchmark interest rate.

Liabilities Present obligations of an enterprise arising from past events, the settlement of which is expected to result in an outflow of resources embodying economic benefits; creditors' claims on the resources of a company.

License The right to use a formula, technique, process, or design.

LIFO layer liquidation With respect to the application of the LIFO inventory method, the liquidation of old, relatively low-priced inventory; happens when the volume of sales rises above the volume of recent purchases so that some sales are made from relatively old, low-priced inventory.

LIFO method The last in, first out, method of accounting for inventory, which matches sales against the costs of items of inventory in the reverse order the items were placed in inventory (i.e., inventory produced or acquired last are assumed to be sold first).

Likelihood The probability of an observation, given a particular set of conditions.

Limit down A limit move in the futures market in which the price at which a transaction would be made is at or below the lower limit.

Limit move A condition in the futures markets in which the price at which a transaction would be made is at or beyond the price limits.

Limit order An order that lasts for a specified time to buy or sell a security when and if it trades at a specified price.

Limit pricing The practice of setting the price at the highest level that inflicts a loss on an entrant.

Limit up A limit move in the futures market in which the price at which a transaction would be made is at or above the upper limit.

Limited Partnership (Private Equity) The legal structure used by most venture and private equity funds. Usually fixed life investment vehicles. The general partner or management firm manages the partnership using the policy laid down in a partnership agreement. The agreement also covers terms, fees, structures, and other items agreed between the limited partners and the general partner.

Linear association A straight-line relationship, as opposed to a relationship that cannot be graphed as a straight line.

Linear interpolation The estimation of an unknown value on the basis of two known values that bracket it, using a straight line between the two known values.

Linear regression Regression that models the straight-line relationship between the dependent and independent variable(s).

Linear relationship A relationship between two variables that is illustrated by a straight line.

Linear trend A trend in which the dependent variable changes at a constant rate with time.

Liquid Term used to describe an asset that can be quickly converted to cash at a price close to fair market value.

Liquid assets Those company assets that are most readily converted to cash.

Liquidity In the context of financial analysis, a company's ability to satisfy its short-term obligations using assets that are most readily converted into cash.

Liquidity premium An extra return that compensates investors for the risk of loss relative to an investment's fair value if the investment needs to be converted to cash quickly.

Liquidity ratios Financial ratios measuring a company's ability to meet its short-term obligations.

Liquidity risk The risk that a financial instrument cannot be purchased or sold without a significant concession in price due to the size of the market.

Living wage An hourly wage rate that enables a person who works a 40-hour week to rent adequate housing for not more than 30 percent of the amount earned.

Lockbox system A payment system in which customer payments are mailed to a post office box and the banking institution retrieves and deposits these payments several times a day, enabling the company to have use of the fund sooner than in a centralized system in which customer payments are sent to the company.

Locked limit A condition in the futures markets in which a transaction cannot take place because the price would be beyond the limits.

Logit model A qualitative-dependent-variable multiple regression model based on the logistic probability distribution.

Log-linear model With reference to time-series models, a model in which the growth rate of the time series as a function of time is constant.

Log-log regression model A regression that expresses the dependent and independent variables as natural logarithms.

London Interbank Offer Rate (LIBOR) The Eurodollar rate at which London banks lend dollars to other London banks; considered to be the best representative rate on a dollar borrowed by a private, high-quality borrower.

Long The buyer of a derivative contract. Also refers to the position of owning a derivative.

Long position The buyer of a commodity or security or, for a forward contract, the counterparty who will be the eventual buyer of the underlying asset.

Long run A period of time in which the quantities of all resources can be varied.

Longitudinal data Observations on characteristic(s) of the same observational unit through time.

Long-lived assets Assets that are expected to provide economic benefits over a future period of time greater than one year.

Long-run aggregate supply curve The relationship between the real GDP supplied and the price level in the long run when real GDP equals potential GDP.

Long-run average cost curve The relationship between the lowest attainable average total cost and output when both capital and labor are varied.

Long-run industry supply curve A curve that shows how the quantity supplied by an industry varies as the market price varies after all the possible adjustments have been made, including changes in plant size and the number of firms in the industry.

Long-run macroeconomic equilibrium A situation that occurs when real GDP equals potential GDP-the economy is on its long-run aggregate supply curve.

Long-run Phillips curve Inflation rate equals the expected inflation rate.

Long-term assets Assets that have a useful life of more than one year, are used in the operation of a business, and are not intended for resale. Less commonly called *fixed assets*.

Long-term contract A contract that spans a number of accounting periods.

Long-term debt-to-assets ratio Ratio of long-term debt to total assets; the proportion of the company's assets that is financed with long-term debt.

Long-term equity anticipatory securities (LEAPS) Options originally created with expirations of several years.

Look-ahead bias A bias caused by using information that was unavailable on the test date.

Losses Asset outflows not directly related to the ordinary activities of the business.

Lower bound The lowest possible value of an option.

Lucas wedge The accumulated loss of output that results from a slowdown in the growth rate of real GDP per person.

M1 A measure of money that consists of currency and traveler's checks plus checking deposits owned by individuals and businesses.

M2 A measure of money that consists of M1 plus time deposits, savings deposits, and money market mutual funds and other deposits.

Macaulay duration The duration without dividing by 1 plus the bond's yield to maturity. The term, named for one of the economists who first derived it, is used to distinguish the calculation from modified duration. See also *modified duration.*

Macroeconomic factor A factor related to the economy, such as the inflation rate, industrial production, or economic sector membership.

Macroeconomic factor model A multifactor model in which the factors are surprises in macroeconomic variables that significantly explain equity returns.

Macroeconomic long run A time frame that is sufficiently long for real GDP to return to potential GDP so that full employment prevails.

Macroeconomic short run A period during which some money prices are sticky and real GDP might be below, above, or at potential GDP and unemployment might be above, below, or at the natural rate of unemployment.

Macroeconomics The study of the performance of the national economy and the global economy.

Maintenance margin The required proportion that the investor's equity value must be to the total market value of the stock. If the proportion drops below this percent, the investor will receive a margin call.

Maintenance margin requirement The margin requirement on any day other than the first day of a transaction.

Management fee The compensation an investment company pays to the investment management company for its services. The average annual fee is about 0.5 percent of fund assets.

Manufacturing resource planning (MRP) The incorporation of production planning into inventory management. A MRP analysis provides both a materials acquisition schedule and a production schedule.

Margin The amount of money that a trader deposits in a margin account. The term is derived from the stock market practice in which an investor borrows a portion of the money required to purchase a certain amount of stock. In futures markets, there is no borrowing so the margin is more of a down payment or performance bond.

Margin account The collateral posted with the futures exchange clearinghouse by an outside counterparty to insure its eventual performance; the *initial* margin is the deposit required at contract origination while the *maintenance* margin is the minimum collateral necessary at all times.

Margin call A request by an investor's broker for additional capital for a security bought on margin if the investor's equity value declines below the required maintenance margin.

Marginal benefit curve A curve that shows the relationship between the marginal benefit of a good and the quantity of that good consumed.

Marginal benefit The benefit that a person receives from consuming one more unit of a good or service. It is measured as the maximum amount that a person is willing to pay for one more unit of the good or service.

Marginal cost The opportunity cost of producing one more unit of a good or service. It is the best alternative forgone. It is calculated as the increase in total cost divided by the increase in output.

Marginal cost pricing rule A rule that sets the price of a good or service equal to the marginal cost of producing it.

Marginal probability *See* Unconditional probability.

Marginal product The increase in total product that results from a one-unit increase in the variable input, with all other inputs remaining the same. It is calculated as the increase in total product divided by the increase in the variable input employed, when the quantities of all other inputs are constant.

Marginal product of labor The additional real GDP produced by an additional hour of labor when all other influences on production remain the same.

Marginal propensity to consume The fraction of a change in disposable income that is consumed. It is calculated as the change in consumption expenditure divided by the change in disposable income.

Marginal revenue The change in total revenue that results from a one-unit increase in the quantity sold. It is calculated as the change in total revenue divided by the change in quantity sold.

Marginal revenue product The change in total revenue that results from employing one more unit of a resource (labor) while the quantity of all other resources remains the same. It is calculated as the increase in total revenue divided by the increase in the quantity of the resource (labor).

Marginal social benefit The marginal benefit enjoyed by society-by the consumer of a good or service (marginal private benefit) plus the marginal benefit enjoyed by others (marginal external benefit).

Marginal social cost The marginal cost incurred by the entire society-by the producer and by everyone else on whom the cost falls-and is the sum of marginal private cost and the marginal external cost.

Marginal tax rate The part of each additional dollar in income that is paid as tax.

Margins (or profit margin ratios and return-on-sales ratios) Ratios that are useful for evaluating a company's ability to manage its expenses to generate profits from its sales.

Marked to market The settlement process used to adjust the margin account of a futures contract for daily changes in the price of the underlying asset.

Market demand The relationship between the total quantity demanded of a good and its price. It is illustrated by the market demand curve.

Market failure A state in which the market does not allocate resources efficiently.

Market order An order to buy or sell a security immediately at the best price available.

Market portfolio The portfolio that includes all risky assets with relative weights equal to their proportional market values.

Market power The ability to influence the market, and in particular the market price, by influencing the total quantity offered for sale.

Market price of risk The slope of the capital market line, indicating the market risk premium for each unit of market risk.

Market risk premium The expected excess return on the market over the risk-free rate.

Market risk The risk associated with interest rates, exchange rates, and equity prices.

Market Value The current listed price at which investors buy or sell securities at a given time.

Market Value (Real Estate) The most probable price that a property should bring in a competitive and open market under all conditions requisite to a fair sale, the buyer and seller each acting prudently and knowledgeably, and assuming the price is not affected by undue stimulus. Implicit in this definition is the consummation of a sale as of a specified date and the passing of title from seller to buyer under conditions whereby: (a) Buyer and seller are typically motivated. (b) Both parties are well informed or well advised and each acting in what they consider their own best interests. (c) A reasonable time is allowed for exposure in the open market. (d) Payment is made in terms of currency or in terms of financial arrangements comparable thereto. (e) The price represents the normal consideration for the property sold unaffected by special or creative financing or sales concessions granted by anyone associated with the sale.

Market value added (MVA) External management performance measure to compare the market value of the company's debt and equity with the total capital invested in the firm.

Market-oriented investors With reference to equity investors, investors whose investment disciplines cannot be clearly categorized as value or growth.

Marking to market A procedure used primarily in futures markets in which the parties to a contract settle the amount owed daily. Also known as the *daily settlement.*

Markowitz decision rule A decision rule for choosing between two investments based on their means and variances.

Mark-to-market The revaluation of a financial asset or liability to its current market value or fair value.

Matching principle The accounting principle that expenses should be recognized when the associated revenue is recognized.

Matching strategy An active investment strategy that includes intentional matching of the timing of cash outflows with investment maturities.

Materiality The condition of being of sufficient importance so that omission or misstatement of the item in a financial report could make a difference to users' decisions.

Matrix pricing In the fixed income markets, to price a security on the basis of valuation-relevant characteristics (e.g. debt-rating approach).

Maturity premium An extra return that compensates investors for the increased sensitivity of the market value of debt to a change in market interest rates as maturity is extended.

McCallum rule A rule that adjusts the growth rate of the monetary base to target the inflation rate but also to take into account changes in the trend productivity growth rate and fluctuations in aggregate demand.

Mean The sum of all values in a distribution or dataset, divided by the number of values summed; a synonym of arithmetic mean.

Mean absolute deviation With reference to a sample, the mean of the absolute values of deviations from the sample mean.

Mean excess return The average rate of return in excess of the risk-free rate.

Mean reversion The tendency of a time series to fall when its level is above its mean and rise when its level is below its mean; a mean-reverting time series tends to return to its long-term mean.

Mean–variance analysis An approach to portfolio analysis using expected means, variances, and covariances of asset returns.

Means of payment A method of settling a debt.

Mean-variance analysis An approach to portfolio analysis using expected means, variances, and covariances of asset returns.

Measure of central tendency A quantitative measure that specifies where data are centered.

Measure of location A quantitative measure that describes the location or distribution of data; includes not only measures of central tendency but also other measures such as percentiles.

Measurement scales A scheme of measuring differences. The four types of measurement scales are nominal, ordinal, interval, and ratio.

Median The value of the middle item of a set of items that has been sorted into ascending or descending order; the 50th percentile.

Mesokurtic Describes a distribution with kurtosis identical to that of the normal distribution.

Microeconomics The study of the choices that individuals and businesses make, the way those choices interact, and the influence governments exert on them.

Minimum efficient scale The smallest quantity of output at which the long-run average cost curve reaches its lowest level.

Minimum wage A regulation that makes the hiring of labor below a specified wage rate illegal.

Minimum-variance frontier The graph of the set of portfolios that have minimum variance for their level of expected return.

Minimum-variance portfolio The portfolio with the minimum variance for each given level of expected return.

Minority interest The portion of consolidated subsidiaries' net assets not owned by the parent.

Mismatching strategy An active investment strategy whereby the timing of cash outflows is not matched with investment maturities.

Mixed factor models Factor models that combine features of more than one type of factor model.

Modal interval With reference to grouped data, the most frequently occurring interval.

Mode The most frequently occurring value in a set of observations.

Model risk The use of an inaccurate pricing model for a particular investment, or the improper use of the right model.

Model specification With reference to regression, the set of variables included in the regression and the regression equation's functional form.

Modified duration A measure of a bond's price sensitivity to interest rate movements. Equal to the Macaulay duration of a bond divided by one plus its yield to maturity.

Monetarist An economist who believes that the economy is self regulating and that it will normally operate at full employment, provided that monetary policy is not erratic and that the pace of money growth is kept steady.

Monetary base The sum of the Federal Reserve notes, coins, and banks' deposits at the Fed.

Monetary policy The Fed conducts the nation's monetary policy by changing interest rates and adjusting the quantity of money.

Money Any commodity or token that is generally acceptable as a means of payment.

Money market fund A fund that invests in short-term securities sold in the money market. (Large companies, banks, and other institutions also invest their surplus cash in the money market for short periods of time.) In the entire investment spectrum, these are generally the safest, most stable securities available. They include Treasury bills, certificates of deposit of large banks, and commercial paper (short-term IOUs of large corporations).

Money market mutual fund A fund operated by a financial institution that sells shares in the fund and holds liquid assets such as U.S. Treasury bills and short-term commercial bills.

Money market yield (or CD equivalent yield) A yield on a basis comparable to the quoted yield on an interest-bearing money market instrument that pays interest on a 360-day basis; the annualized holding period yield, assuming a 360-day year.

Money market The market for short-term debt instruments (one-year maturity or less).

Money multiplier The amount by which a change in the monetary base is multiplied to determine the resulting change in the quantity of money.

Money price The number of dollars that must be given up in exchange for a good or service.

Money wage rate The number of dollars that an hour of labor earns.

Moneyness The relationship between the price of the underlying and an option's exercise price.

Money-weighted rate of return The internal rate of return on a portfolio, taking account of all cash flows.

Monopolistic competition A market structure in which a large number of firms compete by making similar but slightly different products.

Monopoly A market structure in which there is one firm, which produces a good or service that has no close substitute and in which the firm is protected from competition by a barrier preventing the entry of new firms.

Monte Carlo simulation A risk analysis technique in which probable future events are simulated on a computer, generating estimated rates of return and risk indexes.

Monte Carlo simulation method An approach to estimating VAR that produces random outcomes to examine what might happen if a particular risk is faced. This method is widely used in the sciences as well as in business to study a variety of problems.

Mortgage bonds Bonds that pledge specific assets such as buildings and equipment. The proceeds from the sale of these assets are used to pay off bondholders in case of bankruptcy.

Moving average The continually recalculating average of security prices for a period, often 200 days, to serve as an indication of the general trend of prices and also as a benchmark price.

Multicollinearity A regression assumption violation that occurs when two or more independent variables (or combinations of independent variables) are highly but not perfectly correlated with each other.

Multifactor model An empirical version of the APT where the investor chooses the exact number and identity of the common risk factors used to describe an asset's risk-return relationship. Risk factors are often designated as *macroeconomic* variables (e.g., inflation, changes in gross domestic product) or *microeconomic* variables (e.g., security-specific characteristics like firm size or book-to-market ratios).

Multiple linear regression Linear regression involving two or more independent variables.

Multiple linear regression model A linear regression model with two or more independent variables.

Multiple *R* The correlation between the actual and forecasted values of the dependent variable in a regression.

Multiplication rule for probabilities The rule that the joint probability of events A and B equals the probability of A given B times the probability of B.

Multiplier The amount by which a change in autonomous expenditure is magnified or multiplied to determine the change in equilibrium expenditure and real GDP.

Multi-step format With respect to the format of the income statement, a format that presents a subtotal for gross profit (revenue minus cost of goods sold).

Multivariate distribution A probability distribution that specifies the probabilities for a group of related random variables.

Multivariate normal distribution A probability distribution for a group of random variables that is completely defined by the means and variances of the variables plus all the correlations between pairs of the variables.

Must A required provision for claiming compliance with the GIPS standards.

Mutual fund An investment company that pools money from shareholders and invests in a variety of securities, including stocks, bonds, and money market securities. A mutual fund ordinarily stands ready to buy back (redeem) its shares at their current net asset value, which depends on the market value of the fund's portfolio of securities at the time. Mutual funds generally continuously offer new shares to investors.

Mutually exclusive events Events such that only one can occur at a time.

Mutually exclusive projects Mutually exclusive projects compete directly with each other. For example, if Projects A and B are mutually exclusive, you can choose A or B, but you cannot choose both.

***n* Factorial** For a positive integer n, the product of the first n positive integers; 0 factorial equals 1 by definition. n factorial is written as $n!$.

Nasdaq InterMarket A trading system that includes Nasdaq market makers and ECNs that quote and trade stocks listed on the NYSE and the AMEX. It involves dealers from the Nasdaq market and the Intermarket Trading System (ITS). In many ways, this has become what had been labeled the third market.

Nash equilibrium The outcome of a game that occurs when player A takes the best possible action given the action of player B and player B takes the best possible action given the action of player A.

National saving The sum of private saving (saving by households and businesses) and government saving.

Natural monopoly A monopoly that occurs when one firm can supply the entire market at a lower price than two or more firms can.

Natural rate of unemployment The unemployment rate when the economy is at full employment. There is no cyclical unemployment; all unemployment is frictional and structural.

Natural resources Long-term assets purchased for the economic value that can be taken from the land and used up.

Near-term, high-priority goal A short-term financial investment goal of personal importance, such as accumulating funds for making a house down payment or buying a car.

Needs-tested spending Government spending on programs that pay benefits to suitably qualified people and businesses.

Negative relationship A relationship between variables that move in opposite directions.

Negative serial correlation Serial correlation in which a positive error for one observation increases the chance of a negative error for another observation, and vice versa.

Negotiated sales An underwriting arrangement wherein the sale of a security issue by an issuing entity (governmental body or a corporation) is done using an investment banking firm that maintains an ongoing relationship with the issuer. The characteristics of the security issue are determined by the issuer in consultation with the investment banker.

Neoclassical growth theory A theory of economic growth that proposes that real GDP grows because technological change induces a level of saving and investment that makes capital per hour of labor grow.

Net asset value The market value of the assets owned by a fund.

Net book value The remaining (undepreciated) balance of an asset's purchase cost.

Net borrower A country that is borrowing more from the rest of the world than it is lending to it.

Net exports The value of exports minus the value of imports.

Net income (loss) The difference between revenue and expenses; what remains after subtracting all expenses (including depreciation, interest, and taxes) from revenue.

Net investment Net increase in the capital stock–gross investment minus depreciation.

Net lender A country that is lending more to the rest of the world than it is borrowing from it.

Net operating cycle (or cash conversion cycle) An estimate of the average time that elapses between paying suppliers for materials and collecting cash from the subsequent sale of goods produced.

Net present value (NPV) The present value of an investment's cash inflows (benefits) minus the present value of its cash outflows (costs).

Net profit margin (profit margin or return on sales) An indicator of profitability, calculated as net income divided by revenue; indicates how much of each dollar of revenues is left after all costs and expenses.

Net revenue Revenue after adjustments (e.g., for estimated returns or for amounts unlikely to be collected).

Net taxes Taxes paid to governments minus transfer payments received from governments.

Net-of-Fees Return The gross-of-fees return reduced by the investment management fee.

Netting When parties agree to exchange only the net amount owed from one party to the other.

New issue Common stocks or bonds offered by companies for public sale.

New Keynesian A Keynesian who holds the view that not only is the money wage rate sticky but that prices of goods and services are also sticky.

Node Each value on a binomial tree from which successive moves or outcomes branch.

No-load fund A mutual fund that sells its shares at net asset value without adding sales charges.

Nominal GDP The value of the final goods and services produced in a given year valued at the prices that prevailed in that same year. It is a more precise name for GDP.

Nominal rate Rate of interest based on the security's face value.

Nominal risk-free interest rate The sum of the real risk-free interest rate and the inflation premium.

Nominal scale A measurement scale that categorizes data but does not rank them.

Nominal yield A bond's yield as measured by its coupon rate.

Noncash investing and financing transactions Significant investing and financing transactions involving only long-term assets, long-term liabilities, or stockholders' equity that do not affect current cash inflows or outflows.

Nonconventional cash flow In a nonconventional cash flow pattern, the initial outflow is not followed by inflows only, but the cash flows can flip from positive (inflows) to negative (outflows) again (or even change signs several times).

Noncurrent Not due to be consumed, converted into cash, or settled within one year after the balance sheet date.

Noncurrent assets Assets that are expected to benefit the company over an extended period of time (usually more than one year).

Nondeliverable forwards (NDFs) Cash-settled forward contracts, used predominately with respect to foreign exchange forwards.

Nonlinear relation An association or relationship between variables that cannot be graphed as a straight line.

Nonparametric test A test that is not concerned with a parameter, or that makes minimal assumptions about the population from which a sample comes.

Nonrenewable natural resources Natural resources that can be used only once and that cannot be replaced once they have been used.

Nonstationarity With reference to a random variable, the property of having characteristics such as mean and variance that are not constant through time.

Nontariff barrier Any action other than a tariff that restricts international trade.

Normal backwardation The condition in futures markets in which futures prices are lower than expected spot prices.

Normal contango The condition in futures markets in which futures prices are higher than expected spot prices.

Normal distribution A continuous, symmetric probability distribution that is completely described by its mean and its variance.

Normal good A good for which demand increases as income increases.

Normal profit The expected return for supplying entrepreneurial ability.

North American Free Trade Agreement An agreement, which became effective on January 1, 1994, to eliminate all barriers to international trade between the United States, Canada, and Mexico after a 15-year phasing in period.

Notes Intermediate-term debt securities with maturities longer than 1 year but less than 10 years.

Notes payable Amounts owed by a business to creditors as a result of borrowings that are evidenced by (short-term) loan agreements.

Notional principal The principal value of a swap transaction, which is not exchanged but is used as a scale factor to translate interest rate differentials into cash settlement payments.

***n*-Period moving average** The average of the current and immediately prior $n - 1$ values of a time series.

NPV rule An investment decision rule that states that an investment should be undertaken if its NPV is positive but not undertaken if its NPV is negative.

Null hypothesis The hypothesis to be tested.

Number of days of inventory Ratio of the amount of inventory on hand to the average day's cost of goods sold; an indication of the number of days a company ties up funds in inventory.

Number of days of payables An activity ratio equal to the number of days in a period divided by the payables turnover ratio for the period; an estimate of the average number of days it takes a company to pay its suppliers.

Number of days of receivables Ratio of accounts receivable to average day's revenue; an indication of the length of time between a sale (i.e. an account receivable is created) and the collection of the account receivable in cash.

Objective probabilities Probabilities that generally do not vary from person to person; includes a priori and objective probabilities.

Objectives The investor's goals expressed in terms of risk and return and included in the policy statement.

Obsolescence The process of becoming out of date, which is a factor in the limited useful life of tangible assets.

Offensive competitive strategy A strategy whereby a firm attempts to use its strengths to affect the competitive forces in the industry and, in so doing, improves the firm's relative position in the industry.

Official reserves The amount of reserves owned by the central bank of a government in the form of gold, Special Drawing Rights, and foreign cash or marketable securities.

Official settlements account A record of the change in a country's official reserves.

Off-market FRA A contract in which the initial value is intentionally set at a value other than zero and therefore requires a cash payment at the start from one party to the other.

Offsetting A transaction in exchange-listed derivative markets in which a party re-enters the market to close out a position.

Okun gap The gap between real GDP and potential GDP, and so is another name for the output gap.

Oligopoly A market structure in which a small number of firms compete.

One-sided hypothesis test (or one-tailed hypothesis test) A test in which the null hypothesis is rejected only if the evidence indicates that the population parameter is greater than (smaller than) θ_0. The alternative hypothesis also has one side.

Open market operation The purchase or sale of government securities—U.S. Treasury bills and bonds—by the Federal Reserve System in the open market.

Open-End Fund (Private Equity) A type of investment fund where the number of investors and the total committed capital is not fixed (i.e., open for subscriptions and/or redemptions).

Operating activities Activities that are part of the day-to-day business functioning of an entity, such as selling inventory and providing services.

Operating cycle An estimate of the average time needed for a company to convert raw materials into cash from a sale.

Operating efficiency ratios Financial ratios intended to indicate how efficiently management is utilizing the firm's assets in terms of dollar sales generated per dollar of assets. Primary examples would be: total asset turnover, fixed asset turnover, or equity turnover.

Operating leverage The use of fixed costs in operations.

Operating profit (operating income) A company's profits on its usual business activities before deducting taxes.

Operating profit margin A profitability ratio calculated as operating income divided by revenue; indicates how much of each dollar of revenues is left after both cost of goods sold and operating expenses are considered.

Operating profitability ratios Financial ratios intended to indicate how profitable the firm is in terms of the percent of profit generated from sales. Alternative measures would include: operating profit (EBIT)/net sales; pretax profit (EBT)/ net sales; and net profit/sales.

Operating return on assets A profitability ratio calculated as operating income divided by average total assets; a measure of the operating income resulting from the company's investment in total assets.

Operating risk Risk that is attributable to a company's operating cost structure.

Operations risk or operational risk The risk of loss from failures in a company's systems and procedures (for example, due to computer failures or human failures) or events completely outside of the control of organizations (which would include "acts of God" and terrorist actions).

Opportunity cost The value that investors forgo by choosing a particular course of action; the value of something in its best alternative use.

Opportunity set The set of assets available for investment.

Optimal portfolio The portfolio on the efficient frontier that has the highest utility for a given investor. It lies at the point of tangency between the efficient frontier and the curve with the investor's highest possible utility.

Optimizer A specialized computer program or a spreadsheet that solves for the portfolio weights that will result in the lowest risk for a specified level of expected return.

Option A financial instrument that gives one party the right, but not the obligation, to buy or sell an underlying asset from or to another party at a fixed price over a specific period of time. Also referred to as contingent claims.

Option contract An agreement that grants the owner the right, but not the obligation, to make a future transaction in an underlying commodity or security at a fixed price and within a predetermined time in the future.

Option premium The initial price that the option buyer must pay to the option seller to acquire the contract.

Option price, option premium, or premium The amount of money a buyer pays and seller receives to engage in an option transaction.

Option-adjusted spread A type of yield spread that considers changes in the term structure and alternative estimates of the volatility of interest rates.

Ordinal scale A measurement scale that sorts data into categories that are ordered (ranked) with respect to some characteristic.

Ordinary annuity An annuity with a first cash flow that is paid one period from the present.

Ordinary least squares (OLS) An estimation method based on the criterion of minimizing the sum of the squared residuals of a regression.

Ordinary shares (common stock or common shares) Equity shares that are subordinate to all other types of equity (e.g., preferred equity).

Orthogonal Uncorrelated; at a right angle.

OTC Electronic Bulletin Board (OTCBB) A regulated quotation service that displays real-time quotes, last-sale prices, and volume information for a specified set of over-the-counter (OTC) securities that are not traded on the formal Nasdaq market.

Other comprehensive income Items of comprehensive income that are not reported on the income statement; comprehensive income minus net income.

Other receivables Amounts owed to the company from parties other than customers.

Outcome A possible value of a random variable.

Outliers Small numbers of observations at either extreme (small or large) of a sample.

Out-of-sample forecast errors The differences between actual and predicted value of time series outside the sample period used to fit the model.

Out-of-sample test A test of a strategy or model using a sample outside the time period on which the strategy or model was developed.

Out-of-the-money Options that, if exercised, would require the payment of more money than the value received and therefore would not be currently exercised.

Out-of-the-money option (1) An option that has no value if exercised immediately. For example, a call when the strike price is above the current price of the underlying asset, or a put when the strike price is below the current price of the underlying asset. (2) An option that has no intrinsic value. (3) Options that, if exercised, would require the payment of more money than the value received and therefore would not be currently exercised.

Overnight index swap (OIS) A swap in which the floating rate is the cumulative value of a single unit of currency invested at an overnight rate during the settlement period.

Overweighted A condition in which a portfolio, for whatever reason, includes more of a class of securities than the relative market value alone would justify.

Owners' equity The excess of assets over liabilities; the residual interest of shareholders in the assets of an entity after deducting the entity's liabilities.

Paid-In Capital (Private Equity) The amount of committed capital a limited partner has actually transferred to a venture fund. Also known as the cumulative drawdown amount.

Paired comparisons test A statistical test for differences based on paired observations drawn from samples that are dependent on each other.

Paired observations Observations that are dependent on each other.

Pairs arbitrage trade A trade in two closely related stocks involving the short sale of one and the purchase of the other.

Panel data Observations through time on a single characteristic of multiple observational units.

Par value *See* Principal. The principal amount repaid at maturity of a bond. Also called face value.

Parameter A descriptive measure computed from or used to describe a population of data, conventionally represented by Greek letters.

Parameter instability The problem or issue of population regression parameters that have changed over time.

Parametric test Any test (or procedure) concerned with parameters or whose validity depends on assumptions concerning the population generating the sample.

Partial regression coefficients or partial slope coefficients The slope coefficients in a multiple regression.

Passive strategy In reference to short-term cash management, it is an investment strategy characterized by simple decision rules for making daily investments.

Patent A government-sanctioned exclusive right granted to the inventor of a good, service, or productive process to produce, use, and sell the invention for a given number of years.

Payables turnover An activity ratio calculated as purchases divided by average trade payables.

Payback The time required for the added income from the convertible security relative to the stock to offset the conversion premium.

Payer swaption A swaption that allows the holder to enter into a swap as the fixed-rate payer and floating-rate receiver.

Payment date The date on which a firm actually mails dividend checks.

Payment netting A means of settling payments in which the amount owed by the first party to the second is netted with the amount owed by the second party to the first; only the net difference is paid.

Payoff The value of an option at expiration.

Payoff matrix A table that shows the payoffs for every possible action by each player for every possible action by each other player.

Pegged exchange rate regime A system in which a country's exchange rate in relation to a major currency is set at a target value (the peg) but allowed to fluctuate within a small band around the target.

Percentage-of-completion A method of revenue recognition in which, in each accounting period, the company estimates what percentage of the contract is complete and then reports that percentage of the total contract revenue in its income statement.

Percentiles Quantiles that divide a distribution into 100 equal parts.

Perfect collinearity The existence of an exact linear relation between two or more independent variables or combinations of independent variables.

Perfect competition A market in which there are many firms each selling an identical product; there are many buyers; there are no restrictions on entry into the industry; firms in the industry have no advantage over potential new entrants; and firms and buyers are well informed about the price of each firm's product.

Perfect price discrimination Price discrimination that extracts the entire consumer surplus.

Perfectly elastic demand Demand with an infinite price elasticity; the quantity demanded changes by an infinitely large percentage in response to a tiny price change.

Perfectly inelastic demand Demand with a price elasticity of zero; the quantity demanded remains constant when the price changes.

Performance appraisal The evaluation of risk-adjusted performance; the evaluation of investment skill.

Performance guarantee A guarantee from the clearinghouse that if one party makes money on a transaction, the clearinghouse ensures it will be paid.

Performance measurement The calculation of returns in a logical and consistent manner.

Period costs Costs (e.g., executives' salaries) that cannot be directly matched with the timing of revenues and which are thus expensed immediately.

Periodic rate The quoted interest rate per period; the stated annual interest rate divided by the number of compounding periods per year.

Permutation An ordered listing.

Perpetuity A perpetual annuity, or a set of never-ending level sequential cash flows, with the first cash flow occurring one period from now.

Personal trust An amount of money set aside by a grantor and often managed by a third party, the trustee. Often constructed so one party receives income from the trust's investments and another party receives the residual value of the trust after the income beneficiaries' death.

Pet projects Projects in which influential managers want the corporation to invest. Often, unfortunately, pet projects are selected without undergoing normal capital budgeting analysis.

Phillips curve A curve that shows a relationship between inflation and unemployment.

Physical deterioration A decline in the useful life of a depreciable asset resulting from use and from exposure to the elements.

Plain-vanilla Refers to a security, especially a bond or a swap, issued with standard features. Sometimes called generic.

Plain vanilla swap An interest rate swap in which one party pays a fixed rate and the other pays a floating rate, with both sets of payments in the same currency.

Platykurtic Describes a distribution that is less peaked than the normal distribution.

Plowback ratio An indication of the proportion of earnings that are reinvested in the company rather than paid out as dividends; calculated as 1 − dividend payout ratio.

Point estimate A single numerical estimate of an unknown quantity, such as a population parameter.

Point of sale Systems that capture transaction data at the physical location in which the sale is made.

Policy statement A statement in which the investor specifies investment goals, constraints, and risk preferences.

Pooled estimate An estimate of a parameter that involves combining (pooling) observations from two or more samples.

Population All members of a specified group.

Population mean The arithmetic mean value of a population; the arithmetic mean of all the observations or values in the population.

Population standard deviation A measure of dispersion relating to a population in the same unit of measurement as the observations, calculated as the positive square root of the population variance.

Population variance A measure of dispersion relating to a population, calculated as the mean of the squared deviations around the population mean.

Portfolio An individually managed pool of assets. A portfolio may be a subportfolio, account, or pooled fund.

Portfolio performance attribution The analysis of portfolio performance in terms of the contributions from various sources of risk.

Portfolio possibilities curve A graphical representation of the expected return and risk of all portfolios that can be formed using two assets.

Position trader A trader who typically holds positions open overnight.

Positive relationship A relationship between two variables that move in the same direction.

Positive serial correlation Serial correlation in which a positive error for one observation increases the chance of a positive error for another observation, and a negative error for one observation increases the chance of a negative error for another observation.

Posterior probability An updated probability that reflects or comes after new information.

Potential credit risk The risk associated with the possibility that a payment due at a later date will not be made.

Potential GDP The quantity of real GDP at full employment.

Poverty A situation in which a household's income is too low to be able to buy the quantities of food, shelter, and clothing that are deemed necessary.

Power of a test The probability of correctly rejecting the null-that is, rejecting the null hypothesis when it is false.

Precautionary stocks A level of inventory beyond anticipated needs that provides a cushion in the event that it takes longer to replenish inventory than expected or in the case of greater than expected demand.

Predatory pricing Setting a low price to drive competitors out of business with the intention of setting a monopoly price when the competition has gone.

Preferences A description of a person's likes and dislikes.

Preferred stock An equity investment that stipulates the dividend payment either as a coupon or a stated dollar amount. The firm's directors may withhold payments.

Pre-investing The strategy of using futures contracts to enter the market without an immediate outlay of cash.

Premium A bond selling at a price above par value due to capital market conditions.

Prepaid expense A normal operating expense that has been paid in advance of when it is due.

Present (price) value of a basis point (PVBP) The change in the bond price for a 1 basis point change in yield. Also called *basis point value* (BPV).

Present value The amount of money that, if invested today, will grow to be as large as a given future amount when the interest that it will earn is taken into account.

Present value (PV) The present discounted value of future cash flows: for assets, the present discounted value of the future net cash inflows that the asset is expected to generate; for liabilities, the present discounted value of the future net cash outflows that are expected to be required to settle the liabilities.

Pretax profit margin A profitability ratio calculated as earnings before taxes divided by revenue; useful for isolating the effects of taxes on a company's profitability.

Price ceiling A regulation that makes it illegal to charge a price higher than a specified level.

Price continuity A feature of a liquid market in which there are small price changes from one transaction to the next due to the depth of the market.

Price discovery A feature of futures markets in which futures prices provide valuable information about the price of the underlying asset.

Price discrimination The practice of selling different units of a good or service for different prices or of charging one customer different prices for different quantities bought.

Price effect The effect of a change in the price on the quantity of a good consumed, other things remaining the same.

Price elasticity of demand A units-free measure of the responsiveness of the quantity demanded of a good to a change in its price, when all other influences on buyers' plans remain the same.

Price floor A regulation that makes it illegal to charge a price lower than a specified level.

Price level The average level of prices as measured by a price index.

Price limits Limits imposed by a futures exchange on the price change that can occur from one day to the next.

Price momentum A portfolio strategy in which you acquire stocks that have enjoyed above-market stock price increases.

Price multiple The ratio of a stock's market price to some measure of value per share.

Price relative A ratio of an ending price over a beginning price; it is equal to 1 plus the holding period return on the asset.

Price risk The component of interest rate risk due to the uncertainty of the market price of a bond caused by changes in market interest rates.

Price taker A firm that cannot influence the price of the good or service it produces.

Price to book value A valuation ratio calculated as price per share divided by book value per share.

Price to cash flow A valuation ratio calculated as price per share divided by cash flow per share.

Price to sales A valuation ratio calculated as price per share divided by sales per share.

Price/earnings (P/E) ratio The number by which expected earnings per share is multiplied to estimate a stock's value; also called the *earnings multiplier.*

Priced risk Risk for which investors demand compensation for bearing (e.g. equity risk, company-specific factors, macroeconomic factors).

Price-setting option The operational flexibility to adjust prices when demand varies from forecast. For example, when demand exceeds capacity, the company could benefit from the excess demand by increasing prices.

Price-weighted index An index calculated as an arithmetic mean of the current prices of the sampled securities.

Primary market The market in which newly issued securities are sold by their issuers, who receive the proceeds

Principal The amount of funds originally invested in a project or instrument; the face value to be paid at maturity.

Principal-agent problem The problem of devising compensation rules that induce an agent to act in the best interest of a principal.

Prior probabilities Probabilities reflecting beliefs prior to the arrival of new information.

Private Equity Private equity includes, but is not limited to, organizations devoted to venture capital, leveraged buyouts, consolidations, mezzanine and distressed debt investments, and a variety of hybrids, such as venture leasing and venture factoring.

Private information Information that is available to one person but is too costly for anyone else to obtain.

Private placement A new issue sold directly to a small group of investors, usually institutions

Private sector surplus or deficit An amount equal to saving minus investment.

Probability A number between 0 and 1 describing the chance that a stated event will occur.

Probability density function A function with non-negative values such that probability can be described by areas under the curve graphing the function.

Probability distribution A distribution that specifies the probabilities of a random variable's possible outcomes.

Probability function A function that specifies the probability that the random variable takes on a specific value.

Probit model A qualitative-dependent-variable multiple regression model based on the normal distribution.

Producer surplus The price of a good minus the opportunity cost of producing it, summed over the quantity sold.

Product differentiation Making a product slightly different from the product of a competing firm.

Production efficiency A situation in which the economy cannot produce more of one good without producing less of some other good.

Production-flexibility The operational flexibility to alter production when demand varies from forecast. For example, if demand is strong, a company may profit from employees working overtime or from adding additional shifts.

Production function The relationship between real GDP and the quantity of labor when all other influences on production remain the same.

Production method A method of depreciation that assumes depreciation is solely the result of use and that allocates depreciation based on the units of use or output during each period of an asset's useful life.

Production possibilities frontier The boundary between the combinations of goods and services that can be produced and the combinations that cannot.

Production quota An upper limit to the quantity of a good that may be produced in a specified period.

Productivity growth slowdown A slowdown in the growth rate of output per person.

Profit The income earned by entrepreneurship.

Profitability ratios Ratios that measure a company's ability to generate profitable sales from its resources (assets).

Project sequencing To defer the decision to invest in a future project until the outcome of some or all of a current project is known. Projects are sequenced through time, so that investing in a project creates the option to invest in future projects.

Property rights Social arrangements that govern the ownership, use, and disposal of resources or factors of production, goods, and services that are enforceable in the courts.

Prospective P/E *See* Leading P/E.

Protective put An option strategy in which a long position in an asset is combined with a long position in a put.

Provision In accounting, a liability of uncertain timing or amount.

Pseudo-random numbers Numbers produced by random number generators.

Public good A good or service that is both nonrival and nonexcludable—it can be consumed simultaneously by everyone and from which no one can be excluded.

Pull on liquidity When disbursements are paid too quickly or trade credit availability is limited, requiring companies to expend funds before they receive funds from sales that could cover the liability.

Purchasing power parity The equal value of different monies.

Purchasing power parity (PPP) A theory stating that the exchange rate between two currencies will exactly reflect the purchasing power of the two currencies.

Pure discount instruments Instruments that pay interest as the difference between the amount borrowed and the amount paid back.

Pure factor portfolio A portfolio with sensitivity of 1 to the factor in question and a sensitivity of 0 to all other factors.

Pure-play method A method for estimating the beta for a company or project; it requires using a comparable company's beta and adjusting it for financial leverage differences.

Put An option that gives the holder the right to sell an underlying asset to another party at a fixed price over a specific period of time.

Put-call parity An equation expressing the equivalence (parity) of a portfolio of a call and a bond with a portfolio of a put and the underlying, which leads to the relationship between put and call prices

Put-call-forward parity The relationship among puts, calls, and forward contracts.

Put option A contract giving the right to sell an asset at a specified price, on or before a specified date.

***p*-Value** The smallest level of significance at which the null hypothesis can be rejected; also called the marginal significance level.

Qualitative dependent variables Dummy variables used as dependent variables rather than as independent variables.

Quality financial statements Financial statements that most knowledgeable observers (analysts, portfolio managers) would consider conservatively prepared in terms of sales, expenses, earnings, and asset valuations. The results reported would reflect reasonable estimates and indicate what truly happened during the period and the legitimate value of assets and liabilities on the balance sheet.

Quantile (or fractile) A value at or below which a stated fraction of the data lies.

Quantity demanded The amount of a good or service that consumers plan to buy during a given time period at a particular price.

Quantity of labor demanded The labor hours hired by the firms in the economy.

Quantity of labor supplied The number of labor hours that all households in the economy plan to work.

Quantity supplied The amount of a good or service that producers plan to sell during a given time period at a particular price.

Quantity theory of money The proposition that in the long run, an increase in the quantity of money brings an equal percentage increase in the price level.

Quartiles Quantiles that divide a distribution into four equal parts.

Quick assets Assets that can be most readily converted to cash (e.g., cash, short-term marketable investments, receivables).

Quick ratio (or acid test ratio) A liquidity ratio calculated as quick assets (cash + short-term marketable investments + receivables) divided by current liabilities; provides an indication of a company's ability to satisfy current liabilities with its most liquid assets.

Quintiles Quantiles that divide a distribution into five equal parts.

Quota A quantitative restriction on the import of a particular good, which specifies the maximum amount that can be imported in a given time period.

Random number An observation drawn from a uniform distribution.

Random number generator An algorithm that produces uniformly distributed random numbers between 0 and 1.

Random variable A quantity whose future outcomes are uncertain.

Random walk A time series in which the value of the series in one period is the value of the series in the previous period plus an unpredictable random error.

Random walk theory (1) The theory that current stock prices already reflect known information about the future. Therefore, the future movement of stock prices will be determined by surprise occurrences. This will cause them to change in a random fashion. (2) A theory stating that all current information is reflected in current security prices and that future price movements are random because they are caused by unexpected news.

Range The difference between the maximum and minimum values in a dataset.

Range forward A trading strategy based on a variation of the put-call parity model where, for the same underlying asset but different exercise prices, a call option is purchased and a put option is sold (or vice versa).

Ratio scales A measurement scale that has all the characteristics of interval measurement scales as well as a true zero point as the origin.

Ratio spread An option strategy in which a long position in a certain number of options is offset by a short position in a certain number of other options on the same underlying, resulting in a risk-free position.

Rational expectation The most accurate forecast possible, a forecast that uses all the available information, including knowledge of the relevant economic forces that influence the variable being forecasted.

Real business cycle theory A theory that regards random fluctuations in productivity as the main source of economic fluctuations.

Real Estate Real estate Investments include: (a) Wholly owned or partially owned properties, (b) Commingled funds, property unit trusts, and insurance company separate accounts, (c) Unlisted, private placement securities issued by private real estate investment trusts (REITs) and real estate operating companies (REOCs), and (d) Equity-oriented debt, such as participating mortgage loans or any private interest in a property where some portion of return to the investor at the time of investment is related to the performance of the underlying real estate.

Real estate investment trusts (REITs) Investment funds that hold portfolios of real estate investments.

Real income A household's income expressed as a quantity of goods that the household can afford to buy.

Real interest rate The nominal interest rate adjusted for inflation; the nominal interest rate minus the inflation rate.

Real options Options embedded in a firm's real assets that give managers valuable decision-making flexibility, such as the right to either undertake or abandon an investment project.

Real rate of interest The money rate of interest minus the expected rate of inflation. The real rate of interest indicates the interest premium, in terms of real goods and services, that one must pay for earlier availability.

Real risk-free interest rate The single-period interest rate for a completely risk-free security if no inflation were expected.

Real risk-free rate (RRFR) The basic interest rate with no accommodation for inflation or uncertainty. The pure time value of money.

Real wage rate The quantity of goods ands services that an hour's work can buy. It is equal to the money wage rate divided by the price level.

Realizable value (settlement value) With reference to assets, the amount of cash or cash equivalents that could currently be obtained by selling the asset in an orderly disposal; with reference to liabilities, the undiscounted amount of cash or cash equivalents expected to be paid to satisfy the liabilities in the normal course of business.

Realization Multiple (Private Equity) The realization multiple (DPI) is calculated by dividing the cumulative distributions by the paid-in-capital.

Realized capital gains Capital gains that result when an appreciated asset is sold; realized capital gains are taxable.

Receivables turnover An activity ratio equal to revenue divided by average receivables; an indication of the resources tied up in accounts receivable and the speed at which receivables are collected during the period.

Receiver swaption A swaption that allows the holder to enter into a swap as the fixed-rate receiver and floating-rate payer.

Recession There are two common definitions of recession. They are (1) A business cycle phase in which real GDP decreases for at least two successive quarters. (2) A significant decline in activity spread across the economy, lasting for more than a few months, visible in industrial production, employment, real income, and wholesale-retail trade.

Recessionary gap The amount by which potential GDP exceeds real GDP.

Reference base period The period in which the CPI is defined to be 100.

Regime With reference to a time series, the underlying model generating the times series.

Registered competitive market makers (RCMMs) Members of an exchange who are allowed to use their memberships to buy or sell for their own account within the specific trading obligations set down by the exchange.

Registered traders Members of the stock exchange who are allowed to use their memberships to buy and sell for their own account, which means they save commissions on their trading but they provide liquidity to the market, and they abide by exchange regulations on how they can trade.

Regression coefficients The intercept and slope coefficient(s) of a regression.

Regulation Rules administrated by a government agency to influence economic activity by determining prices, product standards and types, and conditions under which new firms may enter an industry.

Regulatory risk The risk associated with the uncertainty of how derivative transactions will be regulated or with changes in regulations.

Rejection point (or critical value) A value against which a computed test statistic is compared to decide whether to reject or not reject the null hypothesis.

Relative dispersion The amount of dispersion relative to a reference value or benchmark.

Relative frequency With reference to an interval of grouped data, the number of observations in the interval divided by the total number of observations in the sample.

Relative price The ratio of the price of one good or service to the price of another good or service. A relative price is an opportunity cost.

Renewable natural resources Natural resources that can be used repeatedly without depleting what is available for future use.

Rent The income that land earns.

Rent ceiling A regulation that makes it illegal to charge a rent higher than a specified level.

Rent seeking Any attempt to capture a consumer surplus, a producer surplus, or an economic profit.

Replacement value The market value of a swap.

Report format With respect to the format of a balance sheet, a format in which assets, liabilities, and equity are listed in a single column.

Required rate of return The return that compensates investors for their time, the expected rate of inflation, and the uncertainty of the return.

Required reserve ratio The ratio of reserves to deposits that banks are required, by regulation, to hold.

Reserve ratio The fraction of a bank's total deposits that are held in reserves.

Reserves Cash in a bank's vault plus the bank's deposits at Federal Reserve banks.

Residual autocorrelations The sample autocorrelations of the residuals.

Residual claim The owners' remaining claim on the company's assets after the liabilities are deducted.

Residual value The estimated net scrap, salvage, or trade-in value of a tangible asset at the estimated date of its disposal. Also called *salvage value* or *disposal value*.

Resistance level A price at which a technician would expect a substantial increase in the supply of a stock to reverse a rising trend.

Retail method An inventory accounting method in which the sales value of an item is reduced by the gross margin to calculate the item's cost.

Return on assets (ROA) A profitability ratio calculated as net income divided by average total assets; indicates the company's net profit generated per dollar invested in total assets.

Return on common equity A profitability ratio calculated as (net income − preferred dividends) divided by average common equity; equal to the return on equity ratio when no preferred equity is outstanding.

Return on equity (ROE) A profitability ratio calculated as net income divided by average shareholders' equity; indicates the return generated per dollar of shareholders' investment in the company.

Return-on-investment ratios Ratios that are useful for comparing the net benefits generated from investments.

Return on total capital A profitability ratio of net income to total capital (i.e., average interest-bearing debt + average total equity); indicates the return to the investments made by both creditors and shareholders.

Return prediction studies Studies wherein investigations attempt to predict the time series of future rates of return using public information. An example would be predicting above-average returns for the stock market based on the aggregate dividend yield—e.g., high dividend yield indicates above average future market returns.

Revenue The amount charged for the delivery of goods or services in the ordinary activities of a business over a stated period; the inflows of economic resources to a company over a stated period.

Revenue bond A bond that is serviced by the income generated from specific revenue-producing projects of the municipality.

Revenue expenditure An expenditure for ordinary repairs and maintenance of a long-term asset, which is recorded by a debit to an expense account.

Revolving credit agreements The strongest form of short-term bank borrowing facilities; they are in effect for multiple years (e.g., 3–5 years) and may have optional medium-term loan features

Rho The sensitivity of the option price to the risk-free rate.

Ricardo-Barro effect The equivalence of financing government purchases by taxes or by borrowing.

Rising trend channel The range defined by security prices as they move progressively higher.

Risk averse The assumption about investors that they will choose the least risky alternative, all else being equal.

Risk budgeting The establishment of objectives for individuals, groups, or divisions of an organization that takes into account the allocation of an acceptable level of risk.

Risk governance The setting of overall policies and standards in risk management

Risk management The process of identifying the level of risk an entity wants, measuring the level of risk the entity currently has, taking actions that bring the actual level of risk to the desired level of risk, and monitoring the new actual level of risk so that it continues to be aligned with the desired level of risk.

Risk premium The expected return on an investment minus the risk-free rate.

Risk premium (RP) (1) The difference between the expected return on an asset and the risk-free interest rate. (2) The increase over the nominal risk-free rate that investors demand as compensation for an investment's uncertainty. (3) The expected return on an investment minus the risk-free rate.

Risk-free asset An asset with returns that exhibit zero variance.

Risk-neutral probabilities Weights that are used to compute a binomial option price. They are the probabilities that would apply if a risk-neutral investor valued an option.

Risk-neutral valuation The process by which options and other derivatives are priced by treating investors as though they were risk neutral.

Risky asset An asset with uncertain future returns.

Rival A good or services or a resource is rival if its use by one person decreases the quantity available for someone else.

Robust The quality of being relatively unaffected by a violation of assumptions.

Robust standard errors Standard errors of the estimated parameters of a regression that correct for the presence of heteroskedasticity in the regression's error term.

Root mean squared error (RMSE) The square root of the average squared forecast error; used to compare the out-of-sample forecasting performance of forecasting models.

Roy's safety first criterion A criterion asserting that the optimal portfolio is the one that minimizes the probability that portfolio return falls below a threshold level.

Rule of 72 The principle that the approximate number of years necessary for an investment to double is 72 divided by the stated interest rate.

Runs test A test of the weak-form efficient market hypothesis that checks for trends that persist longer in terms of positive or negative price changes than one would expect for a random series.

Safety stock A level of inventory beyond anticipated needs that provides a cushion in the event that it takes longer to replenish inventory than expected or in the case of greater than expected demand.

Safety-first rules Rules for portfolio selection that focus on the risk that portfolio value will fall below some minimum acceptable level over some time horizon.

Sales Generally, a synonym for revenue; "sales" is generally understood to refer to the sale of goods, whereas "revenue" is understood to include the sale of goods or services.

Sales returns and allowances An offset to revenue reflecting any cash refunds, credits on account, and discounts from sales prices given to customers who purchased defective or unsatisfactory items.

Salvage value The amount the company estimates that it can sell the asset for at the end of its useful life.

Sample A subset of a population.

Sample excess kurtosis A sample measure of the degree of a distribution's peakedness in excess of the normal distribution's peakedness.

Sample kurtosis A sample measure of the degree of a distribution's peakedness.

Sample mean The sum of the sample observations, divided by the sample size.

Sample selection bias Bias introduced by systematically excluding some members of the population according to a particular attribute-for example, the bias introduced when data availability leads to certain observations being excluded from the analysis.

Sample skewness A sample measure of degree of asymmetry of a distribution.

Sample standard deviation The positive square root of the sample variance.

Sample statistic or statistic A quantity computed from or used to describe a sample.

Sample variance A sample measure of the degree of dispersion of a distribution, calculated by dividing the sum of the squared deviations from the sample mean by the sample size (n) minus 1.

Sampling The process of obtaining a sample.

Sampling distribution The distribution of all distinct possible values that a statistic can assume when computed from samples of the same size randomly drawn from the same population.

Sampling error The difference between the observed value of a statistic and the quantity it is intended to estimate.

Sampling plan The set of rules used to select a sample.

Sandwich spread An option strategy that is equivalent to a short butterfly spread.

Sarbanes-Oxley Act An act passed by the U.S. Congress in 2002 that created the Public Company Accounting Oversight Board (PCAOB) to oversee auditors.

Saving The amount of income that households have left after they have paid their taxes and bought their consumption goods and services.

Saving supply The relationship between saving and the real interest rate, other things remaining the same.

Savings and loan association (S&L) A depository institution that receives checking deposits and savings deposits and that makes personal, commercial, and home-purchase loans.

Savings bank A depository institution, owned by its depositors, that accepts savings deposits and makes mortgage loans.

Scalper A trader who offers to buy or sell futures contracts, holding the position for only a brief period of time. Scalpers attempt to profit by buying at the bid price and selling at the higher ask price.

Scarcity Our inability to satisfy all our wants.

Scatter diagram A diagram that plots the value of one economic variable against the value of another.

Scatter plot A two-dimensional plot of pairs of observations on two data series.

Scenario analysis A risk management technique involving the examination of the performance of a portfolio under specified situations. Closely related to stress testing.

Screening The application of a set of criteria to reduce a set of potential investments to a smaller set having certain desired characteristics.

Search activity The time spent looking for someone with whom to do business.

Seasoned equity issues New equity shares offered by firms that already have stock outstanding.

Seats Memberships in a derivatives exchange.

Secondary market The market in which outstanding securities are bought and sold by owners other than the issuers. Purpose is to provide liquidity for investors.

Sector rotation strategy An active strategy that involves purchasing stocks in specific industries or stocks with specific characteristics (low *P/E*, growth, value) that are anticipated to rise in value more than the overall market.

Securities Act of 1933 An act passed by the U.S. Congress in 1933 that specifies the financial and other significant information that investors must receive when securities are sold, prohibits misrepresentations, and requires initial registration of all public issuances of securities.

Securities Exchange Act of 1934 An act passed by the U.S. Congress in 1934 that created the Securities and Exchange Commission (SEC), gave the SEC authority over all aspects of the securities industry, and empowered the SEC to require periodic reporting by companies with publicly traded securities.

Security market line (SML) The graph of the capital asset pricing model.

Segment debt ratio Segment liabilities divided by segment assets.

Segment margin Segment profit (loss) divided by segment revenue.

Segment ROA Segment profit (loss) divided by segment assets.

Segment turnover Segment revenue divided by segment assets.

SelectNet An order-routing and trade-execution system for institutional investors (brokers and dealers) that allows communication through the Nasdaq system rather than by phone.

Self-interest The choices that you think are the best for you.

Semideviation The positive square root of semivariance (sometimes called semistandard deviation).

Semilogarithmic Describes a scale constructed so that equal intervals on the vertical scale represent equal rates of change, and equal intervals on the horizontal scale represent equal amounts of change.

Semivariance The average squared deviation below the mean.

Sensitivity analysis Analysis that shows the range of possible outcomes as specific assumptions are changed.

Separation theorem The proposition that the investment decision, which involves investing in the market portfolio on the capital market line, is separate from the financing decision, which targets a specific point on the CML based on the investor's risk preference.

Serially correlated With reference to regression errors, errors that are correlated across observations.

Settlement date or payment date The date on which the parties to a swap make payments.

Settlement period The time between settlement dates.

Settlement price The official price, designated by the clearinghouse, from which daily gains and losses will be determined and marked to market.

Settlement risk When settling a contract, the risk that one party could be in the process of paying the counterparty while the counterparty is declaring bankruptcy.

Shareholders' equity Total assets minus total liabilities.

Sharpe measure A relative measure of a portfolio's benefit-to-risk ratio, calculated as its average return in excess of the risk-free rate divided by the standard deviation of portfolio returns.

Sharpe ratio The average return in excess of the risk-free rate divided by the standard deviation of return; a measure of the average excess return earned per unit of standard deviation of return.

Short The seller of a derivative contract. Also refers to the position of being short a derivative.

Short hedge A short position in a forward or futures contract used to offset the price volatility of a long position in the underlying asset.

Short position The seller of a commodity or security or, for a forward contract, the counterparty who will be the eventual seller of the underlying asset.

Short run The short run in microeconomics has two meanings. For the firm, it is the period of time in which the quantity of at least one input is fixed and the quantities of the other inputs can be varied. The fixed input is usually capital-that is, the firm has a given plant size. For the industry, the short run is the period of time in which each firm has a given plant size and the number of firms in the industry is fixed.

Short sale The sale of borrowed securities with the intention of repurchasing them later at a lower price and earning the difference.

Shortfall risk The risk that portfolio value will fall below some minimum acceptable level over some time horizon.

Short-run aggregate supply curve A curve that shows the relationship between the quantity of real GDP supplied and the price level in the short run when the money wage rate, other resource prices, and potential GDP remain constant.

Short-run industry supply curve A curve that shows the quantity supplied by the industry at each price varies when the plant size of each firm and the number of firms in the industry remain the same.

Short-run macroeconomic equilibrium A situation that occurs when the quantity of real GDP demanded equals quantity of real GDP supplied—at the point of intersection of the *AD* curve and the *SAS* curve.

Short-run Phillips curve A curve that shows the tradeoff between inflation and unemployment, when the expected inflation rate and the natural rate of unemployment remain the same.

Should Encouraged (recommended) to follow the recommendation of the GIPS standards but not required.

Shutdown point The output and price at which the firm just covers its total variable cost. In the short run, the firm is indifferent between producing the profit-maximizing output and shutting down temporarily.

Signal An action taken by an informed person (or firm) to send a message to uninformed people or an action taken outside a market that conveys information that can be used by that market.

Simple interest The interest earned each period on the original investment; interest calculated on the principal only.

Simple random sample A subset of a larger population created in such a way that each element of the population has an equal probability of being selected to the subset.

Simple random sampling The procedure of drawing a sample to satisfy the definition of a simple random sample.

Simulation Computer-generated sensitivity or scenario analysis that is based on probability models for the factors that drive outcomes.

Simulation trial A complete pass through the steps of a simulation.

Single-payment loan A loan in which the borrower receives a sum of money at the start and pays back the entire amount with interest in a single payment at maturity.

Single-price monopoly A monopoly that must sell each unit of its output for a same price to all its customers.

Single-step format With respect to the format of the income statement, a format that does not subtotal for gross profit (revenue minus cost of goods sold).

Sinking fund (1) Bond provision that requires the bond to be paid off progressively rather than in full at maturity. (2) Bond provision that requires the issuer to redeem some or all of the bond systematically over the term of the bond rather than in full at maturity.

Skewed Not symmetrical.

Skewness A quantitative measure of skew (lack of symmetry); a synonym of skew.

Slope The change in the value of the variable measured on the *y*-axis divided by the change in the value of the variable measured on the *x*-axis.

Small-firm effect A frequent empirical anomaly where risk-adjusted stock returns for companies with low market capitalization (i.e., share price multiplied by number of outstanding shares) are significantly larger than those generated by high market capitalization (large cap) firms.

Small-Order Execution System (SOES) A quotation and execution system for retail (nonprofessional) investors who place orders with brokers who must honor their prevailing bid-ask for automatic execution up to 1,000 shares.

Social interest Choices that are the best for society as a whole.

Soft dollars A form of compensation to a money manager generated when the manager commits the investor to paying higher brokerage fees in exchange for the manager receiving additional services (e.g., stock research) from the broker.

Software Capitalized costs associated with computer programs developed for sale, lease, or internal use and amortized over the estimated economic life of the programs.

Solvency With respect to financial statement analysis, the ability of a company to fulfill its long-term obligations.

Solvency ratios Ratios that measure a company's ability to meet its long-term obligations.

Sovereign risk The risk that a government may default on its debt.

Sovereign yield spread An estimate of the country spread (country equity premium) for a developing nation that is based on a comparison of bonds yields in country being analyzed and a developed country. The sovereign yield spread is the difference between a government bond yield in the country being analyzed, denominated in the currency of the developed country, and the Treasury bond yield on a similar maturity bond in the developed country.

Spearman rank correlation coefficient A measure of correlation applied to ranked data.

Specialist The major market maker on U.S. stock exchanges who acts as a broker or dealer to ensure the liquidity and smooth functions of the secondary stock market.

Specific identification method An inventory accounting method that identifies which specific inventory items were sold and which remained in inventory to be carried over to later periods.

Speculative company A firm with a great degree of business and/or financial risk, with commensurate high earnings potential.

Speculative stock A stock that appears to be highly overpriced compared to its intrinsic valuation.

Spending phase Phase in the investment life cycle during which individuals' earning years end as they retire. They pay for expenses with income from social security and returns from prior investments and invest to protect against inflation.

Spot price Current market price of an asset. Also called cash price.

Spot rate The required yield for a cash flow to be received at some specific date in the future—for example, the spot rate for a flow to be received in one year, for a cash flow in two years, and so on.

Spread An option strategy involving the purchase of one option and sale of another option that is identical to the first in all respects except either exercise price or expiration.

Spurious correlation A correlation that misleadingly points towards associations between variables.

Stagflation The combination of recession and inflation.

Standard cost With respect to inventory accounting, the planned or target unit cost of inventory items or services.

Standard deviation The positive square root of the variance; a measure of dispersion in the same units as the original data.

Standard normal distribution (or unit normal distribution) The normal density with mean (μ) equal to 0 and standard deviation (σ) equal to 1.

Standardized beta With reference to fundamental factor models, the value of the attribute for an asset minus the average value of the attribute across all stocks, divided by the standard deviation of the attribute across all stocks.

Standardizing A transformation that involves subtracting the mean and dividing the result by the standard deviation.

Stated annual interest rate or quoted interest rate A quoted interest rate that does not account for compounding within the year.

Statement of cash flows (cash flow statement) A financial statement that reconciles beginning-of-period and end-of-period balance sheet values of cash; provides information about an entity's cash inflows and cash outflows as they pertain to operating, investing, and financing activities.

Statement of changes in shareholders' equity (statement of owners' equity) A financial statement that reconciles the beginning-of-period and end-of-period balance sheet values of shareholders' equity; provides information about all factors affecting shareholders' equity.

Statement of retained earnings A financial statement that reconciles beginning-of-period and end-of-period balance sheet values of retained income; shows the linkage between the balance sheet and income statement.

Statistic A quantity computed from or used to describe a sample of data.

Statistical factor models A multifactor model in which statistical methods are applied to a set of historical returns to determine portfolios that best explain either historical return covariances or variances.

Statistical inference Making forecasts, estimates, or judgments about a larger group from a smaller group actually observed; using a sample statistic to infer the value of an unknown population parameter.

Statistically significant A result indicating that the null hypothesis can be rejected; with reference to an estimated regression coefficient, frequently understood to mean a result indicating that the corresponding population regression coefficient is different from 0.

Statistics The science of describing, analyzing, and drawing conclusions from data; also, a collection of numerical data.

Stock A quantity that exists at a point in time.

Stock dividend A dividend paid in the form of additional shares rather than in cash.

Stock split An action taken by a firm to increase the number of shares outstanding, such as doubling the number of shares outstanding by giving each stockholder two new shares for each one formerly held.

Stock-out losses Profits lost from not having sufficient inventory on hand to satisfy demand.

Storage costs or carrying costs The costs of holding an asset, generally a function of the physical characteristics of the underlying asset.

Straddle An option strategy involving the purchase of a put and a call with the same exercise price. A straddle is based on the expectation of high volatility of the underlying.

Straight-line method A method of depreciation that assumes depreciation depends only on the passage of time and that allocates an equal amount of depreciation to each accounting period in an asset's useful life.

Straight-line method A depreciation method that allocates evenly the cost of a long-lived asset less its estimated residual value over the estimated useful life of the asset.

Strangle A variation of a straddle in which the put and call have different exercise prices.

Strap An option strategy involving the purchase of two calls and one put.

Strategies All the possible actions of each player in a game.

Stratified random sampling A procedure by which a population is divided into subpopulations (strata) based on one or more classification criteria. Simple random samples are then drawn from each stratum in sizes proportional to the relative size of each stratum in the population. These samples are then pooled.

Stress testing/scenario analysis A set of techniques for estimating losses in extremely unfavorable combinations of events or scenarios.

Strike price Price at which an option can be exercised (same as exercise price).

Strip An option strategy involving the purchase of two puts and one call.

Structural change Economic trend occurring when the economy is undergoing a major change in organization or in how it functions.

Structural surplus or deficit The budget balance that would occur if the economy were at full employment and real GDP were equal to potential GDP.

Structural unemployment The unemployment that arises when changes in technology or international competition change the skills needed to perform jobs or change the locations of jobs.

Structured note (1) A bond or note issued with some unusual, often option-like, clause. (2) A bond with an embedded derivative designed to create a payoff distribution that satisfies the needs of a specific investor clientele. (3) A variation of a floating-rate note that has some type of unusual characteristic such as a leverage factor or in which the rate moves opposite to interest rates.

Style analysis An attempt to explain the variability in the observed returns to a security portfolio in terms of the movements in the returns to a series of benchmark portfolios designed to capture the essence of a particular security characteristic such as size, value, and growth.

Subjective probability A probability drawing on personal or subjective judgment.

Subsidy A payment that the government makes to a producer.

Substitute A good that can be used in place of another good.

Substitution effect The effect of a change in price of a good or service on the quantity bought when the consumer (hypothetically) remains indifferent between the original and the new consumption situations—that is, the consumer remains on the same indifference curve.

Successful efforts accounting A method of accounting for the costs of exploring and developing oil and gas resources in which successful exploration is recorded as an asset and depleted over the estimated life of the resource and all unsuccessful efforts are immediately written off as losses.

Sunk cost A cost that has already been incurred.

Supplemental Information Any performance-related information included as part of a compliant performance presentation that supplements or enhances the required and/or recommended disclosure and presentation provisions of the GIPS standards.

Supply The relationship between the quantity of a good that producers plan to sell and the price of the good when all other influences on sellers' plans remain the same. It is described by a supply schedule and illustrated by a supply curve.

Supply curve A curve that shows the relationship between the quantity supplied and the price of a good when all other influences on producers' planned sales remain the same.

Supply of labor The relationship between the quantity of labor supplied and the real wage rate when all other influences on work plans remain the same.

Supply-side effects The effects of fiscal policy on employment, potential GDP, and aggregate supply.

Support level A price at which a technician would expect a substantial increase in price and volume for a stock to reverse a declining trend that was due to profit taking.

Surprise The actual value of a variable minus its predicted (or expected) value.

Survey approach An estimate of the equity risk premium that is based upon estimates provided by a panel of finance experts.

Survivorship bias The bias resulting from a test design that fails to account for companies that have gone bankrupt, merged, or are otherwise no longer reported in a database.

Sustainable growth rate The rate of dividend (and earnings) growth that can be sustained over time for a given level of return on equity, keeping the capital structure constant and without issuing additional common stock.

Swap An agreement between two parties to exchange a series of future cash flows.

Swap spread The difference between the fixed rate on an interest rate swap and the rate on a Treasury note with equivalent maturity; it reflects the general level of credit risk in the market.

Swaption An option to enter into a swap.

SWOT analysis An examination of a firm's *S*trengths, *W*eaknesses, *O*pportunities, and *T*hreats. This analysis helps an analyst evaluate a firm's strategies to exploit its competitive advantages or defend against its weaknesses.

Symmetry principle A requirement that people in similar situations be treated similarly.

Synthetic call The combination of puts, the underlying, and risk-free bonds that replicates a call option.

Synthetic forward contract The combination of the underlying, puts, calls, and risk-free bonds that replicates a forward contract.

Synthetic index fund An index fund position created by combining risk-free bonds and futures on the desired index.

Synthetic put The combination of calls, the underlying, and risk-free bonds that replicates a put option.

Systematic factors Factors that affect the average returns of a large number of different assets.

Systematic risk The variability of returns that is due to macroeconomic factors that affect all risky assets. Because it affects all risky assets, it cannot be eliminated by diversification.

Systematic sampling A procedure of selecting every *k*th member until reaching a sample of the desired size. The sample that results from this procedure should be approximately random.

Tangible assets Long-term assets that have physical substance.

Tangible book value per share Common shareholders' equity minus intangible assets from the balance sheet, divided by the number of shares outstanding.

Tap Procedure by which a borrower can keep issuing additional amounts of an old bond at its current market value. This procedure is used for bond issues, notably by the British and French governments, as well as for some short-term debt instruments.

Target balance A minimum level of cash to be held available—estimated in advance and adjusted for known funds transfers, seasonality, or other factors.

Target capital structure The proportion of component sources of capital (e.g. equity, debt) that a company strives to maintain

Target semideviation The positive square root of target semivariance.

Target semivariance The average squared deviation below a target value.

Tariff A tax that is imposed by the importing country when an imported good crosses its international boundary.

Tax incidence The division of the burden of a tax between the buyer and the seller.

Tax multiplier The magnification effect of a change in taxes on aggregate demand.

Tax risk The uncertainty associated with tax laws.

Tax wedge The gap between the before-tax and after-tax wage rates.

Taylor rule A rule that adjusts the federal funds rate to target the inflation rate and to take into account deviations of the inflation rate from its target and deviations of real GDP from potential GDP.

***t*-Distribution** A symmetrical distribution defined by a single parameter, degrees of freedom, that is largely used to make inferences concerning the mean of a normal distribution whose variance is unknown.

Technical analysis Estimation of future security price movements based on past price and volume movements.

Technological change The development of new goods and better ways of producing goods and services.

Technological efficiency A situation that occurs when the firm produces a given output by using the least amount of inputs.

Technology Any method of producing a good or service.

Temporary New Account A tool that firms can use to remove the effect of significant cash flows on a portfolio. When a significant cash flow occurs in a portfolio, the firm may treat this cash flow as a "temporary new account," allowing the firm to implement the mandate of the portfolio without the impact of the cash flow on the performance of the portfolio.

Tenor The original time to maturity on a swap.

Term structure of interest rates The relationship between term to maturity and yield to maturity for a sample of comparable bonds at a given time. Popularly known as the *yield curve.*

Term to maturity Specifies the date or the number of years before a bond matures or expires.

Termination date The date of the final payment on a swap; also, the swap's expiration date.

Terms of trade The quantity of goods and services that a country exports to pay for its imports of goods and services.

Test statistic A quantity, calculated based on a sample, whose value is the basis for deciding whether or not to reject the null hypothesis.

Theta The rate at which an option's time value decays.

Third market Over-the-counter trading of securities listed on an exchange.

Thrift institutions Thrift institutions include savings and loan associations, savings banks, and credit unions.

Tick The minimum price movement for the asset underlying a forward or futures contract; for Treasury bonds, one tick equals 1/32 of 1 percent of par value.

Time series A set of observations on a variable's outcomes in different time periods.

Time to expiration The time remaining in the life of a derivative, typically expressed in years.

Time value decay The loss in the value of an option resulting from movement of the option price toward its payoff value as the expiration day approaches.

Time value of money The principles governing equivalence relationships between cash flows with different dates.

Time value or speculative value The difference between the market price of the option and its intrinsic value, determined by the uncertainty of the underlying over the remaining life of the option.

Time-period bias The possibility that when we use a time-series sample, our statistical conclusion may be sensitive to the starting and ending dates of the sample.

Time-series analysis An examination of a firm's performance data over a period of time.

Time-series data Observations of a variable over time.

Time-series graph A graph that measures time (for example, months or years) on the x-axis and the variable or variables in which we are interested on the y-axis.

Time-weighted rate of return The compound rate of growth of one unit of currency invested in a portfolio during a stated measurement period; a measure of investment performance that is not sensitive to the timing and amount of withdrawals or additions to the portfolio.

Top-down analysis With reference to investment selection processes, an approach that starts with macro selection (i.e., identifying attractive geographic segments and/or industry segments) and then addresses selection of the most attractive investments within those segments.

Total asset turnover An activity ratio calculated as revenue divided by average total assets; indicates the extent to which the investment in total assets results in revenues.

Total cost The cost of all the productive resources that a firm uses.

Total Firm Assets Total firm assets are all assets for which a firm has investment management responsibility. Total firm assets include assets managed outside the firm (e.g., by subadvisors) for which the firm has asset allocation authority.

Total fixed cost The cost of the firm's fixed inputs.

Total invested capital The sum of market value of common equity, book value of preferred equity, and face value of debt.

Total probability rule for expected value A rule explaining the expected value of a random variable in terms of expected values of the random variable conditional on mutually exclusive and exhaustive scenarios.

Total probability rule A rule explaining the unconditional probability of an event in terms of probabilities of the event conditional on mutually exclusive and exhaustive scenarios.

Total product The maximum output that a given quantity of factors of production can produce.

Total return A return objective in which the investor wants to increase the portfolio value to meet a future need by both capital gains and current income reinvestment.

Total return swap A swap in which one party agrees to pay the total return on a security. Often used as a credit derivative, in which the underlying is a bond.

Total revenue The value of a firm's sales. It is calculated as the price of the good multiplied by the quantity sold.

Total revenue test A method of estimating the price elasticity of demand by observing the change in total revenue that results from a change in the price, when all other influences on the quantity sold remain the same.

Total variable cost The cost of all the firm's variable inputs.

Tracking error The standard deviation of the difference in returns between an active investment portfolio and its benchmark portfolio; also called tracking error volatility, tracking risk, and active risk.

Tracking portfolio A portfolio having factor sensitivities that are matched to those of a benchmark or other portfolio.

Tracking risk The standard deviation of the differences between a portfolio's returns and its benchmark's returns; a synonym of active risk.

Trade balance The balance of a country's exports and imports; part of the current account.

Trade credit A spontaneous form of credit in which a purchaser of the goods or service is, effectively, financing its purchase by delaying the date on which payment is made.

Trade Date Accounting The transaction is reflected in the portfolio on the date of the purchase or sale, and not on the settlement date. Recognizing the asset or liability within at least 3 days of the date the transaction is entered into (Trade Date, T 1 1, T 1 2 or T 1 3) all satisfy the trade date accounting requirement for purposes of the GIPS standards. (See settlement date accounting.)

Trade receivables (commercial receivables or accounts receivable) Amounts customers owe the company for products that have been sold as well as amounts that may be due from suppliers (such as for returns of merchandise).

Trademark A registered symbol that can be used only by its owner to identify a product or service.

Tradeoff An exchange–giving up one thing to get something else.

Trading effect The difference in performance of a bond portfolio from that of a chosen index due to short-run changes in the composition of the portfolio.

Trading Expenses The costs of buying or selling a security. These costs typically take the form of brokerage commissions or spreads from either internal or external brokers. Custody fees charged per transaction should be considered custody fees and not direct transaction costs. Estimated trading expenses are not permitted.

Trading rule A formula for deciding on current transactions based on historical data.

Trading securities (held-for-trading securities) Securities held by a company with the intent to trade them.

Trading turnover The percentage of outstanding shares traded during a period of time.

Trailing P/E (or current P/E) A stock's current market price divided by the most recent four quarters of earnings per share.

Tranche Refers to a portion of an issue that is designed for a specific category of investors. French for "slice."

Transaction cost The cost of executing a trade. Low costs characterize an operationally efficient market.

Transaction Expenses (Private Equity) Include all legal, financial, advisory, and investment banking fees related to buying, selling, restructuring, and recapitalizing portfolio companies.

Transaction exposure The risk associated with a foreign exchange rate on a specific business transaction such as a purchase or sale.

Transactions costs The costs that arise from finding someone with whom to do business, of reaching an agreement about the price and other aspects of the exchange, and of ensuring that the terms of the agreement are fulfilled. The opportunity costs of conducting a transaction.

Transactions motive In the context of inventory management, it refers to the need for inventory as part of the routine production–sales cycle.

Translation exposure The risk associated with the conversion of foreign financial statements into domestic currency.

Treasury bill A negotiable U.S. government security with a maturity of less than one year that pays no periodic interest but yields the difference between its par value and its discounted purchase price.

Treasury bond A U.S. government security with a maturity of more than 10 years that pays interest periodically.

Treasury note A U.S. government security with maturities of 1 to 10 years that pays interest periodically.

Treasury stock method A method for accounting for the effect of options (and warrants) on earnings per share (EPS) that specifies what EPS would have been if the options and warrants had been exercised and the company had used the proceeds to repurchase common stock.

Tree diagram A diagram with branches emanating from nodes representing either mutually exclusive chance events or mutually exclusive decisions.

Trend A long-term pattern of movement in a particular direction.

Trimmed mean A mean computed after excluding a stated small percentage of the lowest and highest observations.

Trust receipt arrangement The use of inventory as collateral for a loan. The inventory is segregated and held in trust, and the proceeds of any sale must be remitted to the lender immediately.

***t*-Test** A hypothesis test using a statistic (*t*-statistic) that follows a *t*-distribution.

Two-sided hypothesis test (or two-tailed hypothesis test) A test in which the null hypothesis is rejected in favor of the alternative hypothesis if the evidence indicates that the population parameter is either smaller or larger than a hypothesized value.

Type I error The error of rejecting a true null hypothesis.

Type II error The error of not rejecting a false null hypothesis.

U.S. interest rate differential A gap equal to the U.S. interest rate minus the foreign interest rate.

U.S. Official reserves The government's holdings of foreign currency.

Unbiasedness Lack of bias. A desirable property of estimators, an unbiased estimator is one whose expected value (the mean of its sampling distribution) equals the parameter it is intended to estimate.

Unbilled revenue (accrued revenue) Revenue that has been earned but not yet billed to customers as of the end of an accounting period.

Uncertainty A situation in which more than one event might occur but it is not known which one.

Unclassified balance sheet A balance sheet that does not show subtotals for current assets and current liabilities.

Unconditional heteroskedasticity Heteroskedasticity of the error term that is not correlated with the values of the independent variable(s) in the regression.

Unconditional probability (or marginal probability) The probability of an event *not* conditioned on another event.

Uncovered interest rate parity The assertion that expected currency depreciation should offset the interest differential between two countries over the term of the interest rate.

Underlying An asset that trades in a market in which buyers and sellers meet, decide on a price, and the seller then delivers the asset to the buyer and receives payment. The underlying is the asset or other derivative on which a particular derivative is based. The market for the underlying is also referred to as the spot market.

Underweighted A condition in which a portfolio, for whatever reason, includes less of a class of securities than the relative market value alone would justify.

Unearned fees Unearned fees are recognized when a company receives cash payment for fees prior to earning them.

Unearned revenue (deferred revenue) A liability account for money that has been collected for goods or services that have not yet been delivered.

Unemployment rate The percentage of the people in the labor force who are unemployed.

Unidentifiable intangible An intangible that cannot be acquired singly and that typically possesses an indefinite benefit period; an example is accounting goodwill.

Unit elastic demand Demand with a price elasticity of 1; the percentage change in the quantity demanded equals the percentage change in price.

Unit normal distribution *See* Standard normal distribution.

Unit root A time series that is not covariance stationary is said to have a unit root.

Univariate distribution A distribution that specifies the probabilities for a single random variable.

Unlimited funds An unlimited funds environment assumes that the company can raise the funds it wants for all profitable projects simply by paying the required rate of return.

Unrealized capital gains Capital gains that reflect the price appreciation of currently held unsold assets.

Unsystematic risk Risk that is unique to an asset, derived from its particular characteristics. It can be eliminated in a diversified portfolio.

Unweighted index An indicator series affected equally by the performance of each security in the sample regardless of price or market value. Also referred to as an *equal-weighted series.*

Unwind The negotiated termination of a forward or futures position before contract maturity.

Up transition probability The probability that an asset's value moves up.

Utilitarianism A principle that states that we should strive to achieve "the greatest happiness for the greatest number of people."

Utility The benefit or satisfaction that a person gets from the consumption of a good or service.

Utility of wealth The amount of utility that a person attaches to a given amount of wealth.

Valuation The process of determining the value of an asset or service.

Valuation analysis An active bond portfolio management strategy designed to capitalize on expected price increases in temporarily undervalued issues.

Valuation process Part of the investment decision process in which you estimate the value of a security.

Valuation ratios Ratios that measure the quantity of an asset or flow (e.g., earnings) in relation to the price associated with a specified claim (e.g., a share or ownership of the enterprise).

Value The amount for which one can sell something, or the amount one must pay to acquire something.

Value at risk (VAR) A money measure of the minimum value of losses expected during a specified time period at a given level of probability.

Value chain The set of transformations to move from raw material to product or service delivery.

Value investors With reference to equity investors, investors who are focused on paying a relatively low share price in relation to earnings or assets per share.

Value stocks Stocks that appear to be undervalued for reasons besides earnings growth potential. These stocks are usually identified based on high dividend yields, low *P/E* ratios, or low price-to-book ratios.

Value-weighted index An index calculated as the total market value of the securities in the sample. Market value is equal to the number of shares or bonds outstanding times the market price of the security.

Variable costs Costs that rise proportionally with revenue.

Variance The expected value (the probability-weighted average) of squared deviations from a random variable's expected value.

Variation margin Additional margin that must be deposited in an amount sufficient to bring the balance up to the initial margin requirement.

Vega The relationship between option price and volatility.

Velocity of circulation The average number of times a dollar of money is used annually to buy the goods and services that make up GDP.

Venture Capital (Private Equity) Risk capital in the form of equity and/or loan capital that is provided by an investment institution to back a business venture that is expected to grow in value.

Vertical analysis Common-size analysis using only one reporting period or one base financial statement; for example, an income statement in which all items are stated as percentages of sales.

Vertical common-size analysis An analysis in which financial statement accounts are compared to a benchmark item in that same year. For the income statement, all items are restated as a percentage of revenues; for the balance sheet, all items are restated as a percentage of total assets.

Vintage Year (Private Equity) The year that the venture capital or private equity fund or partnership first draws down or calls capital from its investors.

Volatility As used in option pricing, the standard deviation of the continuously compounded returns on the underlying asset.

Voluntary export restraint An agreement between two governments in which the government of the exporting country agrees to restrain the volume of its own exports.

Wages The income that labor earns.

Warehouse receipt arrangement The use of inventory as collateral for a loan. . It is similar to a trust receipt arrangement except that there is a third part (i.e., a warehouse company) that supervises the inventory.

Warrant An instrument that allows the holder to purchase a specified number of shares of the firm's common stock from the firm at a specified price for a given period of time.

Weak-form efficient market hypothesis The belief that security prices fully reflect all security market information.

Wealth The market value of all the things that people own.

Weighted average cost method An inventory accounting method that averages the total cost of available inventory items over the total units available for sale.

Weighted-average cost of capital A weighted average of the after-tax required rates of return on a company's common stock, preferred stock, and long-term debt, where the weights are the fraction of each source of financing in the company's target capital structure.

Weighted average cost of capital (or marginal cost of capital) The required rate of return that investors demand for the average-risk investment of a company and the cost that a company incurs for additional capital. Found as the average of the company's component costs of capital, weighted by their proportions in the company's capital structure.

Weighted mean An average in which each observation is weighted by an index of its relative importance.

White-corrected standard errors A synonym for robust standard errors.

Winsorized mean A mean computed after assigning a stated percent of the lowest values equal to one specified low value, and a stated percent of the highest values equal to one specified high value.

Working capital The excess of current assets over current liabilities.

Working capital management The management of a company's short-term assets (such as inventory) and short-term liabilities (such as money owed to suppliers).

Working capital turnover An activity ratio calculated as revenue divided by average working capital; an indication of the efficiency with which working capital is employed to produce revenues.

Working-age population The total number of people aged 16 years and over who are not in jail, hospital, or some other form of institutional care.

World Trade Organization An international organization that places greater obligations on its member countries to observe the GATT rules.

Yankee bonds Bonds sold in the United States and denominated in U.S. dollars but issued by a foreign firm or government.

Yield The promised rate of return on an investment under certain assumptions.

Yield beta A measure of the sensitivity of a bond's yield to a general measure of bond yields in the market that is used to refine the hedge ratio.

Yield spread The difference between the yield on a bond and the yield on a default-free security, usually a government note, of the same maturity. The yield spread is primarily determined by the market's perception of the credit risk on the bond.

Yield to maturity The total yield on a bond obtained by equating the bond's current market value to the discounted cash flows promised by the bond.

Yield to worst Given a bond with multiple potential maturity dates and prices due to embedded call options, the practice is to calculate a yield to maturity for each of the call dates and prices and select the lowest yield (the most conservative possible yield) as yield to worst.

Zero-cost collar A transaction in which a position in the underlying is protected by buying a put and selling a call with the premium from the sale of the call offsetting the premium from the purchase of the put. It can also be used to protect a floating-rate borrower against interest rate increases with the premium on a long cap offsetting the premium on a short floor.

INDEX

Page numbers followed by n refer to footnotes.

C

G

J

K

L